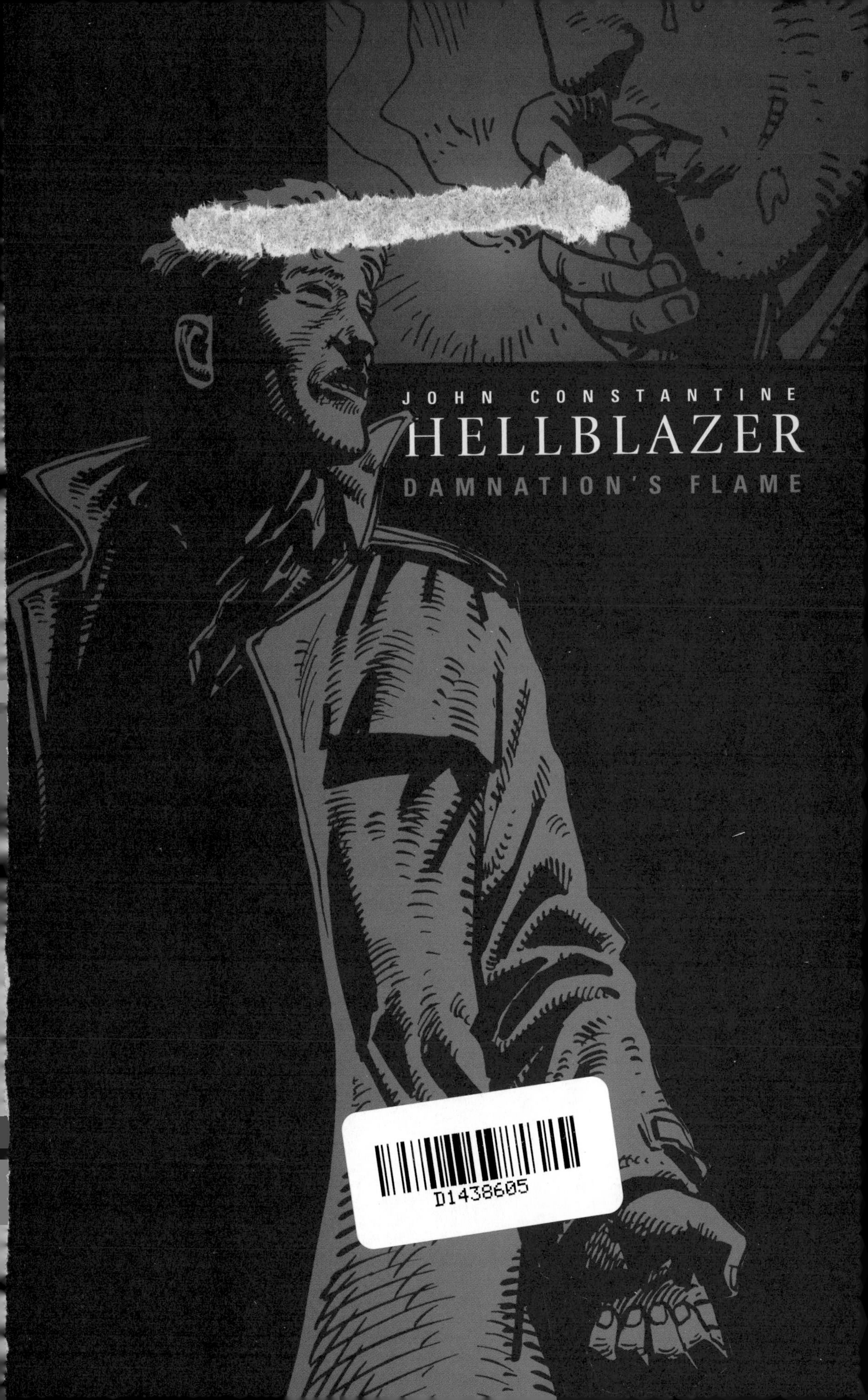
JOHN CONSTANTINE
HELLBLAZER
DAMNATION'S FLAME

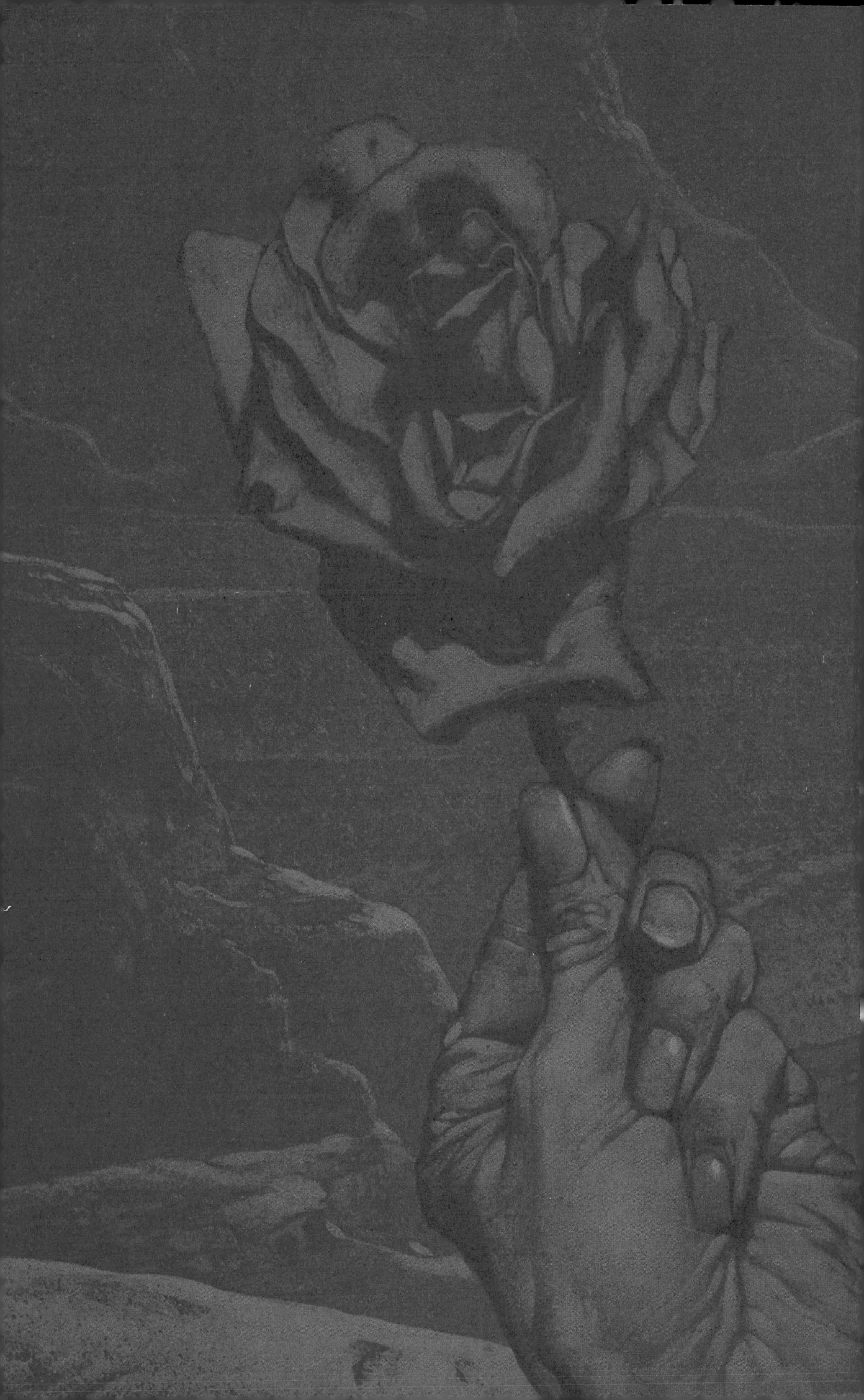

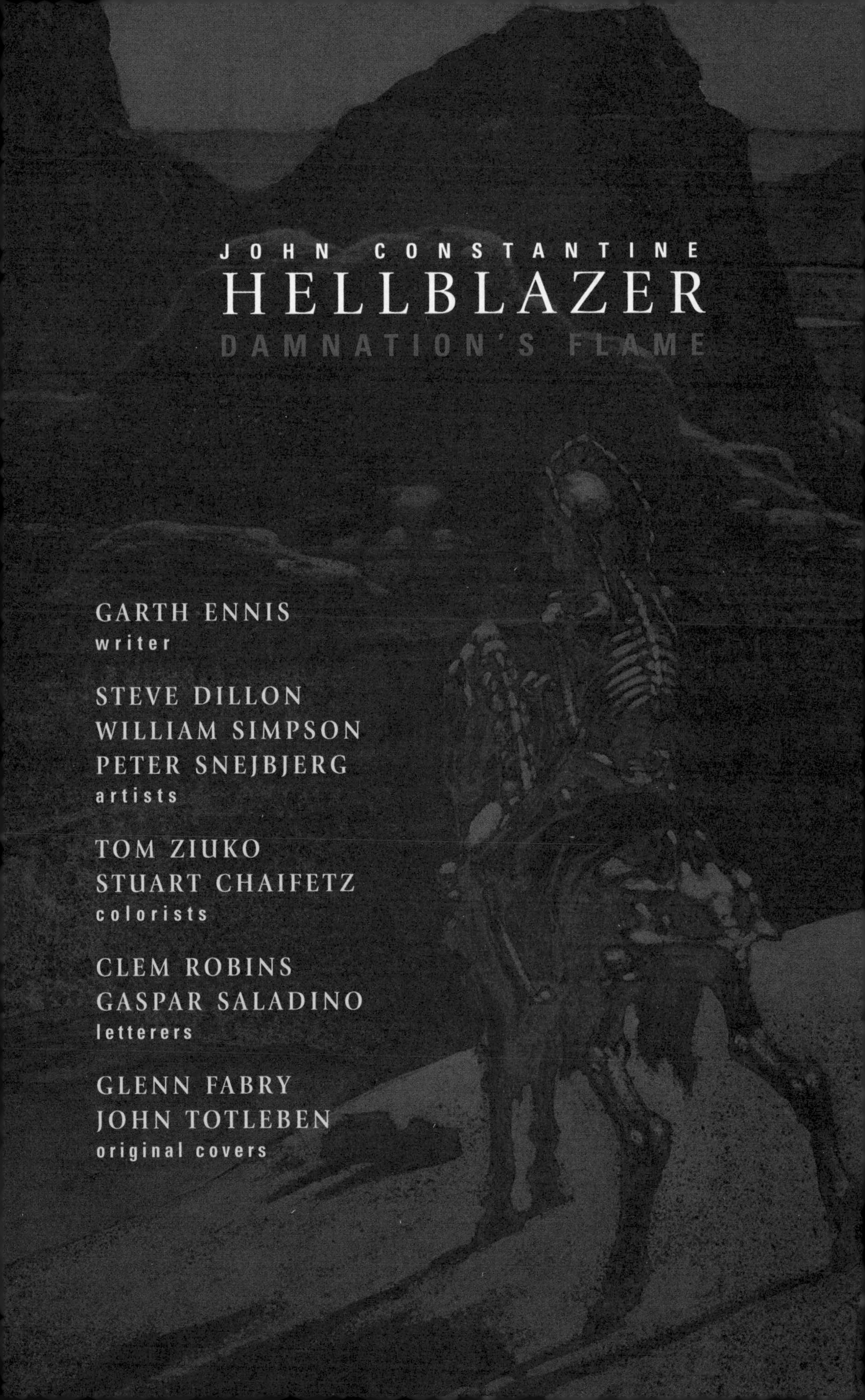

JOHN CONSTANTINE

HELLBLAZER

DAMNATION'S FLAME

GARTH ENNIS
writer

STEVE DILLON
WILLIAM SIMPSON
PETER SNEJBJERG
artists

TOM ZIUKO
STUART CHAIFETZ
colorists

CLEM ROBINS
GASPAR SALADINO
letterers

GLENN FABRY
JOHN TOTLEBEN
original covers

KAREN BERGER
VP-EXECUTIVE EDITOR

STUART MOORE
EDITOR-ORIGINAL SERIES

JULIE ROTTENBERG
ASSISTANT EDITOR-ORIGINAL SERIES

DALE CRAIN
EDITOR-COLLECTED EDITION

JIM SPIVEY
ASSOCIATE EDITOR-COLLECTED EDITION

AXEL ALONSO
CONSULTING EDITOR

ROBBIN BROSTERMAN
SENIOR ART DIRECTOR

PAUL LEVITZ
PRESIDENT & PUBLISHER

GEORG BREWER
VP-DESIGN & RETAIL PRODUCT DEVELOPMENT

RICHARD BRUNING
SENIOR VP-CREATIVE DIRECTOR

PATRICK CALDON
SENIOR VP-FINANCE & OPERATIONS

CHRIS CARAMALIS
VP-FINANCE

TERRI CUNNINGHAM
VP-MANAGING EDITOR

STEPHANIE FIERMAN
SENIOR VP-SALES & MARKETING

ALISON GILL
VP-MANUFACTURING

RICH JOHNSON
VP-BOOK TRADE SALES

HANK KANALZ
VP-GENERAL MANAGER, WILDSTORM

LILLIAN LASERSON
SENIOR VP & GENERAL COUNSEL

JIM LEE
EDITORIAL DIRECTOR-WILDSTORM

PAULA LOWITT
SENIOR VP-BUSINESS & LEGAL AFFAIRS

DAVID McKILLIPS
VP-ADVERTISING & CUSTOM PUBLISHING

JOHN NEE
VP-BUSINESS DEVELOPMENT

GREGORY NOVECK
SENIOR VP-CREATIVE AFFAIRS

CHERYL RUBIN
SENIOR VP-BRAND MANAGEMENT

BOB WAYNE
VP-SALES

JOHN CONSTANTINE, HELLBLAZER:
DAMNATION'S FLAME

DC COMICS, 1700 BROADWAY, NEW YORK, NY 10019

A WARNER BROS. ENTERTAINMENT COMPANY

PRINTED IN CANADA. THIRD PRINTING.

ISBN: 1-56389-508-0

COVER ILLUSTRATION BY GLENN FABRY.
LOGO DESIGN BY NESSIM HIGSON.
PUBLICATION DESIGN BY MURPHY FOGELNEST.

JOHN CONSTANTINE

A trenchcoated mystic with an instinct for trouble, John Constantine has made more enemies than he can count. Chief among them is the First of the Fallen, ruler of Hell, who has sworn a bloody and eternal vengeance.

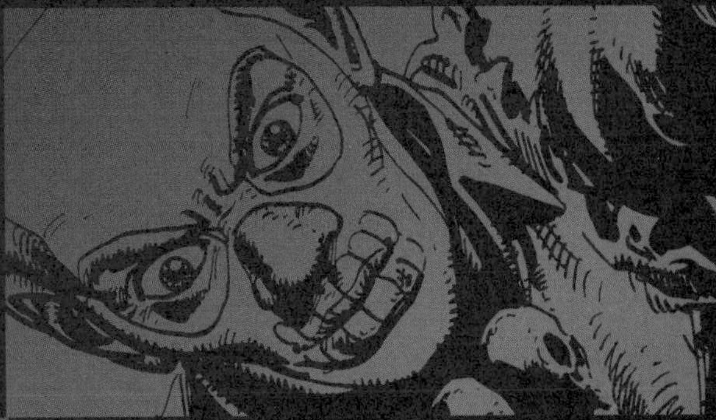

But more earthly concerns have preoccupied Constantine lately. Devastated by the departure of his lover Kit, he spent several months living homeless and derelict on the streets before pulling his world together.

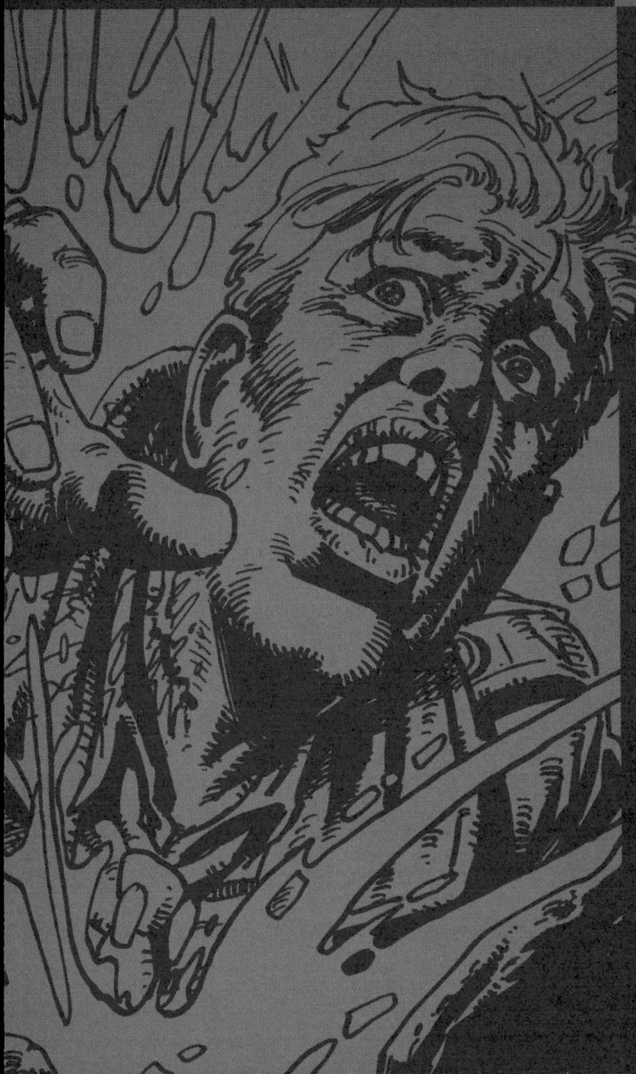

Now the time has come for another chapter in the magus's life—and a change of scene from his usual London haunts. But the First of the Fallen isn't the only supernatural force with a grudge against Constantine....

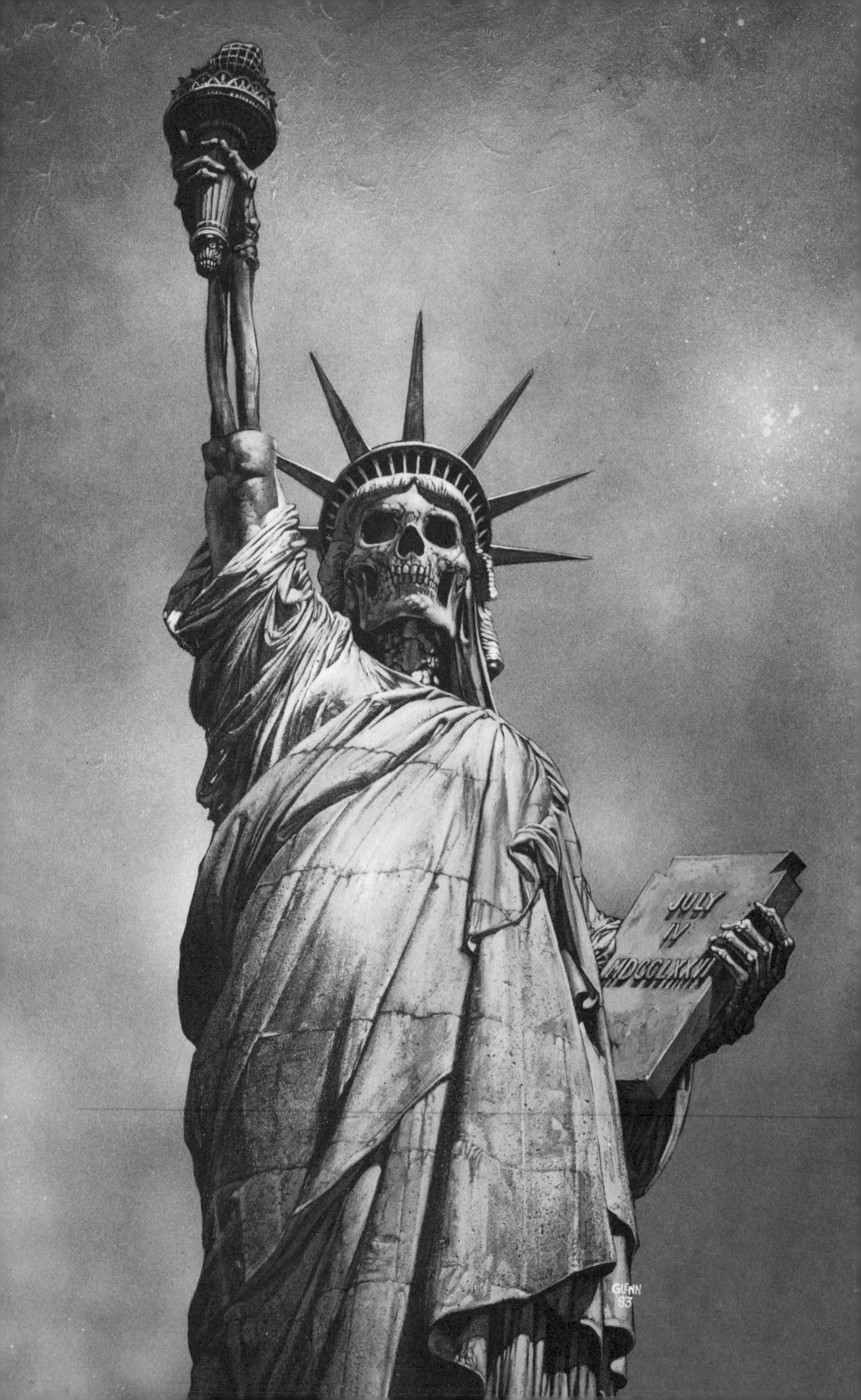
JULY
IV
MDCCLXXVI
GLENN
93

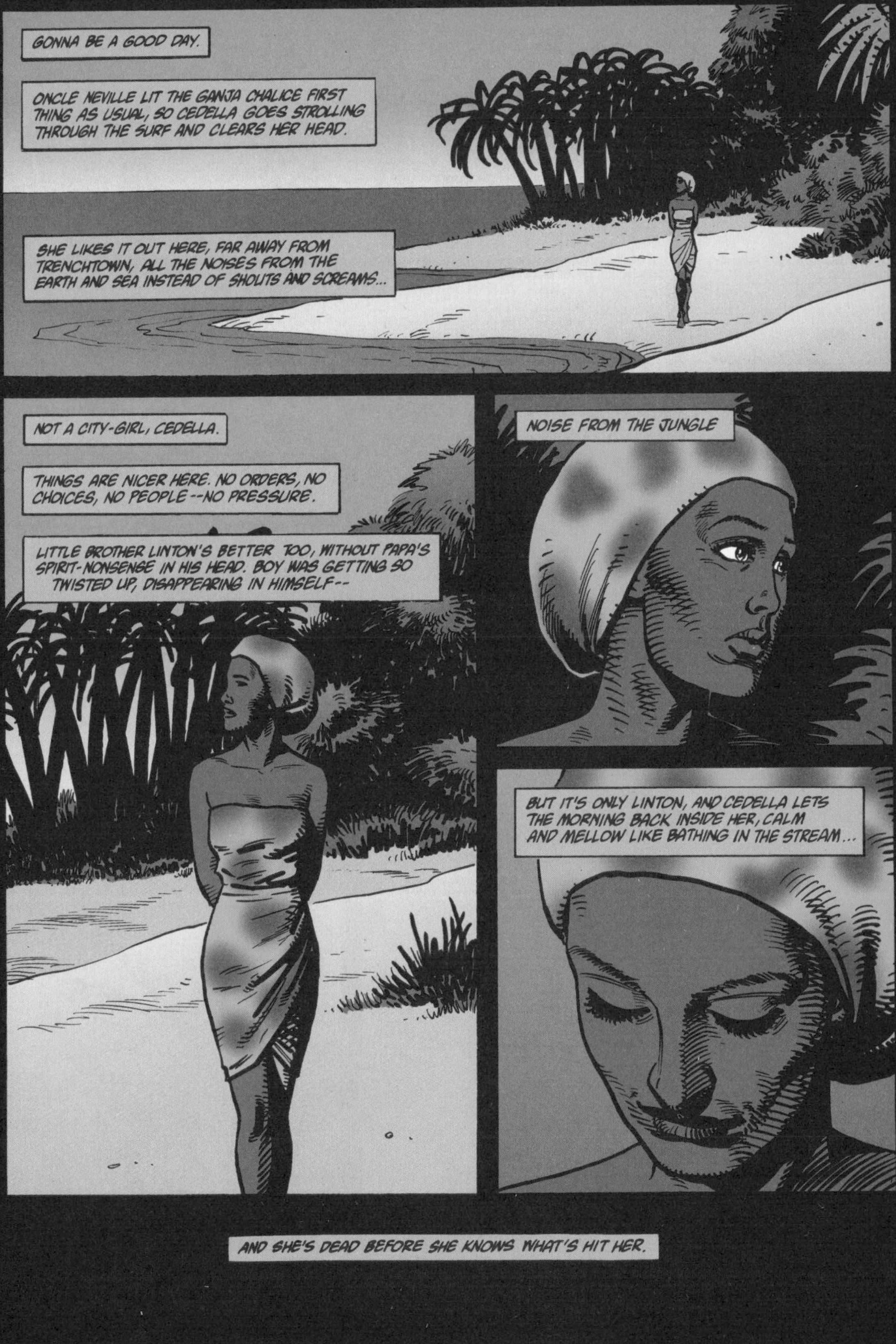
GONNA BE A GOOD DAY.
ONCLE NEVILLE LIT THE GANJA CHALICE FIRST THING AS USUAL, SO CEDELLA GOES STROLLING THROUGH THE SURF AND CLEARS HER HEAD.
SHE LIKES IT OUT HERE, FAR AWAY FROM TRENCHTOWN, ALL THE NOISES FROM THE EARTH AND SEA INSTEAD OF SHOUTS AND SCREAMS...
NOT A CITY-GIRL, CEDELLA.
THINGS ARE NICER HERE. NO ORDERS, NO CHOICES, NO PEOPLE--NO PRESSURE.
LITTLE BROTHER LINTON'S BETTER TOO, WITHOUT PAPA'S SPIRIT-NONSENSE IN HIS HEAD. BOY WAS GETTING SO TWISTED UP, DISAPPEARING IN HIMSELF--
NOISE FROM THE JUNGLE
BUT IT'S ONLY LINTON, AND CEDELLA LETS THE MORNING BACK INSIDE HER, CALM AND MELLOW LIKE BATHING IN THE STREAM...
AND SHE'S DEAD BEFORE SHE KNOWS WHAT'S HIT HER.

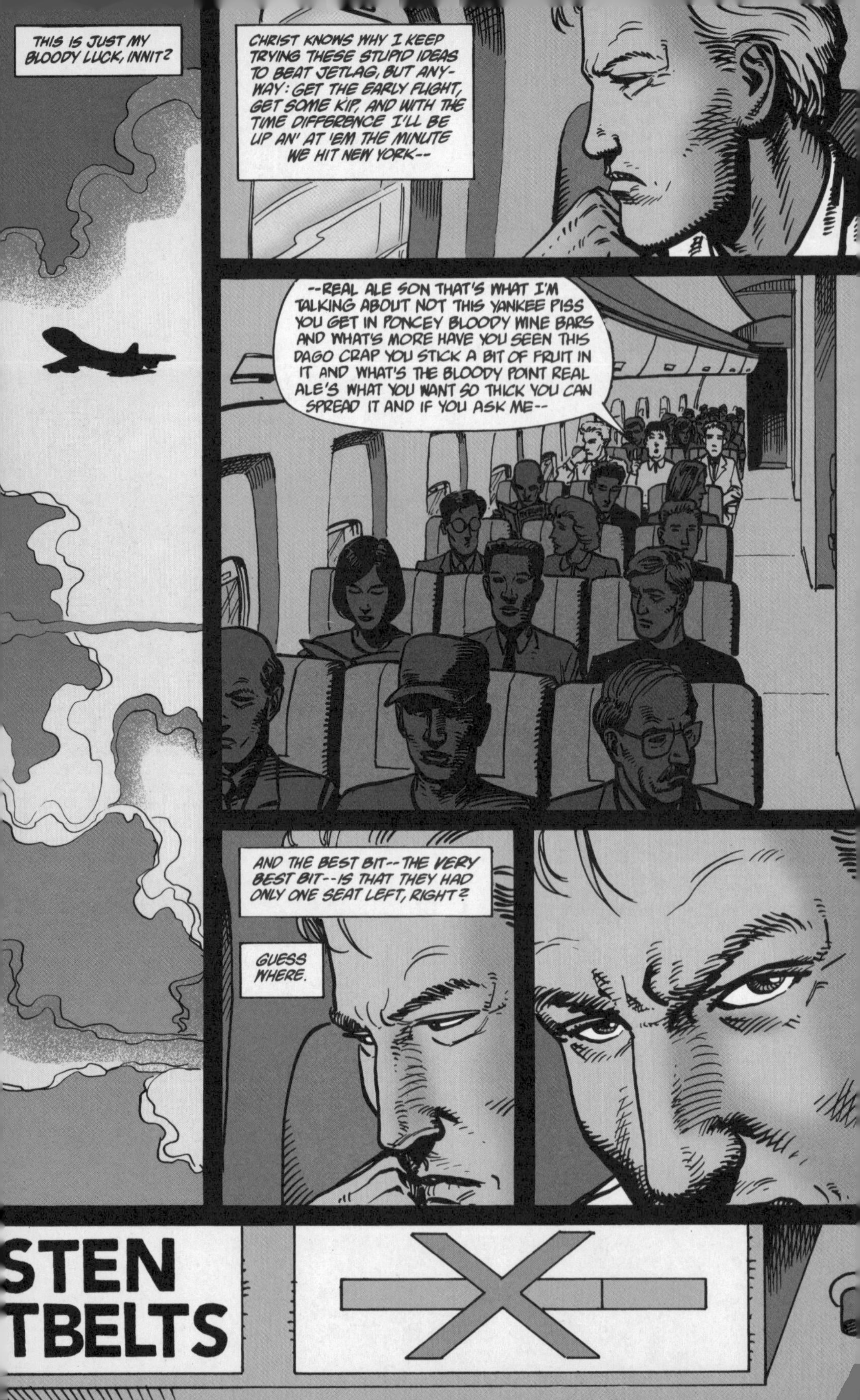
THIS IS JUST MY BLOODY LUCK, INNIT?
CHRIST KNOWS WHY I KEEP TRYING THESE STUPID IDEAS TO BEAT JETLAG, BUT ANYWAY: GET THE EARLY FLIGHT, GET SOME KIP, AND WITH THE TIME DIFFERENCE I'LL BE UP AN' AT 'EM THE MINUTE WE HIT NEW YORK--
--REAL ALE SON THAT'S WHAT I'M TALKING ABOUT NOT THIS YANKEE PISS YOU GET IN PONCEY BLOODY WINE BARS AND WHAT'S MORE HAVE YOU SEEN THIS DAGO CRAP YOU STICK A BIT OF FRUIT IN IT AND WHAT'S THE BLOODY POINT REAL ALE'S WHAT YOU WANT SO THICK YOU CAN SPREAD IT AND IF YOU ASK ME--
AND THE BEST BIT--THE VERY BEST BIT--IS THAT THEY HAD ONLY ONE SEAT LEFT, RIGHT?
GUESS WHERE.
STEN
TBELTS

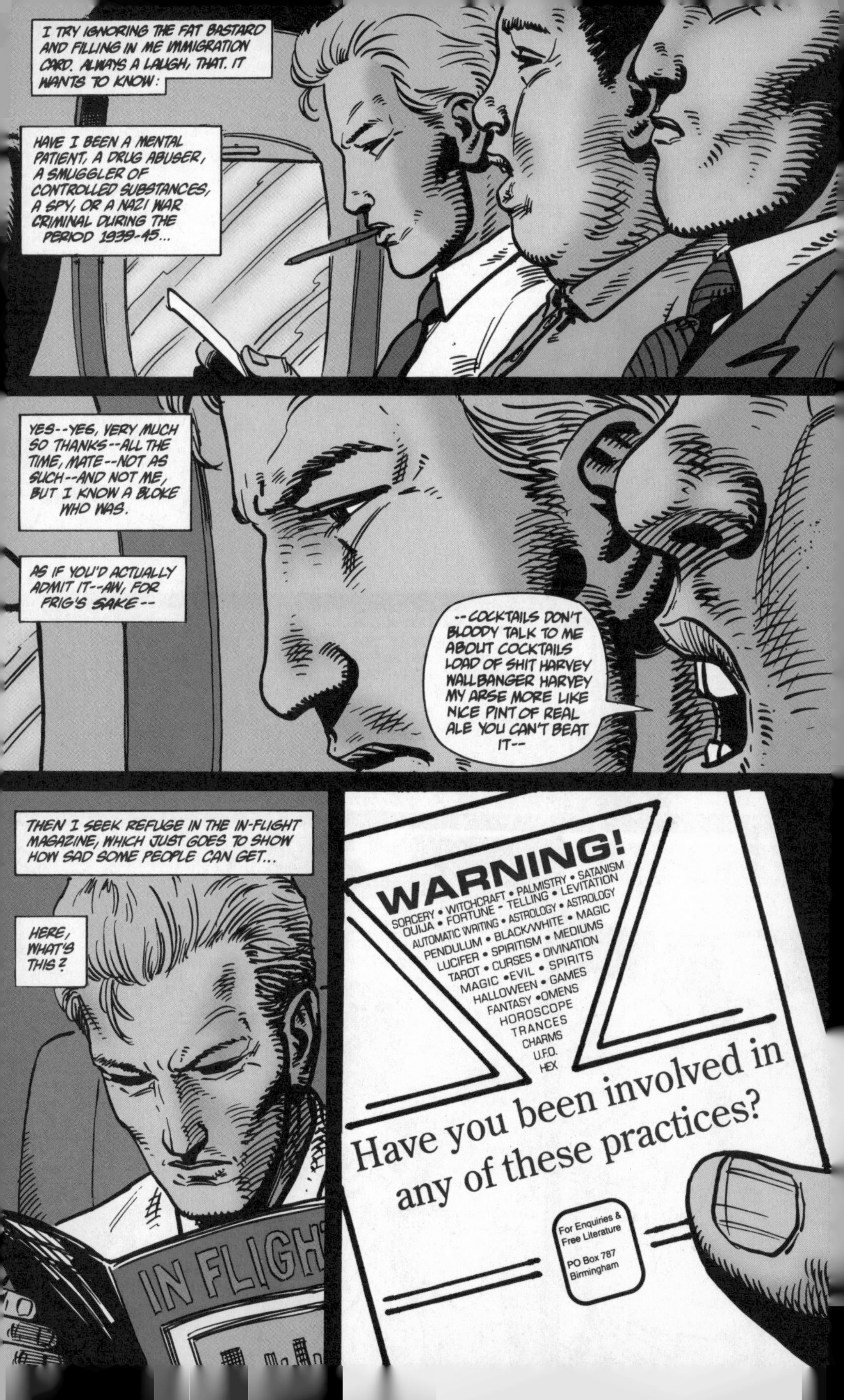

I TRY IGNORING THE FAT BASTARD AND FILLING IN ME IMMIGRATION CARD. ALWAYS A LAUGH, THAT. IT WANTS TO KNOW:
HAVE I BEEN A MENTAL PATIENT, A DRUG ABUSER, A SMUGGLER OF CONTROLLED SUBSTANCES, A SPY, OR A NAZI WAR CRIMINAL DURING THE PERIOD 1939-45...
YES--YES, VERY MUCH SO THANKS--ALL THE TIME, MATE--NOT AS SUCH--AND NOT ME, BUT I KNOW A BLOKE WHO WAS.
AS IF YOU'D ACTUALLY ADMIT IT--AW, FOR FRIG'S SAKE--
--COCKTAILS DON'T BLOODY TALK TO ME ABOUT COCKTAILS LOAD OF SHIT HARVEY WALLBANGER HARVEY MY ARSE MORE LIKE NICE PINT OF REAL ALE YOU CAN'T BEAT IT--
THEN I SEEK REFUGE IN THE IN-FLIGHT MAGAZINE, WHICH JUST GOES TO SHOW HOW SAD SOME PEOPLE CAN GET...
HERE, WHAT'S THIS?
IN FLIGHT
WARNING!
SORCERY • WITCHCRAFT • PALMISTRY • SATANISM
OUIJA • FORTUNE - TELLING • LEVITATION
AUTOMATIC WRITING • ASTROLOGY • ASTROLOGY
PENDULUM • BLACK/WHITE • MAGIC
LUCIFER • SPIRITISM • MEDIUMS
TAROT • CURSES • DIVINATION
MAGIC • EVIL • SPIRITS
HALLOWEEN • GAMES
FANTASY • OMENS
HOROSCOPE
TRANCES
CHARMS
U.F.O.
HEX
Have you been involved in any of these practices?
For Enquiries & Free Literature
PO Box 787 Birmingham

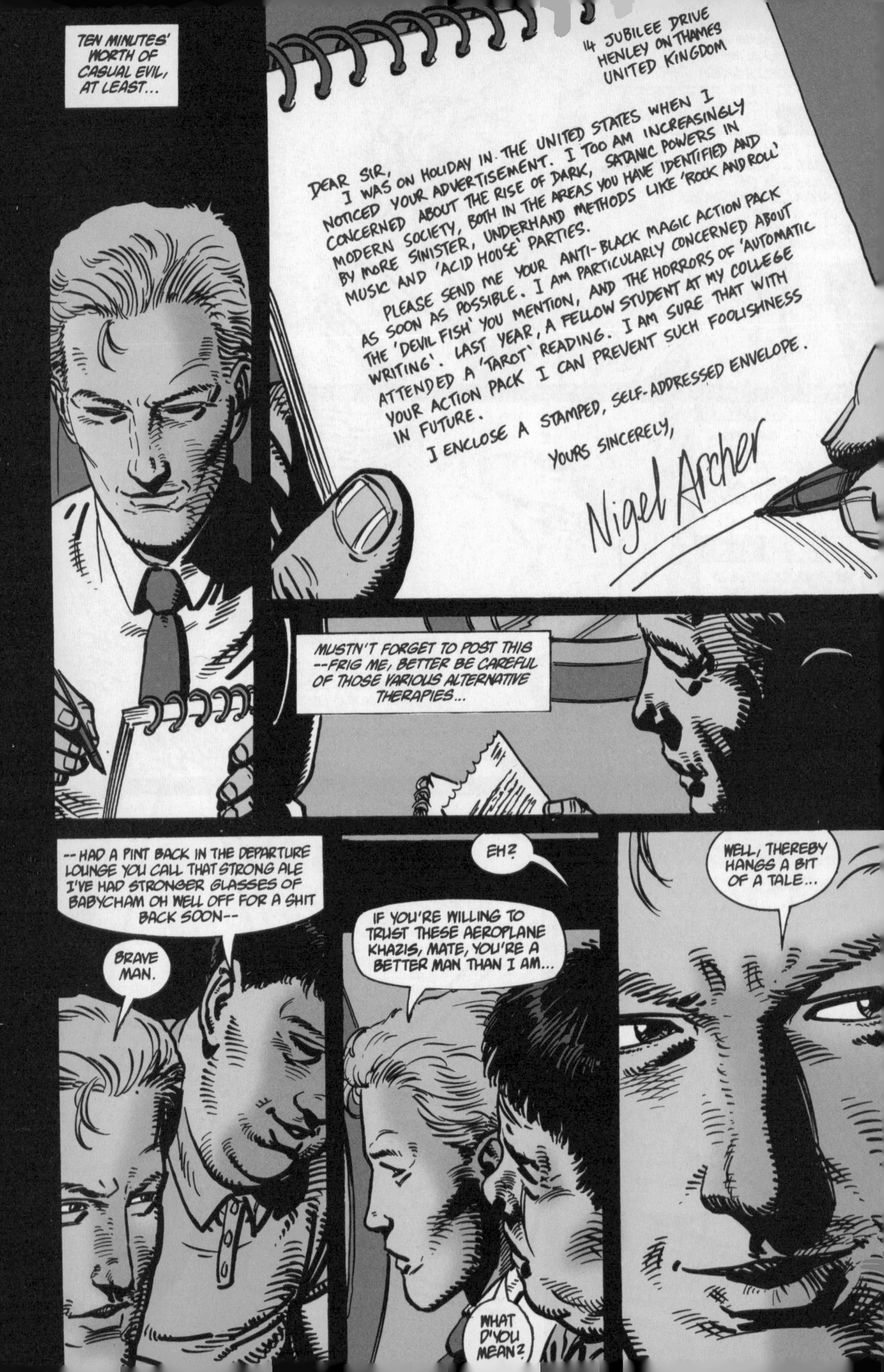
TEN MINUTES' WORTH OF CASUAL EVIL, AT LEAST...
14 JUBILEE DRIVE
HENLEY ON THAMES
UNITED KINGDOM
DEAR SIR,
I WAS ON HOLIDAY IN THE UNITED STATES WHEN I NOTICED YOUR ADVERTISEMENT. I TOO AM INCREASINGLY CONCERNED ABOUT THE RISE OF DARK, SATANIC POWERS IN MODERN SOCIETY, BOTH IN THE AREAS YOU HAVE IDENTIFIED AND BY MORE SINISTER, UNDERHAND METHODS LIKE 'ROCK AND ROLL' MUSIC AND 'ACID HOUSE' PARTIES.
PLEASE SEND ME YOUR ANTI-BLACK MAGIC ACTION PACK AS SOON AS POSSIBLE. I AM PARTICULARLY CONCERNED ABOUT THE 'DEVIL FISH' YOU MENTION, AND THE HORRORS OF 'AUTOMATIC WRITING'. LAST YEAR, A FELLOW STUDENT AT MY COLLEGE ATTENDED A 'TAROT' READING. I AM SURE THAT WITH YOUR ACTION PACK I CAN PREVENT SUCH FOOLISHNESS IN FUTURE.
I ENCLOSE A STAMPED, SELF-ADDRESSED ENVELOPE.
YOURS SINCERELY,
Nigel Archer
MUSTN'T FORGET TO POST THIS --FRIG ME, BETTER BE CAREFUL OF THOSE VARIOUS ALTERNATIVE THERAPIES...
--HAD A PINT BACK IN THE DEPARTURE LOUNGE YOU CALL THAT STRONG ALE I'VE HAD STRONGER GLASSES OF BABYCHAM OH WELL OFF FOR A SHIT BACK SOON--
BRAVE MAN.
EH?
IF YOU'RE WILLING TO TRUST THESE AEROPLANE KHAZIS, MATE, YOU'RE A BETTER MAN THAN I AM...
WHAT D'YOU MEAN?
WELL, THEREBY HANGS A BIT OF A TALE...

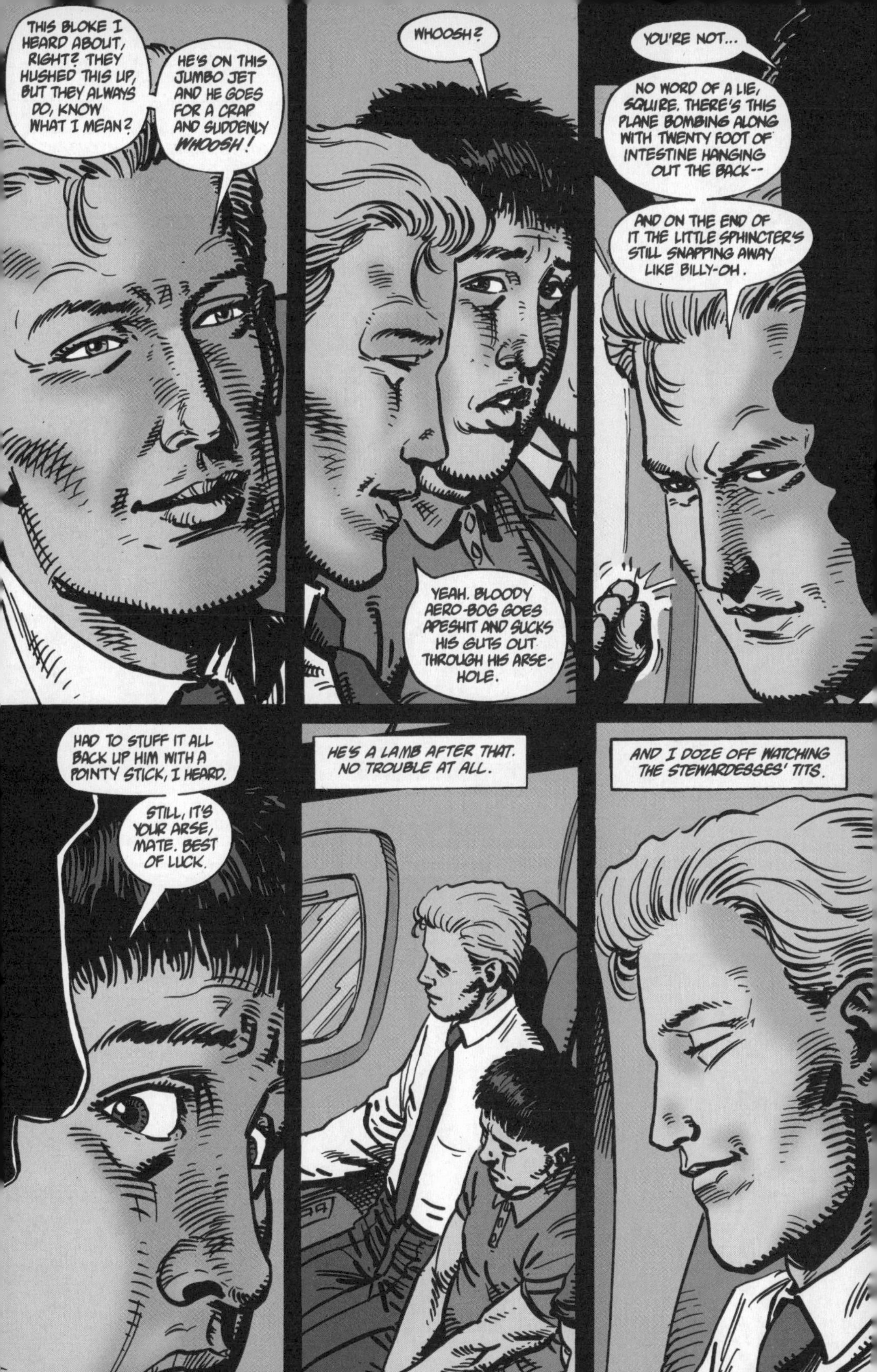

THIS BLOKE I HEARD ABOUT, RIGHT? THEY HUSHED THIS UP, BUT THEY ALWAYS DO, KNOW WHAT I MEAN?
HE'S ON THIS JUMBO JET AND HE GOES FOR A CRAP AND SUDDENLY WHOOSH!
WHOOSH?
YEAH. BLOODY AERO-BOG GOES APESHIT AND SUCKS HIS GUTS OUT THROUGH HIS ARSE-HOLE.
YOU'RE NOT...
NO WORD OF A LIE, SQUIRE. THERE'S THIS PLANE BOMBING ALONG WITH TWENTY FOOT OF INTESTINE HANGING OUT THE BACK--
AND ON THE END OF IT THE LITTLE SPHINCTER'S STILL SNAPPING AWAY LIKE BILLY-OH.
HAD TO STUFF IT ALL BACK UP HIM WITH A POINTY STICK, I HEARD.
STILL, IT'S YOUR ARSE, MATE. BEST OF LUCK.
HE'S A LAMB AFTER THAT. NO TROUBLE AT ALL.
AND I DOZE OFF WATCHING THE STEWARDESSES' TITS.

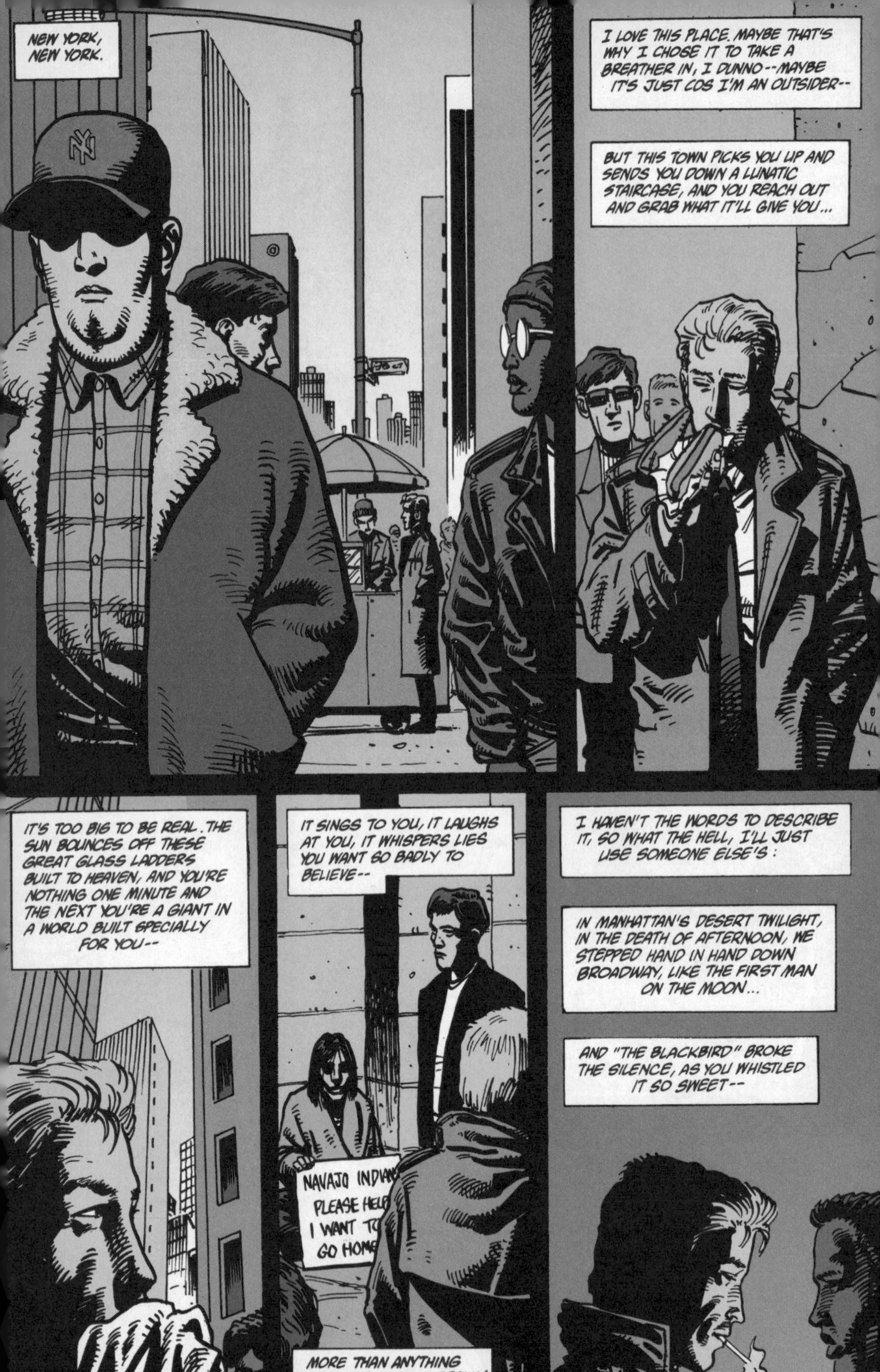
NEW YORK, NEW YORK.
I LOVE THIS PLACE. MAYBE THAT'S WHY I CHOSE IT TO TAKE A BREATHER IN, I DUNNO--MAYBE IT'S JUST COS I'M AN OUTSIDER--
BUT THIS TOWN PICKS YOU UP AND SENDS YOU DOWN A LUNATIC STAIRCASE, AND YOU REACH OUT AND GRAB WHAT IT'LL GIVE YOU...
IT'S TOO BIG TO BE REAL. THE SUN BOUNCES OFF THESE GREAT GLASS LADDERS BUILT TO HEAVEN, AND YOU'RE NOTHING ONE MINUTE AND THE NEXT YOU'RE A GIANT IN A WORLD BUILT SPECIALLY FOR YOU--
IT SINGS TO YOU, IT LAUGHS AT YOU, IT WHISPERS LIES YOU WANT SO BADLY TO BELIEVE--
NAVAJO INDIAN
PLEASE HEL
I WANT TO
GO HOME
MORE THAN ANYTHING ELSE, AND THIS IS REALLY WHY I CAME HERE, IT'S SOMETHING NEW.
I HAVEN'T THE WORDS TO DESCRIBE IT, SO WHAT THE HELL, I'LL JUST USE SOMEONE ELSE'S:
IN MANHATTAN'S DESERT TWILIGHT, IN THE DEATH OF AFTERNOON, WE STEPPED HAND IN HAND DOWN BROADWAY, LIKE THE FIRST MAN ON THE MOON...
AND "THE BLACKBIRD" BROKE THE SILENCE, AS YOU WHISTLED IT SO SWEET--

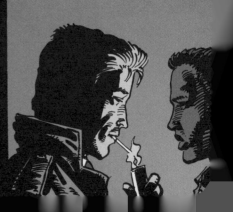

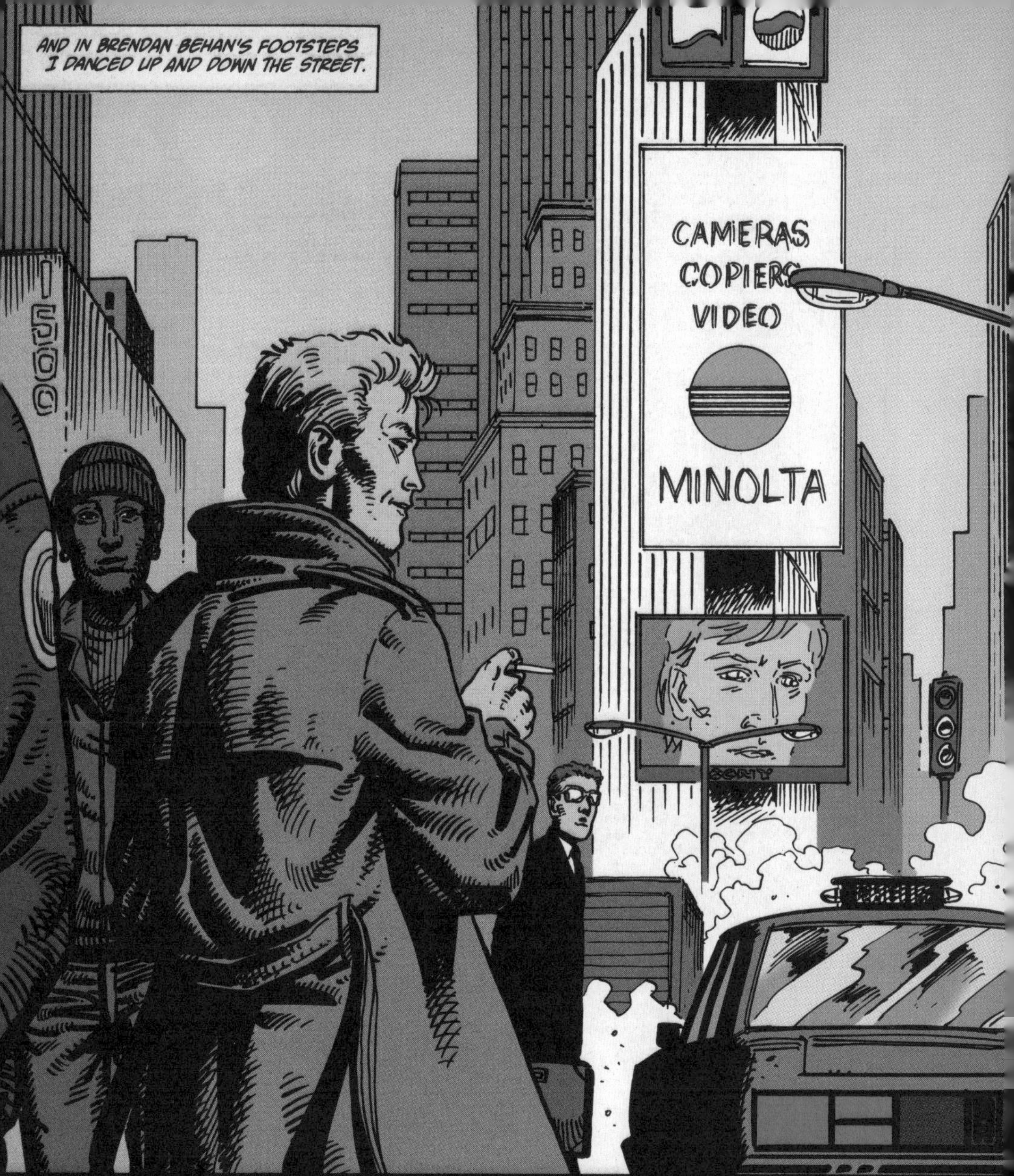
AND IN BRENDAN BEHAN'S FOOTSTEPS I DANCED UP AND DOWN THE STREET.
CAMERAS
COPIERS
VIDEO
MINOLTA

DAMNATION'S FLAME PART ONE

BRAVE NEW WORLD

GARTH ENNIS • *writer* **STEVE DILLON** • *artist*
TOM ZIUKO • *colors* **CLEM ROBINS** • *letters*
JULIE ROTTENBERG • *asst. editor* **STUART MOORE** • *editor*

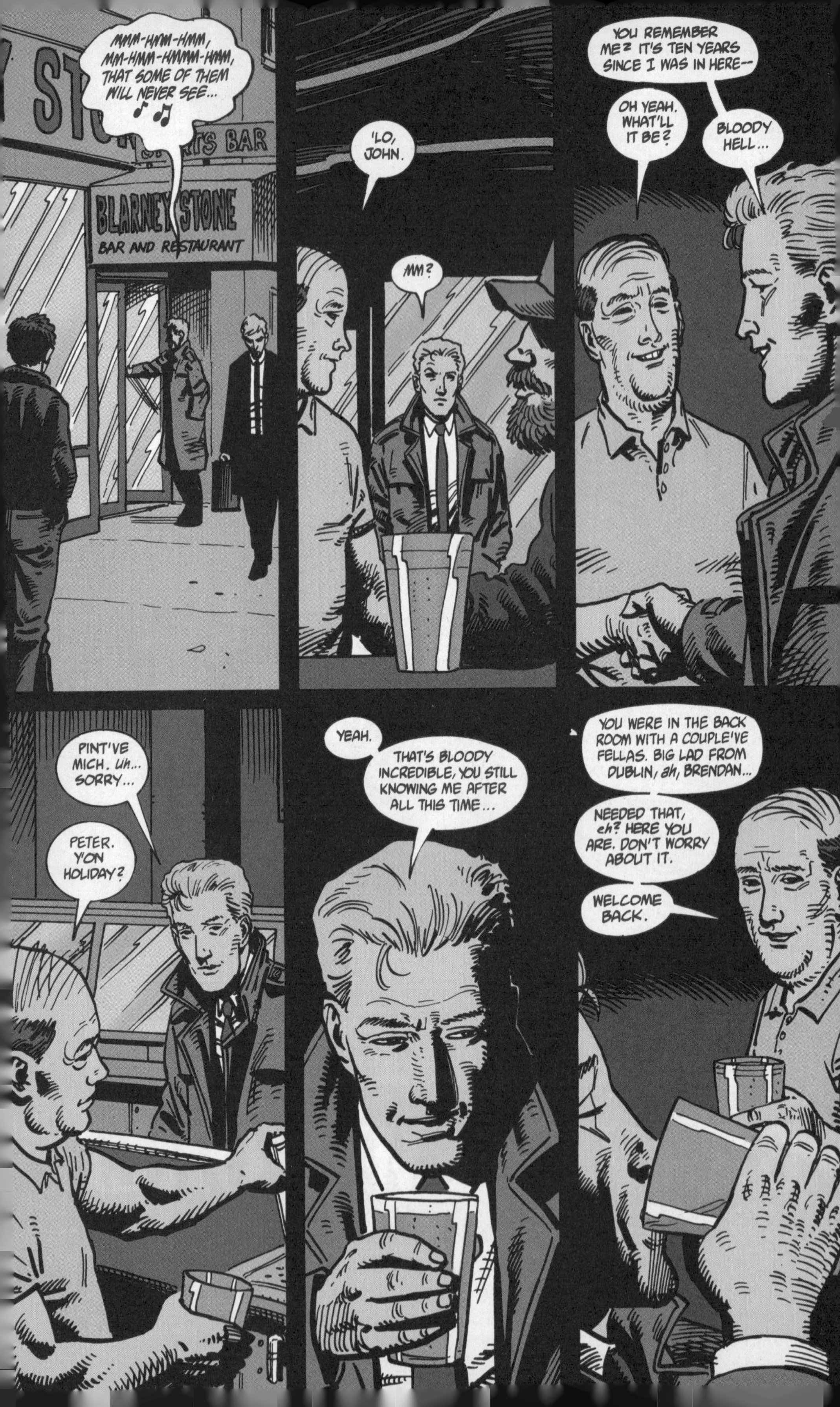
MMM-HMM-HMM, MM-HMM-HMMM-HMM, THAT SOME OF THEM WILL NEVER SEE...
SPORTS BAR
BLARNEY STONE
BAR AND RESTAURANT
'LO, JOHN.
MM?
YOU REMEMBER ME? IT'S TEN YEARS SINCE I WAS IN HERE--
OH YEAH. WHAT'LL IT BE?
BLOODY HELL...
PINT'VE MICH. UH... SORRY...
PETER. Y'ON HOLIDAY?
YEAH.
THAT'S BLOODY INCREDIBLE, YOU STILL KNOWING ME AFTER ALL THIS TIME...
YOU WERE IN THE BACK ROOM WITH A COUPLE'VE FELLAS. BIG LAD FROM DUBLIN, AH, BRENDAN...
NEEDED THAT, EH? HERE YOU ARE. DON'T WORRY ABOUT IT.
WELCOME BACK.

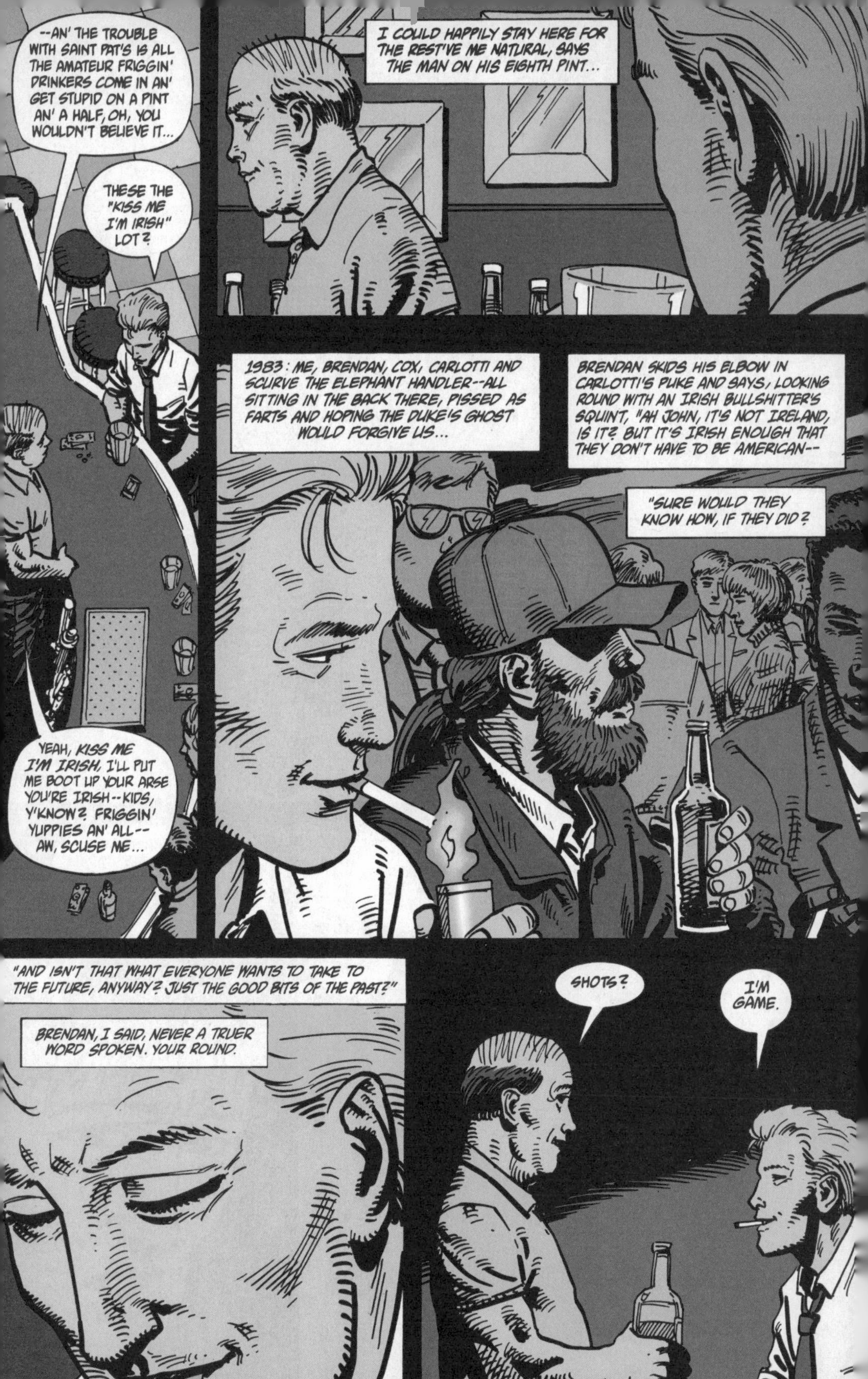
--AN' THE TROUBLE WITH SAINT PAT'S IS ALL THE AMATEUR FRIGGIN' DRINKERS COME IN AN' GET STUPID ON A PINT AN' A HALF, OH, YOU WOULDN'T BELIEVE IT...
THESE THE "KISS ME I'M IRISH" LOT?
YEAH, KISS ME I'M IRISH, I'LL PUT ME BOOT UP YOUR ARSE YOU'RE IRISH--KIDS, Y'KNOW? FRIGGIN' YUPPIES AN' ALL--AW, SCUSE ME...
I COULD HAPPILY STAY HERE FOR THE REST'VE ME NATURAL, SAYS THE MAN ON HIS EIGHTH PINT...
1983: ME, BRENDAN, COX, CARLOTTI AND SCURVE THE ELEPHANT HANDLER--ALL SITTING IN THE BACK THERE, PISSED AS FARTS AND HOPING THE DUKE'S GHOST WOULD FORGIVE US...
BRENDAN SKIDS HIS ELBOW IN CARLOTTI'S PUKE AND SAYS, LOOKING ROUND WITH AN IRISH BULLSHITTER'S SQUINT, "AH JOHN, IT'S NOT IRELAND, IS IT? BUT IT'S IRISH ENOUGH THAT THEY DON'T HAVE TO BE AMERICAN--
"SURE WOULD THEY KNOW HOW, IF THEY DID?
"AND ISN'T THAT WHAT EVERYONE WANTS TO TAKE TO THE FUTURE, ANYWAY? JUST THE GOOD BITS OF THE PAST?"
BRENDAN, I SAID, NEVER A TRUER WORD SPOKEN. YOUR ROUND.
SHOTS?
I'M GAME.

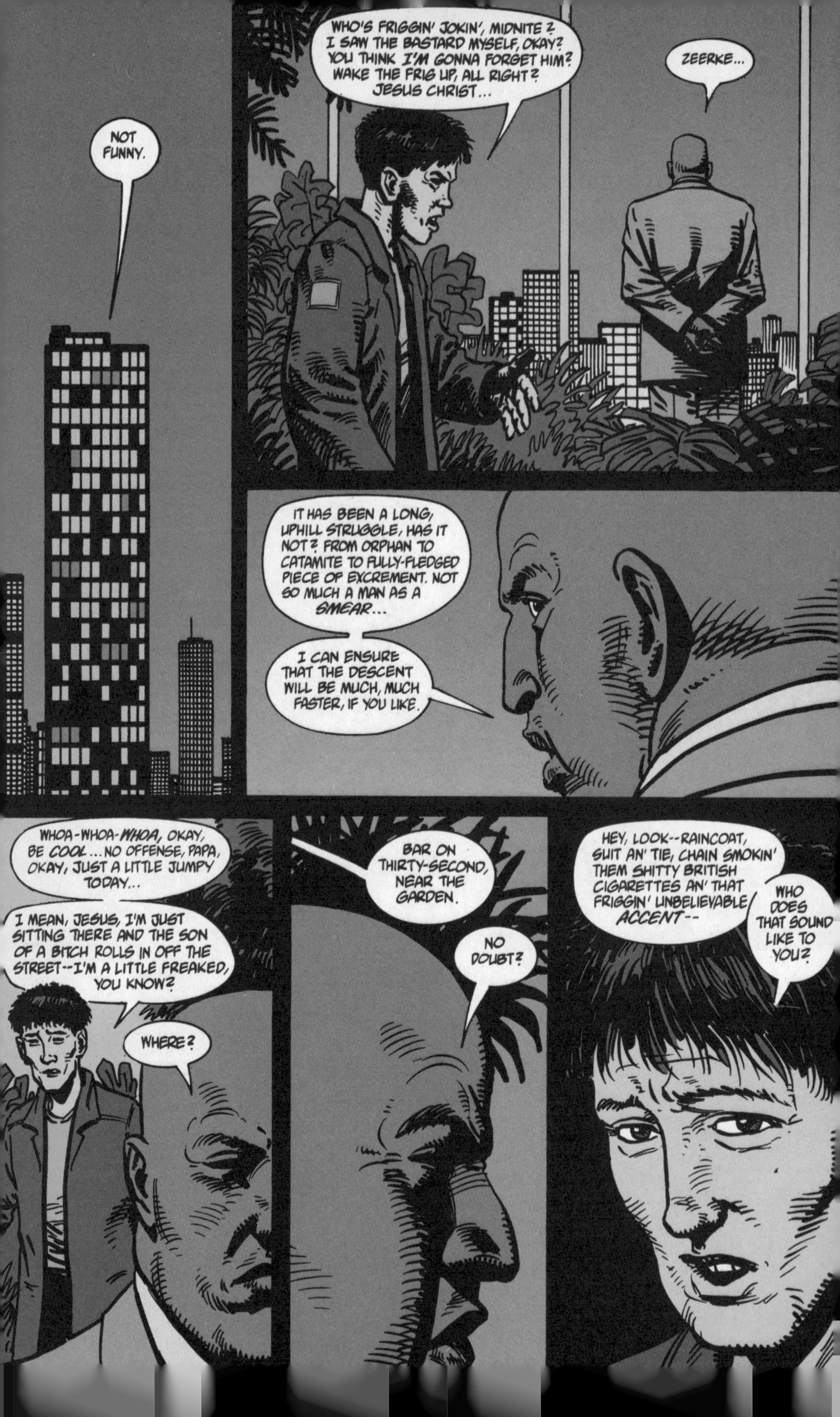
NOT FUNNY.
WHO'S FRIGGIN' JOKIN', MIDNITE? I SAW THE BASTARD MYSELF, OKAY? YOU THINK I'M GONNA FORGET HIM? WAKE THE FRIG UP, ALL RIGHT? JESUS CHRIST...
ZEERKE...
IT HAS BEEN A LONG, UPHILL STRUGGLE, HAS IT NOT? FROM ORPHAN TO CATAMITE TO FULLY-FLEDGED PIECE OF EXCREMENT. NOT SO MUCH A MAN AS A SMEAR...
I CAN ENSURE THAT THE DESCENT WILL BE MUCH, MUCH FASTER, IF YOU LIKE.
WHOA-WHOA-WHOA, OKAY, BE COOL... NO OFFENSE, PAPA, OKAY, JUST A LITTLE JUMPY TODAY...
I MEAN, JESUS, I'M JUST SITTING THERE AND THE SON OF A BITCH ROLLS IN OFF THE STREET--I'M A LITTLE FREAKED, YOU KNOW?
WHERE?
BAR ON THIRTY-SECOND, NEAR THE GARDEN.
NO DOUBT?
HEY, LOOK--RAINCOAT, SUIT AN' TIE, CHAIN SMOKIN' THEM SHITTY BRITISH CIGARETTES AN' THAT FRIGGIN' UNBELIEVABLE ACCENT--
WHO DOES THAT SOUND LIKE TO YOU?

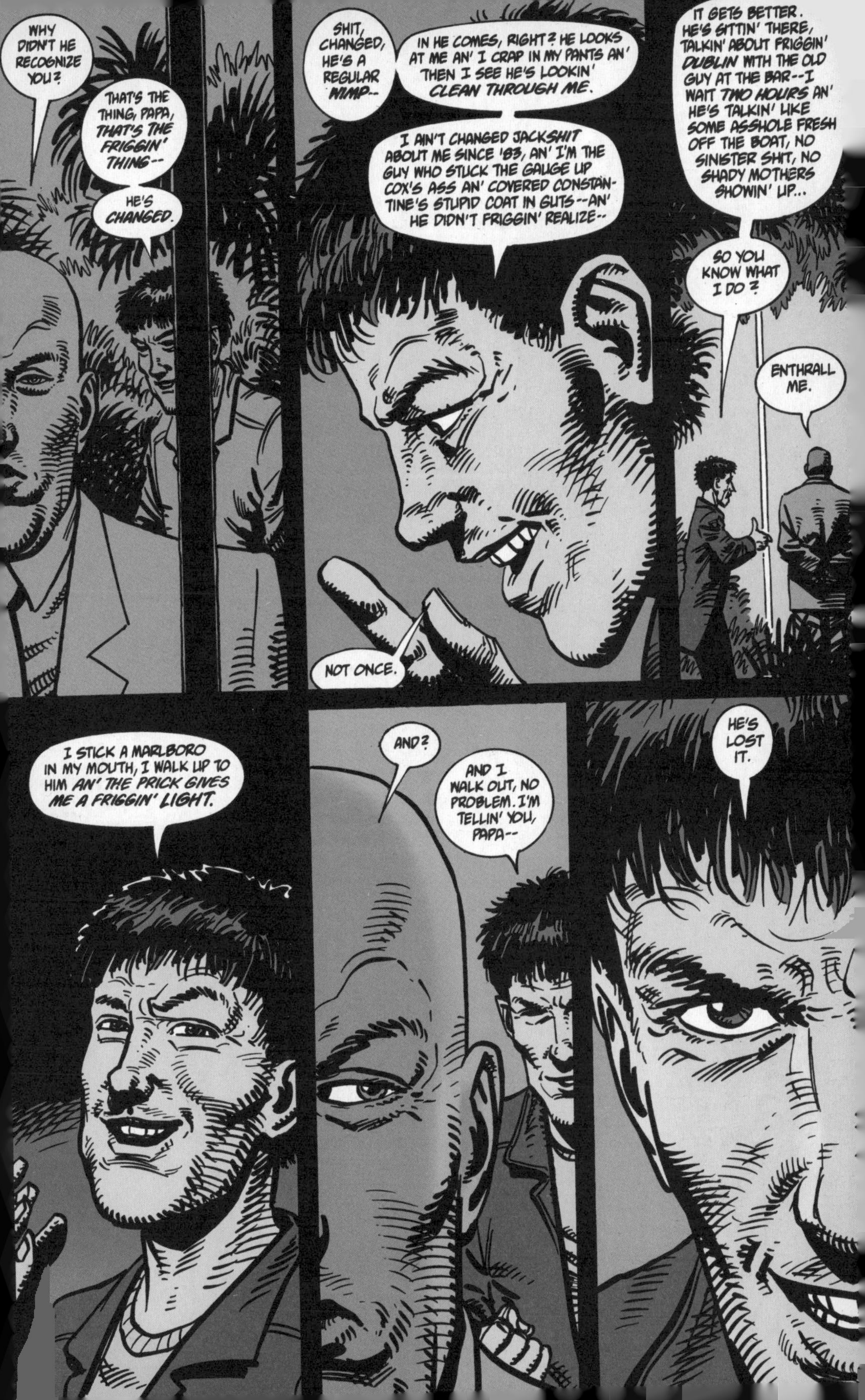
WHY DIDN'T HE RECOGNIZE YOU?
THAT'S THE THING, PAPA, THAT'S THE FRIGGIN' THING--
HE'S CHANGED.
SHIT, CHANGED, HE'S A REGULAR WIMP--
IN HE COMES, RIGHT? HE LOOKS AT ME AN' I CRAP IN MY PANTS AN' THEN I SEE HE'S LOOKIN' CLEAN THROUGH ME.
I AIN'T CHANGED JACKSHIT ABOUT ME SINCE '83, AN' I'M THE GUY WHO STUCK THE GAUGE UP COX'S ASS AN' COVERED CONSTANTINE'S STUPID COAT IN GUTS--AN' HE DIDN'T FRIGGIN' REALIZE--
NOT ONCE.
IT GETS BETTER. HE'S SITTIN' THERE, TALKIN' ABOUT FRIGGIN' DUBLIN WITH THE OLD GUY AT THE BAR--I WAIT TWO HOURS AN' HE'S TALKIN' LIKE SOME ASSHOLE FRESH OFF THE BOAT, NO SINISTER SHIT, NO SHADY MOTHERS SHOWIN' UP...
SO YOU KNOW WHAT I DO?
ENTHRALL ME.
I STICK A MARLBORO IN MY MOUTH, I WALK UP TO HIM AN' THE PRICK GIVES ME A FRIGGIN' LIGHT.
AND?
AND I WALK OUT, NO PROBLEM. I'M TELLIN' YOU, PAPA--
HE'S LOST IT.

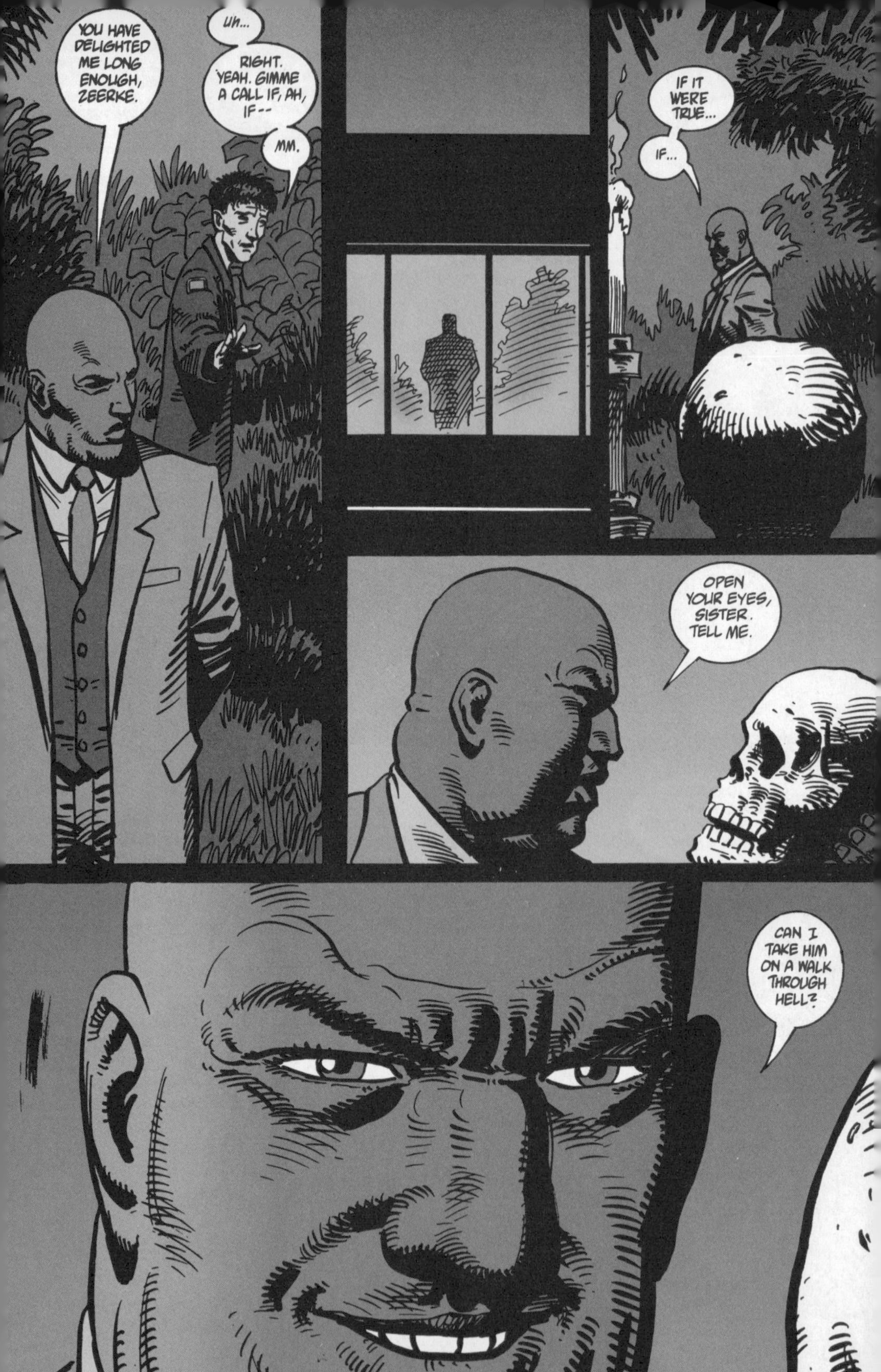
YOU HAVE DELIGHTED ME LONG ENOUGH, ZEERKE.
uh...
RIGHT. YEAH. GIMME A CALL IF, AH, IF--
MM.
IF IT WERE TRUE...
IF...
OPEN YOUR EYES, SISTER. TELL ME.
CAN I TAKE HIM ON A WALK THROUGH HELL?

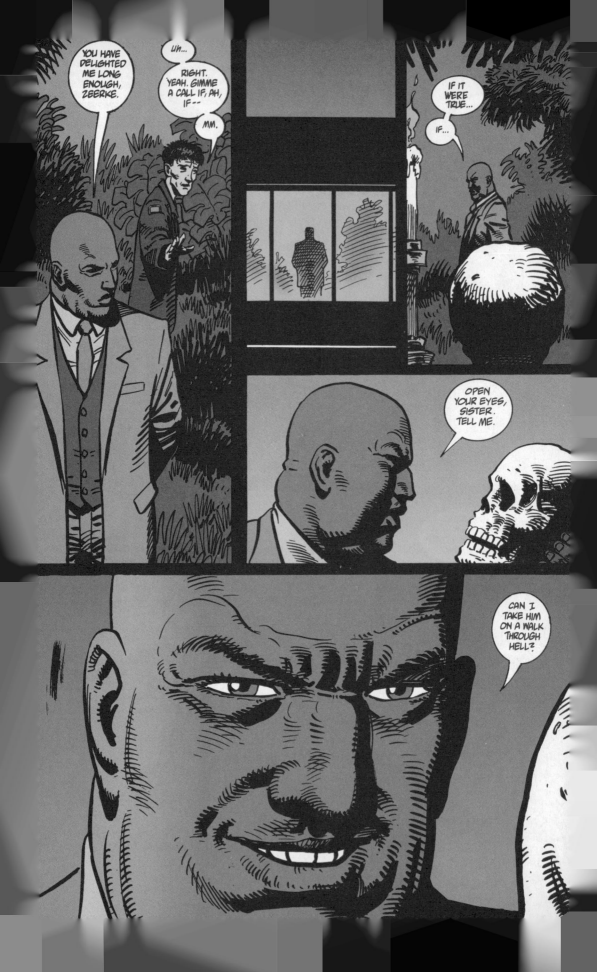

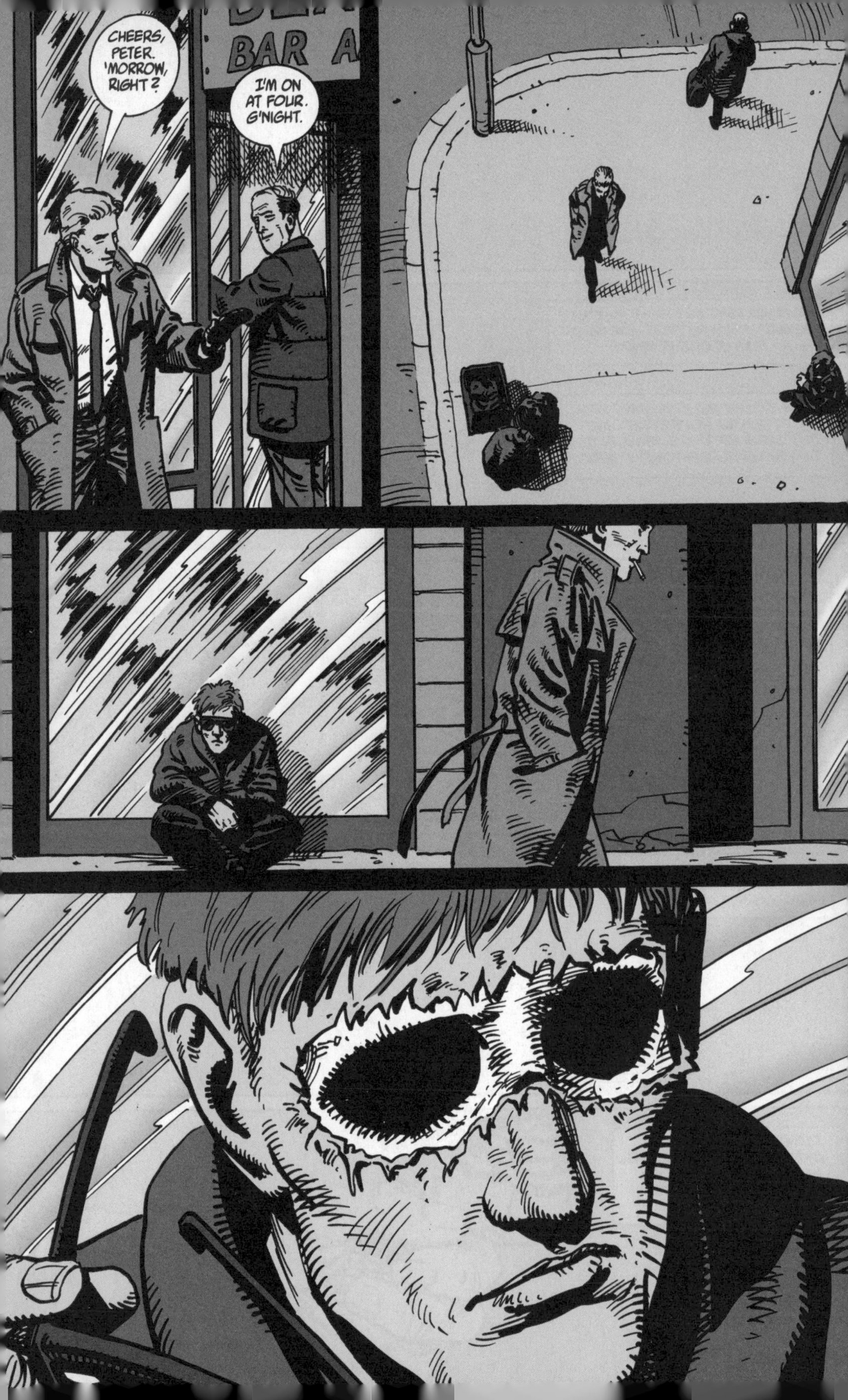
BAR A
CHEERS, PETER. 'MORROW, RIGHT?
I'M ON AT FOUR. G'NIGHT.

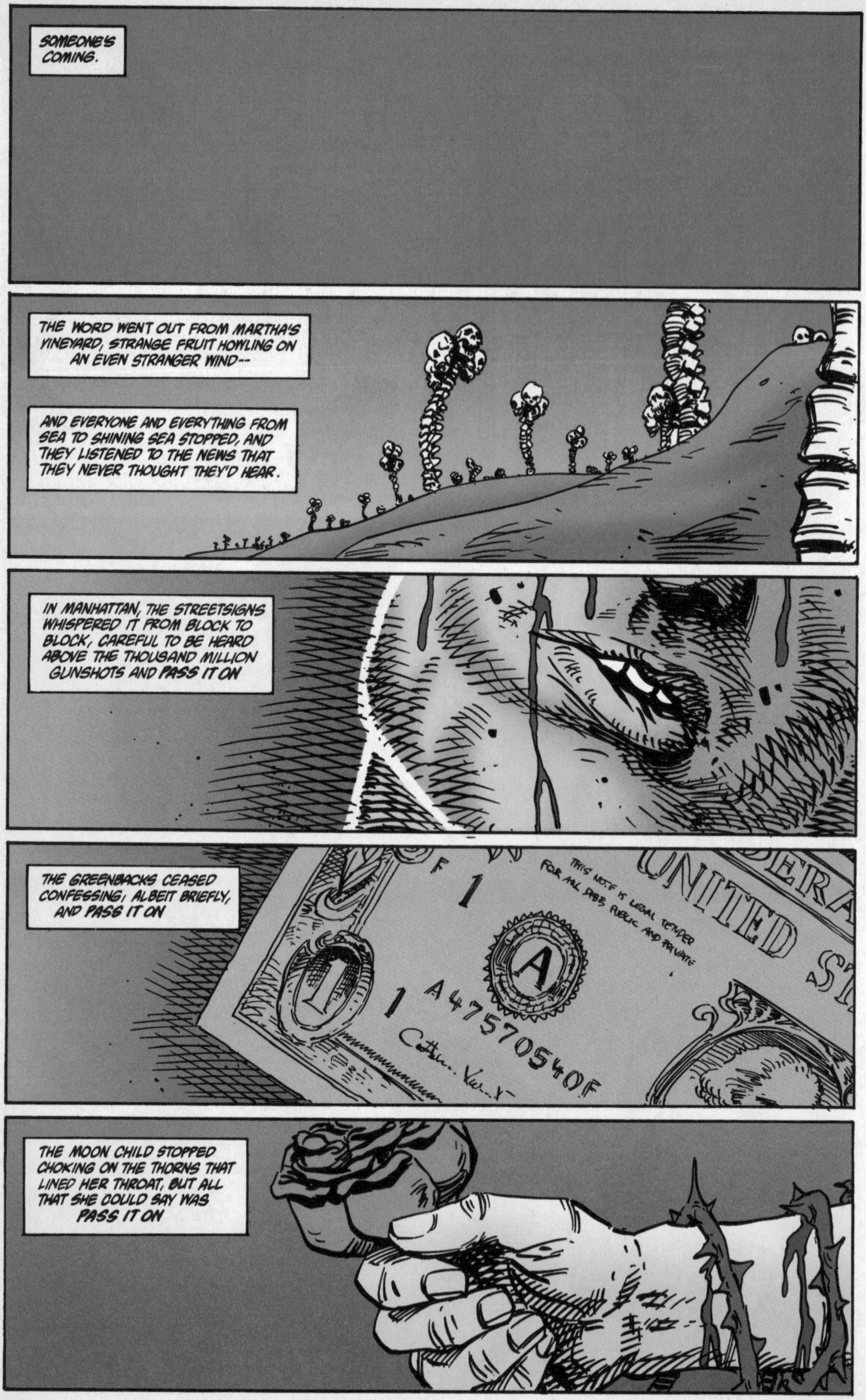

SOMEONE'S COMING.
THE WORD WENT OUT FROM MARTHA'S VINEYARD, STRANGE FRUIT HOWLING ON AN EVEN STRANGER WIND--
AND EVERYONE AND EVERYTHING FROM SEA TO SHINING SEA STOPPED, AND THEY LISTENED TO THE NEWS THAT THEY NEVER THOUGHT THEY'D HEAR.
IN MANHATTAN, THE STREETSIGNS WHISPERED IT FROM BLOCK TO BLOCK, CAREFUL TO BE HEARD ABOVE THE THOUSAND MILLION GUNSHOTS AND PASS IT ON
THE GREENBACKS CEASED CONFESSING, ALBEIT BRIEFLY, AND PASS IT ON
UNITED
A47570540F
THE MOON CHILD STOPPED CHOKING ON THE THORNS THAT LINED HER THROAT, BUT ALL THAT SHE COULD SAY WAS PASS IT ON

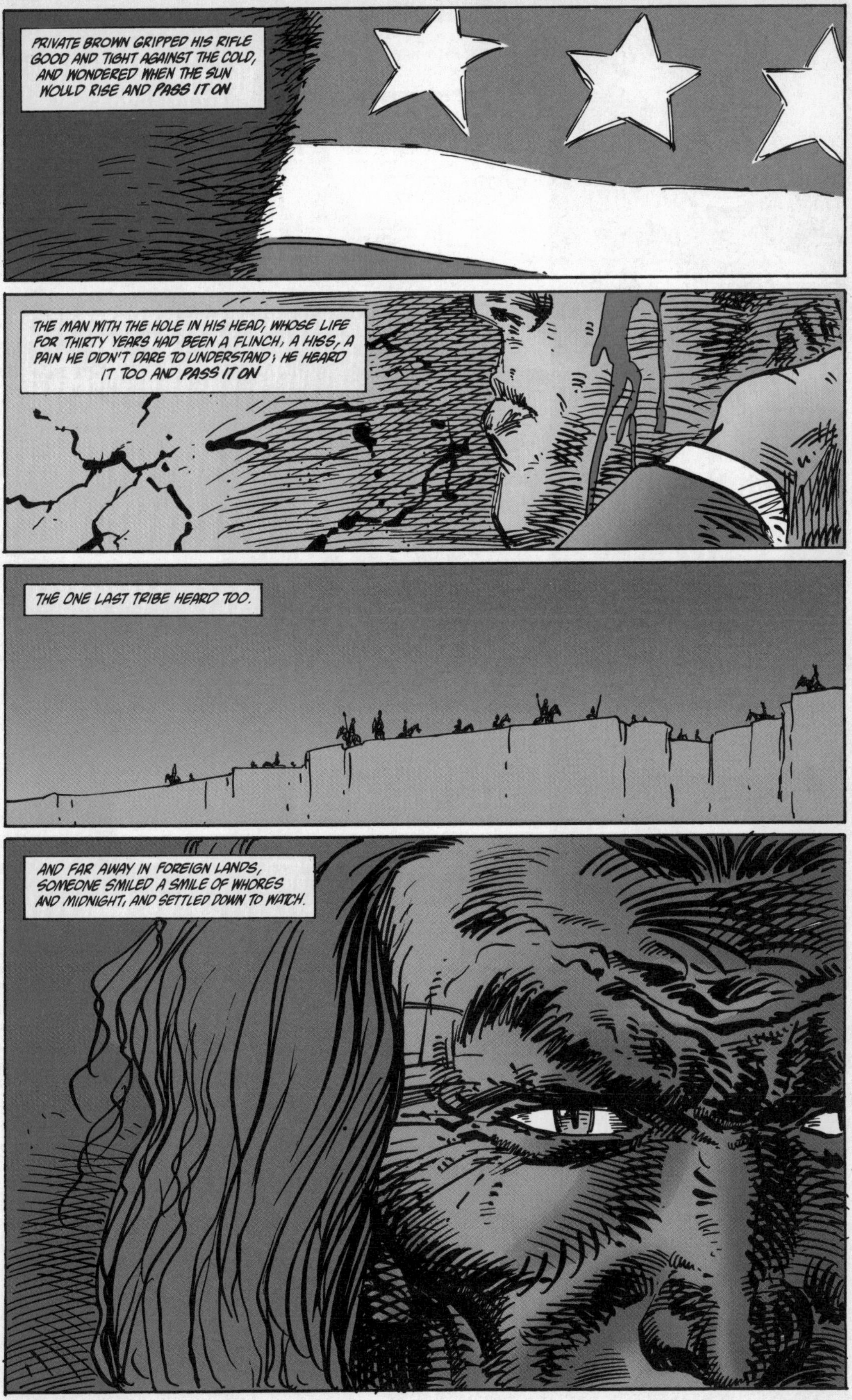
PRIVATE BROWN GRIPPED HIS RIFLE GOOD AND TIGHT AGAINST THE COLD, AND WONDERED WHEN THE SUN WOULD RISE AND PASS IT ON
THE MAN WITH THE HOLE IN HIS HEAD, WHOSE LIFE FOR THIRTY YEARS HAD BEEN A FLINCH, A HISS, A PAIN HE DIDN'T DARE TO UNDERSTAND; HE HEARD IT TOO AND PASS IT ON
THE ONE LAST TRIBE HEARD TOO.
AND FAR AWAY IN FOREIGN LANDS, SOMEONE SMILED A SMILE OF WHORES AND MIDNIGHT, AND SETTLED DOWN TO WATCH.

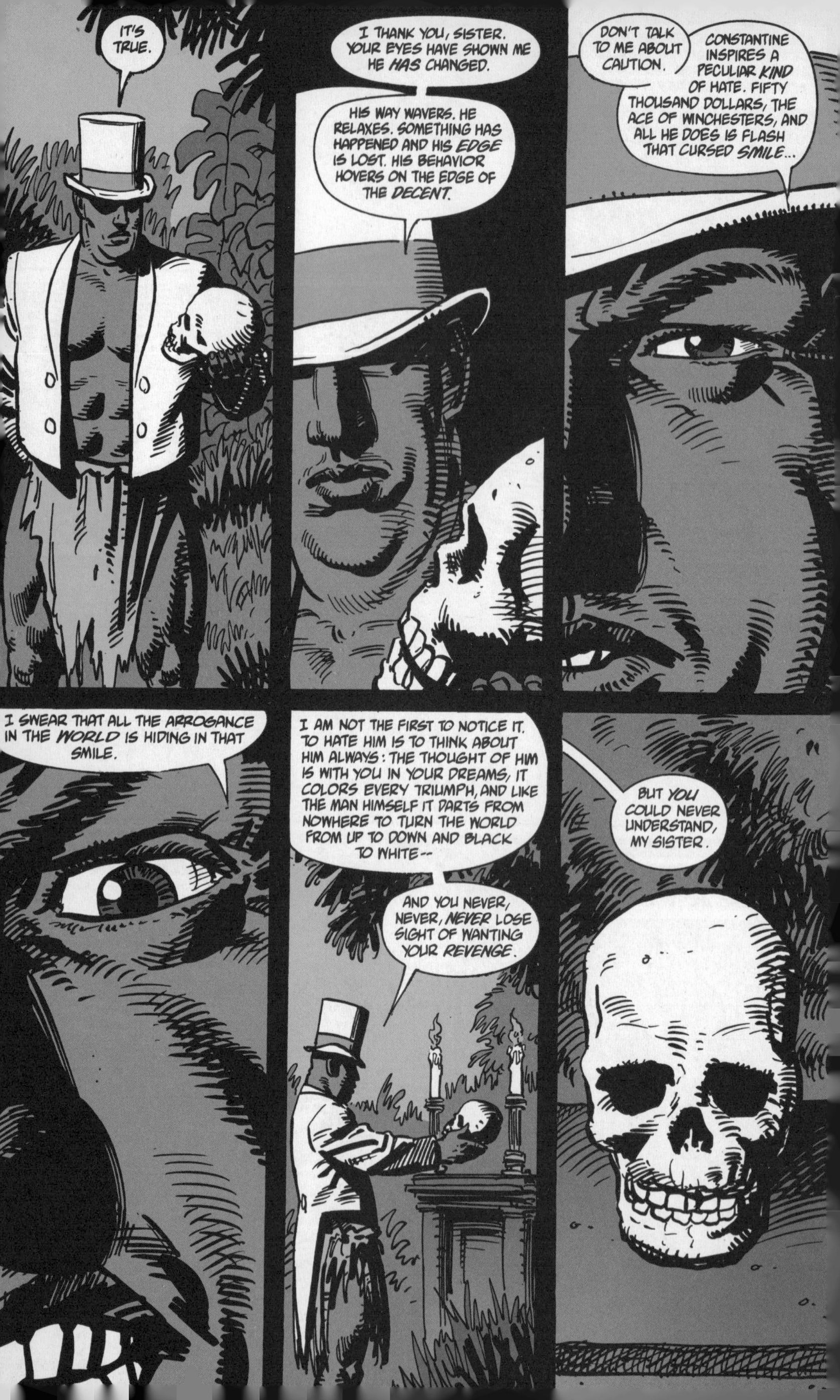
IT'S TRUE.
I THANK YOU, SISTER. YOUR EYES HAVE SHOWN ME HE HAS CHANGED.
HIS WAY WAVERS. HE RELAXES. SOMETHING HAS HAPPENED AND HIS EDGE IS LOST. HIS BEHAVIOR HOVERS ON THE EDGE OF THE DECENT.
DON'T TALK TO ME ABOUT CAUTION.
CONSTANTINE INSPIRES A PECULIAR KIND OF HATE. FIFTY THOUSAND DOLLARS, THE ACE OF WINCHESTERS, AND ALL HE DOES IS FLASH THAT CURSED SMILE...
I SWEAR THAT ALL THE ARROGANCE IN THE WORLD IS HIDING IN THAT SMILE.
I AM NOT THE FIRST TO NOTICE IT. TO HATE HIM IS TO THINK ABOUT HIM ALWAYS: THE THOUGHT OF HIM IS WITH YOU IN YOUR DREAMS, IT COLORS EVERY TRIUMPH, AND LIKE THE MAN HIMSELF IT DARTS FROM NOWHERE TO TURN THE WORLD FROM UP TO DOWN AND BLACK TO WHITE--
AND YOU NEVER, NEVER, NEVER LOSE SIGHT OF WANTING YOUR REVENGE.
BUT YOU COULD NEVER UNDERSTAND, MY SISTER.

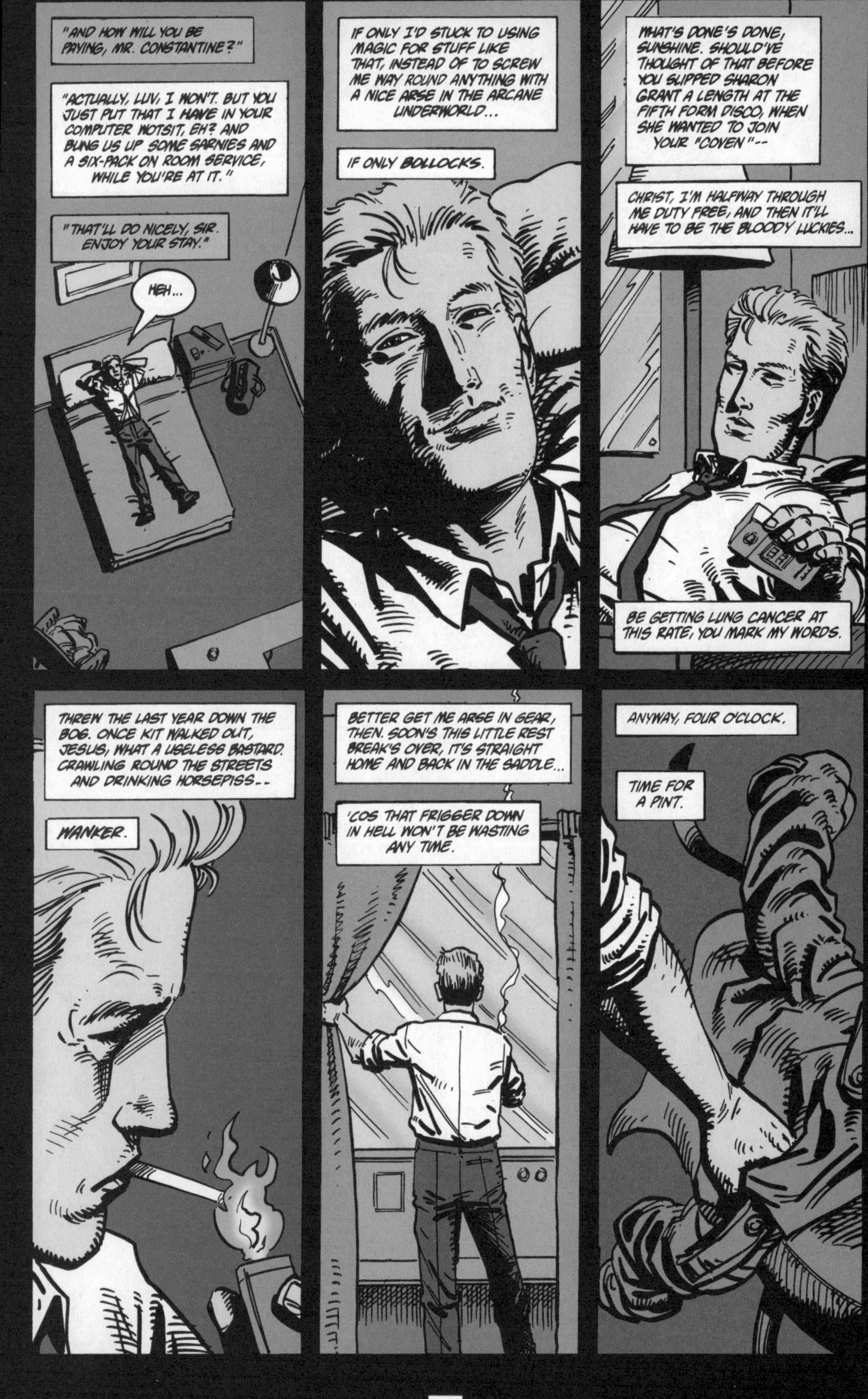
"AND HOW WILL YOU BE PAYING, MR. CONSTANTINE?"
"ACTUALLY, LUV, I WON'T. BUT YOU JUST PUT THAT I HAVE IN YOUR COMPUTER WOTSIT, EH? AND BUNG US UP SOME SARNIES AND A SIX-PACK ON ROOM SERVICE, WHILE YOU'RE AT IT."
"THAT'LL DO NICELY, SIR. ENJOY YOUR STAY."
HEH...
IF ONLY I'D STUCK TO USING MAGIC FOR STUFF LIKE THAT, INSTEAD OF TO SCREW ME WAY ROUND ANYTHING WITH A NICE ARSE IN THE ARCANE UNDERWORLD...
IF ONLY BOLLOCKS.
WHAT'S DONE'S DONE, SUNSHINE. SHOULD'VE THOUGHT OF THAT BEFORE YOU SLIPPED SHARON GRANT A LENGTH AT THE FIFTH FORM DISCO, WHEN SHE WANTED TO JOIN YOUR "COVEN"--
CHRIST, I'M HALFWAY THROUGH ME DUTY FREE, AND THEN IT'LL HAVE TO BE THE BLOODY LUCKIES...
BE GETTING LUNG CANCER AT THIS RATE, YOU MARK MY WORDS.
THREW THE LAST YEAR DOWN THE BOG. ONCE KIT WALKED OUT, JESUS, WHAT A USELESS BASTARD. CRAWLING ROUND THE STREETS AND DRINKING HORSEPISS--
WANKER.
BETTER GET ME ARSE IN GEAR, THEN. SOON'S THIS LITTLE REST BREAK'S OVER, IT'S STRAIGHT HOME AND BACK IN THE SADDLE...
'COS THAT FRIGGER DOWN IN HELL WON'T BE WASTING ANY TIME.
ANYWAY, FOUR O'CLOCK.
TIME FOR A PINT.

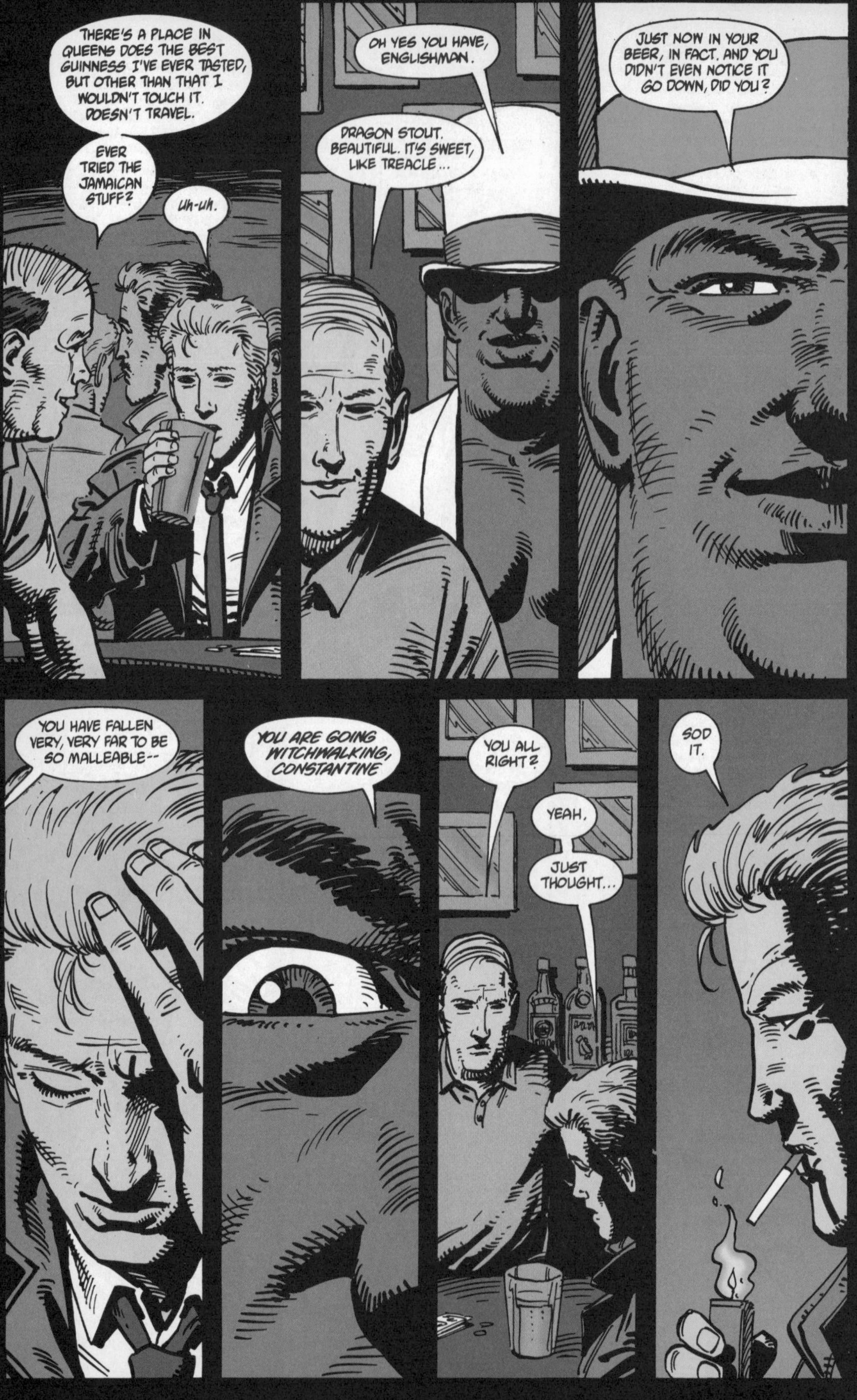
THERE'S A PLACE IN QUEENS DOES THE BEST GUINNESS I'VE EVER TASTED, BUT OTHER THAN THAT I WOULDN'T TOUCH IT. DOESN'T TRAVEL.
EVER TRIED THE JAMAICAN STUFF?
Uh-uh.
OH YES YOU HAVE, ENGLISHMAN.
DRAGON STOUT. BEAUTIFUL. IT'S SWEET, LIKE TREACLE...
JUST NOW IN YOUR BEER, IN FACT. AND YOU DIDN'T EVEN NOTICE IT GO DOWN, DID YOU?
YOU HAVE FALLEN VERY, VERY FAR TO BE SO MALLEABLE--
YOU ARE GOING WITCHWALKING, CONSTANTINE
YOU ALL RIGHT?
YEAH.
JUST THOUGHT...
SOD IT.

TO TELL YOU THE TRUTH, MATE, I DOUBT THE BLOODY THING'LL MAKE MONEY...

HEY, WE'LL AT LEAST CLEAN UP ON THE ADVERTISING!

NO ONE'S GONNA WATCH IT. LOOK, AMERICANS DON'T LIKE FOOTBA--SOCCER, EVEN--'COS THERE'S NOT ENOUGH BREAKS AN' NO CHANCE OF THE ODD *MAIMING*--

AND ANYWAY, ALL THE IRISH SUPPORTERS'LL GET STOPPED AT IMMIGRATION, WON'T THEY?

HAHAHA!

"LOOK, I'M A FRIGGIN' FOOTBALL FAN"--"MY ASS. NO GREEN CARD, SHIT, YOU MICKS'LL TRY ANYTHING..."

UH...

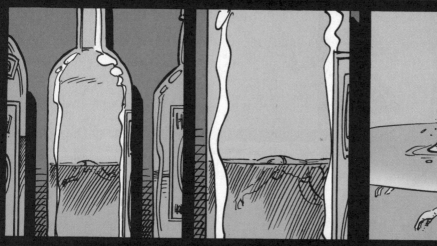

YOU SEE THAT?

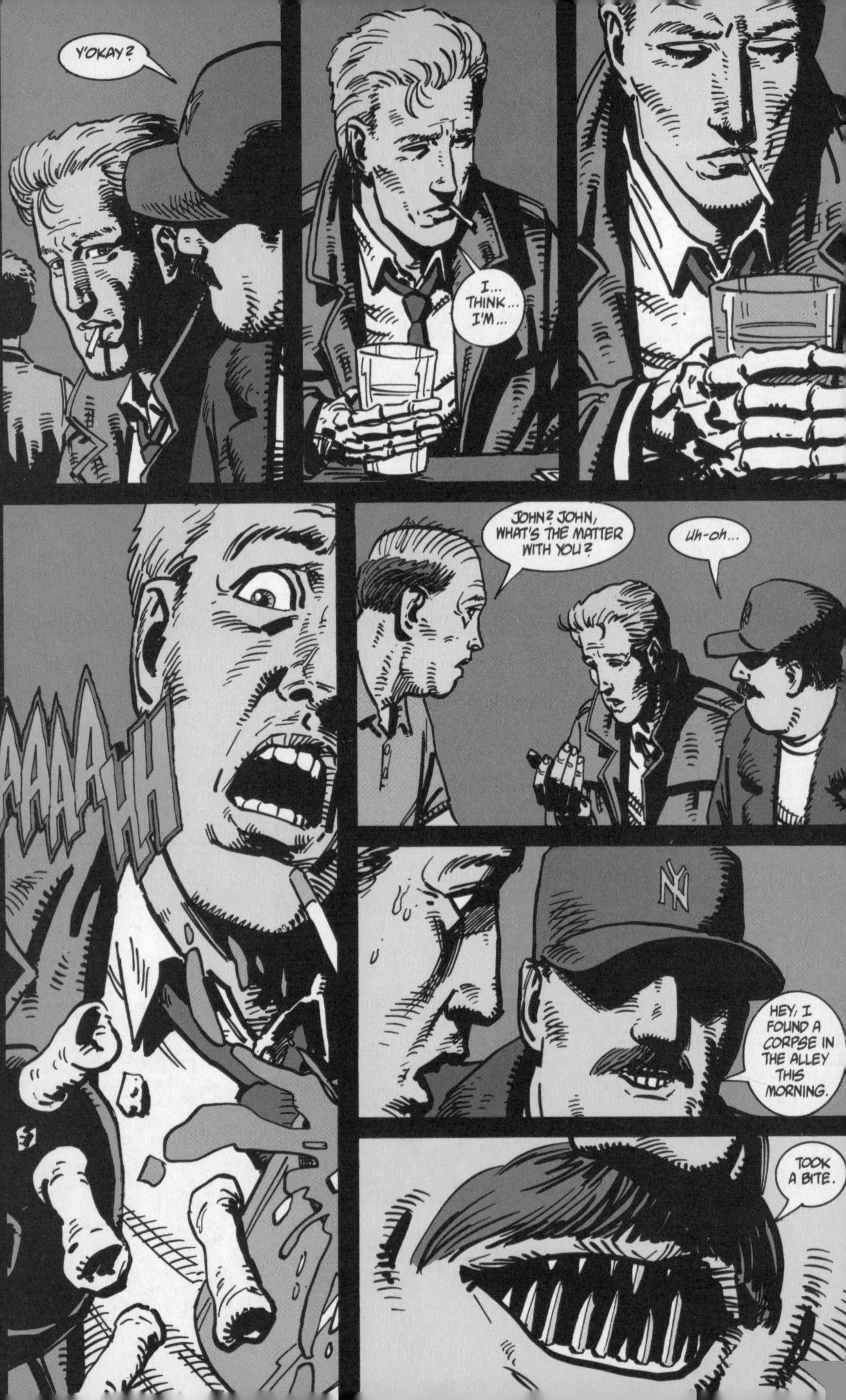

Y'OKAY?
I... THINK... I'M...
AAAAHH
JOHN? JOHN, WHAT'S THE MATTER WITH YOU?
Uh-oh...
HEY, I FOUND A CORPSE IN THE ALLEY THIS MORNING.
TOOK A BITE.

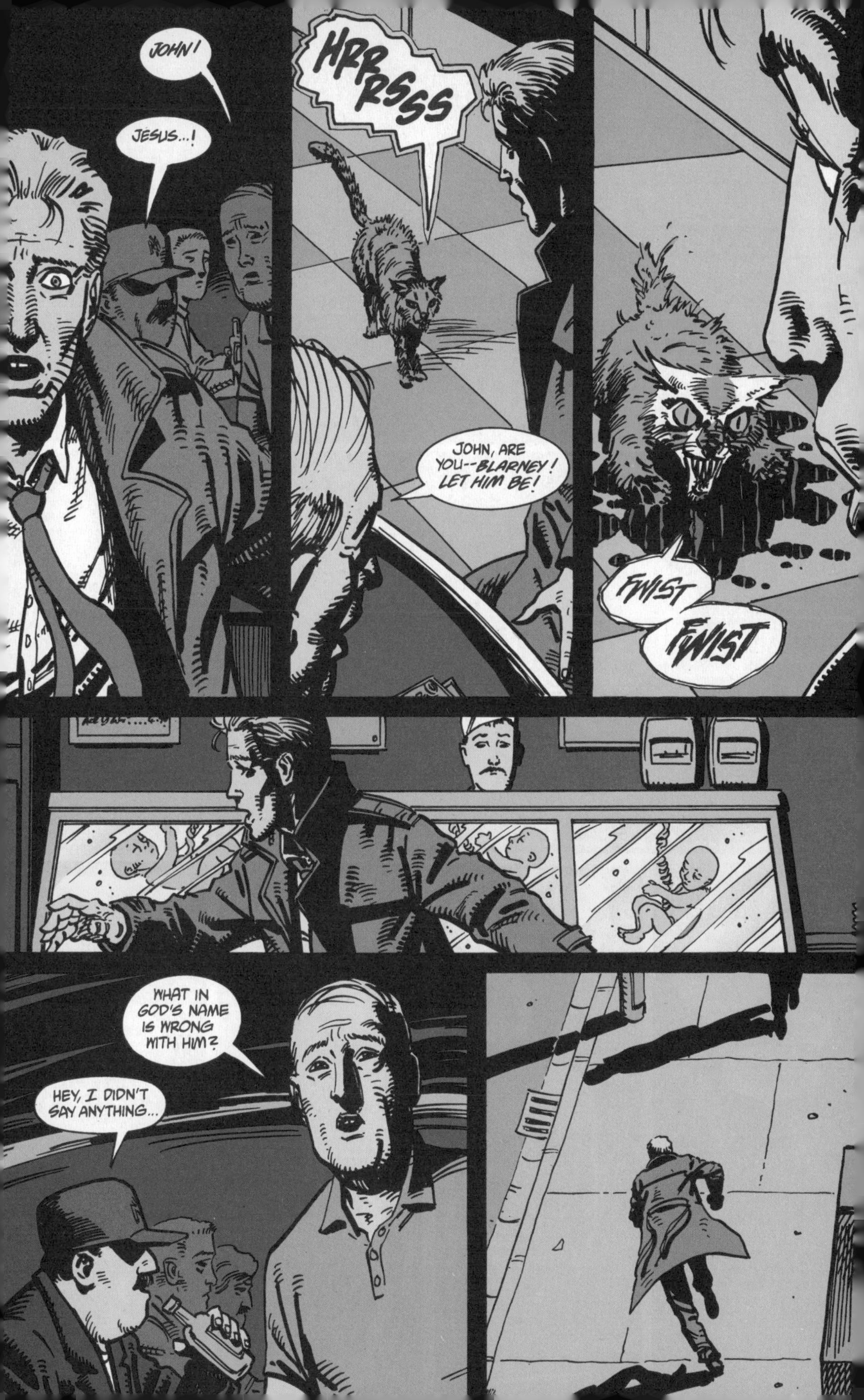
JOHN!
JESUS...!
HRRRSSSS
JOHN, ARE YOU--BLARNEY! LET HIM BE!
FWIST
FWIST
WHAT IN GOD'S NAME IS WRONG WITH HIM?
HEY, I DIDN'T SAY ANYTHING...

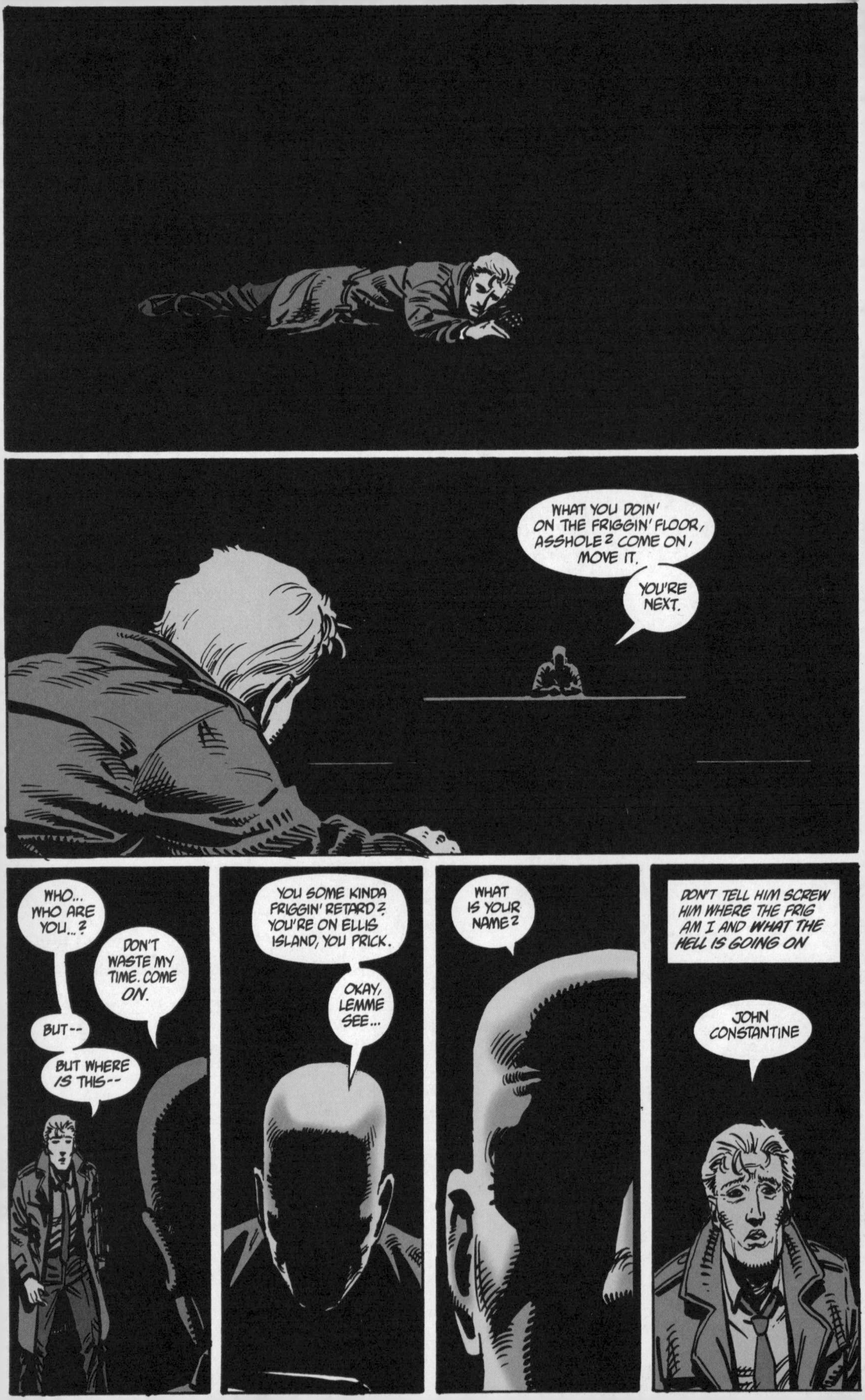
WHAT YOU DOIN' ON THE FRIGGIN' FLOOR, ASSHOLE? COME ON, MOVE IT.
YOU'RE NEXT.
WHO... WHO ARE YOU...?
DON'T WASTE MY TIME. COME ON.
BUT--
BUT WHERE IS THIS--
YOU SOME KINDA FRIGGIN' RETARD? YOU'RE ON ELLIS ISLAND, YOU PRICK.
OKAY, LEMME SEE...
WHAT IS YOUR NAME?
DON'T TELL HIM SCREW HIM WHERE THE FRIG AM I AND WHAT THE HELL IS GOING ON
JOHN CONSTANTINE

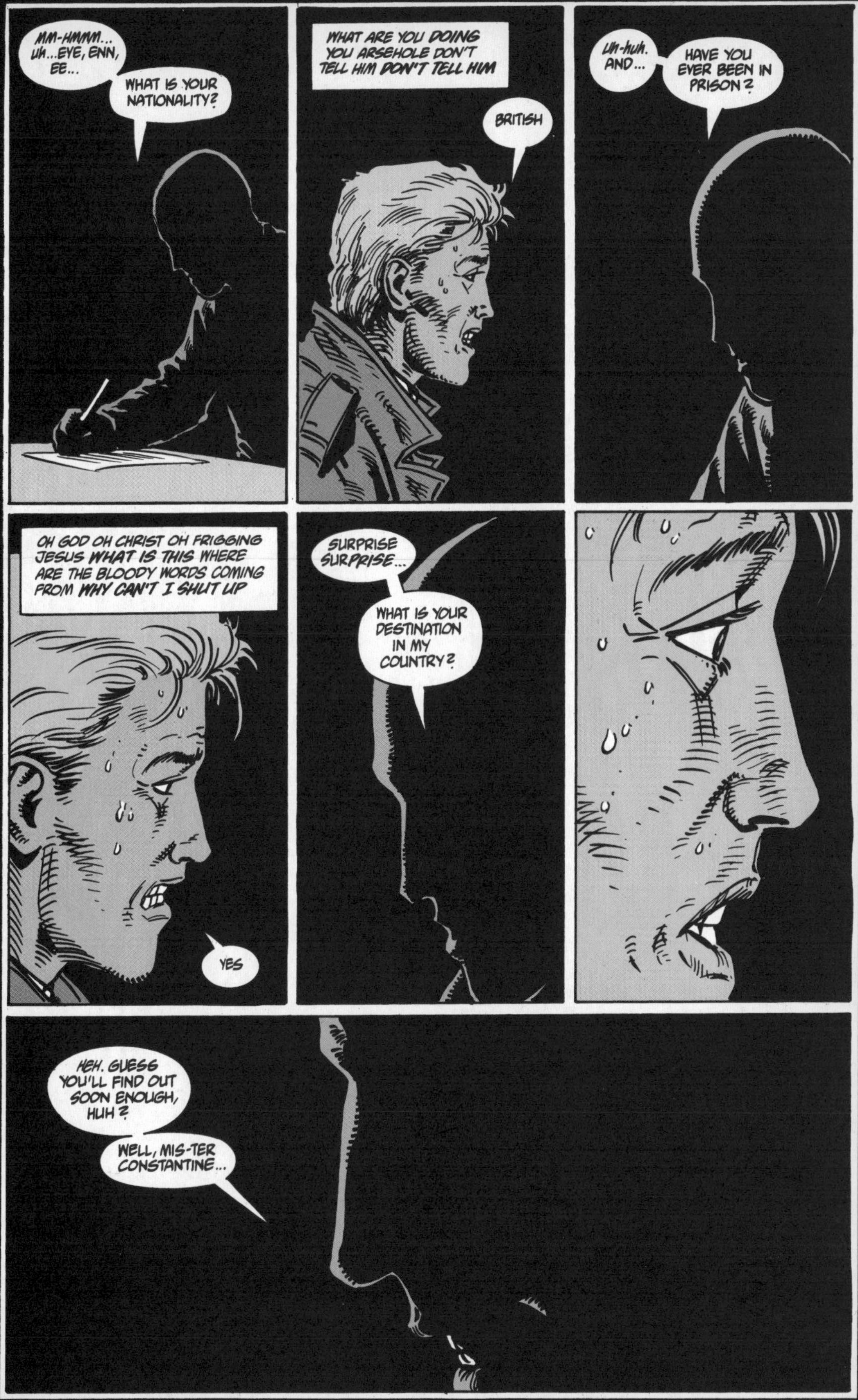
MM-HMMM... UH...EYE, ENN, EE...
WHAT IS YOUR NATIONALITY?
WHAT ARE YOU DOING YOU ARSEHOLE DON'T TELL HIM DON'T TELL HIM
BRITISH
UH-HUH. AND...
HAVE YOU EVER BEEN IN PRISON?
OH GOD OH CHRIST OH FRIGGING JESUS WHAT IS THIS WHERE ARE THE BLOODY WORDS COMING FROM WHY CAN'T I SHUT UP
YES
SURPRISE SURPRISE...
WHAT IS YOUR DESTINATION IN MY COUNTRY?
HEH. GUESS YOU'LL FIND OUT SOON ENOUGH, HUH?
WELL, MIS-TER CONSTANTINE...

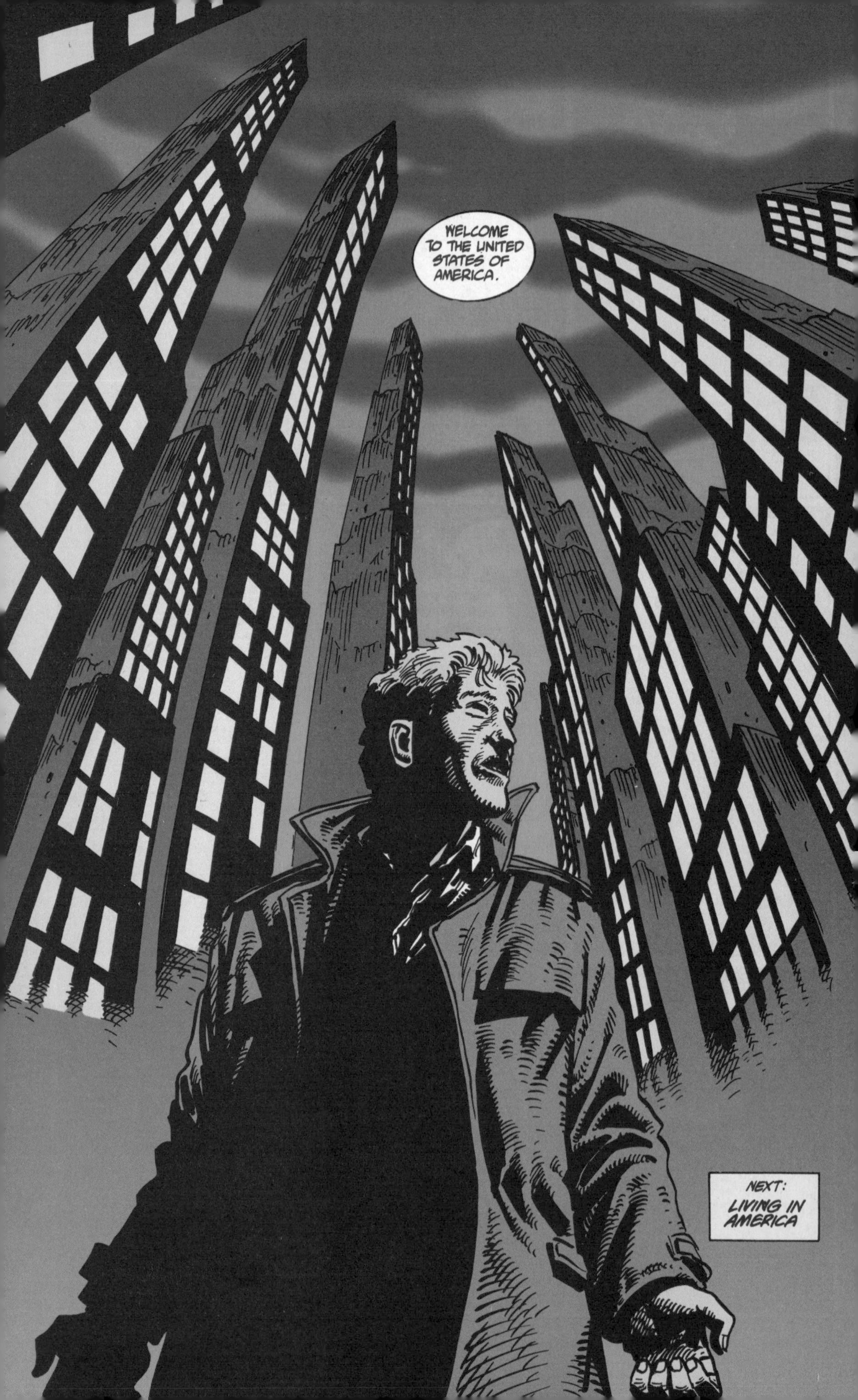
WELCOME TO THE UNITED STATES OF AMERICA.
NEXT: LIVING IN AMERICA

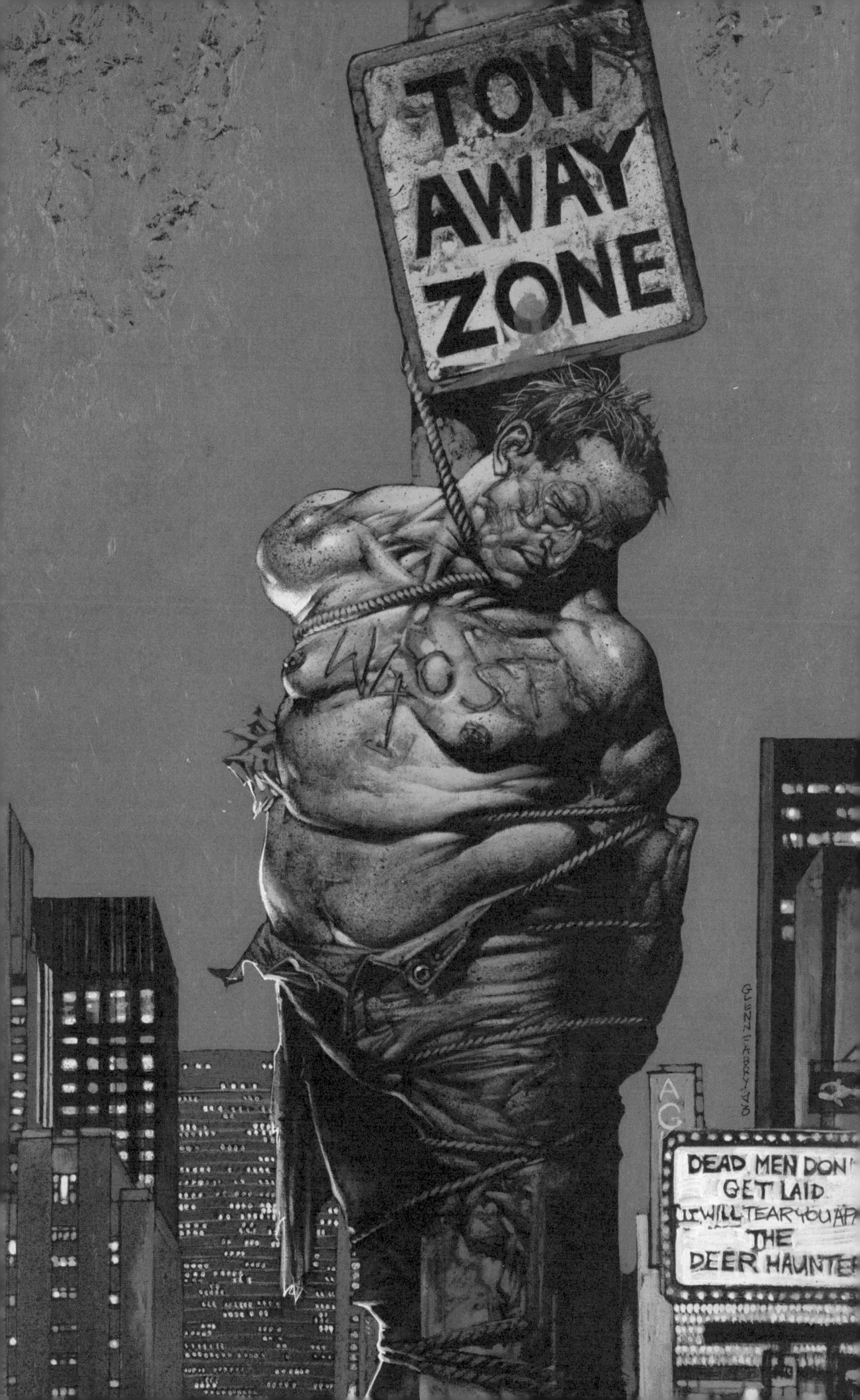
TOW AWAY ZONE
DEAD MEN DON'
GET LAID
IT WILL TEAR YOU AP
THE
DEER HAUNTE

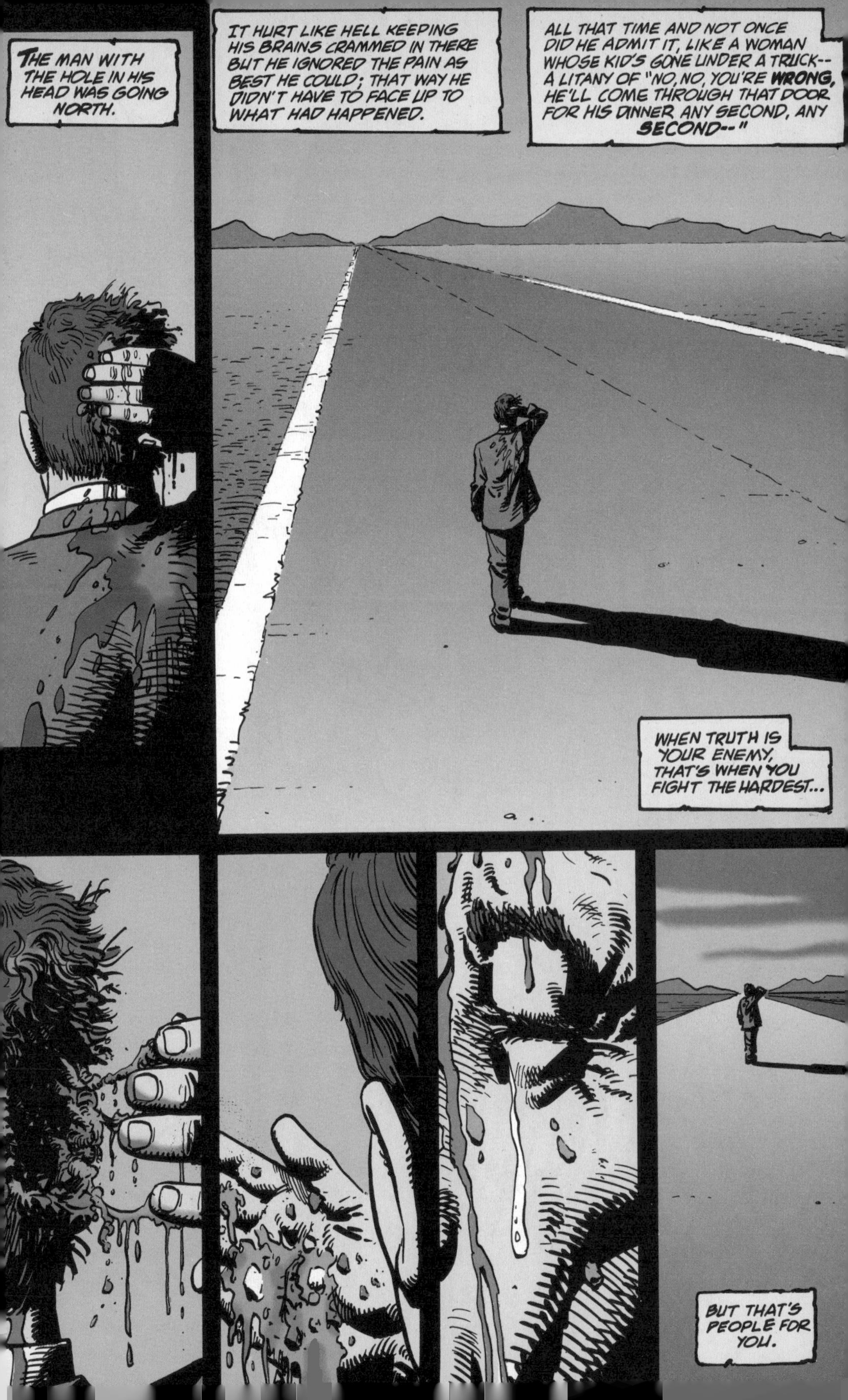
THE MAN WITH THE HOLE IN HIS HEAD WAS GOING NORTH.
IT HURT LIKE HELL KEEPING HIS BRAINS CRAMMED IN THERE BUT HE IGNORED THE PAIN AS BEST HE COULD; THAT WAY HE DIDN'T HAVE TO FACE UP TO WHAT HAD HAPPENED.
ALL THAT TIME AND NOT ONCE DID HE ADMIT IT, LIKE A WOMAN WHOSE KID'S GONE UNDER A TRUCK-- A LITANY OF "NO, NO, YOU'RE WRONG, HE'LL COME THROUGH THAT DOOR FOR HIS DINNER ANY SECOND, ANY SECOND--"
WHEN TRUTH IS YOUR ENEMY, THAT'S WHEN YOU FIGHT THE HARDEST...
BUT THAT'S PEOPLE FOR YOU.

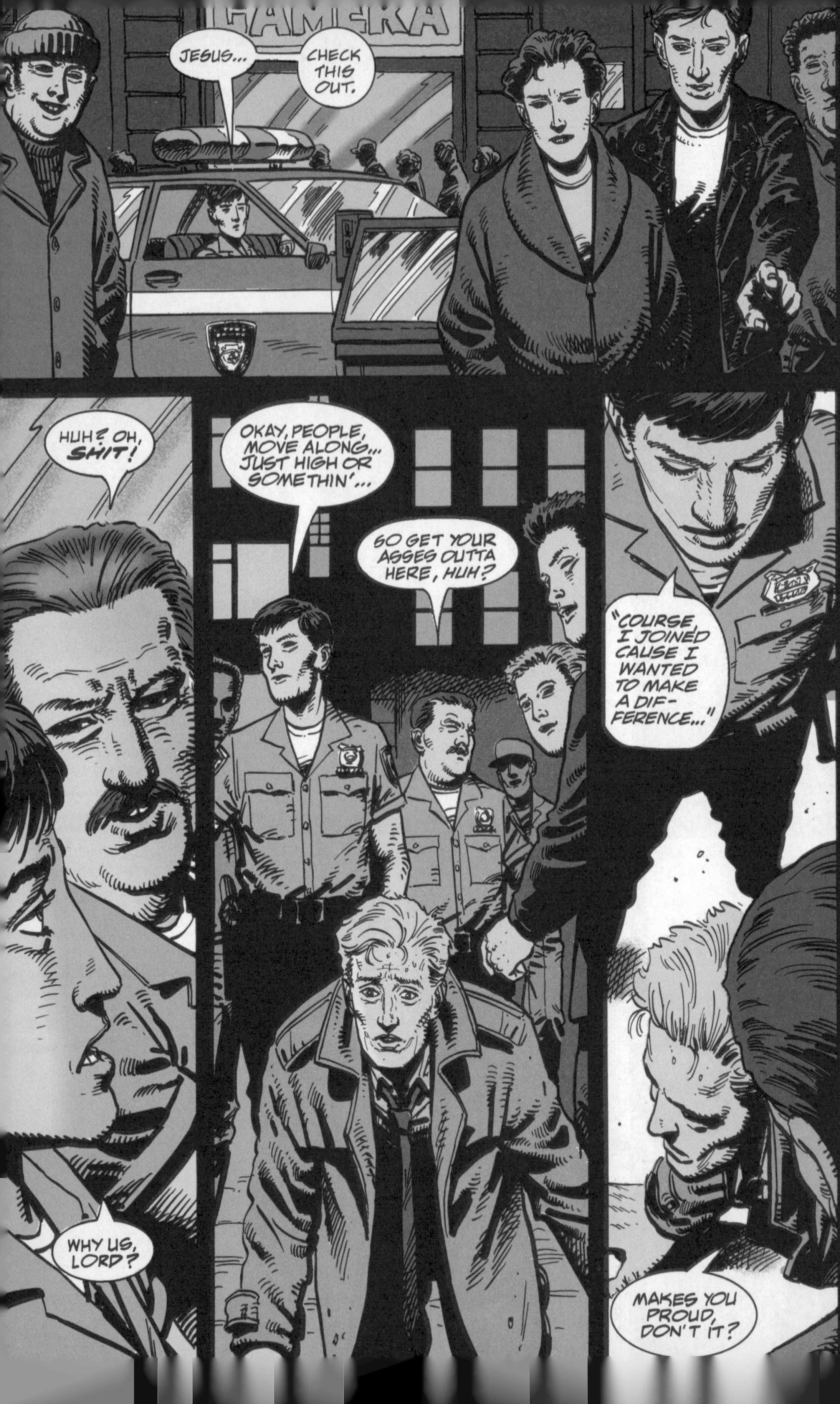
CAMERA
JESUS...
CHECK THIS OUT.
HUH? OH, SHIT!
WHY US, LORD?
OKAY, PEOPLE, MOVE ALONG... JUST HIGH OR SOMETHIN'...
SO GET YOUR ASSES OUTTA HERE, HUH?
"COURSE, I JOINED CAUSE I WANTED TO MAKE A DIF-FERENCE..."
MAKES YOU PROUD, DON'T IT?

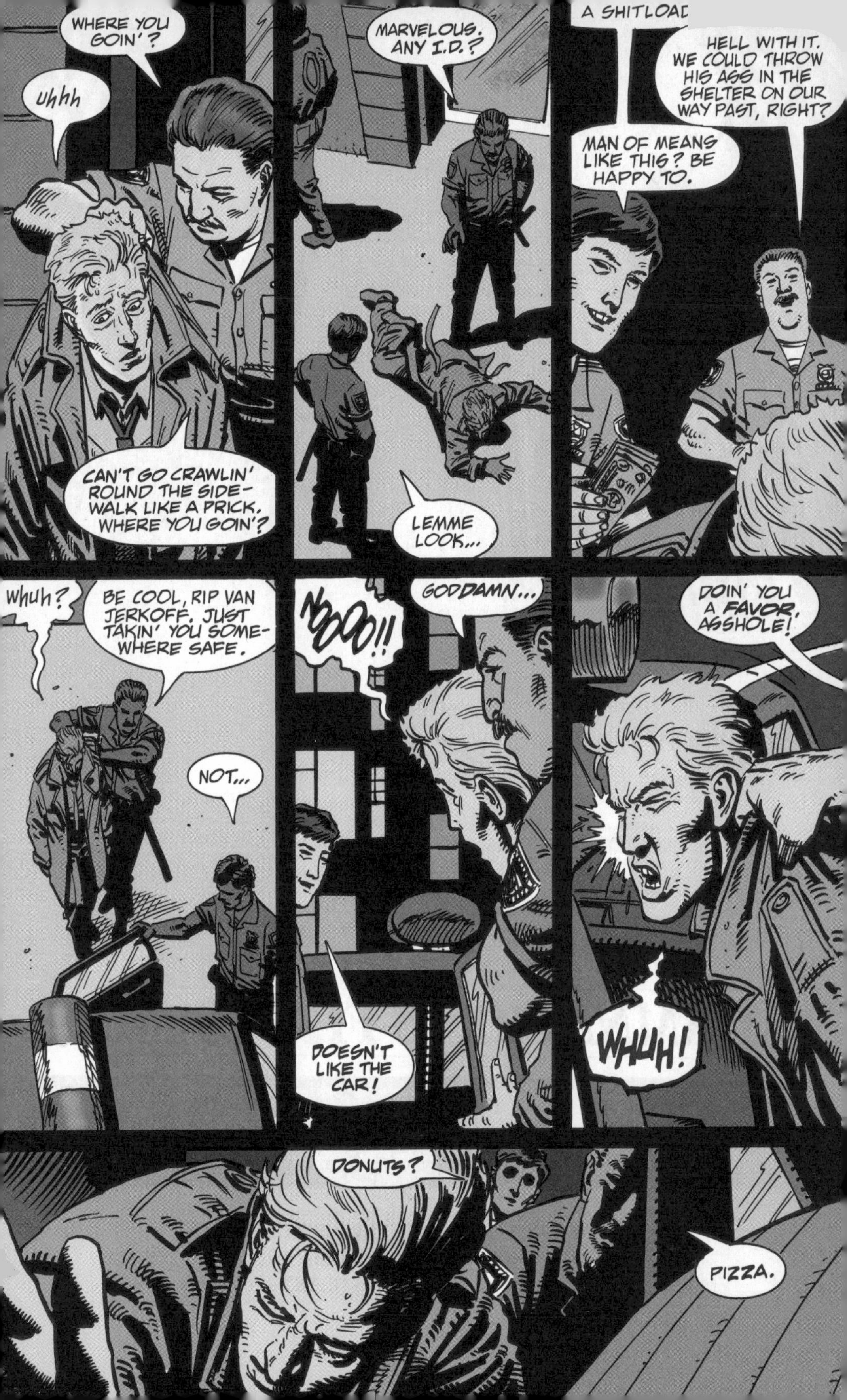

WHERE YOU GOIN'?
uhhh
CAN'T GO CRAWLIN' ROUND THE SIDE-WALK LIKE A PRICK. WHERE YOU GOIN'?
MARVELOUS. ANY I.D.?
LEMME LOOK...
A SHITLOAD
MAN OF MEANS LIKE THIS? BE HAPPY TO.
HELL WITH IT. WE COULD THROW HIS ASS IN THE SHELTER ON OUR WAY PAST, RIGHT?
Whuh?
BE COOL, RIP VAN JERKOFF. JUST TAKIN' YOU SOME-WHERE SAFE.
NOT...
NOOOO!!
GODDAMN...
DOESN'T LIKE THE CAR!
DOIN' YOU A FAVOR, ASSHOLE!
WHUH!
DONUTS?
PIZZA.

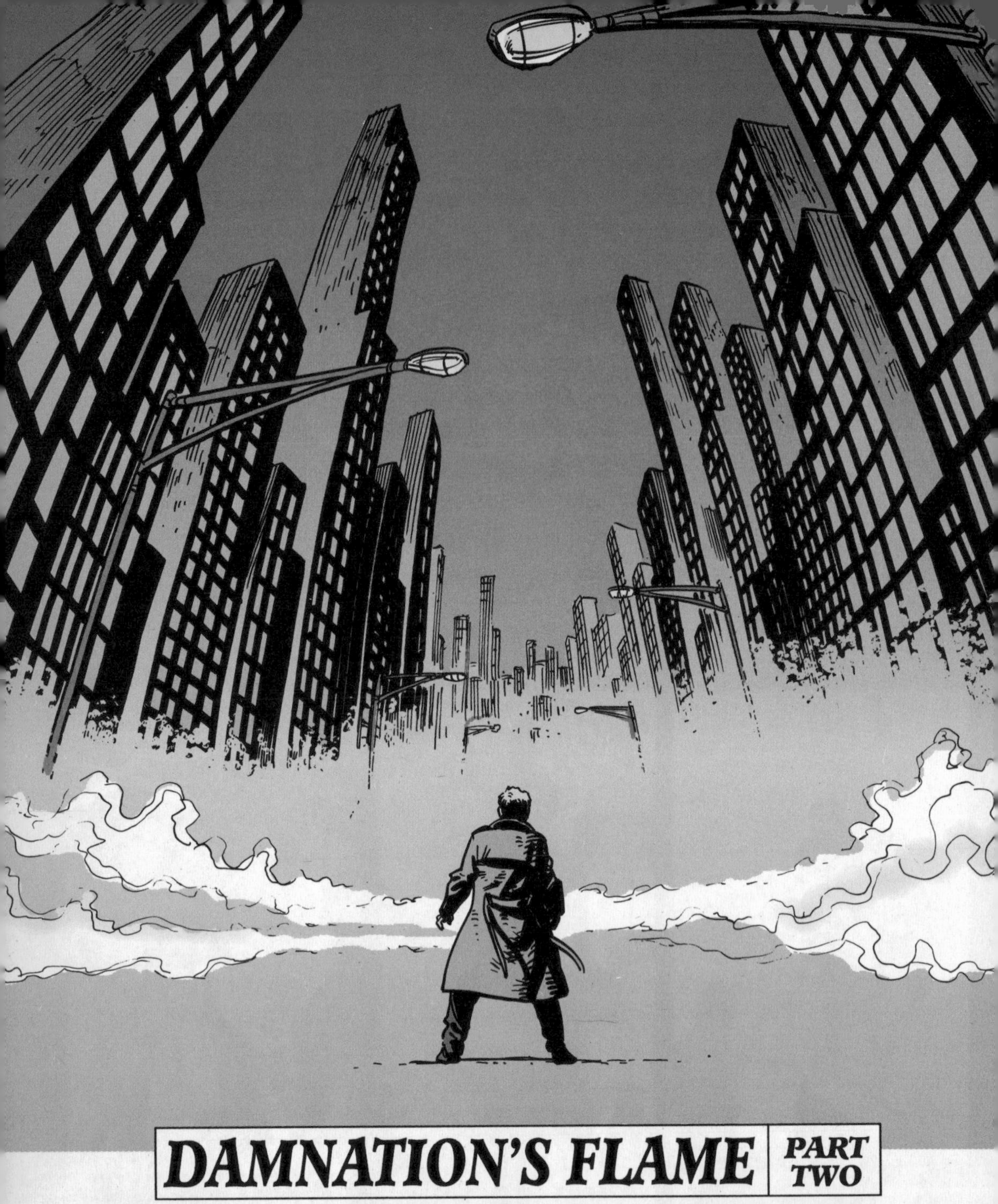

DAMNATION'S FLAME PART TWO

BROADWAY THE HARD WAY

GARTH ENNIS • *writer* **STEVE DILLON** • *artist*
TOM ZIUKO • *colors* **GASPAR** • *letters*
JULIE ROTTENBERG • *asst. editor* **STUART MOORE** • *editor*

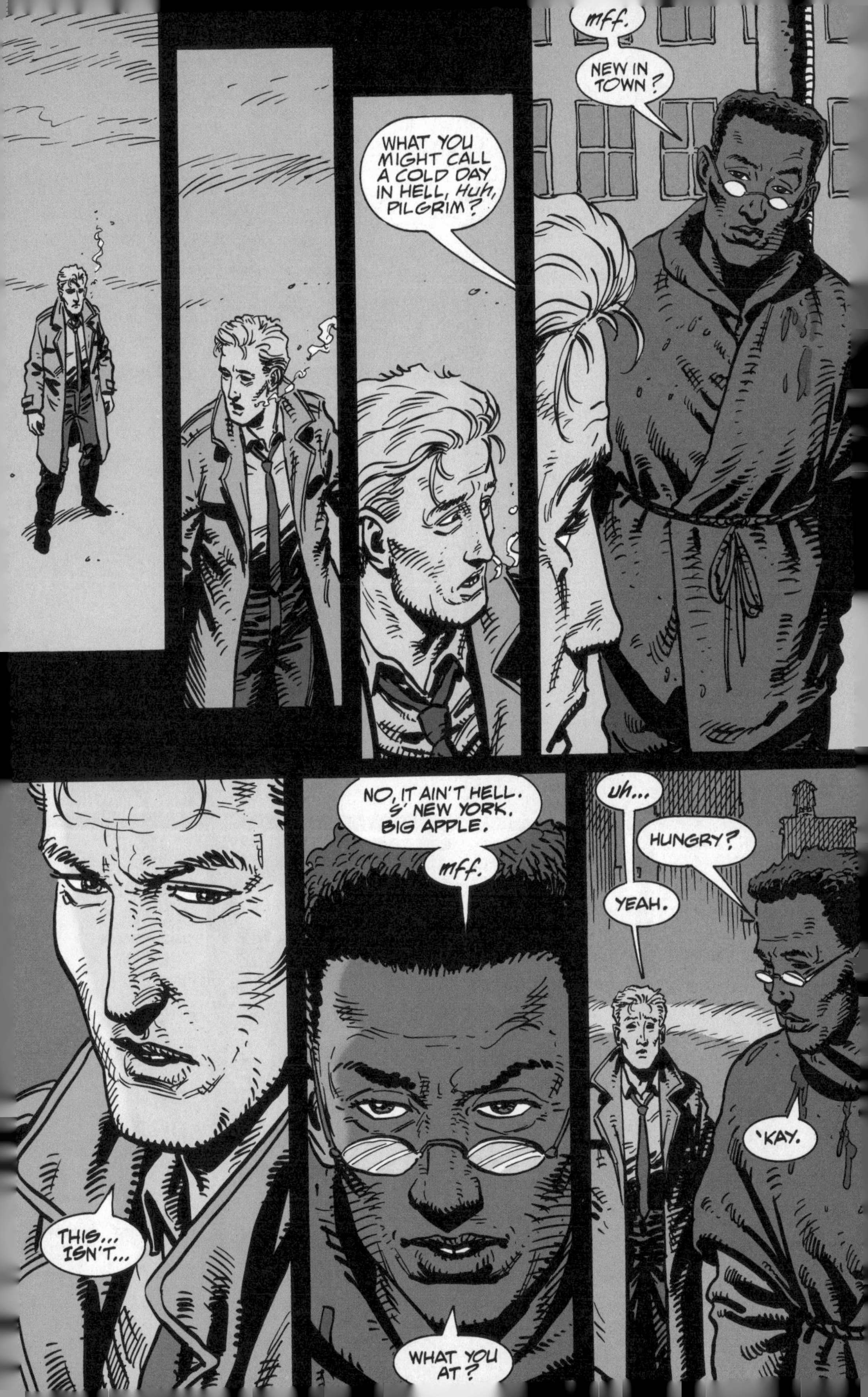
WHAT YOU MIGHT CALL A COLD DAY IN HELL, HUH, PILGRIM?
MFF.
NEW IN TOWN?
THIS... ISN'T...
NO, IT AIN'T HELL. 'S' NEW YORK. BIG APPLE.
MFF.
WHAT YOU AT?
UH...
HUNGRY?
YEAH.
'KAY.

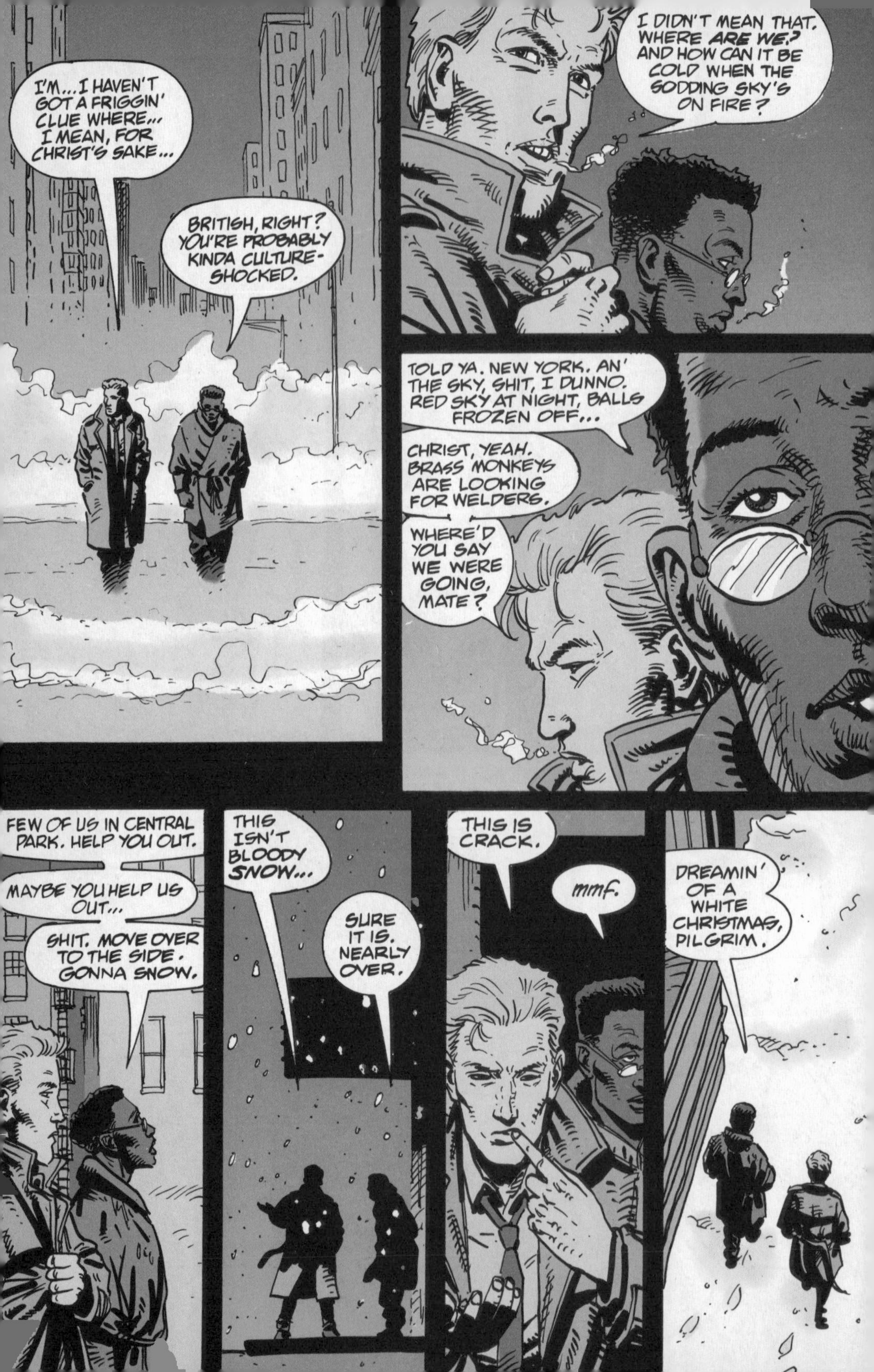
I'M... I HAVEN'T GOT A FRIGGIN' CLUE WHERE... I MEAN, FOR CHRIST'S SAKE...
BRITISH, RIGHT? YOU'RE PROBABLY KINDA CULTURE-SHOCKED.
I DIDN'T MEAN THAT. WHERE ARE WE? AND HOW CAN IT BE COLD WHEN THE SODDING SKY'S ON FIRE?
TOLD YA. NEW YORK. AN' THE SKY, SHIT, I DUNNO. RED SKY AT NIGHT, BALLS FROZEN OFF...
CHRIST, YEAH. BRASS MONKEYS ARE LOOKING FOR WELDERS.
WHERE'D YOU SAY WE WERE GOING, MATE?
FEW OF US IN CENTRAL PARK. HELP YOU OUT.
MAYBE YOU HELP US OUT...
SHIT. MOVE OVER TO THE SIDE. GONNA SNOW.
THIS ISN'T BLOODY SNOW...
SURE IT IS. NEARLY OVER.
THIS IS CRACK.
mmf.
DREAMIN' OF A WHITE CHRISTMAS, PILGRIM.

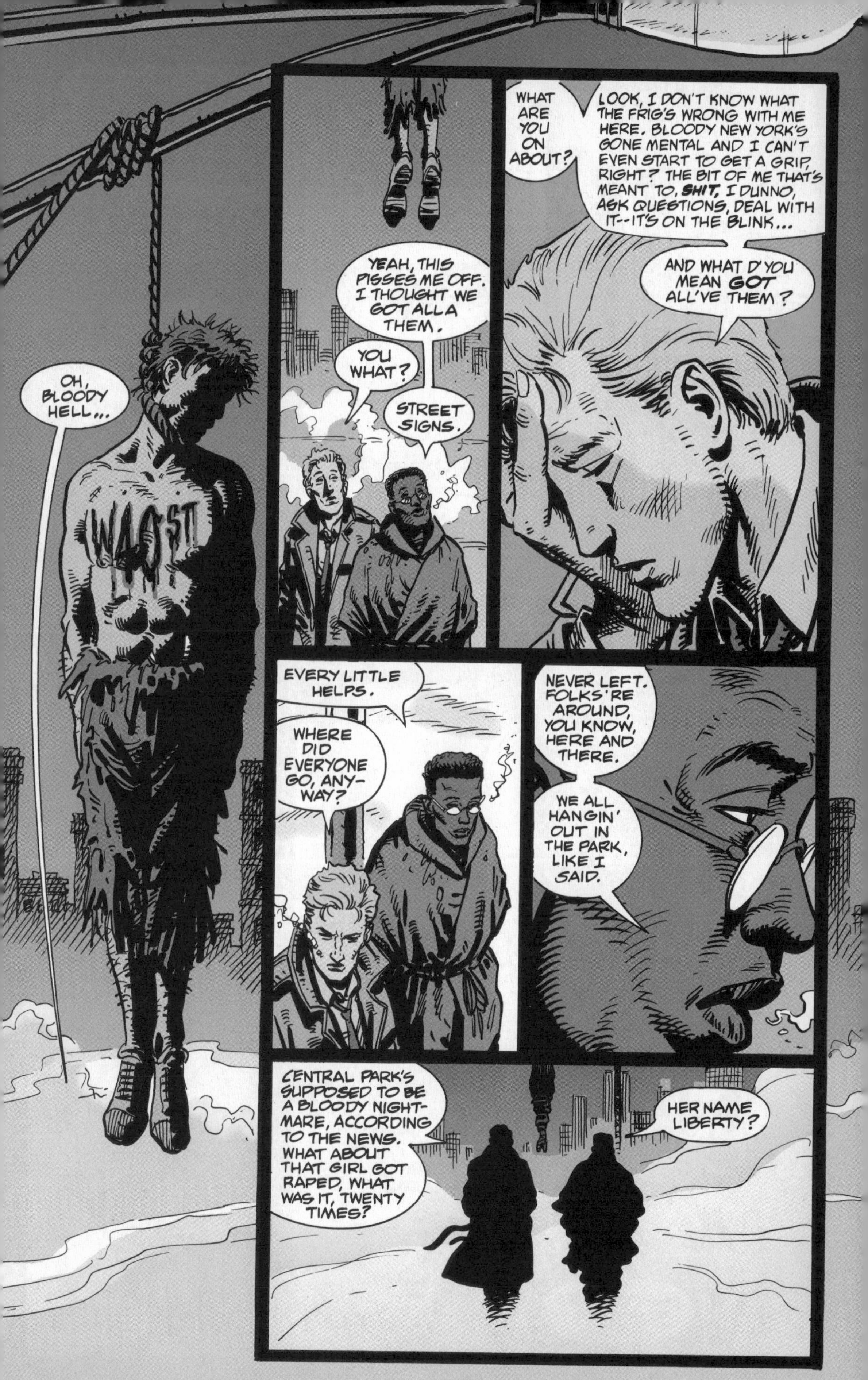
OH, BLOODY HELL...
WASTE
YEAH, THIS PISSES ME OFF. I THOUGHT WE GOT ALL A THEM.
YOU WHAT?
STREET SIGNS.
WHAT ARE YOU ON ABOUT?
LOOK, I DON'T KNOW WHAT THE FRIG'S WRONG WITH ME HERE. BLOODY NEW YORK'S GONE MENTAL AND I CAN'T EVEN START TO GET A GRIP, RIGHT? THE BIT OF ME THAT'S MEANT TO, **SHIT,** I DUNNO, ASK QUESTIONS, DEAL WITH IT--IT'S ON THE BLINK...
AND WHAT D'YOU MEAN **GOT** ALL'VE THEM?
EVERY LITTLE HELPS.
WHERE DID EVERYONE GO, ANYWAY?
NEVER LEFT. FOLKS'RE AROUND, YOU KNOW, HERE AND THERE.
WE ALL HANGIN' OUT IN THE PARK, LIKE I SAID.
CENTRAL PARK'S SUPPOSED TO BE A BLOODY NIGHTMARE, ACCORDING TO THE NEWS. WHAT ABOUT THAT GIRL GOT RAPED, WHAT WAS IT, TWENTY TIMES?
HER NAME LIBERTY?

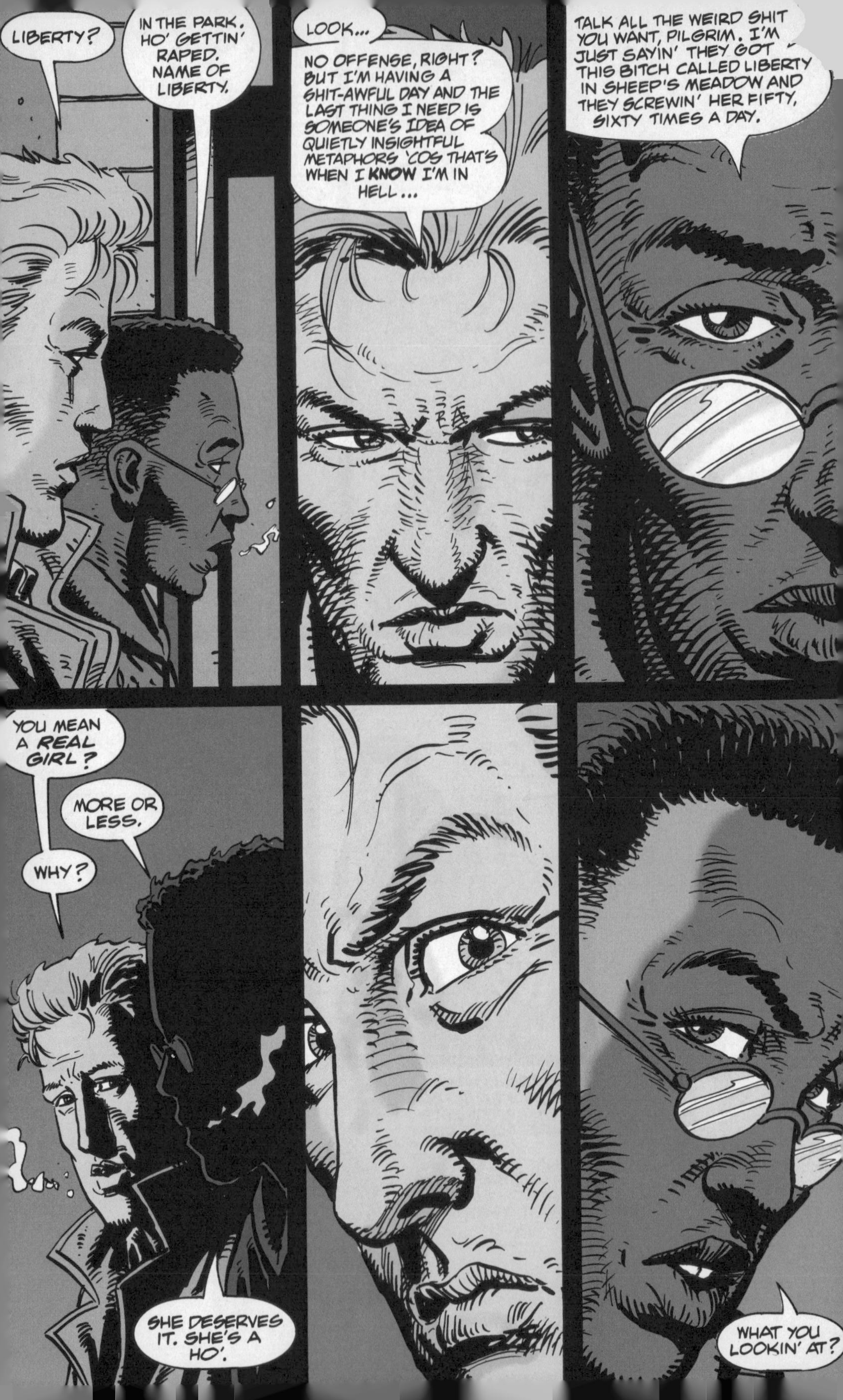
LIBERTY?
IN THE PARK. HO' GETTIN' RAPED. NAME OF LIBERTY.
LOOK...
NO OFFENSE, RIGHT? BUT I'M HAVING A SHIT-AWFUL DAY AND THE LAST THING I NEED IS SOMEONE'S IDEA OF QUIETLY INSIGHTFUL METAPHORS 'COS THAT'S WHEN I KNOW I'M IN HELL...
TALK ALL THE WEIRD SHIT YOU WANT, PILGRIM. I'M JUST SAYIN' THEY GOT THIS BITCH CALLED LIBERTY IN SHEEP'S MEADOW AND THEY SCREWIN' HER FIFTY, SIXTY TIMES A DAY.
YOU MEAN A REAL GIRL?
MORE OR LESS.
WHY?
SHE DESERVES IT. SHE'S A HO'.
WHAT YOU LOOKIN' AT?

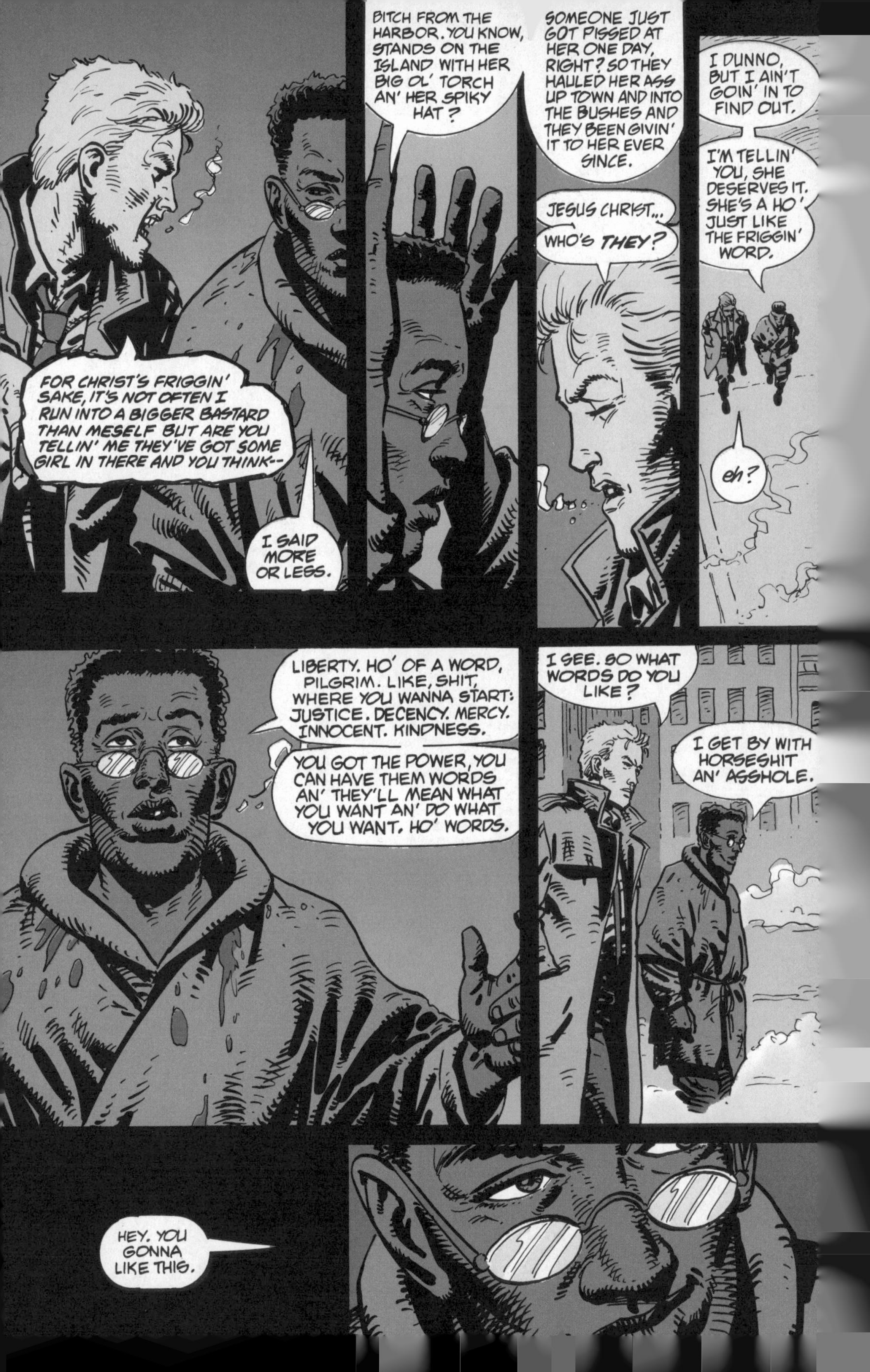
FOR CHRIST'S FRIGGIN' SAKE, IT'S NOT OFTEN I RUN INTO A BIGGER BASTARD THAN MESELF BUT ARE YOU TELLIN' ME THEY'VE GOT SOME GIRL IN THERE AND YOU THINK--
I SAID MORE OR LESS.
BITCH FROM THE HARBOR. YOU KNOW, STANDS ON THE ISLAND WITH HER BIG OL' TORCH AN' HER SPIKY HAT?
SOMEONE JUST GOT PISSED AT HER ONE DAY, RIGHT? SO THEY HAULED HER ASS UP TOWN AND INTO THE BUSHES AND THEY BEEN GIVIN' IT TO HER EVER SINCE.
JESUS CHRIST...
WHO'S THEY?
I DUNNO, BUT I AIN'T GOIN' IN TO FIND OUT.
I'M TELLIN' YOU, SHE DESERVES IT. SHE'S A HO' JUST LIKE THE FRIGGIN' WORD.
eh?
LIBERTY. HO' OF A WORD, PILGRIM. LIKE, SHIT, WHERE YOU WANNA START: JUSTICE. DECENCY. MERCY. INNOCENT. KINDNESS.
YOU GOT THE POWER, YOU CAN HAVE THEM WORDS AN' THEY'LL MEAN WHAT YOU WANT AN' DO WHAT YOU WANT. HO' WORDS.
I SEE. SO WHAT WORDS DO YOU LIKE?
I GET BY WITH HORSESHIT AN' ASSHOLE.
HEY. YOU GONNA LIKE THIS.

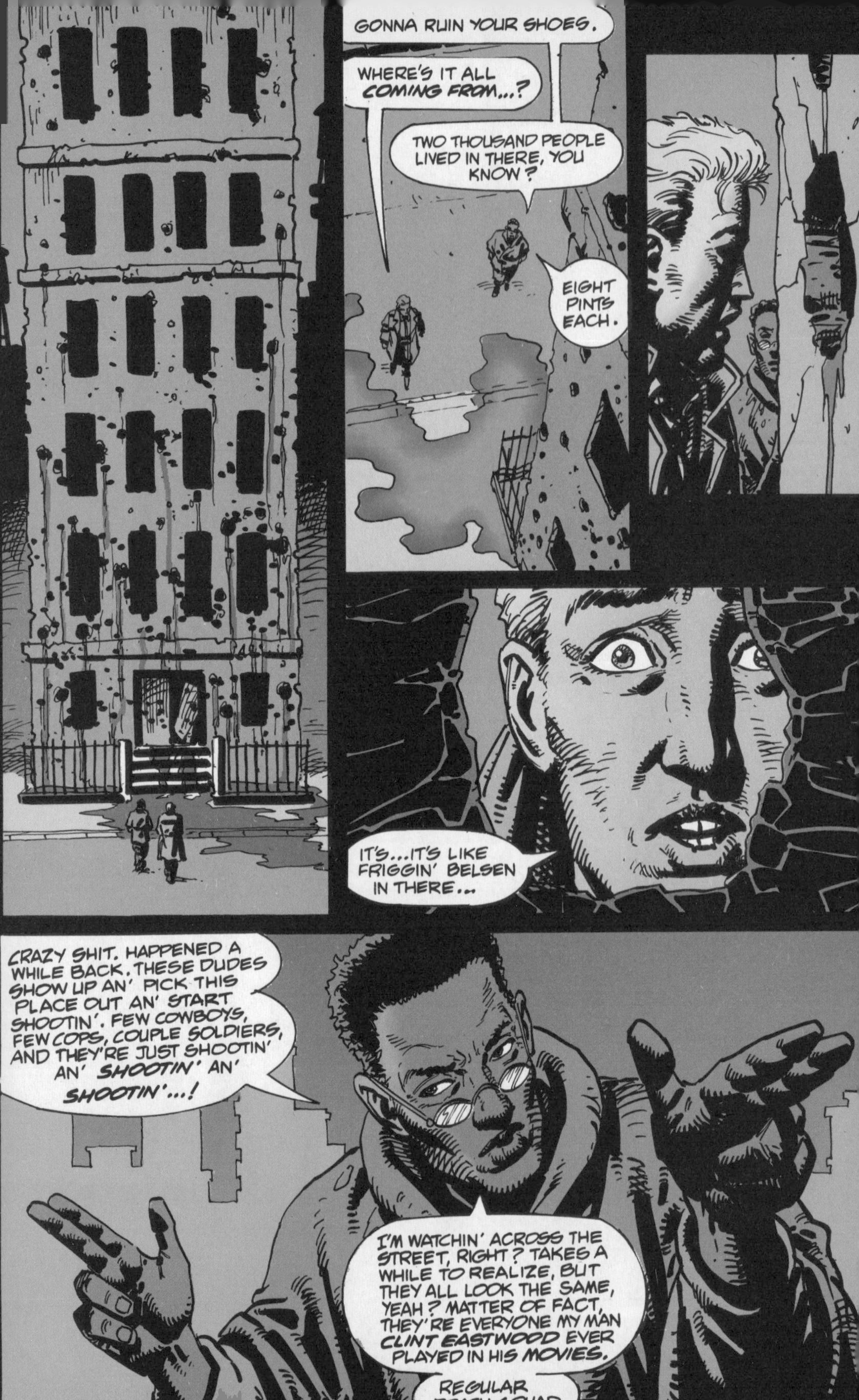
GONNA RUIN YOUR SHOES.
WHERE'S IT ALL COMING FROM...?
TWO THOUSAND PEOPLE LIVED IN THERE, YOU KNOW?
EIGHT PINTS EACH.
IT'S...IT'S LIKE FRIGGIN' BELSEN IN THERE...
CRAZY SHIT. HAPPENED A WHILE BACK. THESE DUDES SHOW UP AN' PICK THIS PLACE OUT AN' START SHOOTIN'. FEW COWBOYS, FEW COPS, COUPLE SOLDIERS, AND THEY'RE JUST SHOOTIN' AN' SHOOTIN' AN' SHOOTIN'...!
I'M WATCHIN' ACROSS THE STREET, RIGHT? TAKES A WHILE TO REALIZE, BUT THEY ALL LOOK THE SAME, YEAH? MATTER OF FACT, THEY'RE EVERYONE MY MAN CLINT EASTWOOD EVER PLAYED IN HIS MOVIES.
REGULAR DEATH SQUAD.

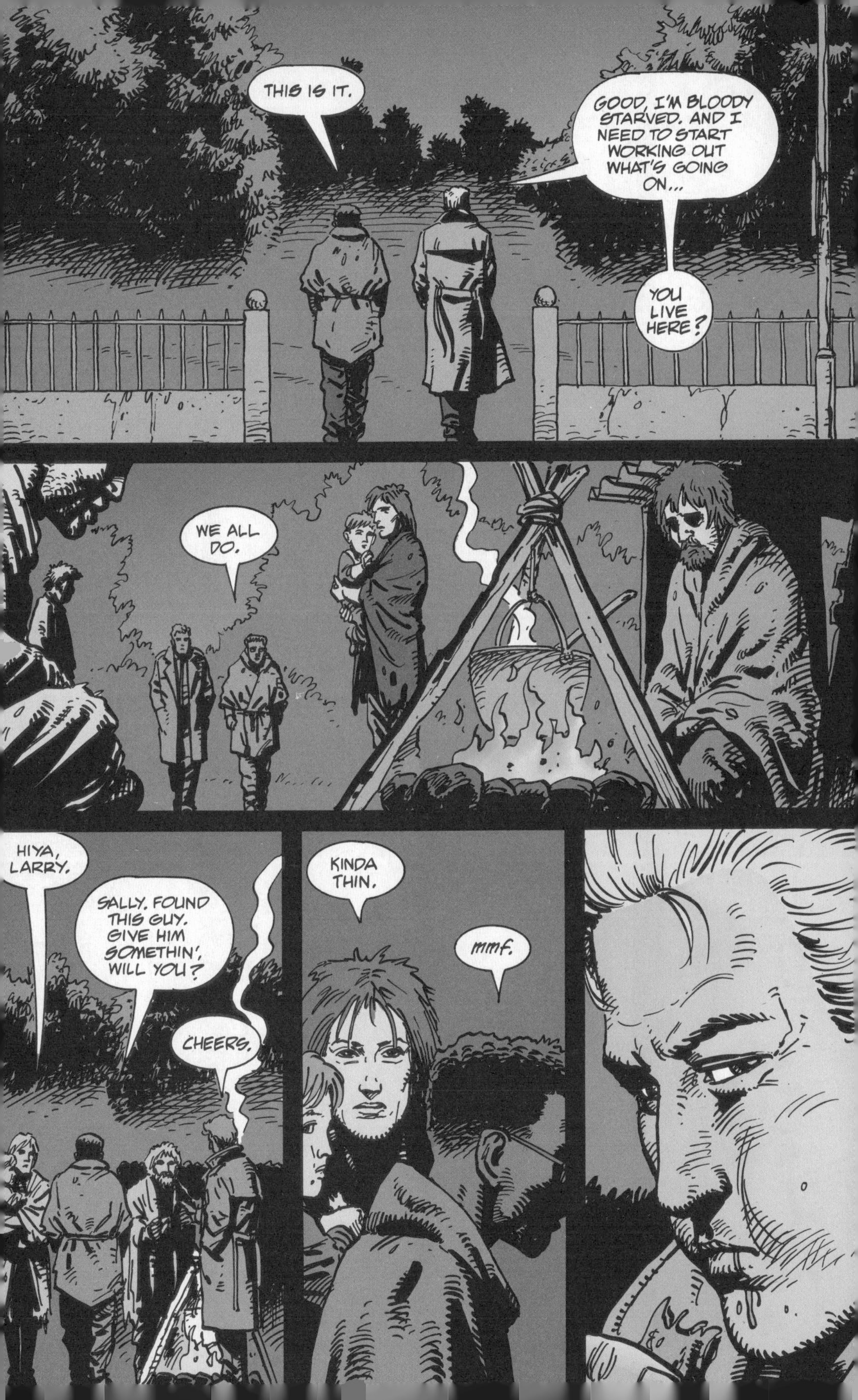
THIS IS IT.
GOOD, I'M BLOODY STARVED. AND I NEED TO START WORKING OUT WHAT'S GOING ON...
YOU LIVE HERE?
WE ALL DO.
HIYA, LARRY.
SALLY. FOUND THIS GUY. GIVE HIM SOMETHIN', WILL YOU?
CHEERS.
KINDA THIN.
mmf.

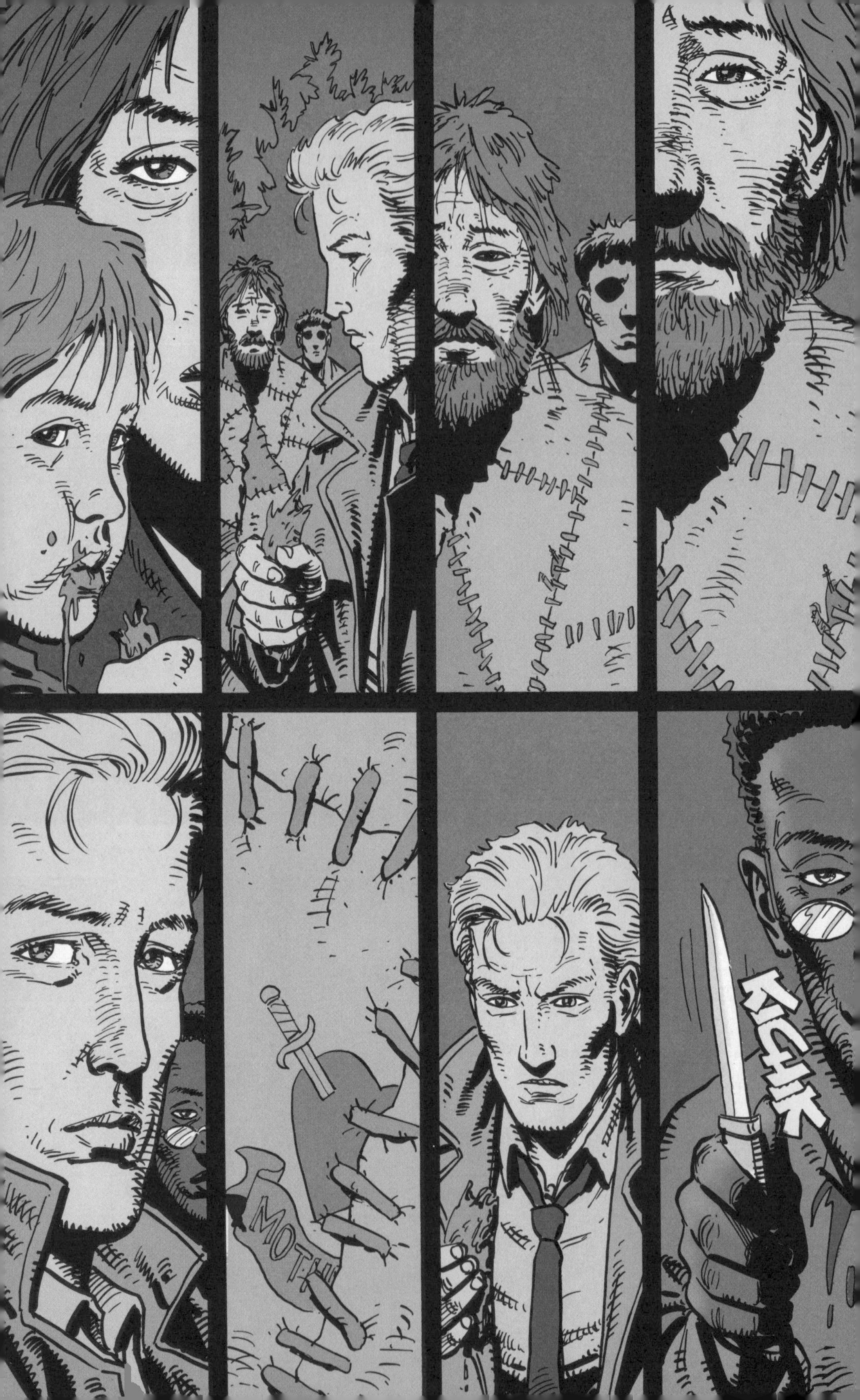
MOTH
KICHK

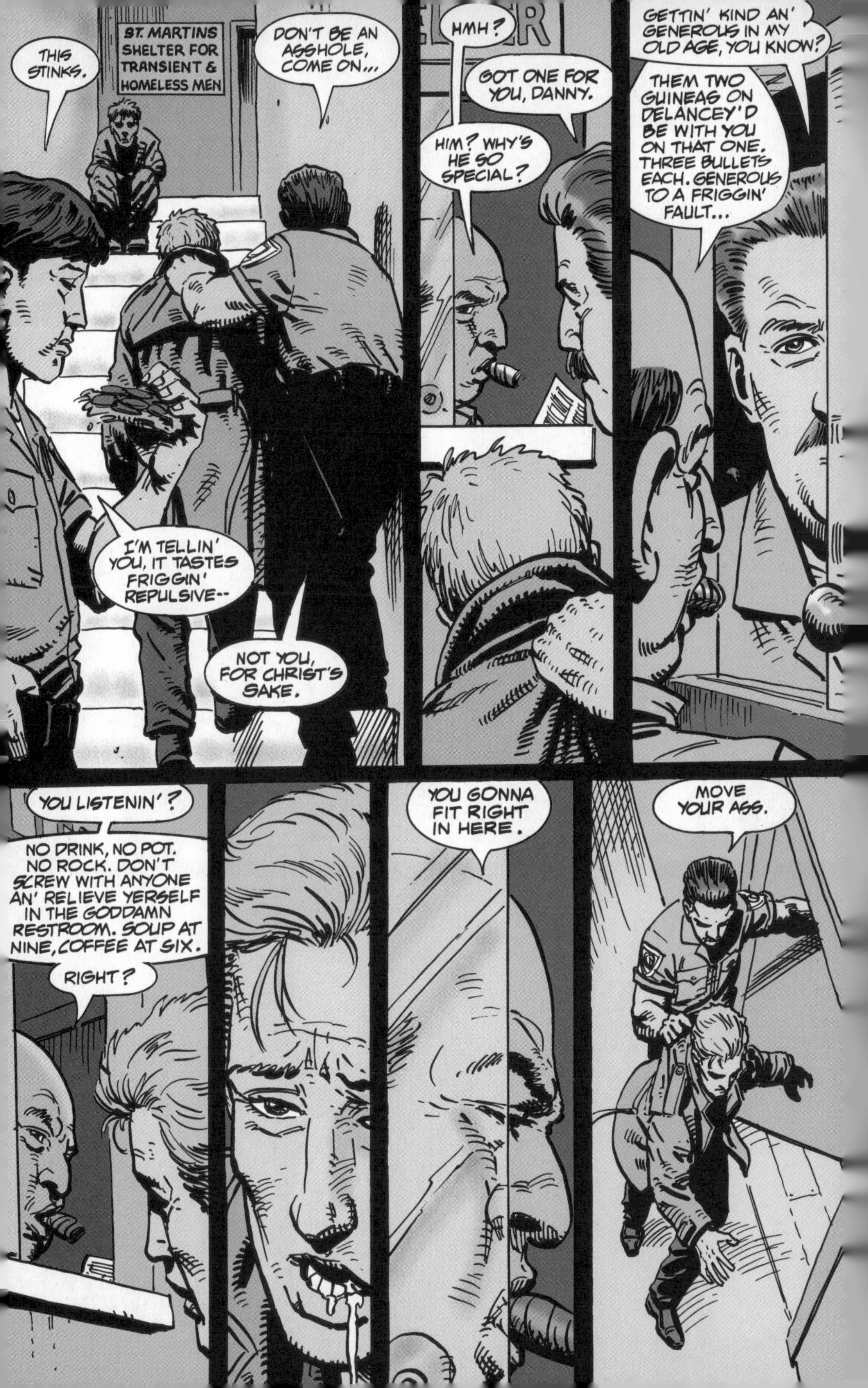

ST. MARTINS SHELTER FOR TRANSIENT & HOMELESS MEN
THIS STINKS.
DON'T BE AN ASSHOLE, COME ON...
I'M TELLIN' YOU, IT TASTES FRIGGIN' REPULSIVE--
NOT YOU, FOR CHRIST'S SAKE.
HMH?
GOT ONE FOR YOU, DANNY.
HIM? WHY'S HE SO SPECIAL?
GETTIN' KIND AN' GENEROUS IN MY OLD AGE, YOU KNOW?
THEM TWO GUINEAS ON DELANCEY'D BE WITH YOU ON THAT ONE. THREE BULLETS EACH. GENEROUS TO A FRIGGIN' FAULT...
YOU LISTENIN'?
NO DRINK, NO POT. NO ROCK. DON'T SCREW WITH ANYONE AN' RELIEVE YERSELF IN THE GODDAMN RESTROOM. SOUP AT NINE, COFFEE AT SIX.
RIGHT?
YOU GONNA FIT RIGHT IN HERE.
MOVE YOUR ASS.

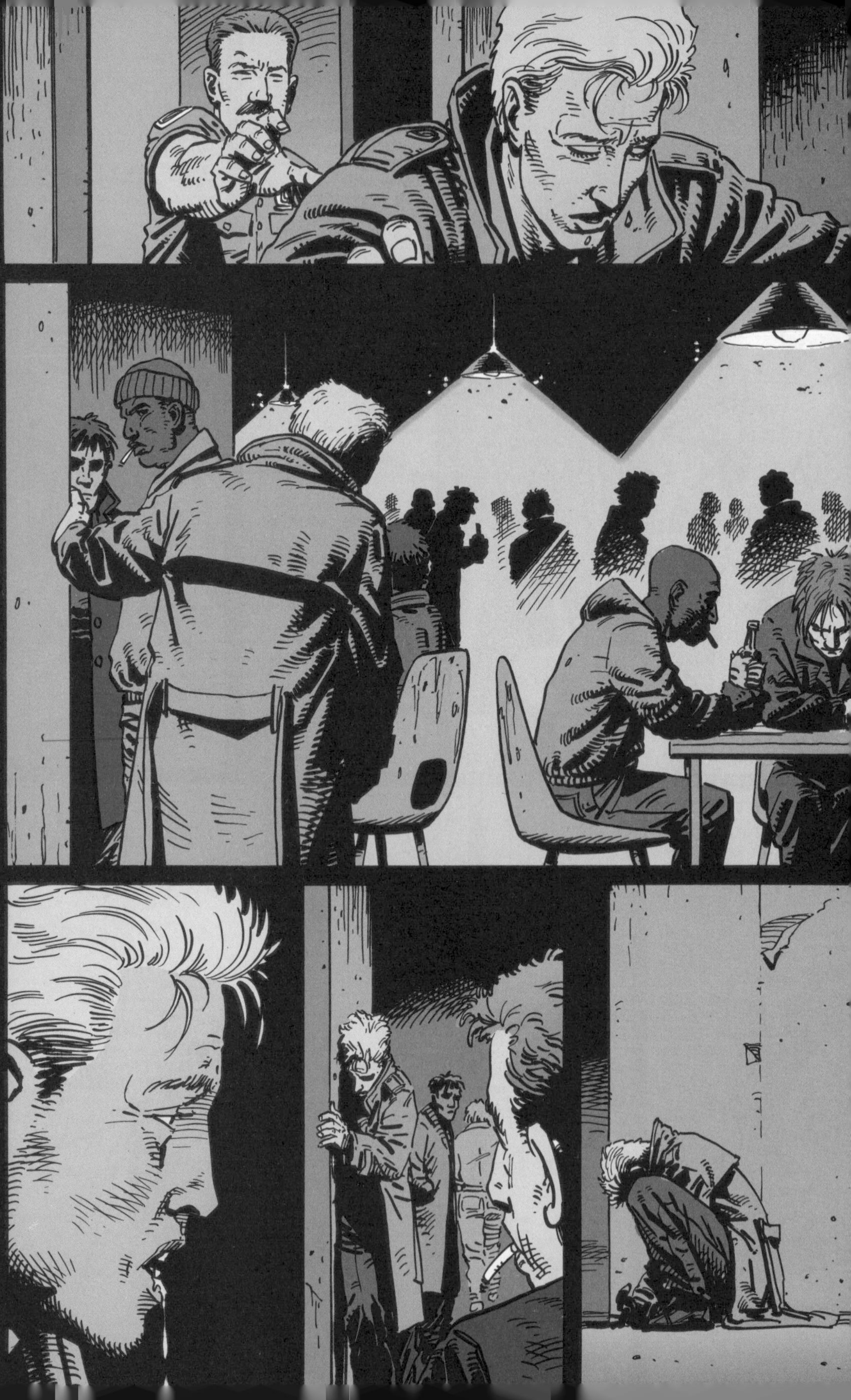

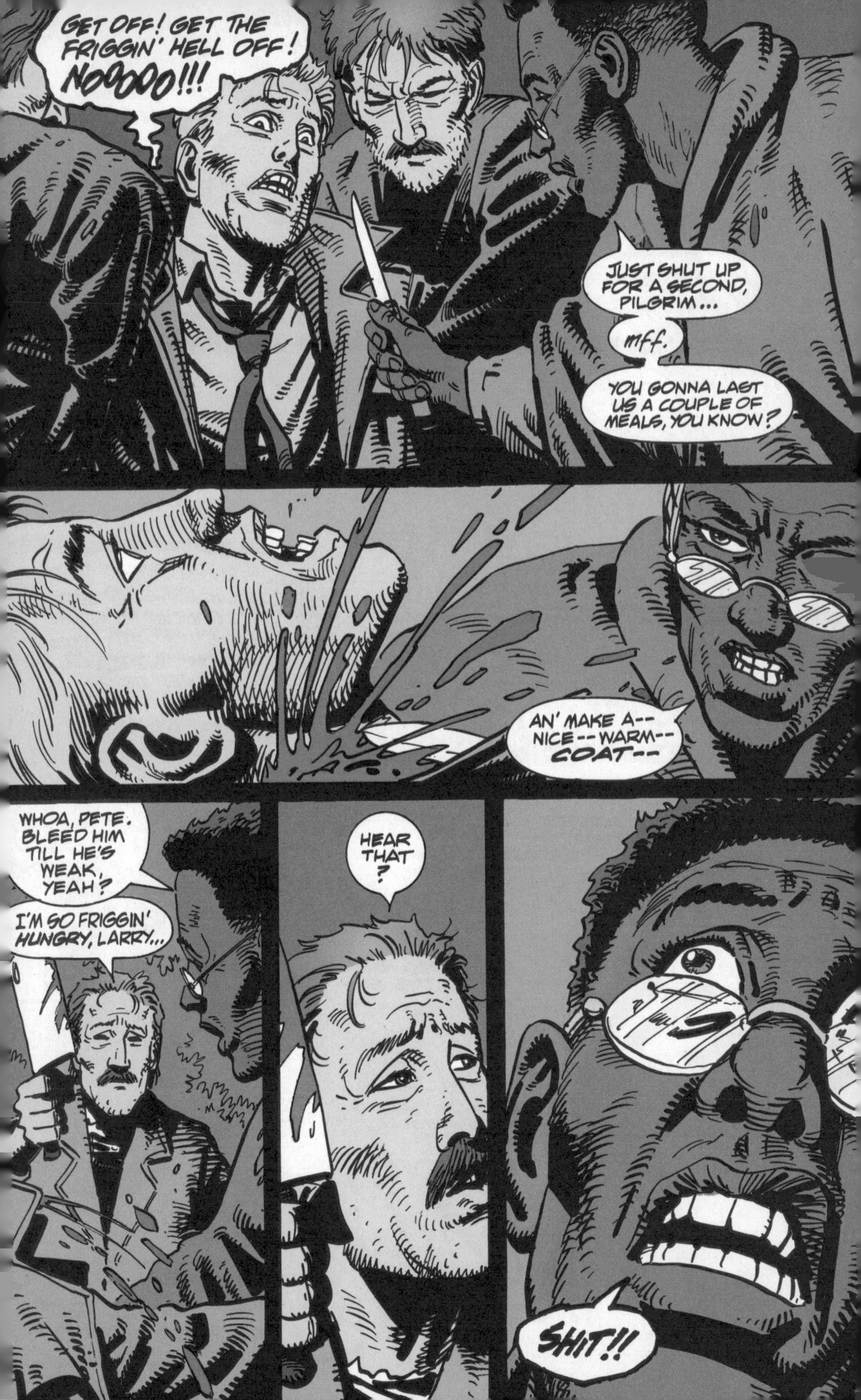
GET OFF! GET THE FRIGGIN' HELL OFF! NOOOOO!!!
JUST SHUT UP FOR A SECOND, PILGRIM...
mff.
YOU GONNA LAST US A COUPLE OF MEALS, YOU KNOW?
AN' MAKE A-- NICE--WARM-- COAT--
WHOA, PETE. BLEED HIM TILL HE'S WEAK, YEAH?
I'M SO FRIGGIN' HUNGRY, LARRY...
HEAR THAT?
SHIT!!

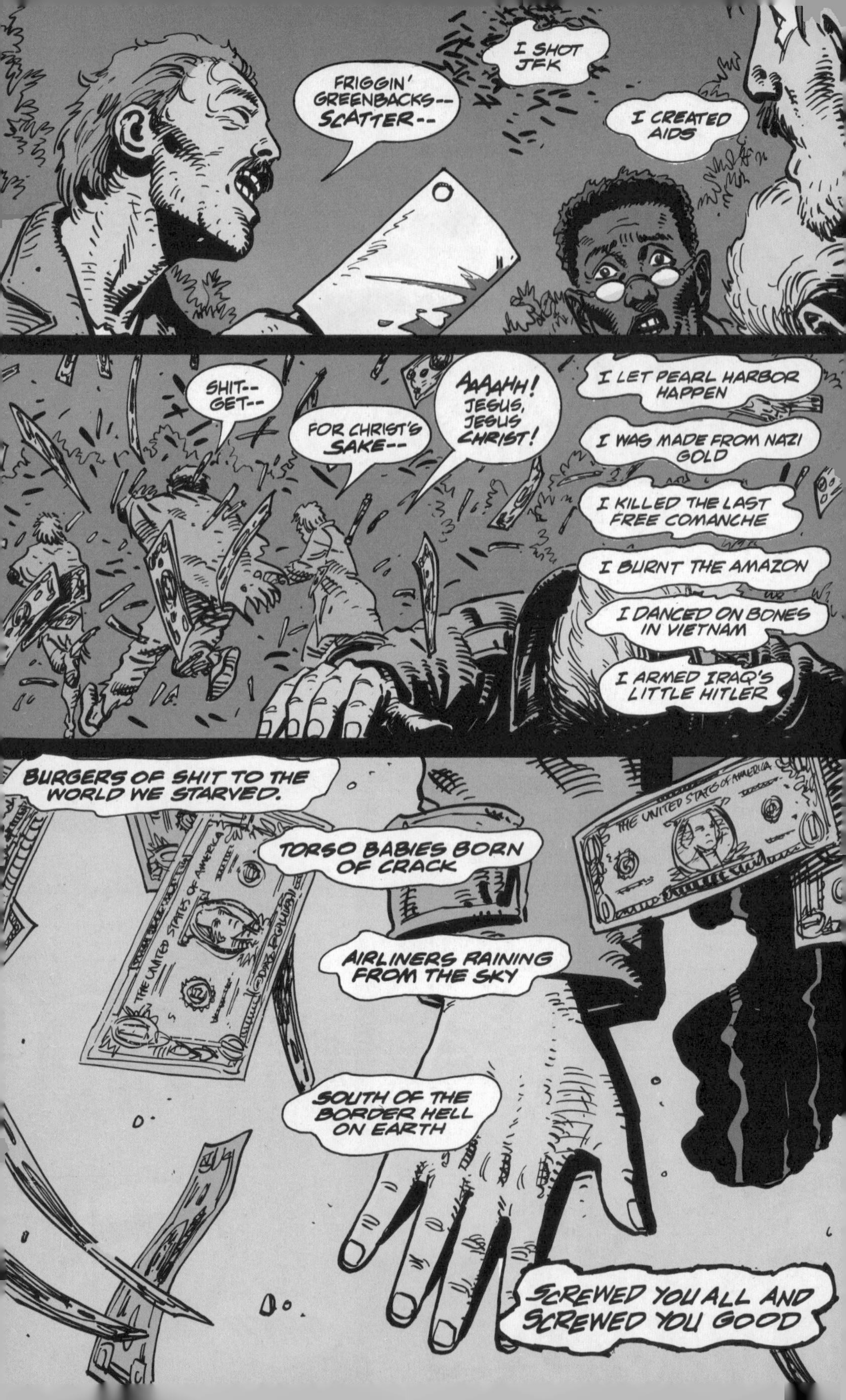
FRIGGIN' GREENBACKS-- SCATTER--
I SHOT JFK
I CREATED AIDS
SHIT-- GET--
FOR CHRIST'S SAKE--
AAAAHH! JESUS, JESUS CHRIST!
I LET PEARL HARBOR HAPPEN
I WAS MADE FROM NAZI GOLD
I KILLED THE LAST FREE COMANCHE
I BURNT THE AMAZON
I DANCED ON BONES IN VIETNAM
I ARMED IRAQ'S LITTLE HITLER
BURGERS OF SHIT TO THE WORLD WE STARVED.
TORSO BABIES BORN OF CRACK
AIRLINERS RAINING FROM THE SKY
SOUTH OF THE BORDER HELL ON EARTH
SCREWED YOU ALL AND SCREWED YOU GOOD

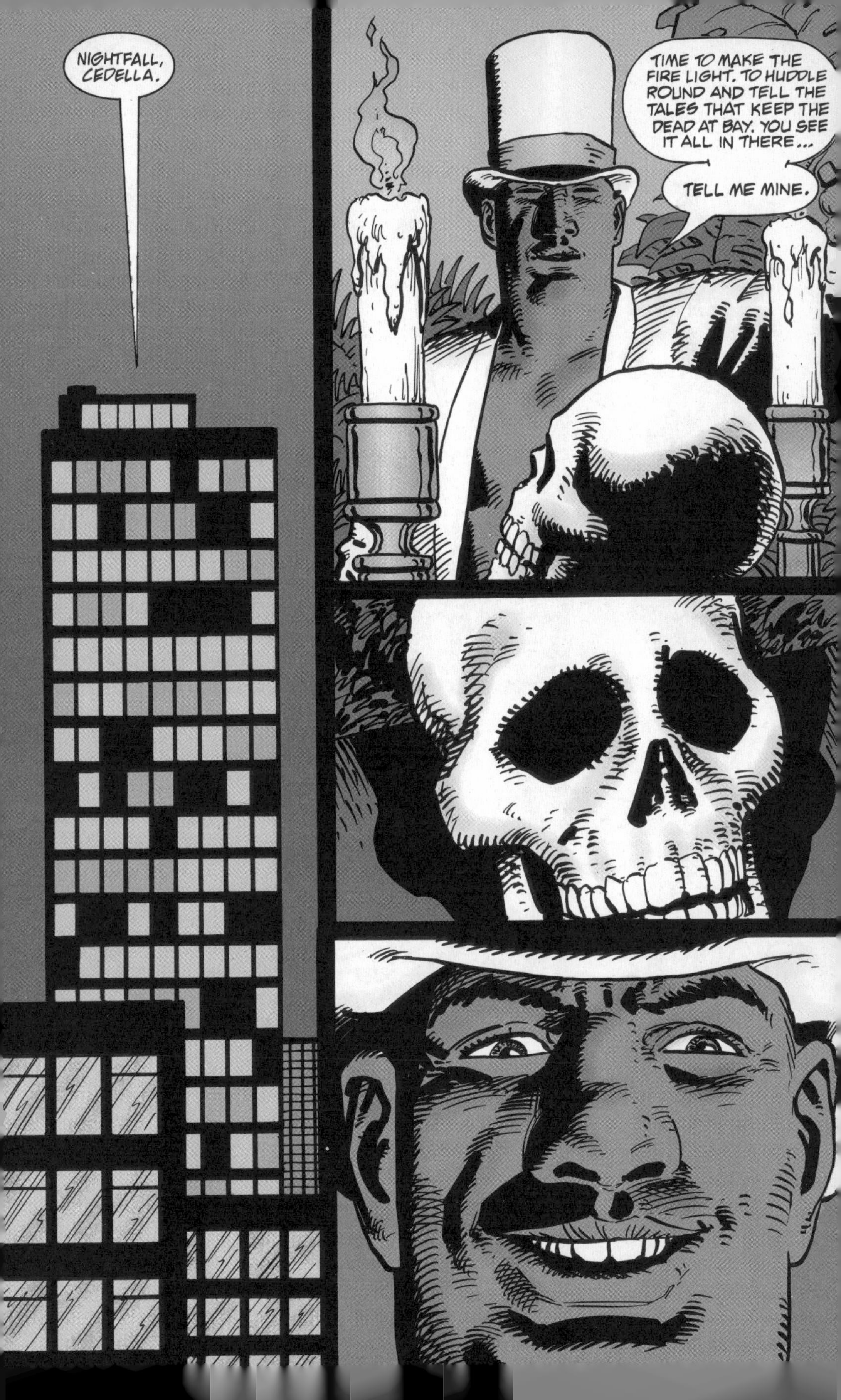
NIGHTFALL, CEDELLA.
TIME TO MAKE THE FIRE LIGHT. TO HUDDLE ROUND AND TELL THE TALES THAT KEEP THE DEAD AT BAY. YOU SEE IT ALL IN THERE...
TELL ME MINE.

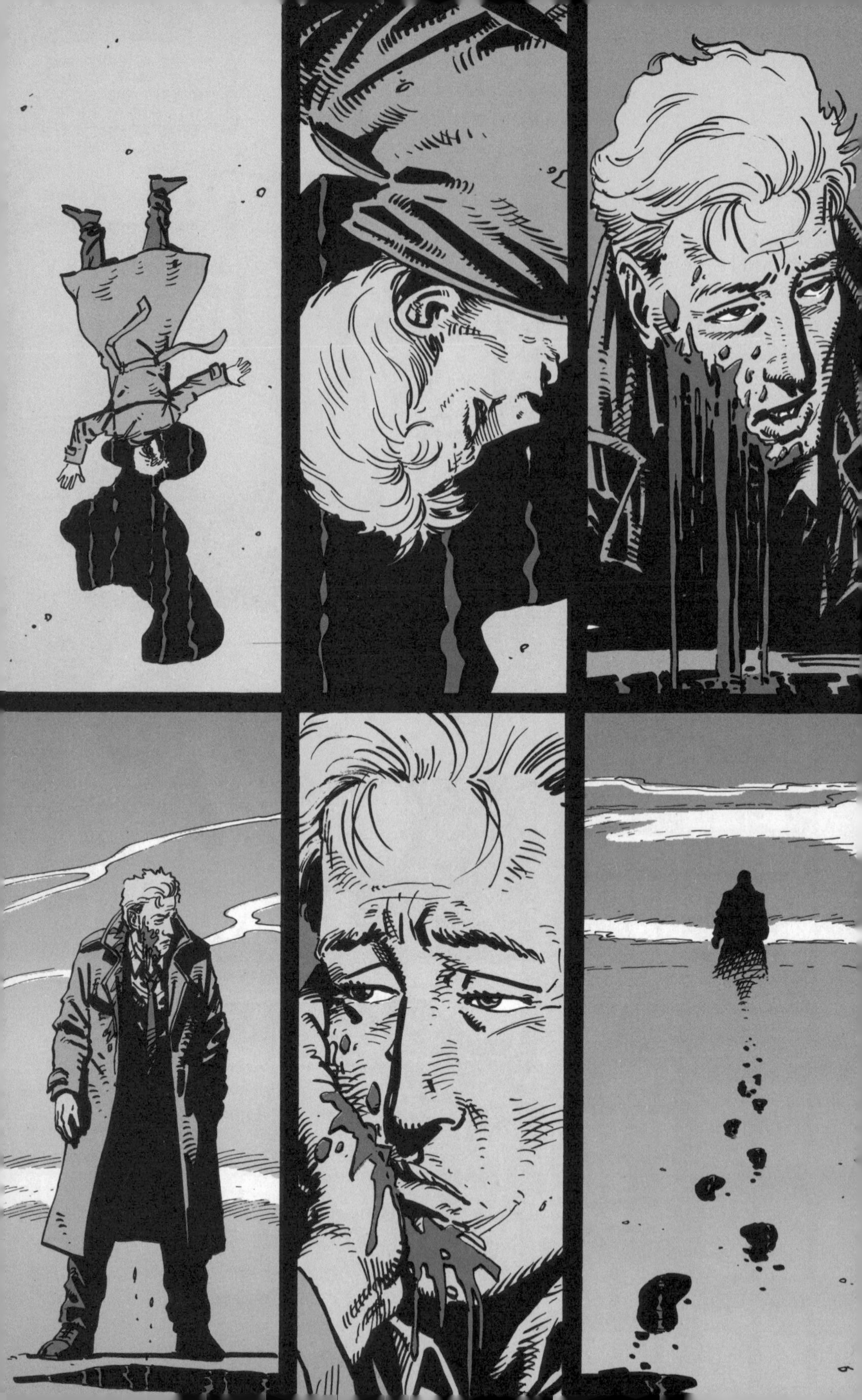

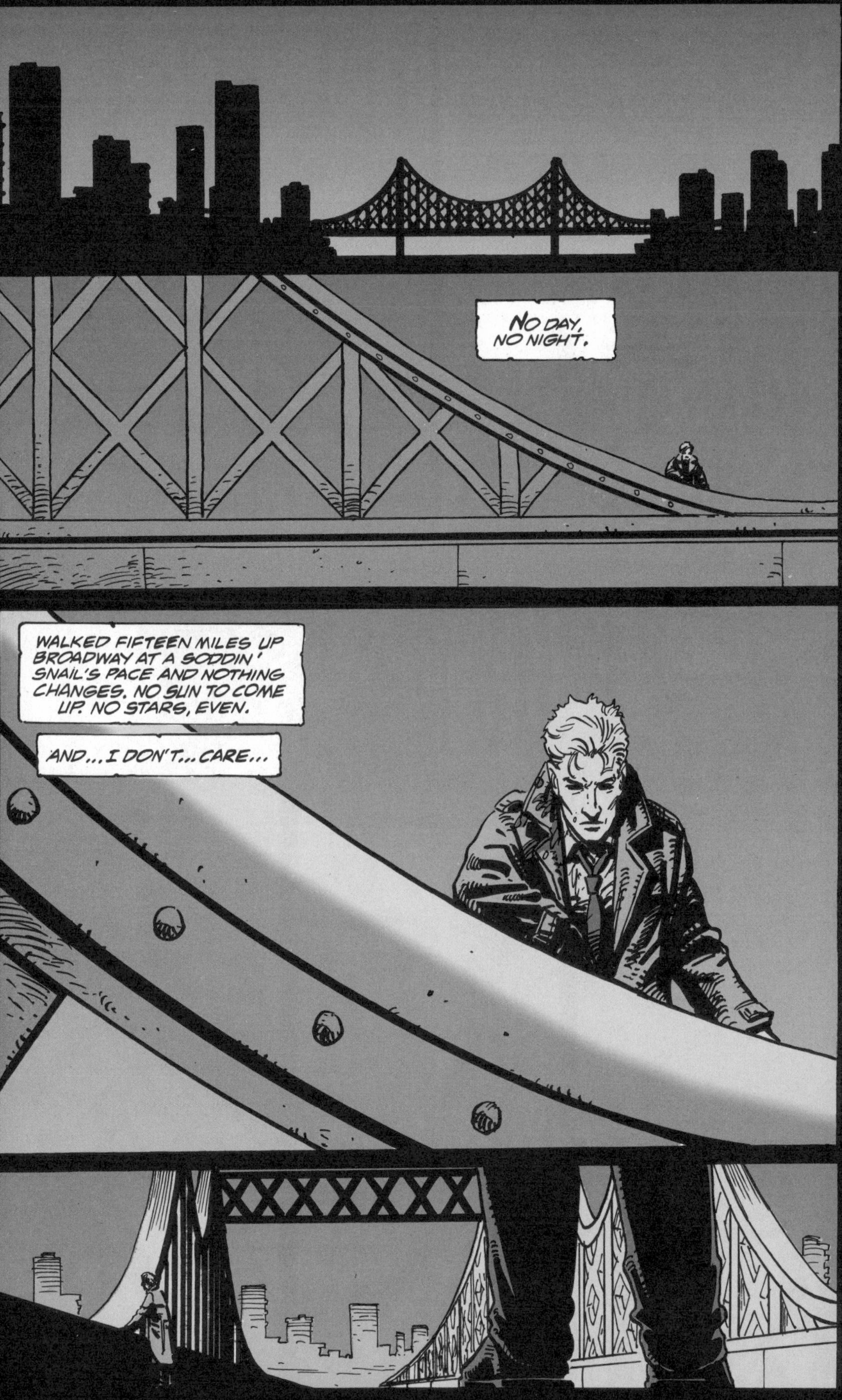

NO DAY, NO NIGHT.
WALKED FIFTEEN MILES UP BROADWAY AT A SODDIN' SNAIL'S PACE AND NOTHING CHANGES. NO SUN TO COME UP. NO STARS, EVEN.
AND...I DON'T...CARE...

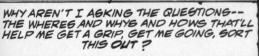

WHY DON'T I CARE?

WHY AREN'T I ASKING THE QUESTIONS-- THE WHERES AND WHYS AND HOWS THAT'LL HELP ME GET A GRIP, GET ME GOING, SORT THIS OUT?

EVERYTHING'S GONE OUT THE BLOODY WINDOW AND THE SKY'S BRIGHT RED BUT THAT'S NOT THE WORST I'VE EVER HAD HAPPEN, IS IT? I'M USED TO THIS SORT'VE MALARKEY--JUST GRIST TO THE MILL --

I SHOULD BE ABLE TO WALK IT--

BUT NO QUESTIONS.

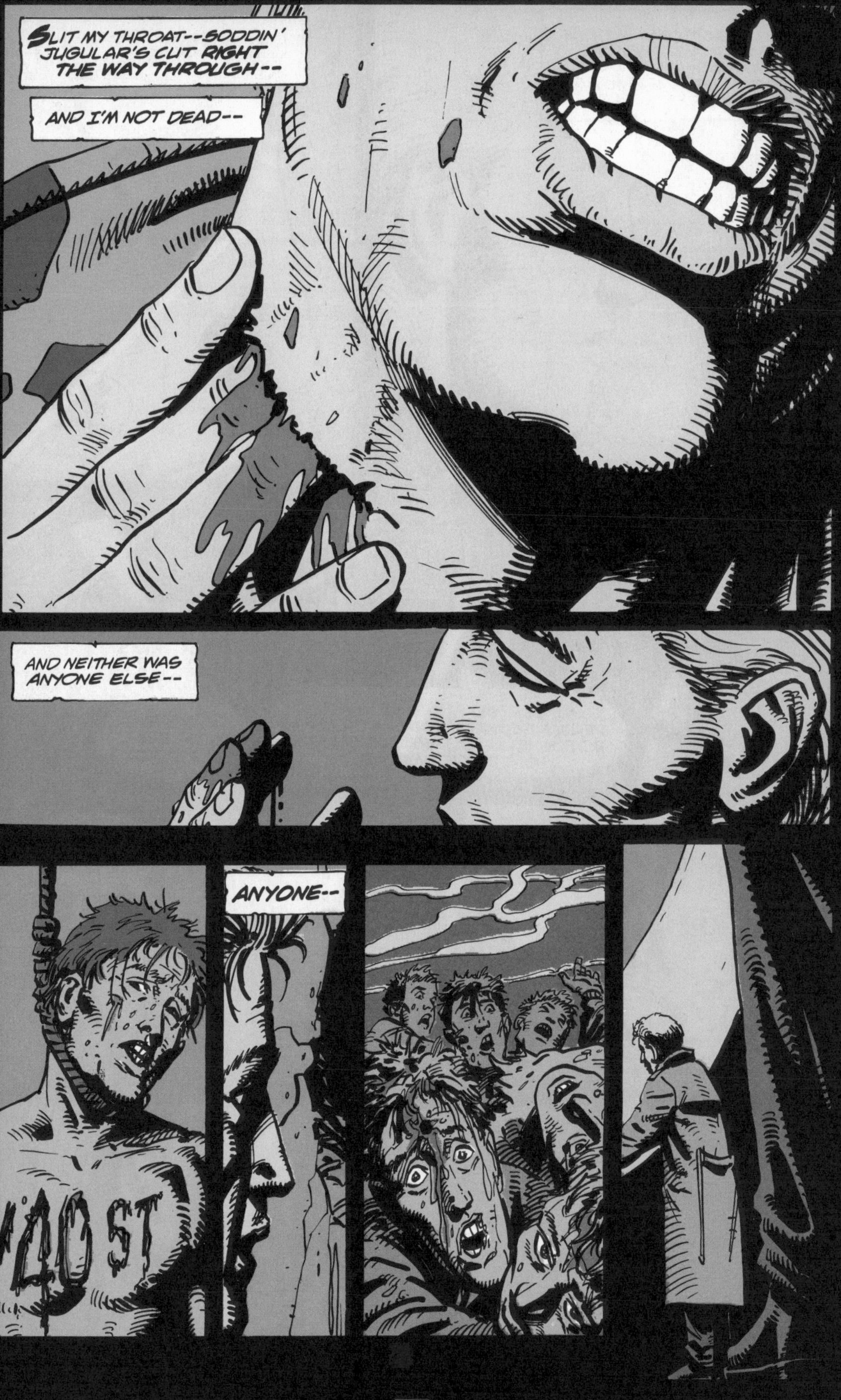
SLIT MY THROAT--SODDIN' JUGULAR'S CUT RIGHT THE WAY THROUGH--
AND I'M NOT DEAD--
AND NEITHER WAS ANYONE ELSE--
ANYONE--
40 ST

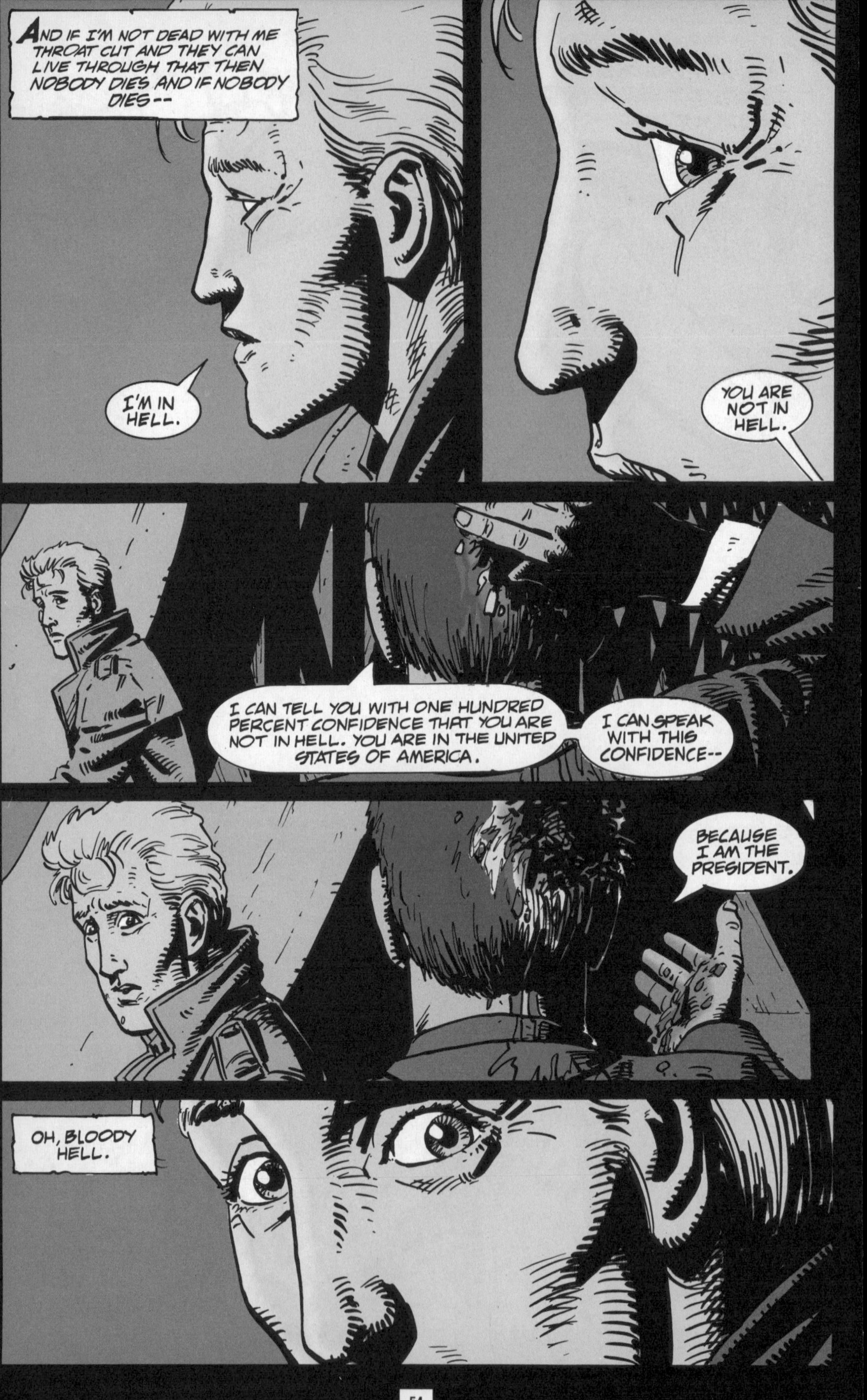

AND IF I'M NOT DEAD WITH ME THROAT CUT AND THEY CAN LIVE THROUGH THAT THEN NOBODY DIES AND IF NOBODY DIES--
I'M IN HELL.
YOU ARE NOT IN HELL.
I CAN TELL YOU WITH ONE HUNDRED PERCENT CONFIDENCE THAT YOU ARE NOT IN HELL. YOU ARE IN THE UNITED STATES OF AMERICA.
I CAN SPEAK WITH THIS CONFIDENCE--
BECAUSE I AM THE PRESIDENT.
OH, BLOODY HELL.

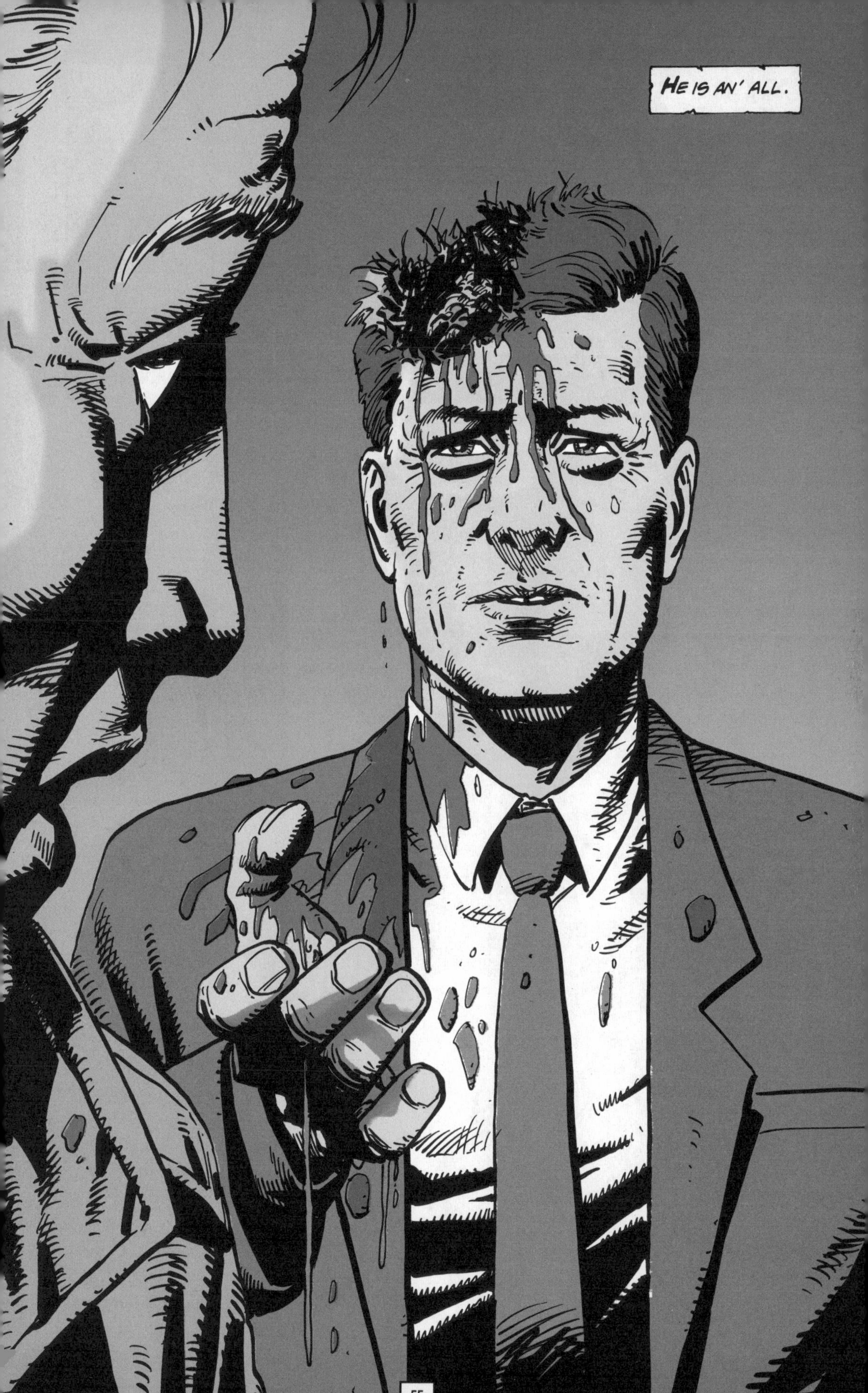
HE IS AN' ALL.

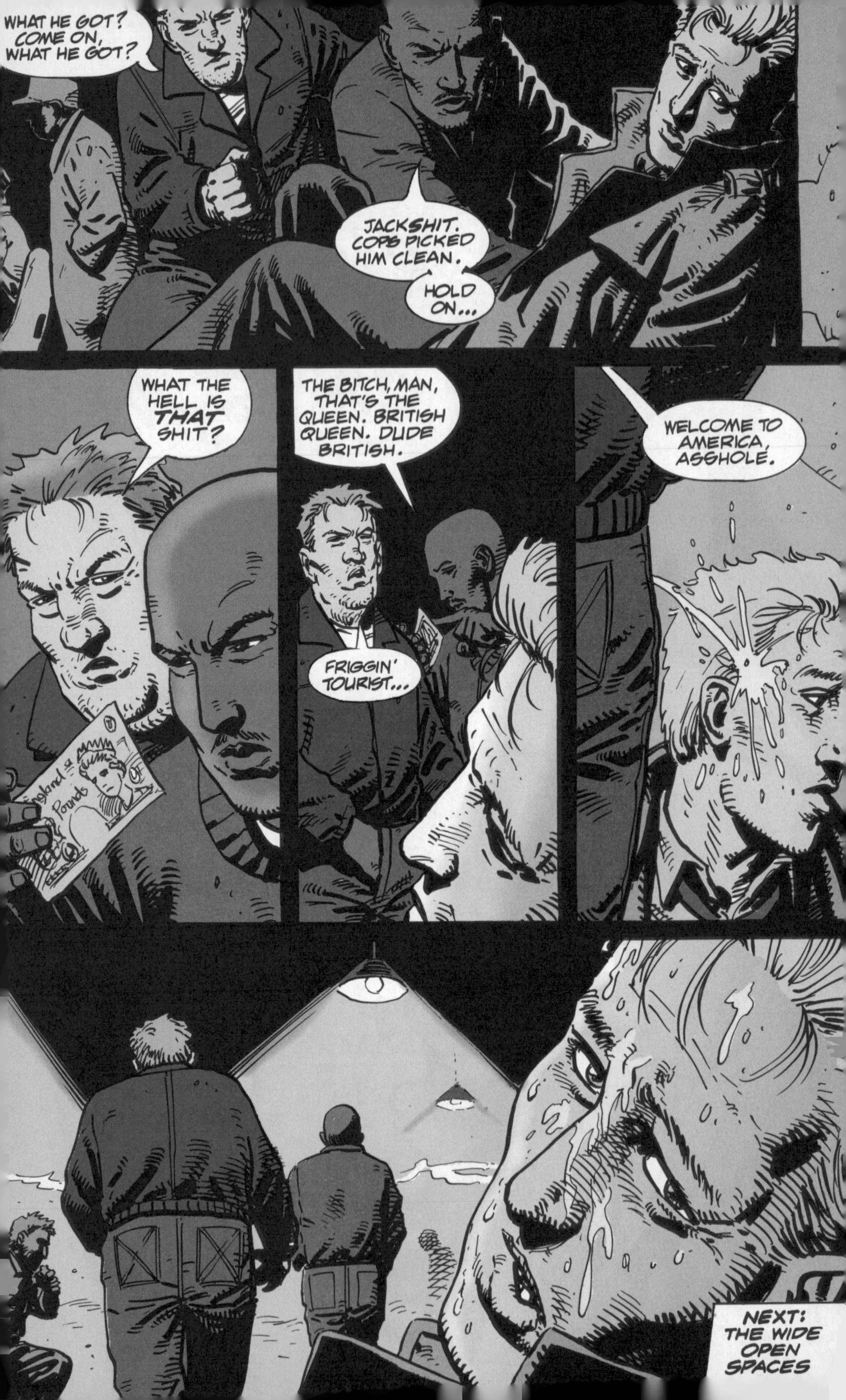
WHAT HE GOT? COME ON, WHAT HE GOT?
JACKSHIT. COPS PICKED HIM CLEAN.
HOLD ON...
WHAT THE HELL IS THAT SHIT?
THE BITCH, MAN, THAT'S THE QUEEN. BRITISH QUEEN. DUDE BRITISH.
FRIGGIN' TOURIST...
WELCOME TO AMERICA, ASSHOLE.
NEXT: THE WIDE OPEN SPACES

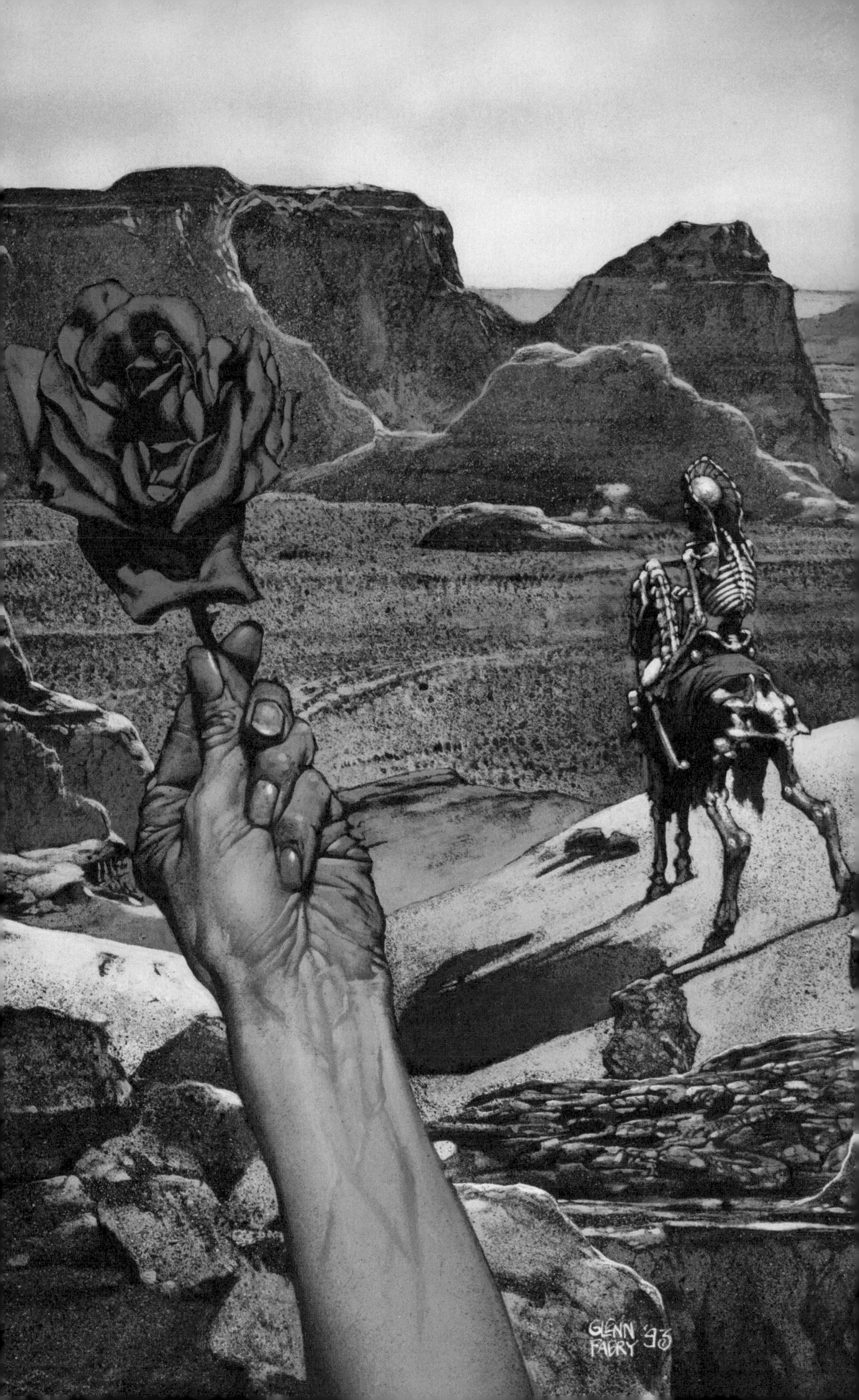
GLENN
FABRY '93

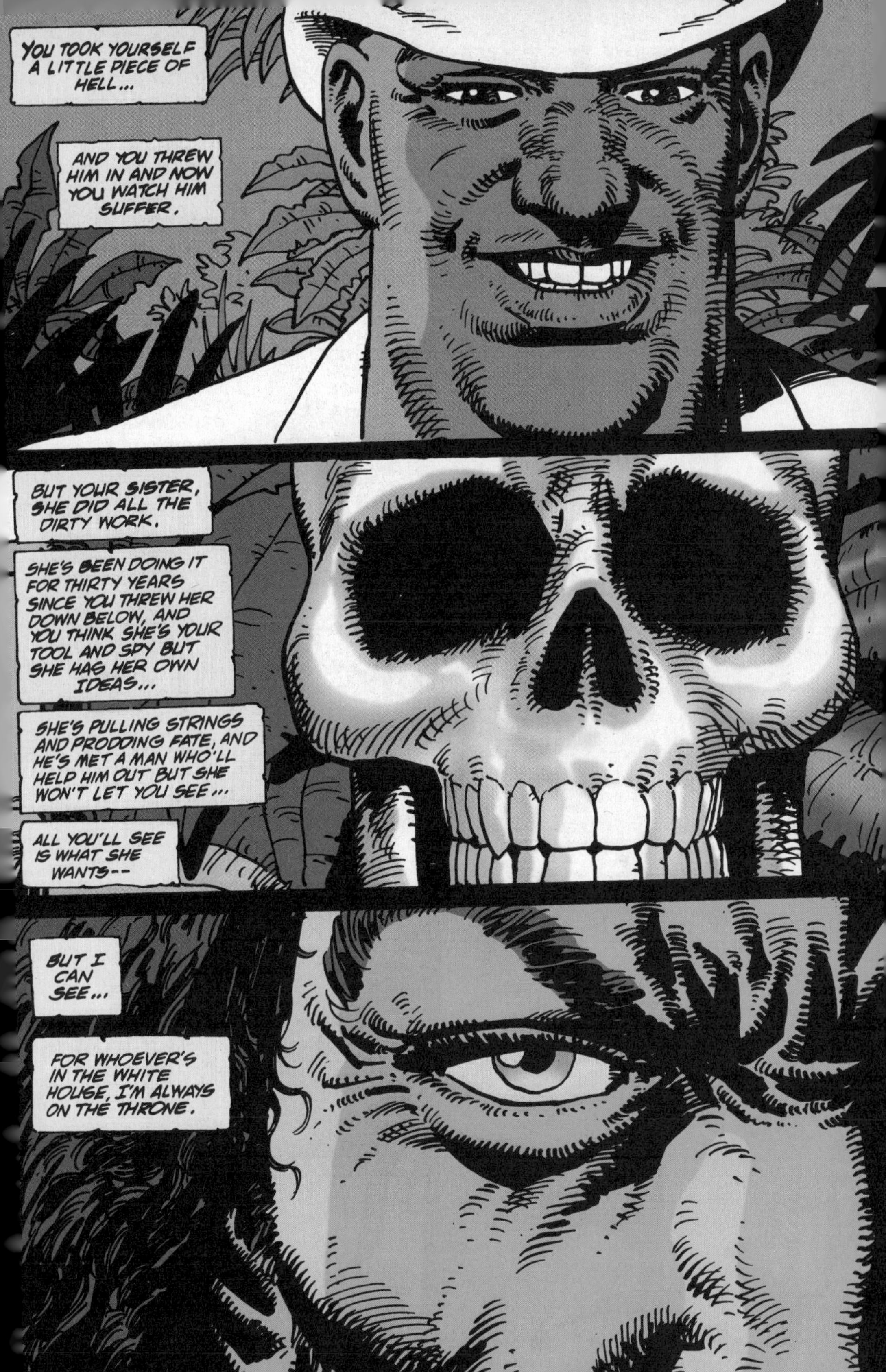
YOU TOOK YOURSELF A LITTLE PIECE OF HELL...
AND YOU THREW HIM IN AND NOW YOU WATCH HIM SUFFER.
BUT YOUR SISTER, SHE DID ALL THE DIRTY WORK.
SHE'S BEEN DOING IT FOR THIRTY YEARS SINCE YOU THREW HER DOWN BELOW, AND YOU THINK SHE'S YOUR TOOL AND SPY BUT SHE HAS HER OWN IDEAS...
SHE'S PULLING STRINGS AND PRODDING FATE, AND HE'S MET A MAN WHO'LL HELP HIM OUT BUT SHE WON'T LET YOU SEE...
ALL YOU'LL SEE IS WHAT SHE WANTS--
BUT I CAN SEE...
FOR WHOEVER'S IN THE WHITE HOUSE, I'M ALWAYS ON THE THRONE.

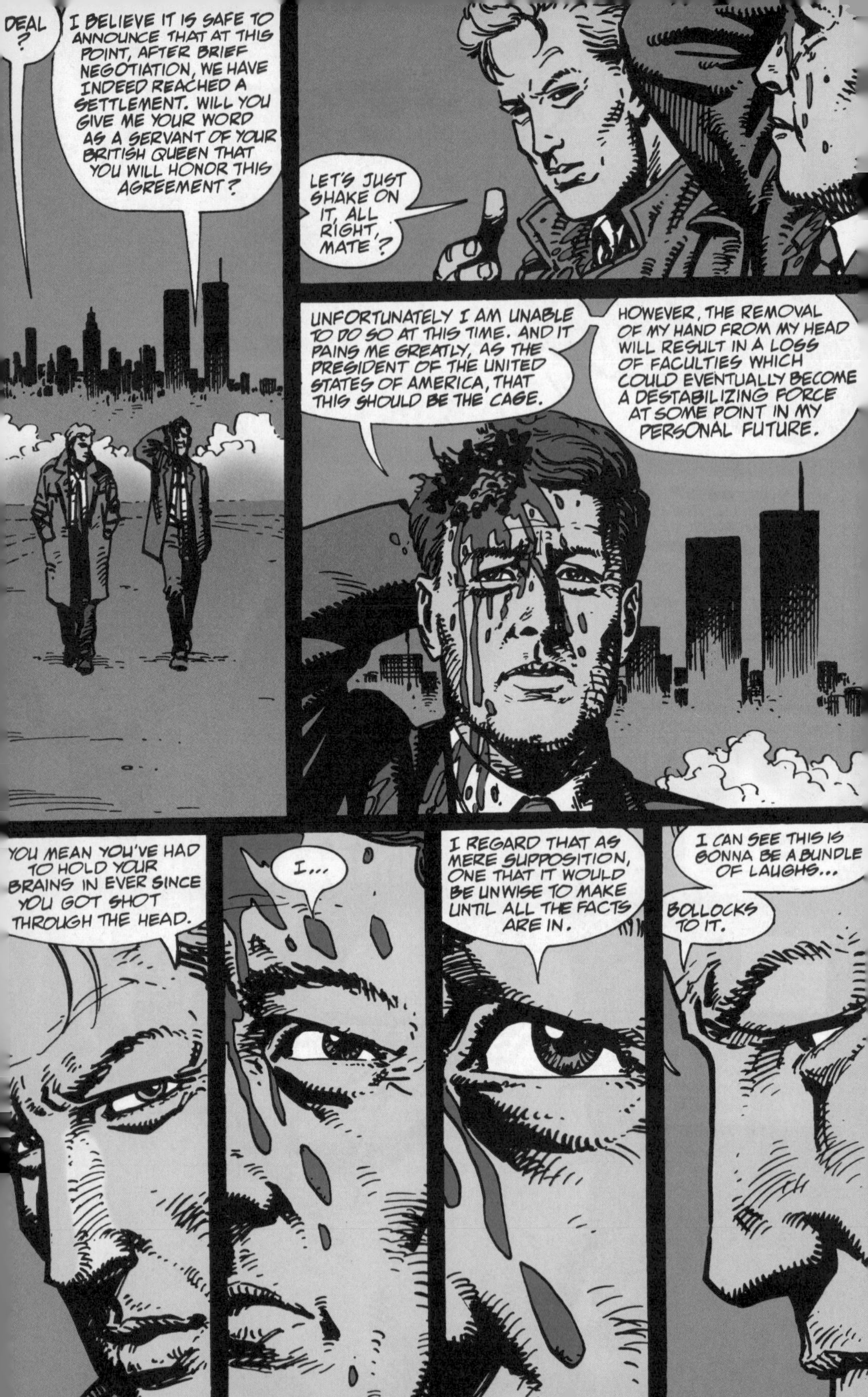
DEAL?
I BELIEVE IT IS SAFE TO ANNOUNCE THAT AT THIS POINT, AFTER BRIEF NEGOTIATION, WE HAVE INDEED REACHED A SETTLEMENT. WILL YOU GIVE ME YOUR WORD AS A SERVANT OF YOUR BRITISH QUEEN THAT YOU WILL HONOR THIS AGREEMENT?
LET'S JUST SHAKE ON IT, ALL RIGHT, MATE?
UNFORTUNATELY I AM UNABLE TO DO SO AT THIS TIME. AND IT PAINS ME GREATLY, AS THE PRESIDENT OF THE UNITED STATES OF AMERICA, THAT THIS SHOULD BE THE CASE.
HOWEVER, THE REMOVAL OF MY HAND FROM MY HEAD WILL RESULT IN A LOSS OF FACULTIES WHICH COULD EVENTUALLY BECOME A DESTABILIZING FORCE AT SOME POINT IN MY PERSONAL FUTURE.
YOU MEAN YOU'VE HAD TO HOLD YOUR BRAINS IN EVER SINCE YOU GOT SHOT THROUGH THE HEAD.
I...
I REGARD THAT AS MERE SUPPOSITION, ONE THAT IT WOULD BE UNWISE TO MAKE UNTIL ALL THE FACTS ARE IN.
I CAN SEE THIS IS GONNA BE A BUNDLE OF LAUGHS...
BOLLOCKS TO IT.

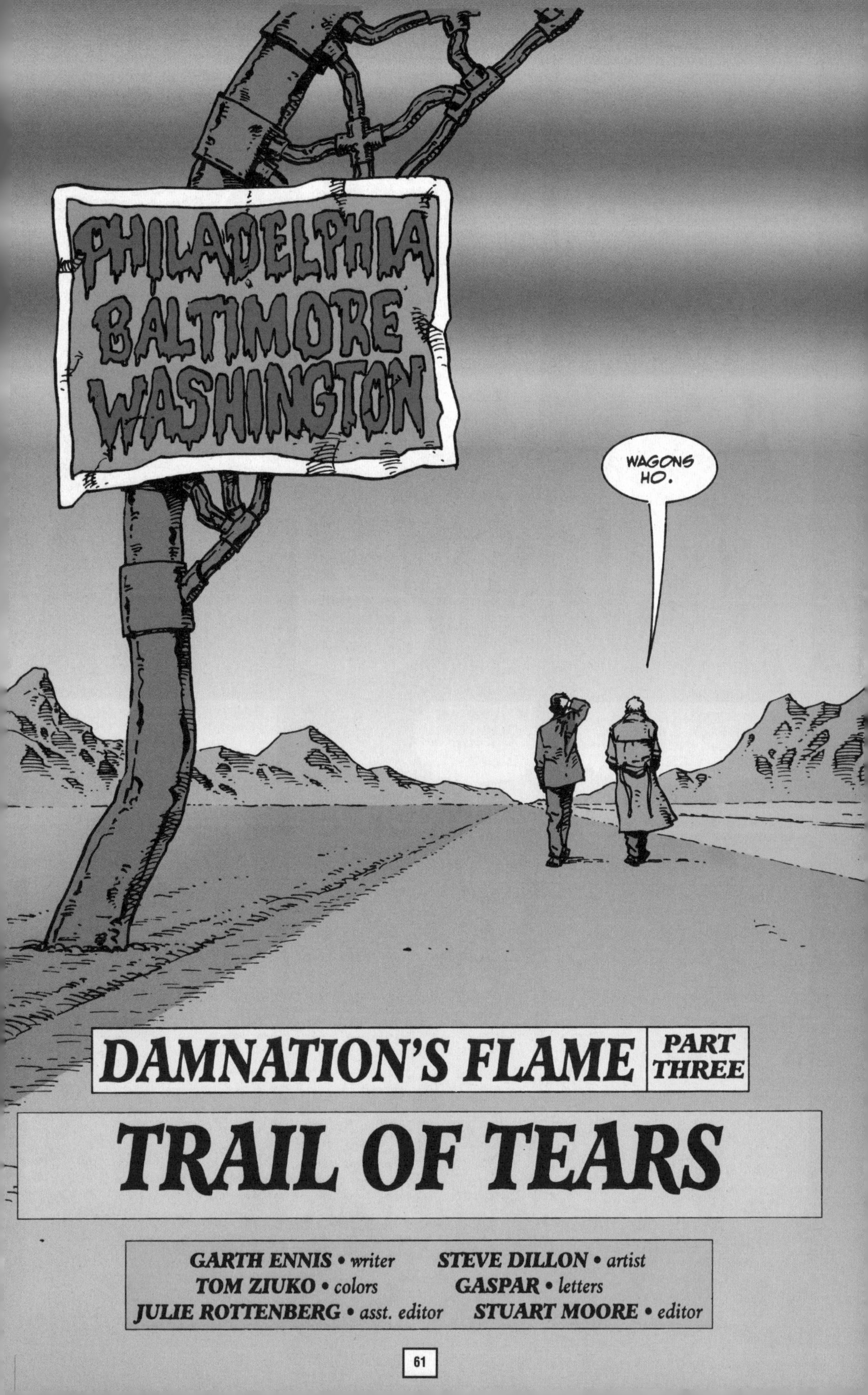
PHILADELPHIA
BALTIMORE
WASHINGTON
WAGONS HO.

DAMNATION'S FLAME PART THREE

TRAIL OF TEARS

GARTH ENNIS • *writer* **STEVE DILLON** • *artist*
TOM ZIUKO • *colors* **GASPAR** • *letters*
JULIE ROTTENBERG • *asst. editor* **STUART MOORE** • *editor*

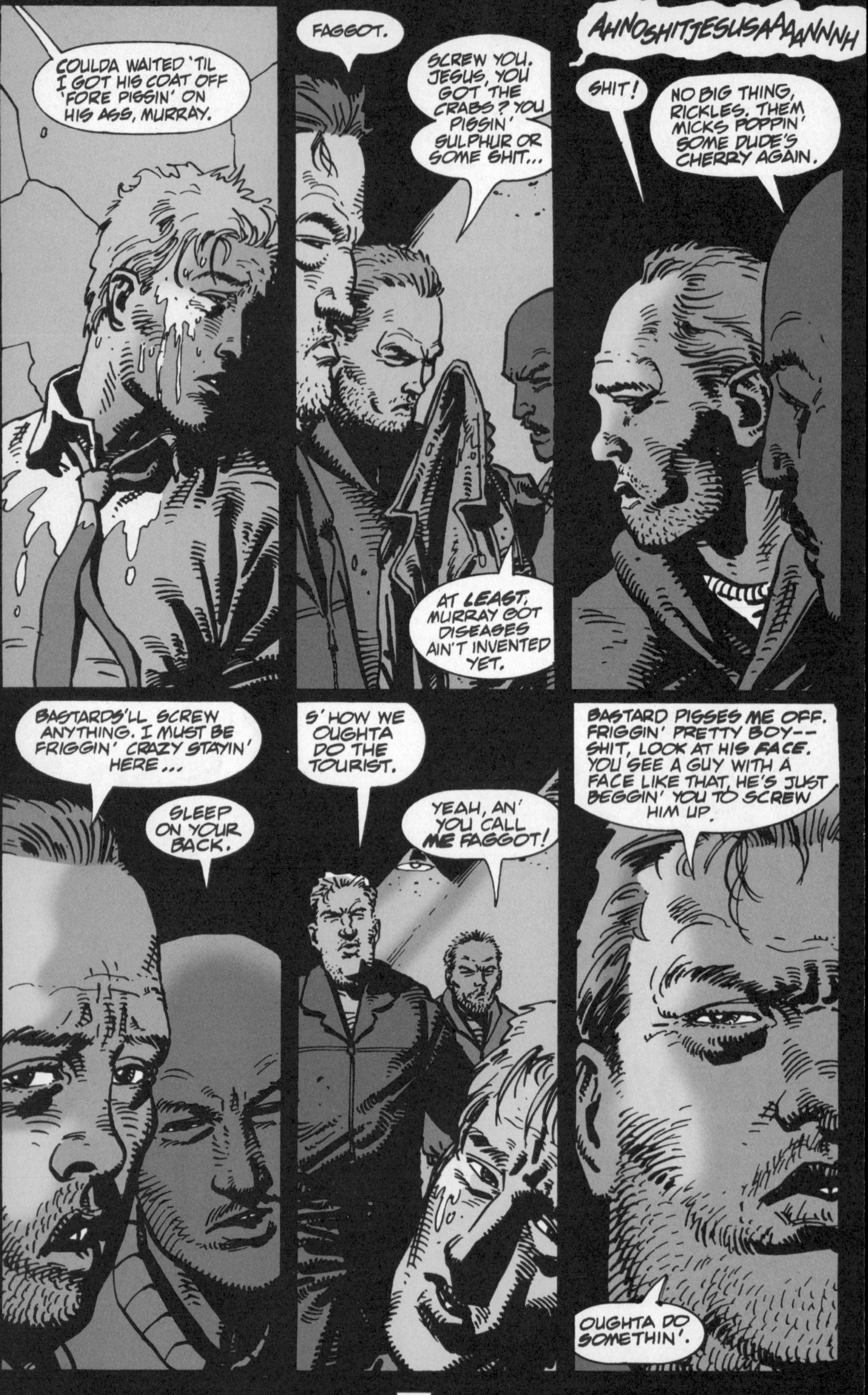
COULDA WAITED 'TIL I GOT HIS COAT OFF 'FORE PISSIN' ON HIS ASS, MURRAY.
FAGGOT.
SCREW YOU. JESUS, YOU GOT THE CRABS? YOU PISSIN' SULPHUR OR SOME SHIT...
AT LEAST, MURRAY GOT DISEASES AIN'T INVENTED YET.
AHNOSHITJESUSAAAANNNH
SHIT!
NO BIG THING, RICKLES. THEM MICKS POPPIN' SOME DUDE'S CHERRY AGAIN.
BASTARDS'LL SCREW ANYTHING. I MUST BE FRIGGIN' CRAZY STAYIN' HERE...
SLEEP ON YOUR BACK.
S' HOW WE OUGHTA DO THE TOURIST.
YEAH, AN' YOU CALL ME FAGGOT!
BASTARD PISSES ME OFF. FRIGGIN' PRETTY BOY-- SHIT, LOOK AT HIS FACE. YOU SEE A GUY WITH A FACE LIKE THAT, HE'S JUST BEGGIN' YOU TO SCREW HIM UP.
OUGHTA DO SOMETHIN'.

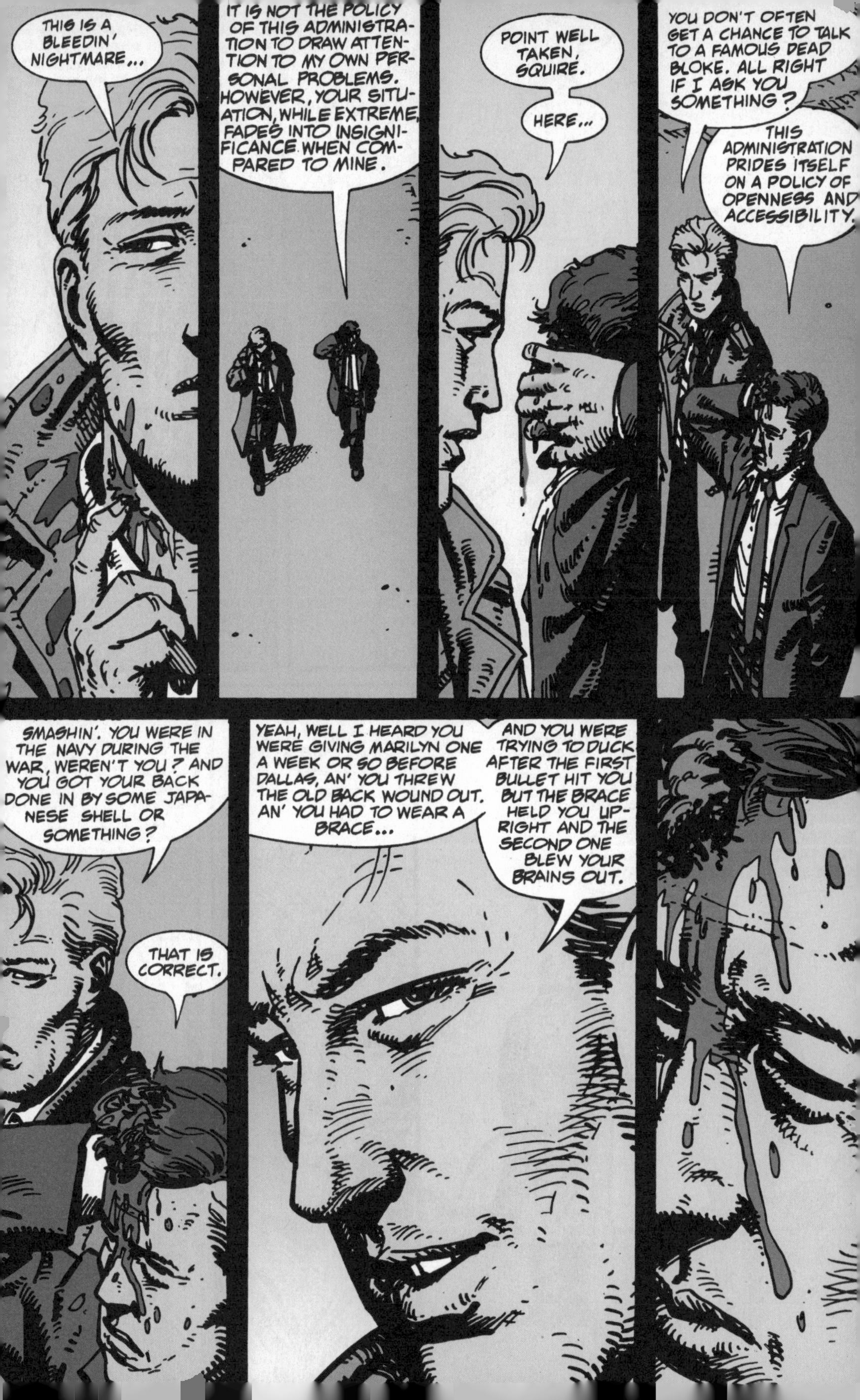
THIS IS A BLEEDIN' NIGHTMARE...
IT IS NOT THE POLICY OF THIS ADMINISTRATION TO DRAW ATTENTION TO MY OWN PERSONAL PROBLEMS. HOWEVER, YOUR SITUATION, WHILE EXTREME, FADES INTO INSIGNIFICANCE WHEN COMPARED TO MINE.
POINT WELL TAKEN, SQUIRE.
HERE...
YOU DON'T OFTEN GET A CHANCE TO TALK TO A FAMOUS DEAD BLOKE. ALL RIGHT IF I ASK YOU SOMETHING?
THIS ADMINISTRATION PRIDES ITSELF ON A POLICY OF OPENNESS AND ACCESSIBILITY.
SMASHIN'. YOU WERE IN THE NAVY DURING THE WAR, WEREN'T YOU? AND YOU GOT YOUR BACK DONE IN BY SOME JAPANESE SHELL OR SOMETHING?
THAT IS CORRECT.
YEAH, WELL I HEARD YOU WERE GIVING MARILYN ONE A WEEK OR SO BEFORE DALLAS, AN' YOU THREW THE OLD BACK WOUND OUT, AN' YOU HAD TO WEAR A BRACE...
AND YOU WERE TRYING TO DUCK AFTER THE FIRST BULLET HIT YOU BUT THE BRACE HELD YOU UPRIGHT AND THE SECOND ONE BLEW YOUR BRAINS OUT.

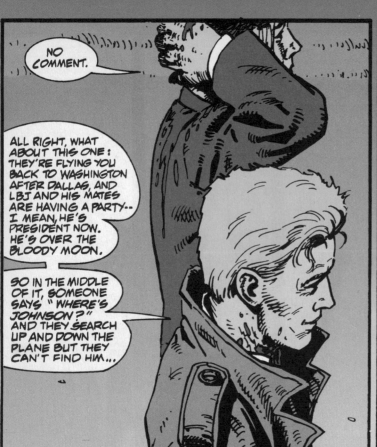

NO COMMENT.

ALL RIGHT, WHAT ABOUT THIS ONE: THEY'RE FLYING YOU BACK TO WASHINGTON AFTER DALLAS, AND LBJ AND HIS MATES ARE HAVING A PARTY-- I MEAN, HE'S PRESIDENT NOW. HE'S OVER THE BLOODY MOON.

SO IN THE MIDDLE OF IT, SOMEONE SAYS "WHERE'S JOHNSON?" AND THEY SEARCH UP AND DOWN THE PLANE BUT THEY CAN'T FIND HIM...

EVENTUALLY SOMEONE LOOKS IN THE BIT THEY'RE KEEPING YOU IN, AND THERE HE IS-- PISSED AS A FART, LAUGHING HIS HEAD OFF AND SCREWING THE HOLE IN THE BACK OF YOUR HEAD.

AND HE'S GOING, "WHO'S LAUGHING NOW, JACK? WHO'S LAUGHING NOW?"

NO COMMENT.

SUIT YOURSELF MATE.

S'ME FAVORITE ONE, THAT IS...

I SEE NO POINT IN CONTINUING THIS LINE OF QUESTIONING. IN FACT I MUST DENOUNCE THE TACTLESSNESS AND CRUELTY YOU ARE DISPLAYING.

JUST TAKING THE PISS. I FIND IT HELPS AT TIMES LIKE THESE...

THAT'S RIGHT, INNIT? I DO TAKE THE PISS. MORE THAN THAT, I CAN BE A RIGHT BASTARD WHEN I WANT TO BE...

THAT'S WHAT THEY ALL SAY: "JOHN CONSTANTINE, HE'S A SHIFTY LITTLE SOD. HE'D SELL YOU DOWN THE RIVER SOON AS LOOK AT YOU," HE WOULD."

FOR CHRIST'S SAKE, THAT'S WHAT KEEPS ME GOING--BUT IN THE THREE WEEKS SINCE I GOT OFF THE STREETS, I'VE BEEN GOING AROUND FULL OF THE JOYS OF SPRING AND HAPPY TO BE ALIVE--

AND SO--WHATEVER THIS IS THAT'S CLOBBERED ME, WHENEVER IT CAME...

I WASN'T FRIGGIN' READY.

I FEEL IT APPROPRIATE TO MAKE A STATEMENT AT THIS TIME.

THE WIDESPREAD RUMOR, SPECULATION AND SLANDER THAT HAS OCCURRED SINCE THE INCIDENT IN DALLAS YOU REFER TO, HAS AT ITS CORE THE ASSUMPTION THAT THIS ADMINISTRATION WAS IN SOME WAY THE LAST HOPE FOR FAIRNESS AND DECENCY IN AMERICA.

IT IS THIS ASSUMPTION-- MORE ACCURATELY, ACCUSATION-- THAT HAS KEPT ME IN A PERSONAL, SPIRITUAL AND SPATIAL LIMBO FOR OVER THIRTY YEARS...

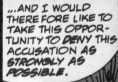

...AND I WOULD THEREFORE LIKE TO TAKE THIS OPPOR- TUNITY TO DENY THIS ACCUSATION AS STRONGLY AS POSSIBLE.

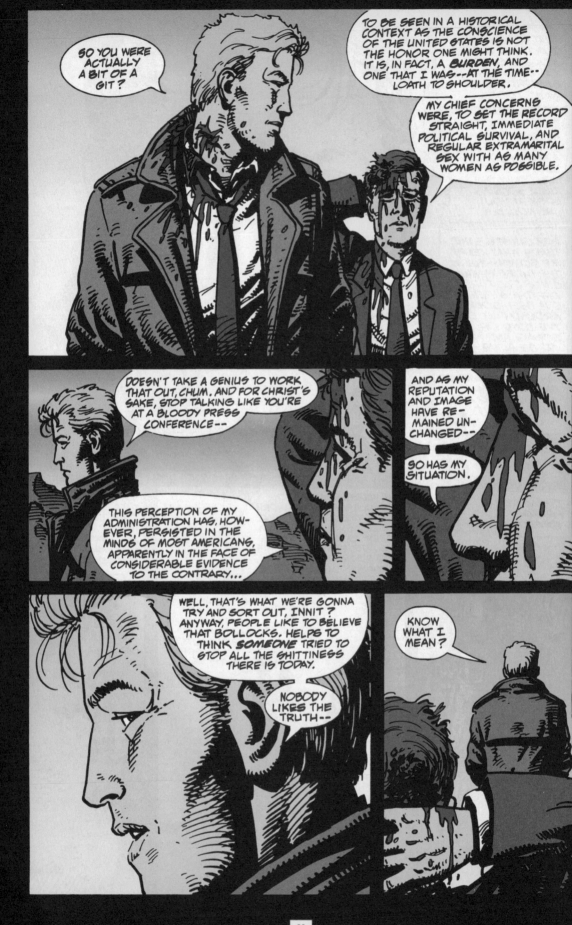

SO YOU WERE ACTUALLY A BIT OF A GIT?

TO BE SEEN IN A HISTORICAL CONTEXT AS THE CONSCIENCE OF THE UNITED STATES IS NOT THE HONOR ONE MIGHT THINK. IT IS, IN FACT, A *BURDEN*, AND ONE THAT I WAS--AT THE TIME-- LOATH TO SHOULDER.

MY CHIEF CONCERNS WERE, TO SET THE RECORD STRAIGHT, IMMEDIATE POLITICAL SURVIVAL, AND REGULAR EXTRAMARITAL SEX WITH AS MANY WOMEN AS POSSIBLE.

DOESN'T TAKE A GENIUS TO WORK THAT OUT, CHUM. AND FOR CHRIST'S SAKE, STOP TALKING LIKE YOU'RE AT A BLOODY PRESS CONFERENCE--

AND AS MY REPUTATION AND IMAGE HAVE RE- MAINED UN- CHANGED--

SO HAS MY SITUATION.

THIS PERCEPTION OF MY ADMINISTRATION HAS, HOW- EVER, PERSISTED IN THE MINDS OF MOST AMERICANS, APPARENTLY IN THE FACE OF CONSIDERABLE EVIDENCE TO THE CONTRARY...

WELL, THAT'S WHAT WE'RE GONNA TRY AND SORT OUT, INNIT? ANYWAY, PEOPLE LIKE TO BELIEVE THAT BOLLOCKS. HELPS TO THINK *SOMEONE* TRIED TO STOP ALL THE SHITTINESS THERE IS TODAY.

NOBODY LIKES THE TRUTH--

KNOW WHAT I MEAN?

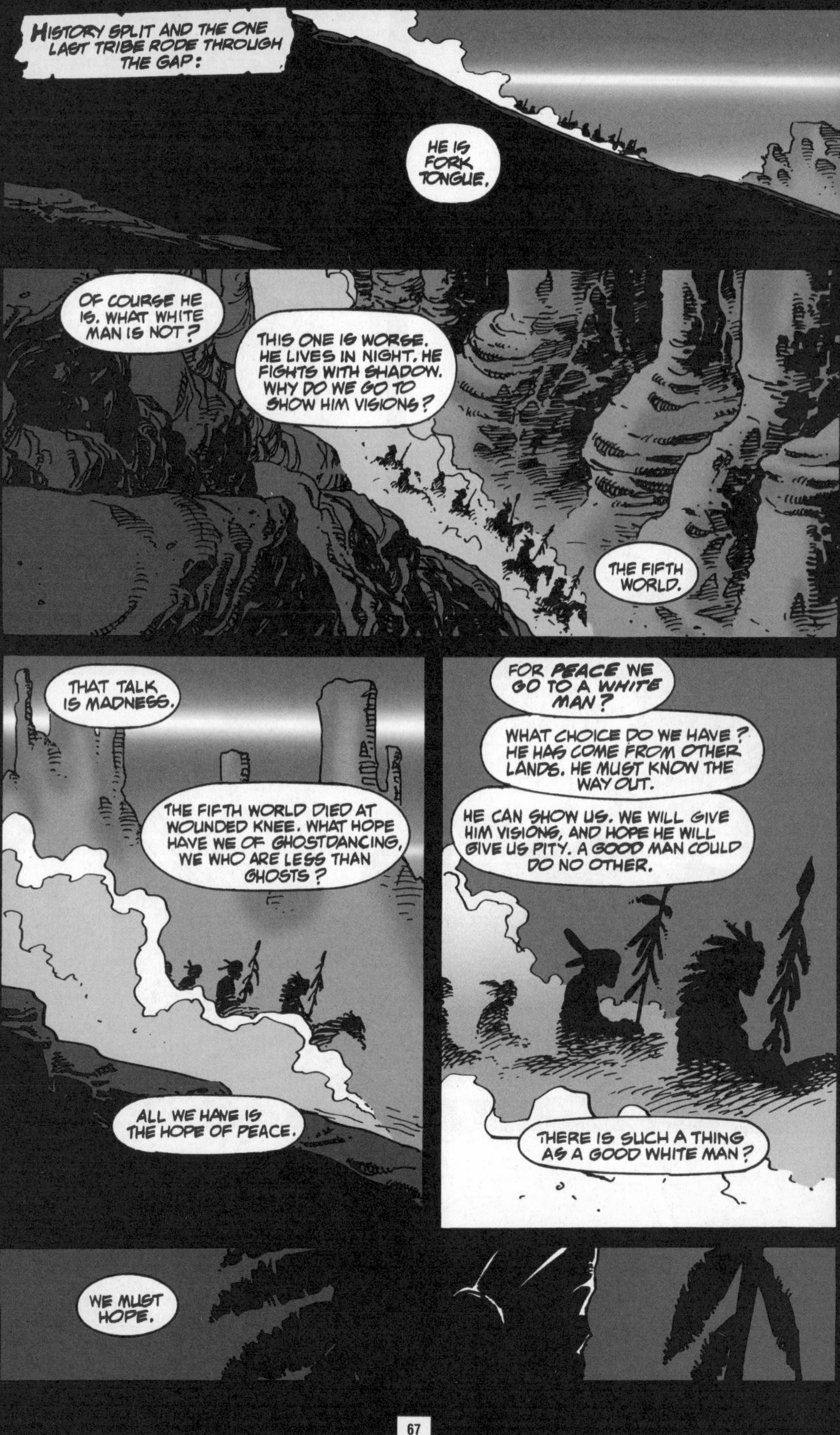
HISTORY SPLIT AND THE ONE LAST TRIBE RODE THROUGH THE GAP:
HE IS FORK TONGUE.
OF COURSE HE IS. WHAT WHITE MAN IS NOT?
THIS ONE IS WORSE. HE LIVES IN NIGHT. HE FIGHTS WITH SHADOW. WHY DO WE GO TO SHOW HIM VISIONS?
THE FIFTH WORLD.
THAT TALK IS MADNESS.
THE FIFTH WORLD DIED AT WOUNDED KNEE. WHAT HOPE HAVE WE OF GHOSTDANCING, WE WHO ARE LESS THAN GHOSTS?
ALL WE HAVE IS THE HOPE OF PEACE.
FOR PEACE WE GO TO A WHITE MAN?
WHAT CHOICE DO WE HAVE? HE HAS COME FROM OTHER LANDS. HE MUST KNOW THE WAY OUT.
HE CAN SHOW US. WE WILL GIVE HIM VISIONS, AND HOPE HE WILL GIVE US PITY. A GOOD MAN COULD DO NO OTHER.
THERE IS SUCH A THING AS A GOOD WHITE MAN?
WE MUST HOPE.

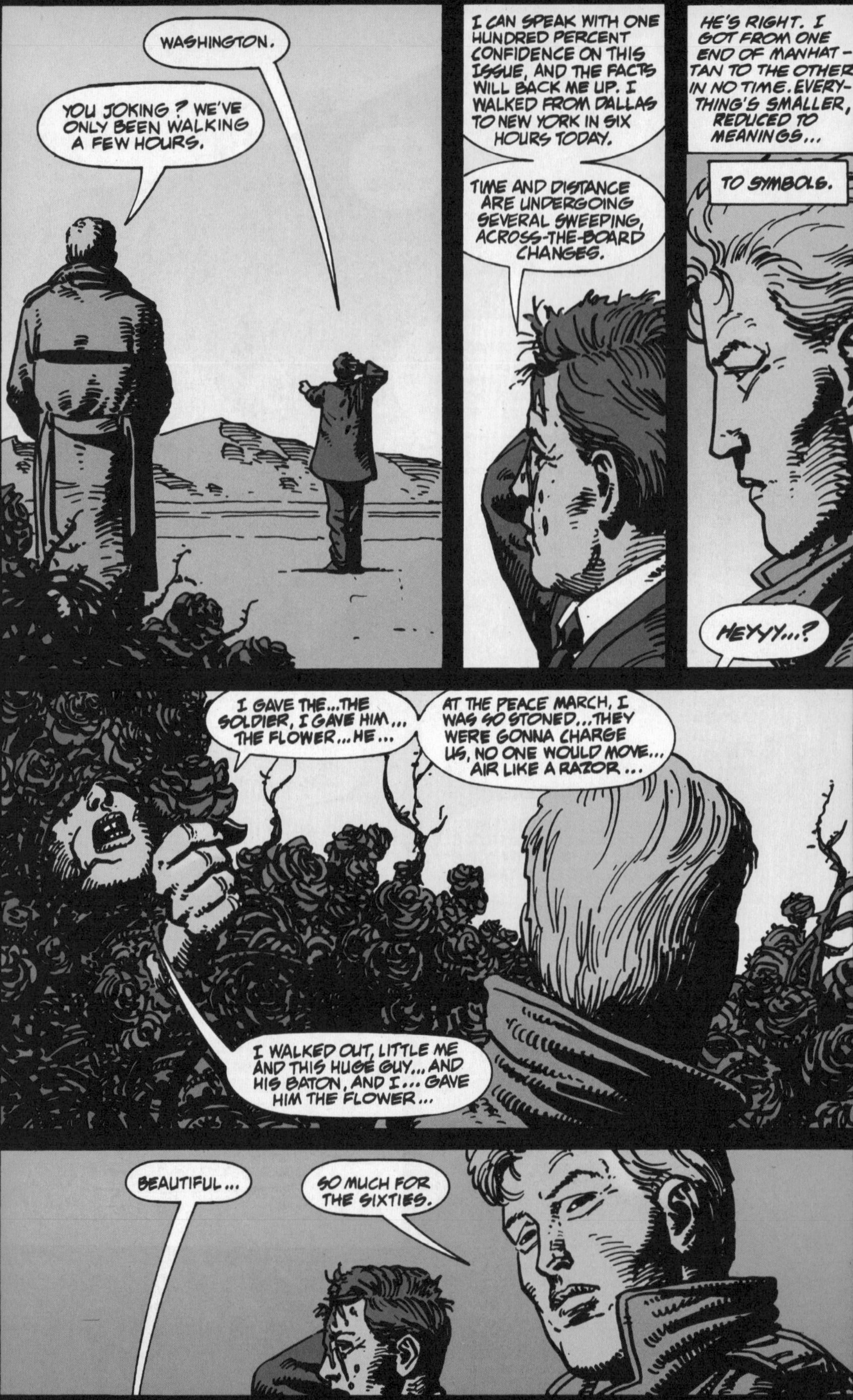

WASHINGTON.
YOU JOKING? WE'VE ONLY BEEN WALKING A FEW HOURS.
I CAN SPEAK WITH ONE HUNDRED PERCENT CONFIDENCE ON THIS ISSUE, AND THE FACTS WILL BACK ME UP. I WALKED FROM DALLAS TO NEW YORK IN SIX HOURS TODAY.
TIME AND DISTANCE ARE UNDERGOING SEVERAL SWEEPING, ACROSS-THE-BOARD CHANGES.
HE'S RIGHT. I GOT FROM ONE END OF MANHAT-TAN TO THE OTHER IN NO TIME. EVERY-THING'S SMALLER, REDUCED TO MEANINGS...
TO SYMBOLS.
HEYYY...?
I GAVE THE...THE SOLDIER, I GAVE HIM... THE FLOWER...HE...
AT THE PEACE MARCH, I WAS SO STONED...THEY WERE GONNA CHARGE US, NO ONE WOULD MOVE... AIR LIKE A RAZOR...
I WALKED OUT, LITTLE ME AND THIS HUGE GUY...AND HIS BATON, AND I... GAVE HIM THE FLOWER...
BEAUTIFUL...
SO MUCH FOR THE SIXTIES.

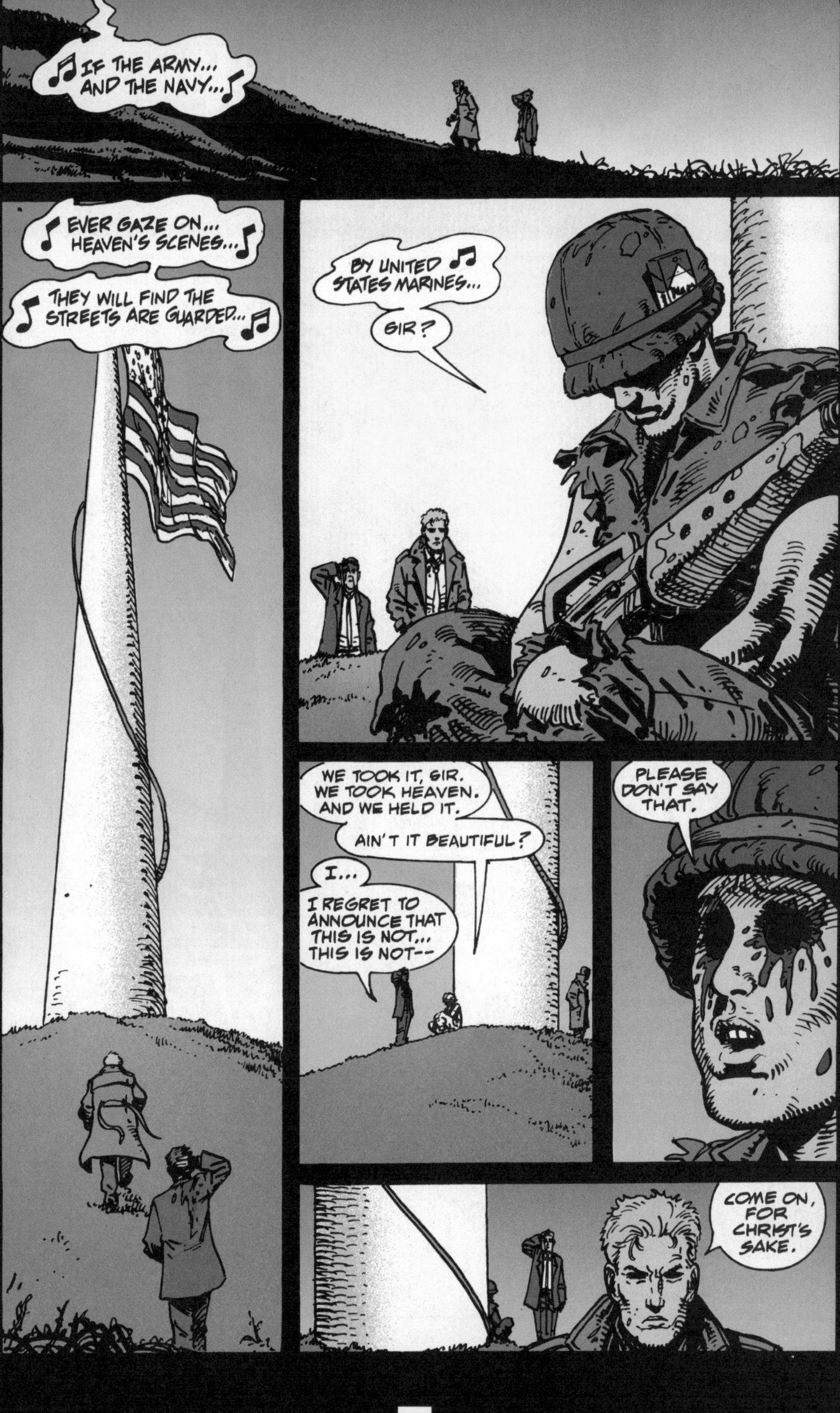
IF THE ARMY... AND THE NAVY...
EVER GAZE ON... HEAVEN'S SCENES...
THEY WILL FIND THE STREETS ARE GUARDED...
BY UNITED STATES MARINES...
SIR?
WE TOOK IT, SIR. WE TOOK HEAVEN. AND WE HELD IT.
AIN'T IT BEAUTIFUL?
I...
I REGRET TO ANNOUNCE THAT THIS IS NOT... THIS IS NOT--
PLEASE DON'T SAY THAT.
COME ON, FOR CHRIST'S SAKE.

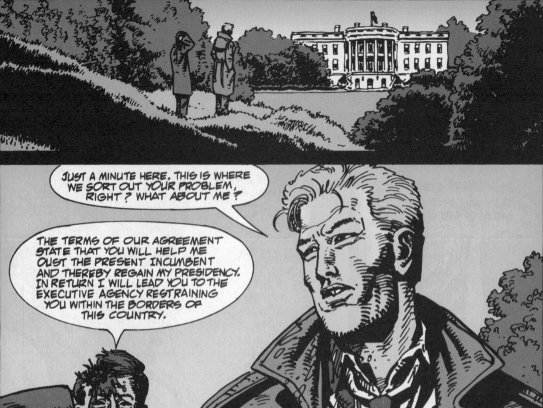

JUST A MINUTE HERE. THIS IS WHERE WE SORT OUT YOUR PROBLEM, RIGHT? WHAT ABOUT ME?

THE TERMS OF OUR AGREEMENT STATE THAT YOU WILL HELP ME OUST THE PRESENT INCUMBENT AND THEREBY REGAIN MY PRESIDENCY. IN RETURN I WILL LEAD YOU TO THE EXECUTIVE AGENCY RESTRAINING YOU WITHIN THE BORDERS OF THIS COUNTRY.

AS ULTIMATE POWER IN THE UNITED STATES RESIDES WITHIN THE WALLS OF THE WHITE HOUSE, I HAVE IN NO WAY VIOLATED ANY OF THE ARTICLES OF OUR AGREEMENT.

SO I'M SUPPOSED TO HELP YOU THROW THIS BLOKE OUT ON HIS ARSE AND THEN ASK HIM FOR HELP? BLOODY STROLL ON!

THAT ASSUMPTION IS FUNDAMENTALLY FLAWED. EXECUTIVE POWER AND THE PRESIDENCY ARE BY NO MEANS ONE AND THE SAME.

IT WAS THIS DILEMMA, IN FACT, WHICH LED TO THE INCIDENT IN DALLAS MENTIONED EARLIER IN OUR ONGOING DIALOGUE.

AND I HAVE, INCIDENTALLY, LOCATED OUR MEANS OF GAINING ACCESS.

SOUND. YOU GO FIRST.

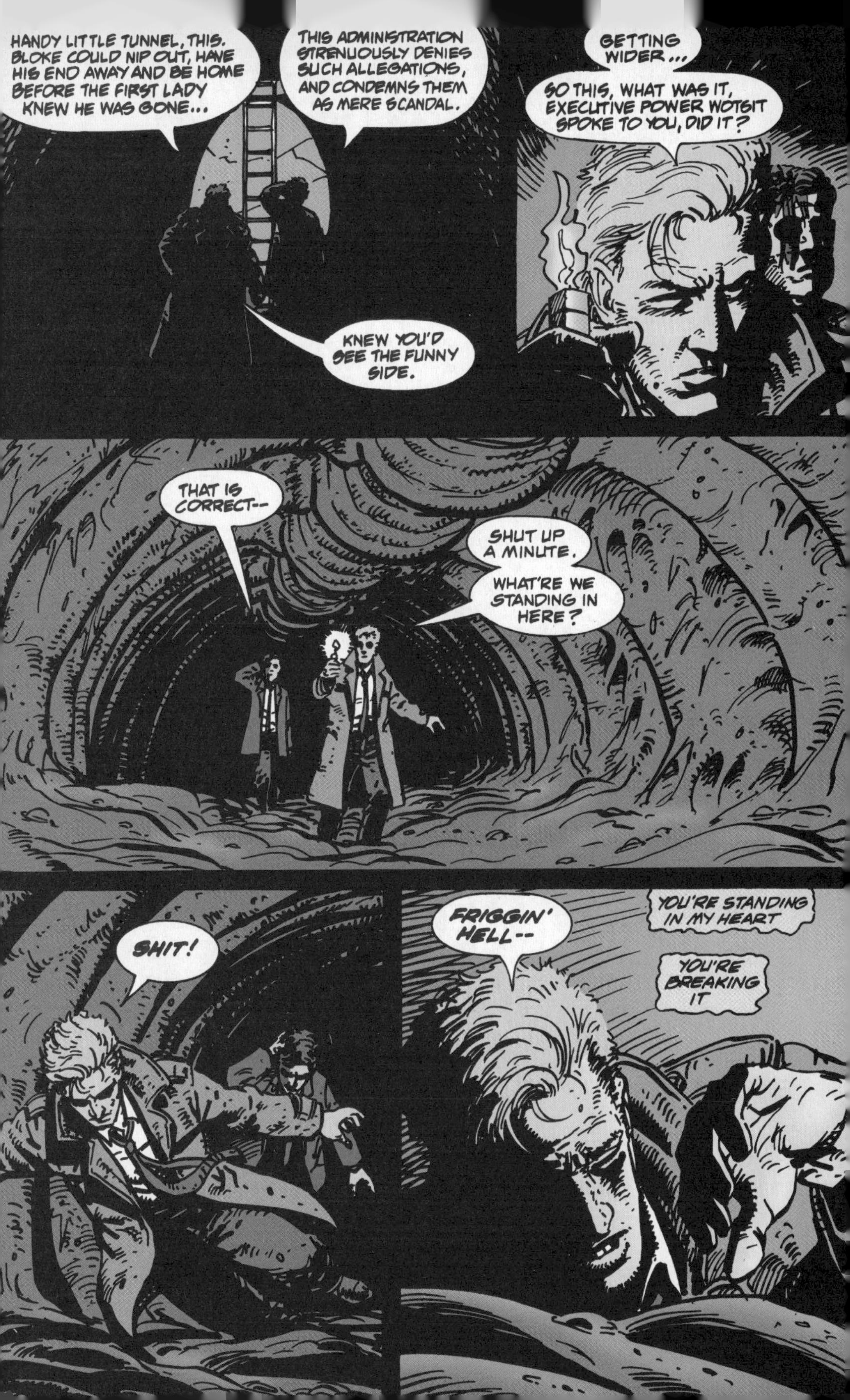
HANDY LITTLE TUNNEL, THIS. BLOKE COULD NIP OUT, HAVE HIS END AWAY AND BE HOME BEFORE THE FIRST LADY KNEW HE WAS GONE...
THIS ADMINISTRATION STRENUOUSLY DENIES SUCH ALLEGATIONS, AND CONDEMNS THEM AS MERE SCANDAL.
KNEW YOU'D SEE THE FUNNY SIDE.
GETTING WIDER...
SO THIS, WHAT WAS IT, EXECUTIVE POWER WOTSIT SPOKE TO YOU, DID IT?
THAT IS CORRECT--
SHUT UP A MINUTE.
WHAT'RE WE STANDING IN HERE?
SHIT!
FRIGGIN' HELL--
YOU'RE STANDING IN MY HEART
YOU'RE BREAKING IT

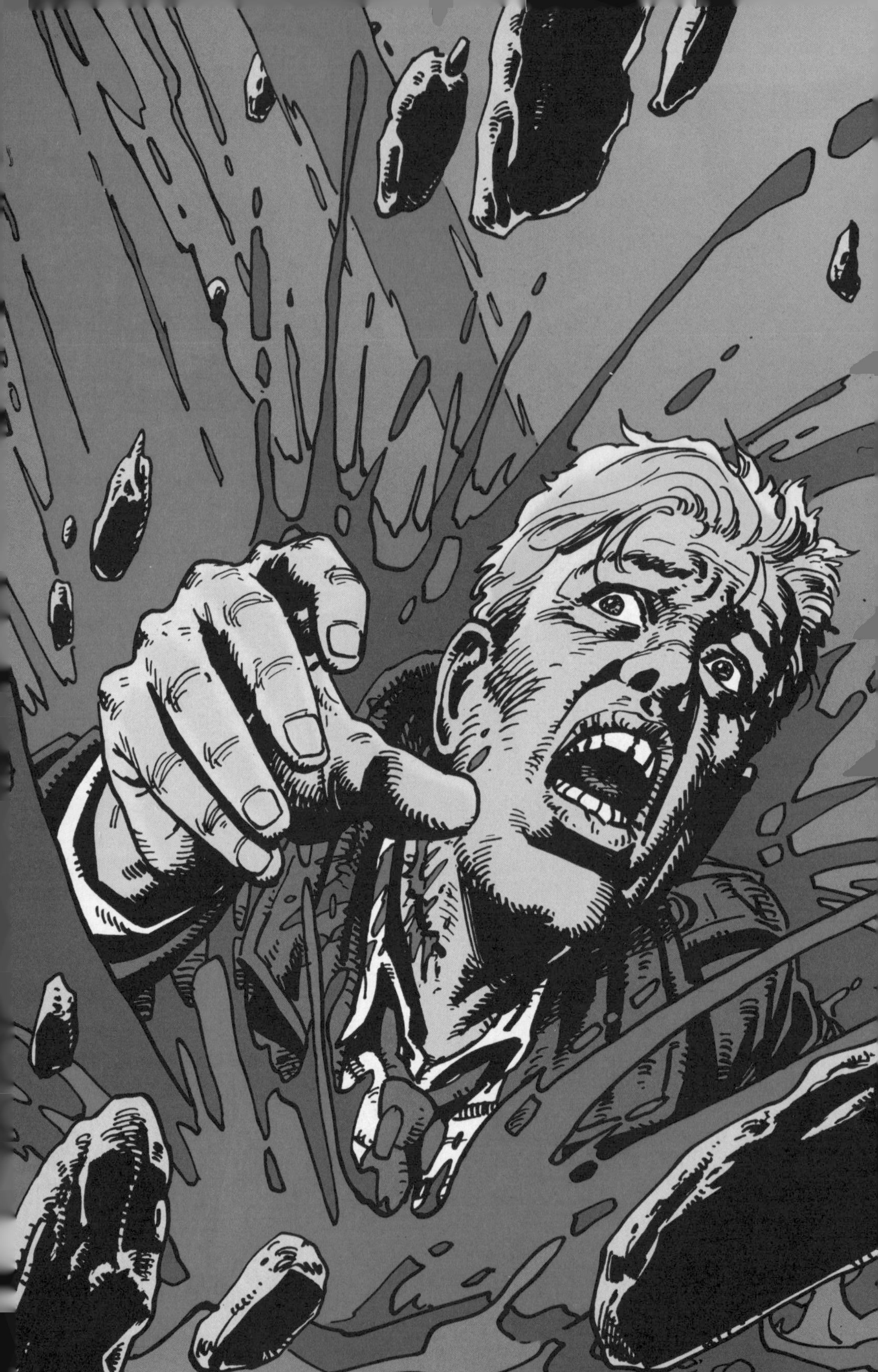

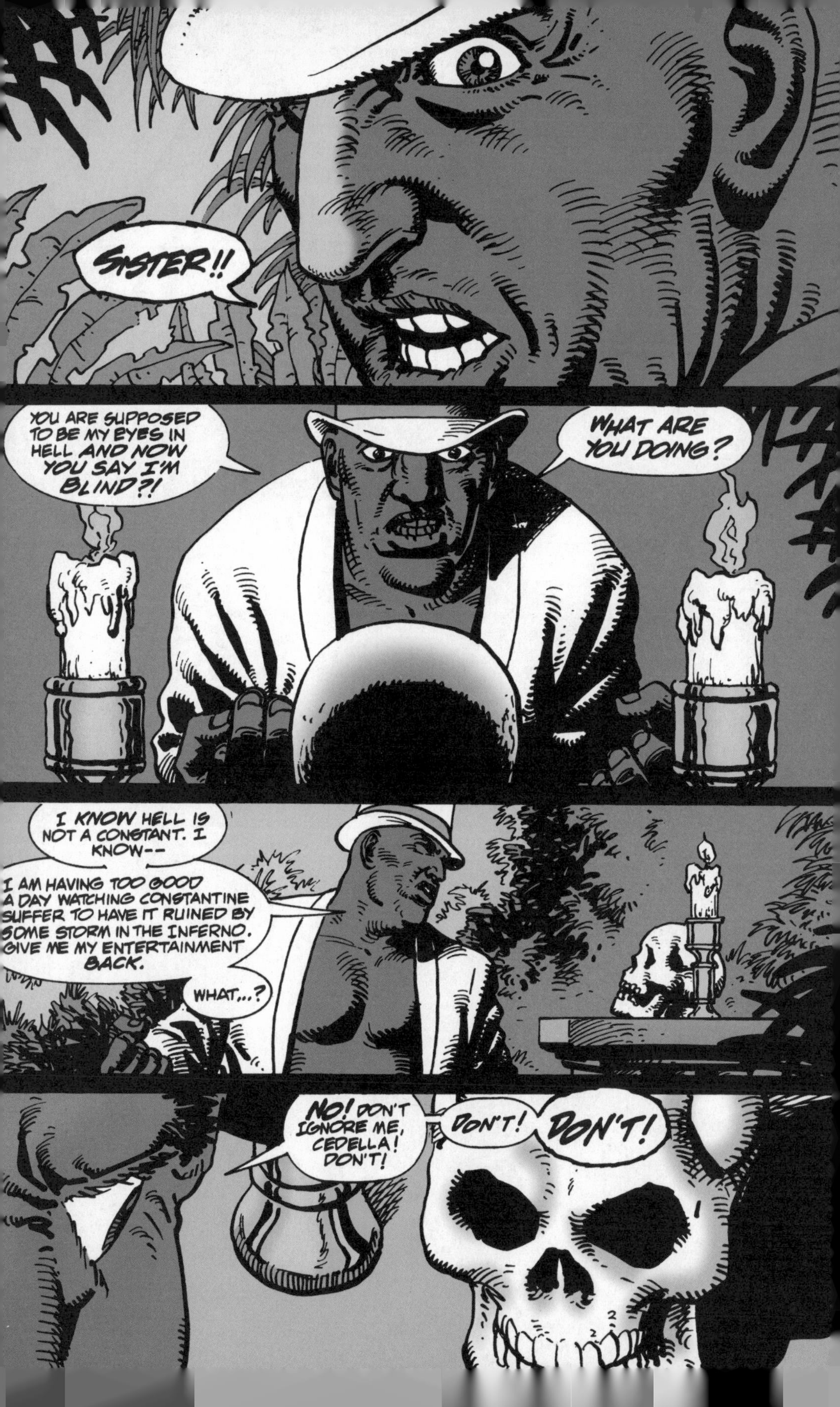
SISTER!!
YOU ARE SUPPOSED TO BE MY EYES IN HELL AND NOW YOU SAY I'M BLIND?!
WHAT ARE YOU DOING?
I KNOW HELL IS NOT A CONSTANT. I KNOW--
I AM HAVING TOO GOOD A DAY WATCHING CONSTANTINE SUFFER TO HAVE IT RUINED BY SOME STORM IN THE INFERNO. GIVE ME MY ENTERTAINMENT BACK.
WHAT...?
NO! DON'T IGNORE ME, CEDELLA! DON'T!
DON'T!
DON'T!

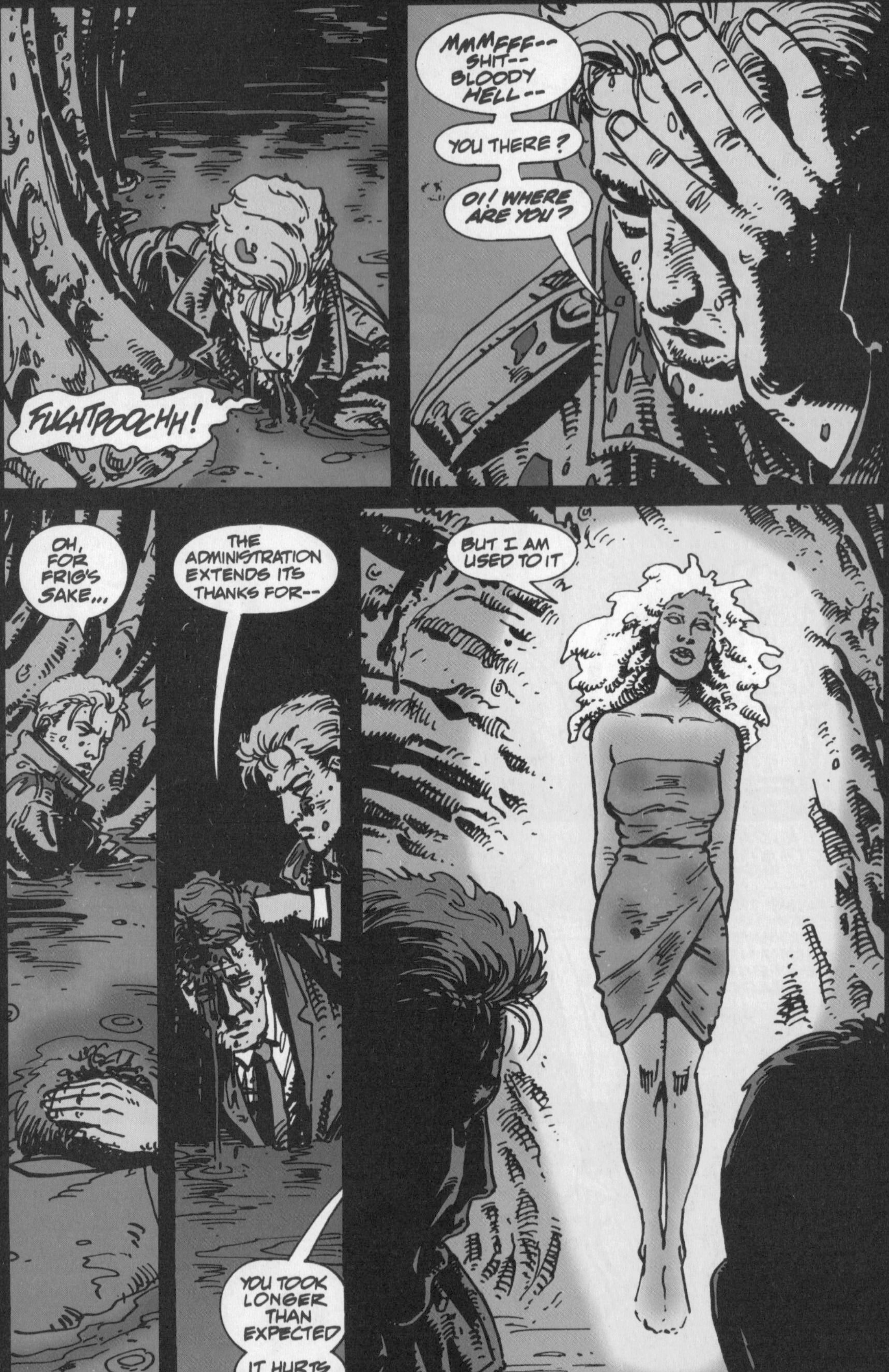
FLGHTPOOCHH!
MMMFFF-- SHIT-- BLOODY HELL--
YOU THERE?
OI! WHERE ARE YOU?
OH, FOR FRIG'S SAKE...
THE ADMINISTRATION EXTENDS ITS THANKS FOR--
YOU TOOK LONGER THAN EXPECTED
IT HURTS TO WAIT
BUT I AM USED TO IT

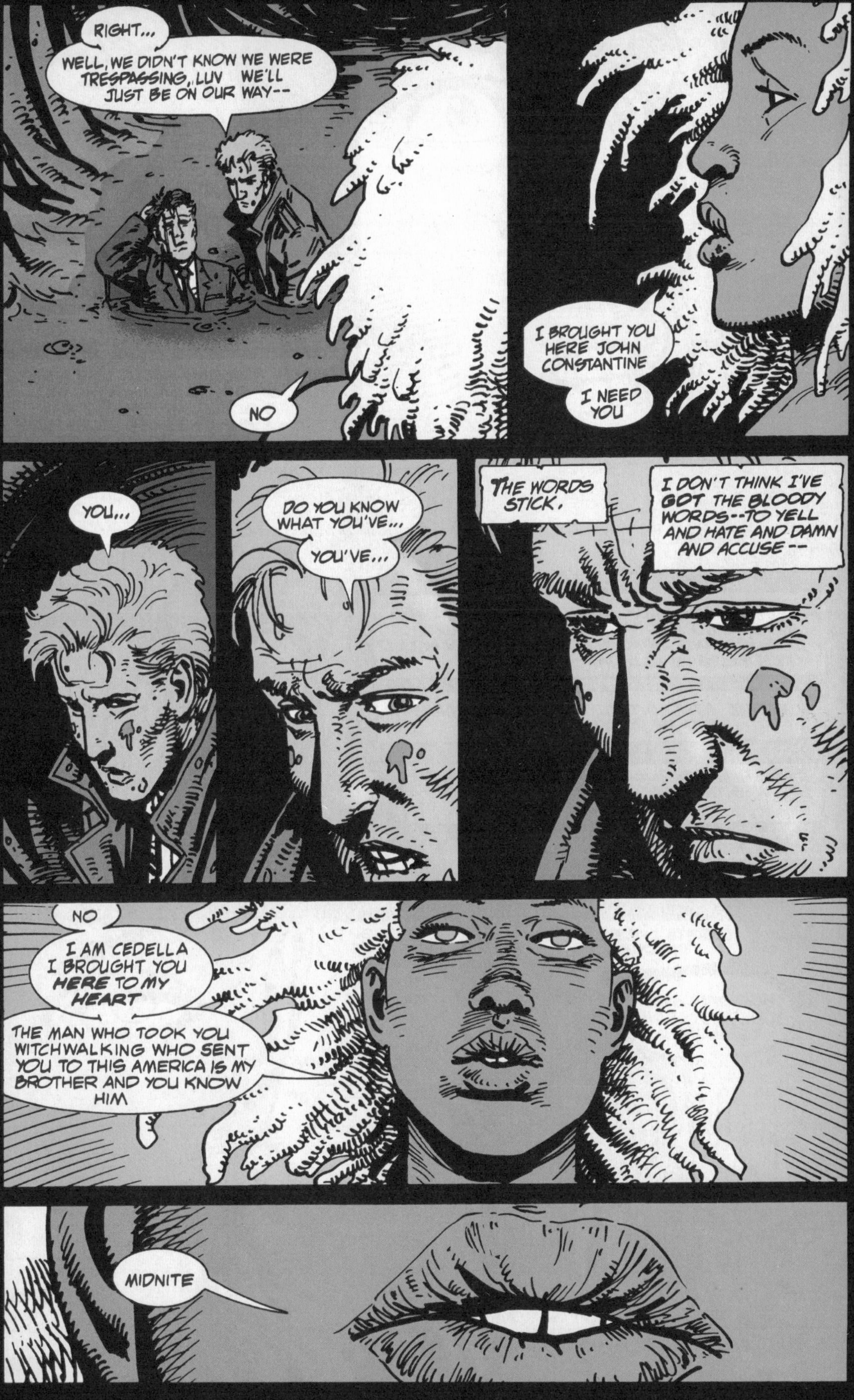
RIGHT...
WELL, WE DIDN'T KNOW WE WERE TRESPASSING, LUV WE'LL JUST BE ON OUR WAY--
NO
I BROUGHT YOU HERE JOHN CONSTANTINE
I NEED YOU
YOU...
DO YOU KNOW WHAT YOU'VE...
YOU'VE...
THE WORDS STICK.
I DON'T THINK I'VE GOT THE BLOODY WORDS--TO YELL AND HATE AND DAMN AND ACCUSE--
NO
I AM CEDELLA I BROUGHT YOU HERE TO MY HEART
THE MAN WHO TOOK YOU WITCHWALKING WHO SENT YOU TO THIS AMERICA IS MY BROTHER AND YOU KNOW HIM
MIDNITE

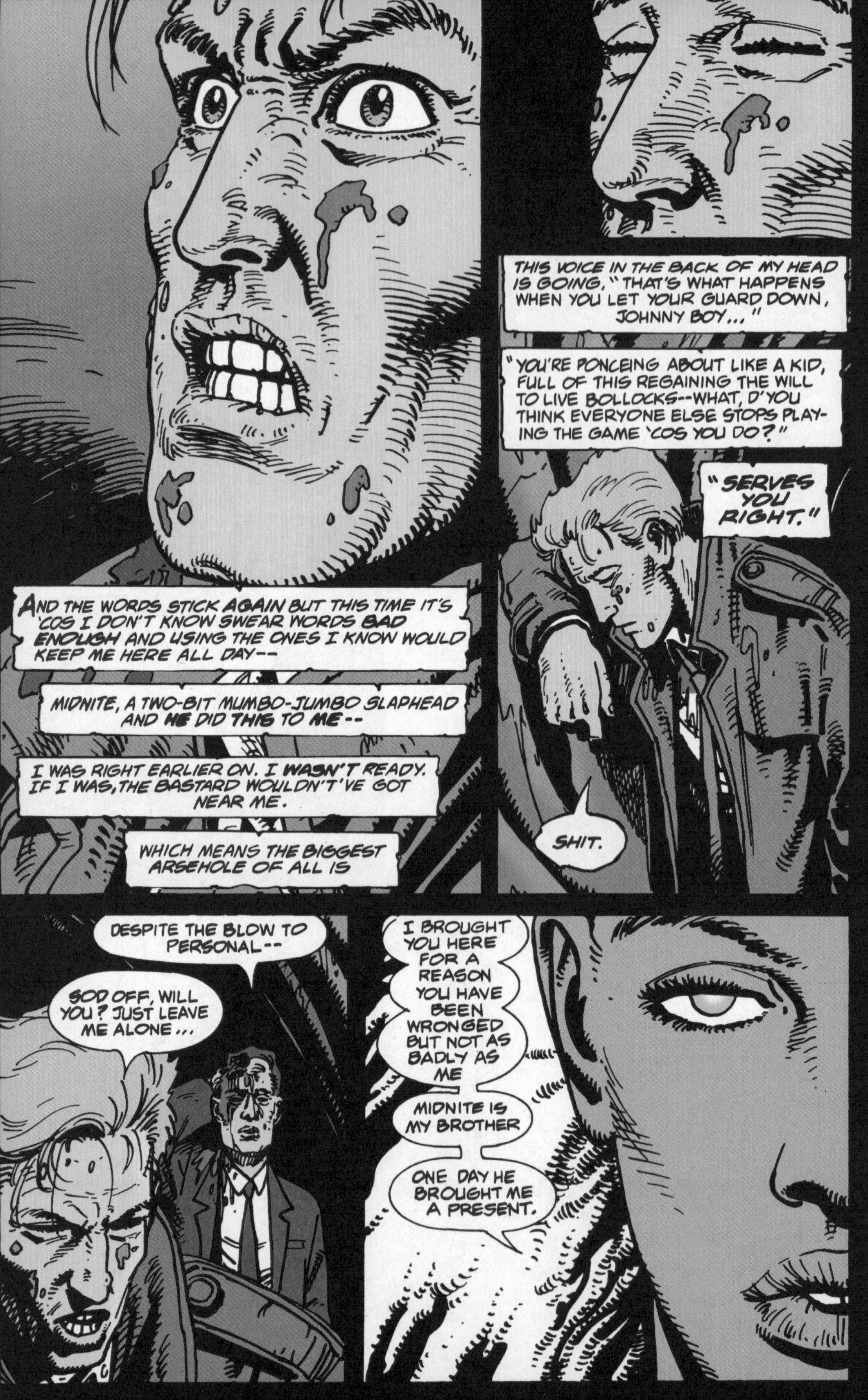
THIS VOICE IN THE BACK OF MY HEAD IS GOING, "THAT'S WHAT HAPPENS WHEN YOU LET YOUR GUARD DOWN, JOHNNY BOY..."
"YOU'RE PONCEING ABOUT LIKE A KID, FULL OF THIS REGAINING THE WILL TO LIVE BOLLOCKS--WHAT, D'YOU THINK EVERYONE ELSE STOPS PLAYING THE GAME 'COS YOU DO?"
"SERVES YOU RIGHT."
SHIT.
AND THE WORDS STICK AGAIN BUT THIS TIME IT'S 'COS I DON'T KNOW SWEAR WORDS BAD ENOUGH AND USING THE ONES I KNOW WOULD KEEP ME HERE ALL DAY--
MIDNITE, A TWO-BIT MUMBO-JUMBO SLAPHEAD AND HE DID THIS TO ME--
I WAS RIGHT EARLIER ON. I WASN'T READY. IF I WAS, THE BASTARD WOULDN'T'VE GOT NEAR ME.
WHICH MEANS THE BIGGEST ARSEHOLE OF ALL IS
DESPITE THE BLOW TO PERSONAL--
SOD OFF, WILL YOU? JUST LEAVE ME ALONE...
I BROUGHT YOU HERE FOR A REASON
YOU HAVE BEEN WRONGED
BUT NOT AS BADLY AS ME
MIDNITE IS MY BROTHER
ONE DAY HE BROUGHT ME A PRESENT.

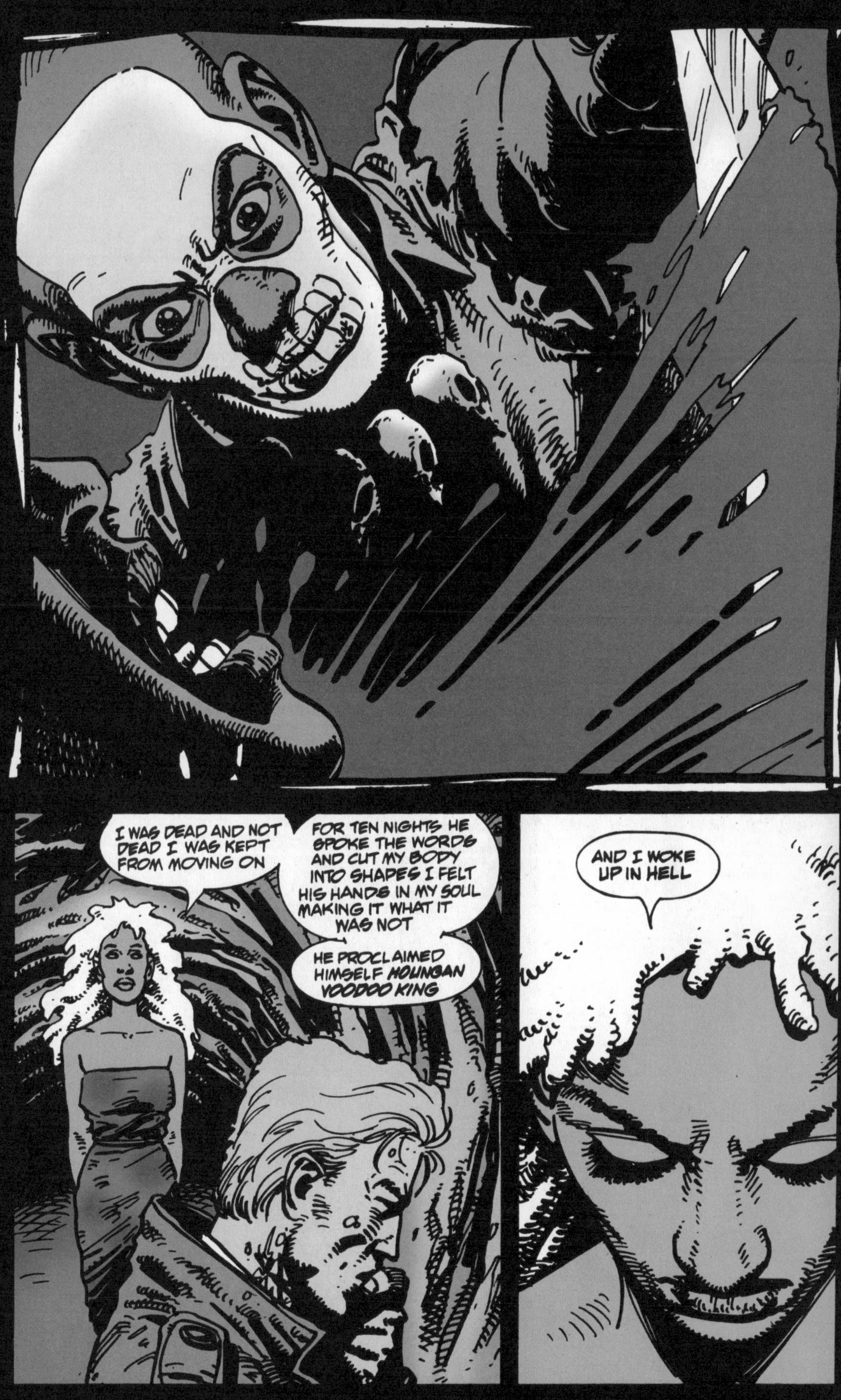
I WAS DEAD AND NOT DEAD I WAS KEPT FROM MOVING ON
FOR TEN NIGHTS HE SPOKE THE WORDS AND CUT MY BODY INTO SHAPES I FELT HIS HANDS IN MY SOUL MAKING IT WHAT IT WAS NOT
HE PROCLAIMED HIMSELF HOUNGAN VOODOO KING
AND I WOKE UP IN HELL

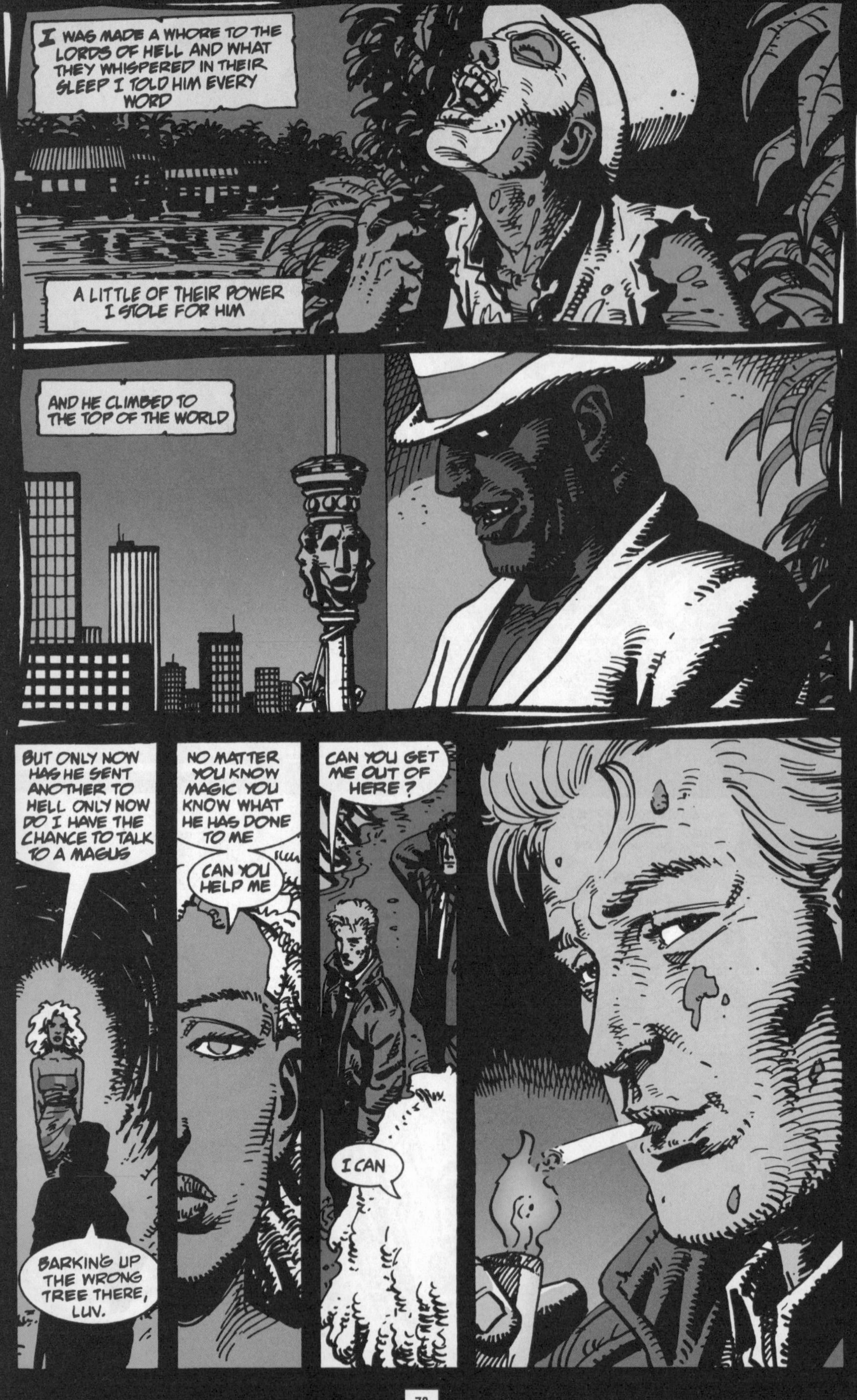

I WAS MADE A WHORE TO THE LORDS OF HELL AND WHAT THEY WHISPERED IN THEIR SLEEP I TOLD HIM EVERY WORD
A LITTLE OF THEIR POWER I STOLE FOR HIM
AND HE CLIMBED TO THE TOP OF THE WORLD
BUT ONLY NOW HAS HE SENT ANOTHER TO HELL ONLY NOW DO I HAVE THE CHANCE TO TALK TO A MAGUS
BARKING UP THE WRONG TREE THERE, LUV.
NO MATTER YOU KNOW MAGIC YOU KNOW WHAT HE HAS DONE TO ME
CAN YOU HELP ME
CAN YOU GET ME OUT OF HERE?
I CAN

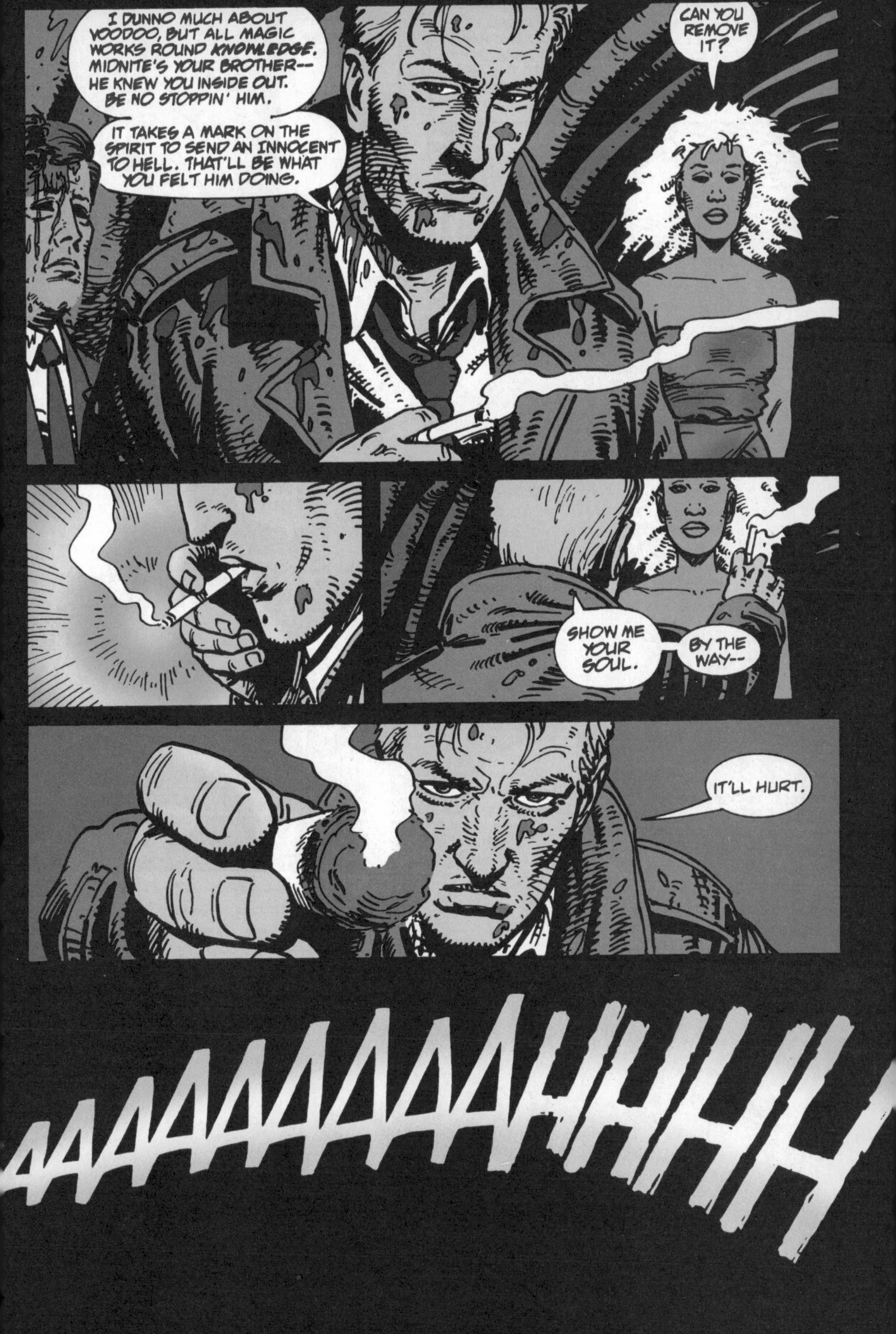
I DUNNO MUCH ABOUT VOODOO, BUT ALL MAGIC WORKS ROUND KNOWLEDGE. MIDNITE'S YOUR BROTHER-- HE KNEW YOU INSIDE OUT. BE NO STOPPIN' HIM.
IT TAKES A MARK ON THE SPIRIT TO SEND AN INNOCENT TO HELL. THAT'LL BE WHAT YOU FELT HIM DOING.
CAN YOU REMOVE IT?
SHOW ME YOUR SOUL.
BY THE WAY--
IT'LL HURT.
AAAAAAAAAHHHHH

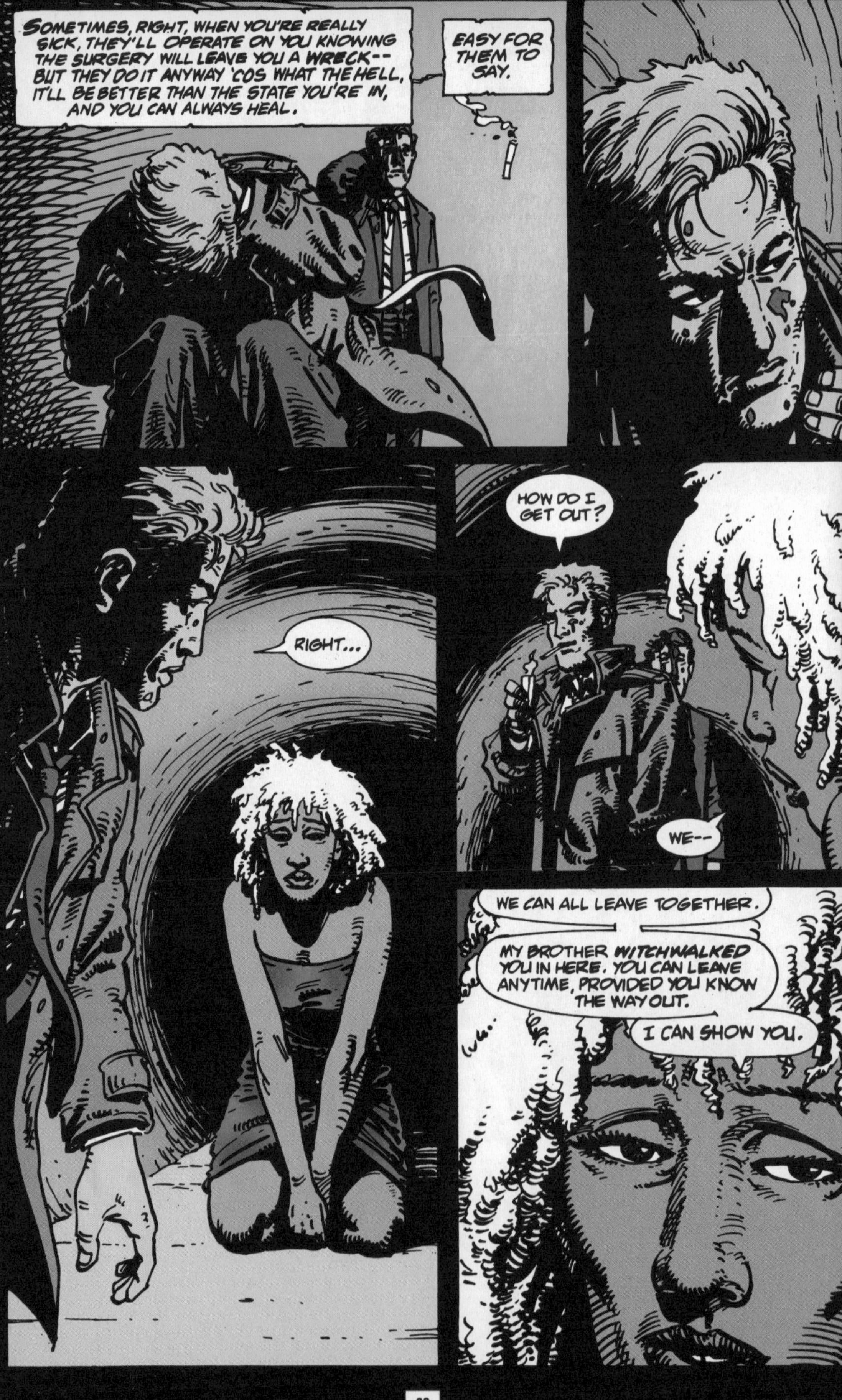

SOMETIMES, RIGHT, WHEN YOU'RE REALLY SICK, THEY'LL OPERATE ON YOU KNOWING THE SURGERY WILL LEAVE YOU A WRECK-- BUT THEY DO IT ANYWAY 'COS WHAT THE HELL, IT'LL BE BETTER THAN THE STATE YOU'RE IN, AND YOU CAN ALWAYS HEAL.
EASY FOR THEM TO SAY.
RIGHT...
HOW DO I GET OUT?
WE--
WE CAN ALL LEAVE TOGETHER.
MY BROTHER WITCHWALKED YOU IN HERE. YOU CAN LEAVE ANYTIME, PROVIDED YOU KNOW THE WAY OUT.
I CAN SHOW YOU.

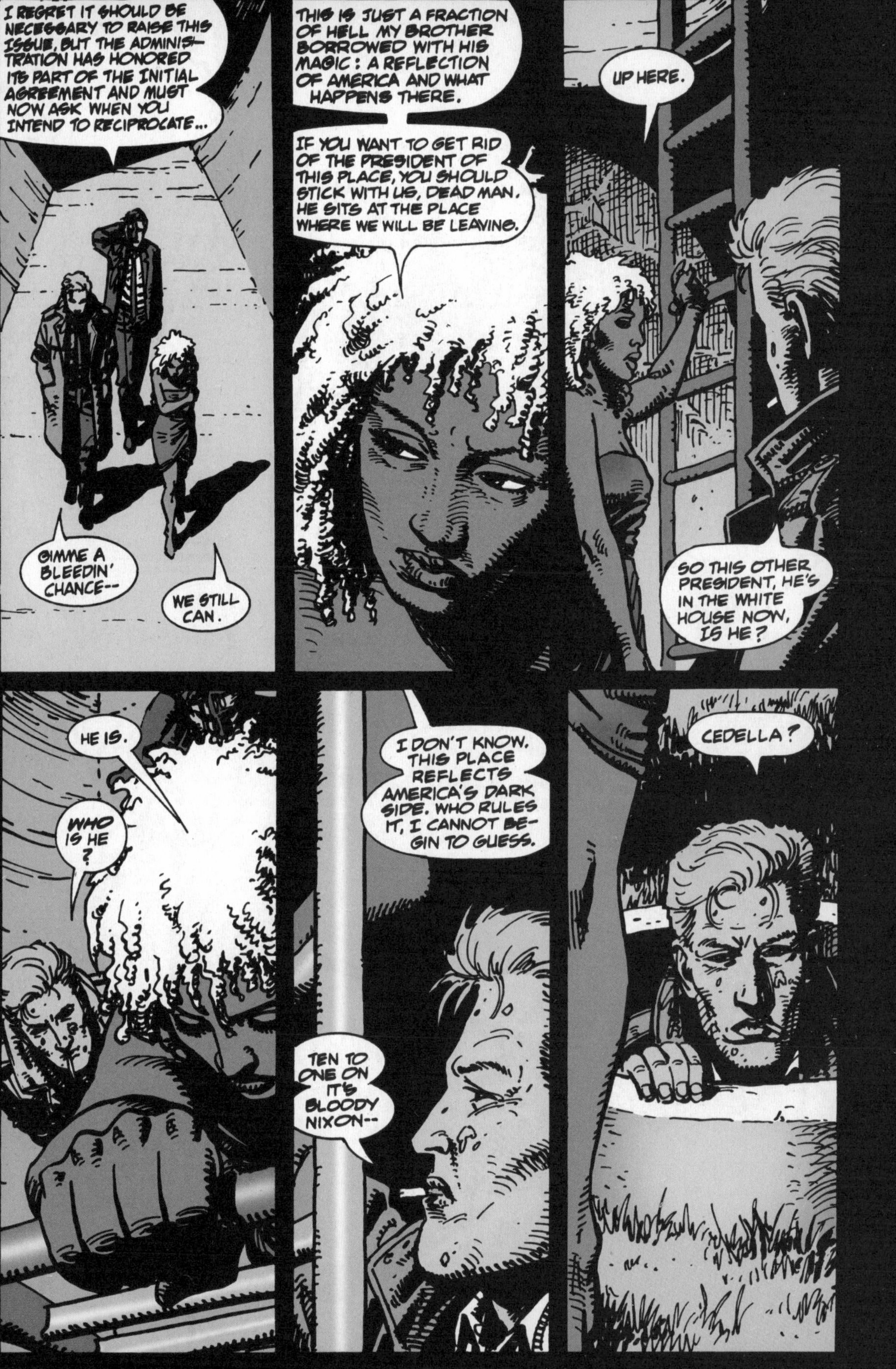
I REGRET IT SHOULD BE NECESSARY TO RAISE THIS ISSUE, BUT THE ADMINISTRATION HAS HONORED ITS PART OF THE INITIAL AGREEMENT AND MUST NOW ASK WHEN YOU INTEND TO RECIPROCATE...
GIMME A BLEEDIN' CHANCE--
WE STILL CAN.
THIS IS JUST A FRACTION OF HELL MY BROTHER BORROWED WITH HIS MAGIC: A REFLECTION OF AMERICA AND WHAT HAPPENS THERE.
IF YOU WANT TO GET RID OF THE PRESIDENT OF THIS PLACE, YOU SHOULD STICK WITH US, DEAD MAN. HE SITS AT THE PLACE WHERE WE WILL BE LEAVING.
UP HERE.
SO THIS OTHER PRESIDENT, HE'S IN THE WHITE HOUSE NOW, IS HE?
HE IS.
WHO IS HE?
I DON'T KNOW. THIS PLACE REFLECTS AMERICA'S DARK SIDE. WHO RULES IT, I CANNOT BEGIN TO GUESS.
TEN TO ONE ON IT'S BLOODY NIXON--
CEDELLA?

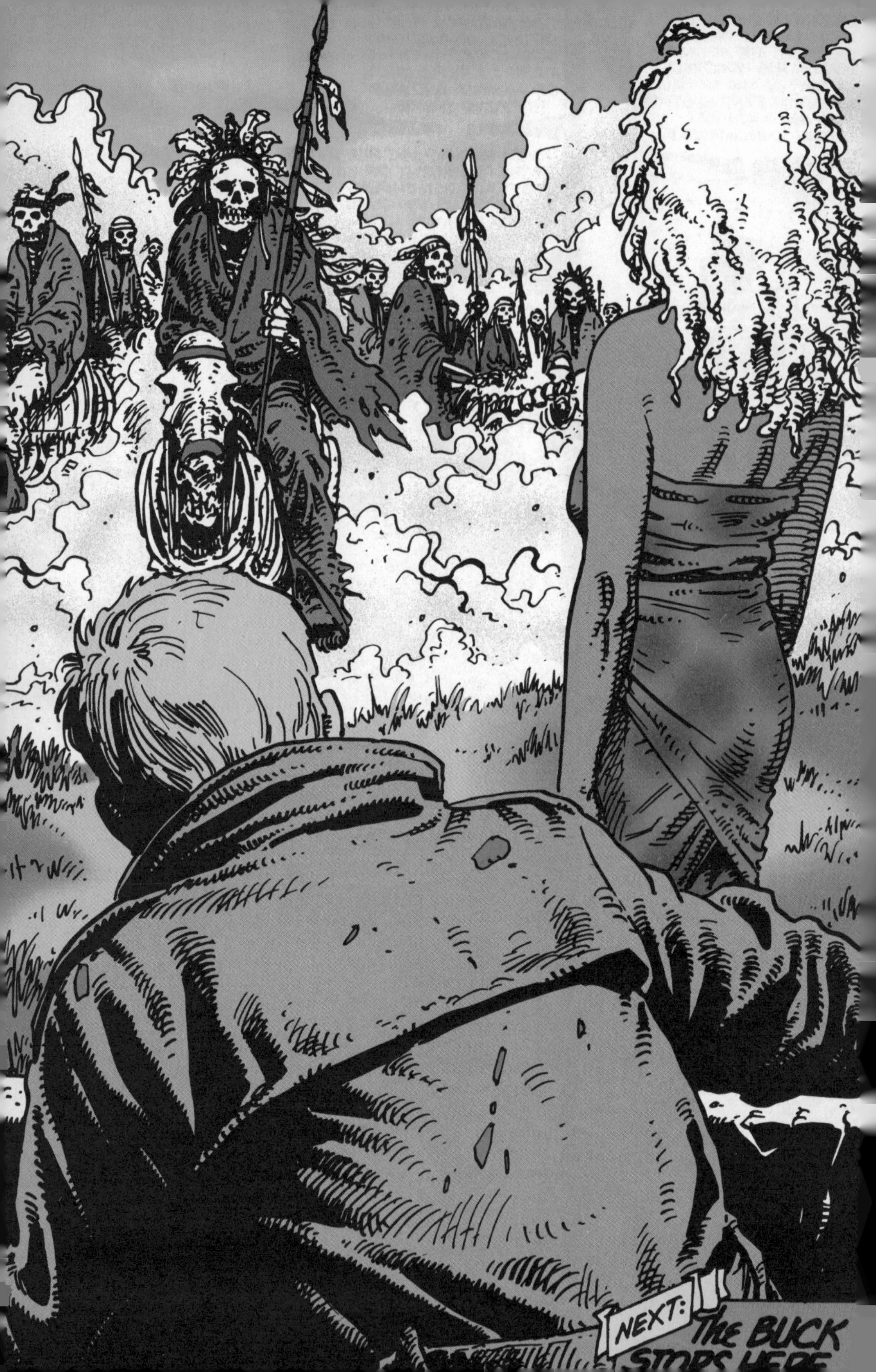
NEXT:
The BUCK STOPS HERE

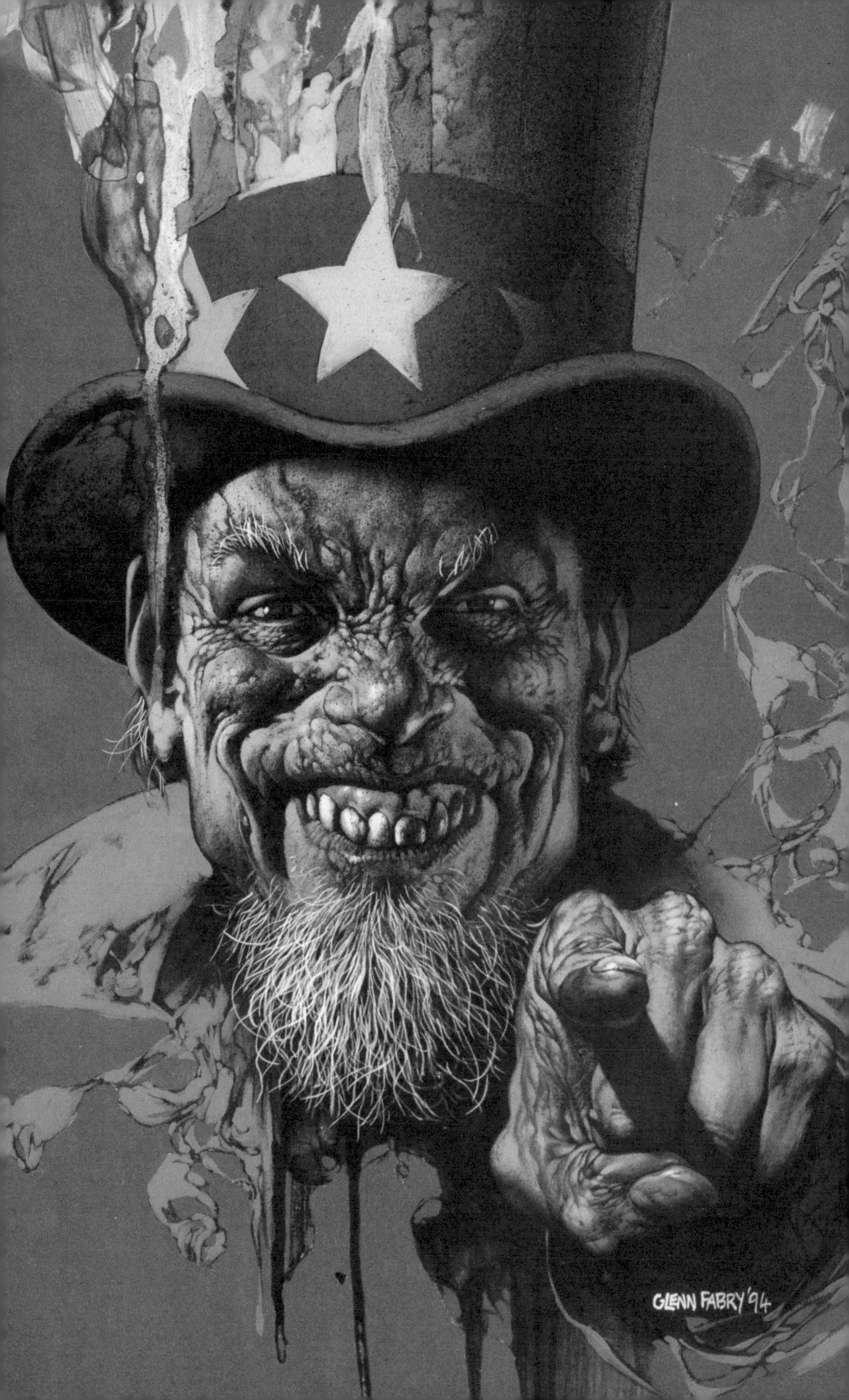
GLENN FABRY '94

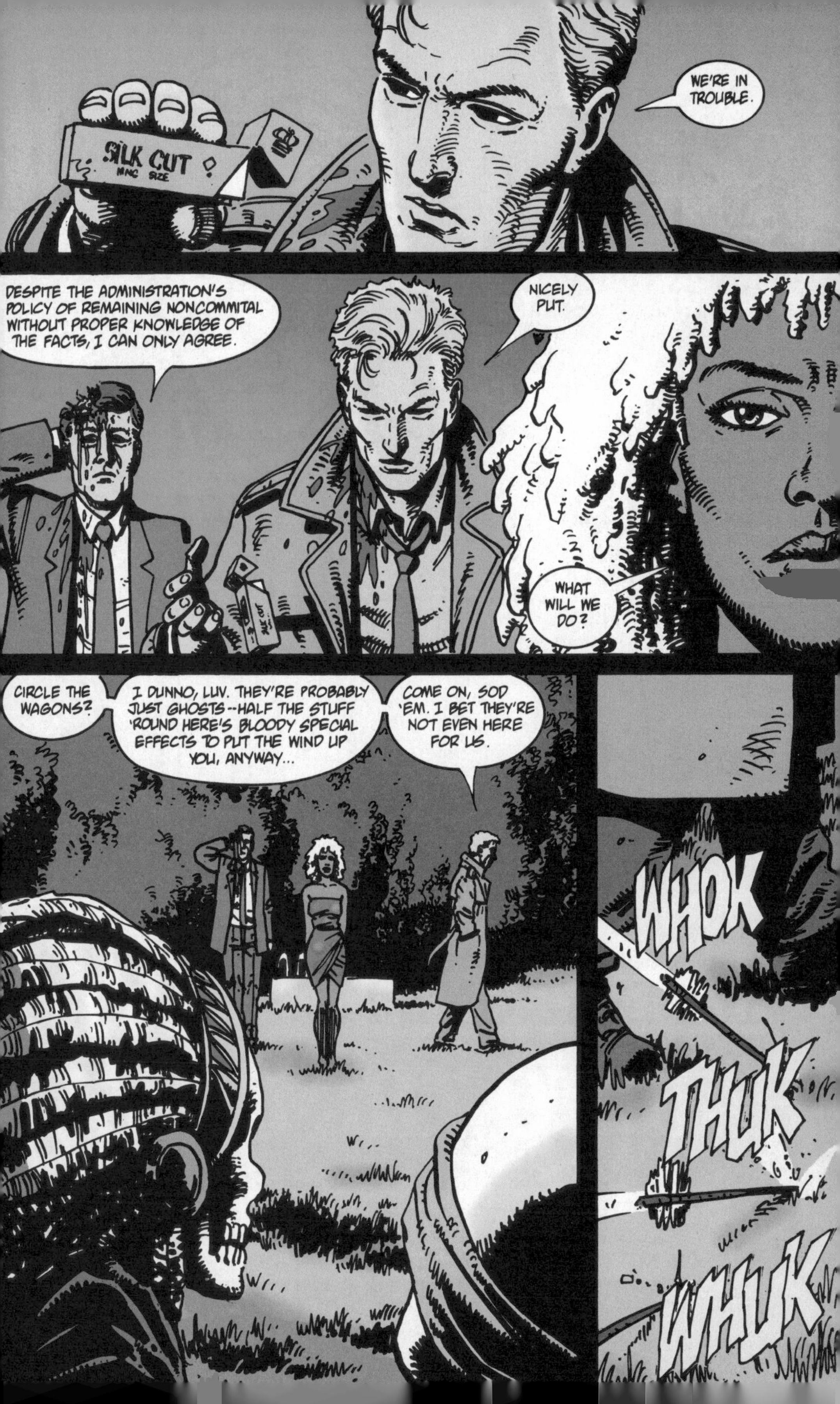
SILK CUT
KING SIZE
WE'RE IN TROUBLE.
DESPITE THE ADMINISTRATION'S POLICY OF REMAINING NONCOMMITAL WITHOUT PROPER KNOWLEDGE OF THE FACTS, I CAN ONLY AGREE.
NICELY PUT.
WHAT WILL WE DO?
CIRCLE THE WAGONS?
I DUNNO, LUV. THEY'RE PROBABLY JUST GHOSTS--HALF THE STUFF 'ROUND HERE'S BLOODY SPECIAL EFFECTS TO PUT THE WIND UP YOU, ANYWAY...
COME ON, SOD 'EM. I BET THEY'RE NOT EVEN HERE FOR US.
WHOK
THUK
WHUK

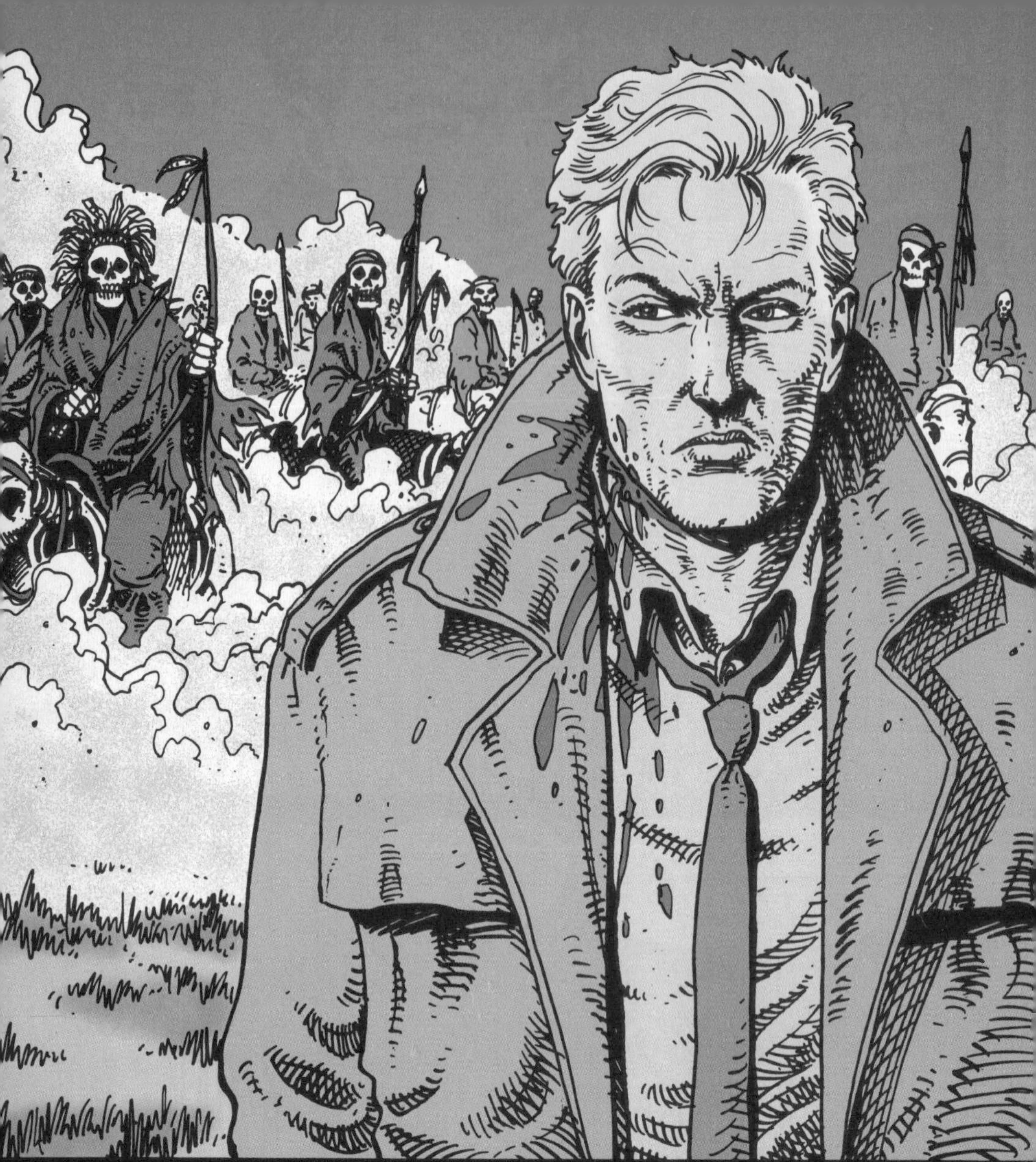

DAMNATION'S FLAME PART FOUR

HAIL TO THE CHIEF

GARTH ENNIS • writer STEVE DILLON • artist
TOM ZIUKO • colors CLEM ROBINS • letters
JULIE ROTTENBERG • asst. editor STUART MOORE • editor

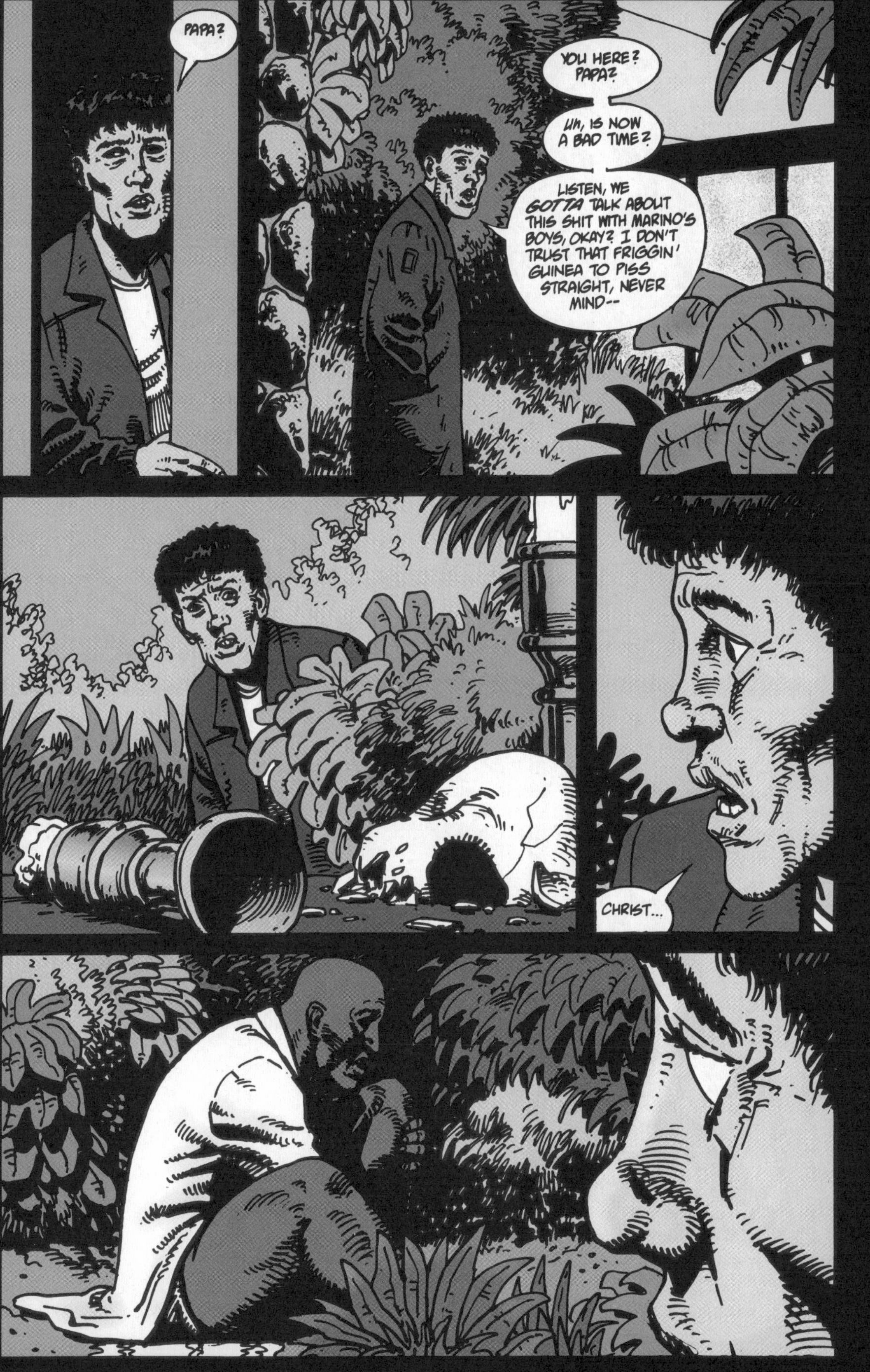
PAPA?
YOU HERE? PAPA?
UH, IS NOW A BAD TIME?
LISTEN, WE GOTTA TALK ABOUT THIS SHIT WITH MARINO'S BOYS, OKAY? I DON'T TRUST THAT FRIGGIN' GUINEA TO PISS STRAIGHT, NEVER MIND--
CHRIST...

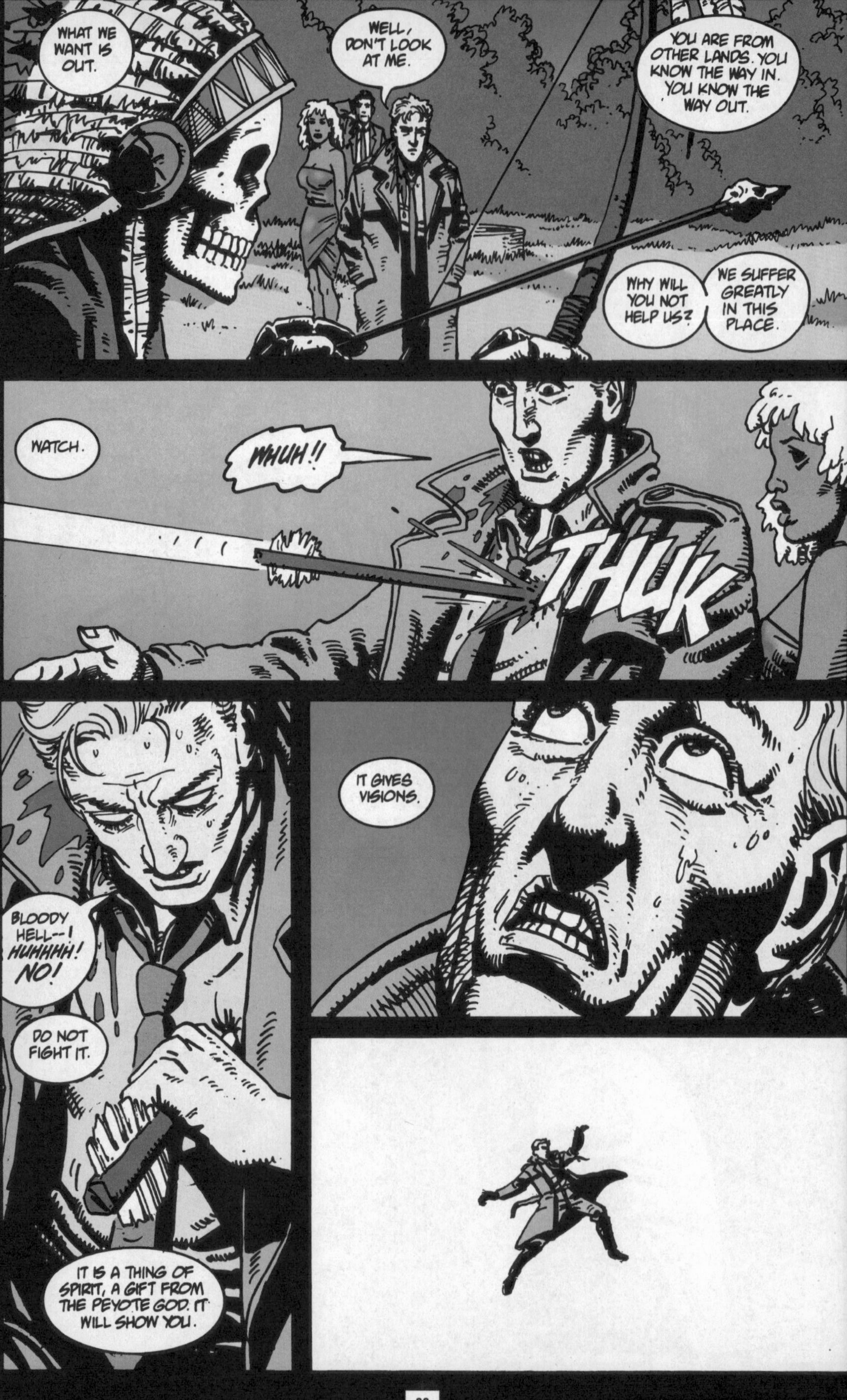
WHAT WE WANT IS OUT.
WELL, DON'T LOOK AT ME.
YOU ARE FROM OTHER LANDS. YOU KNOW THE WAY IN. YOU KNOW THE WAY OUT.
WHY WILL YOU NOT HELP US?
WE SUFFER GREATLY IN THIS PLACE.
WATCH.
WHUH!!
THUK
IT GIVES VISIONS.
BLOODY HELL--! HUHHHH! NO!
DO NOT FIGHT IT.
IT IS A THING OF SPIRIT, A GIFT FROM THE PEYOTE GOD. IT WILL SHOW YOU.

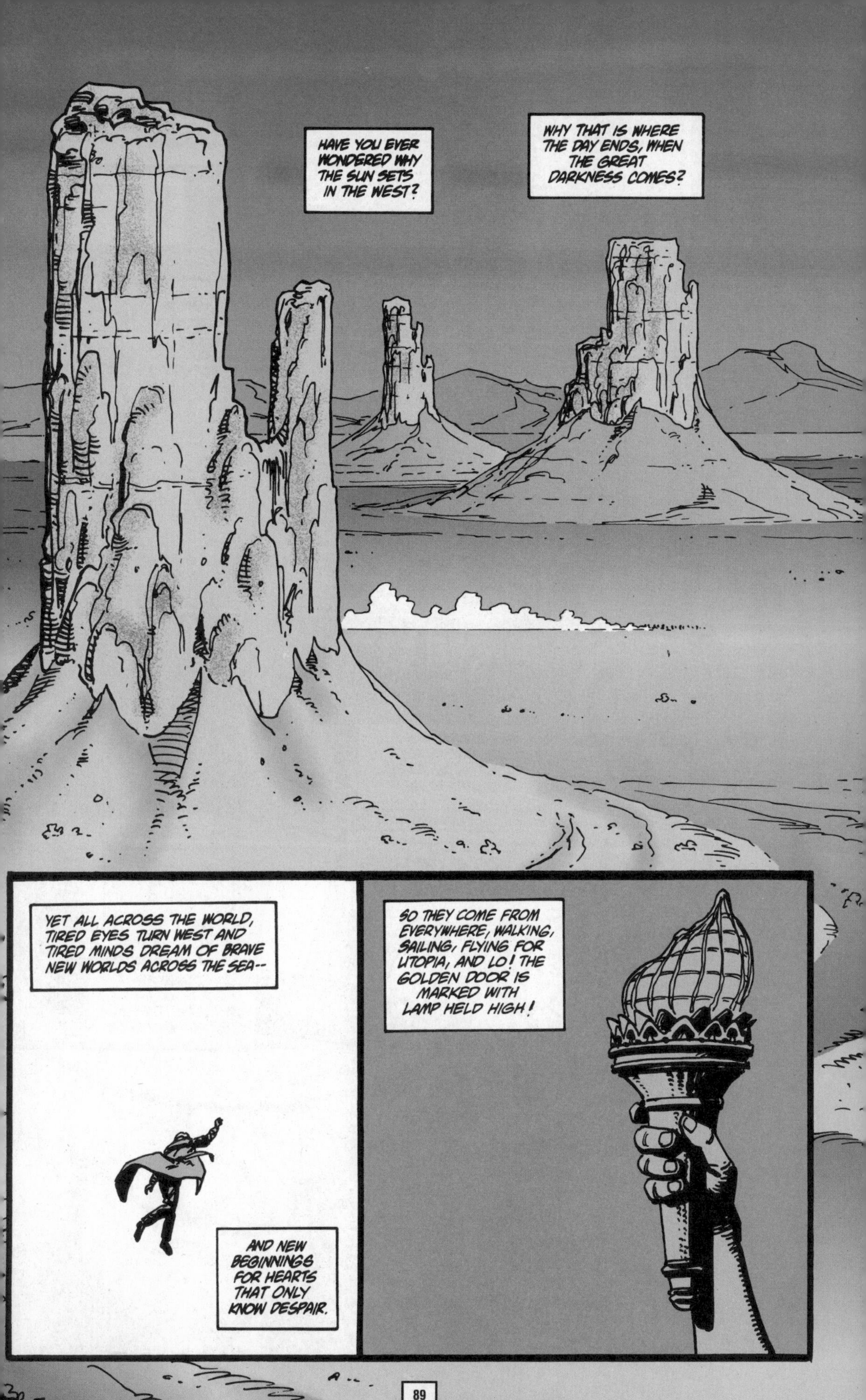
HAVE YOU EVER WONDERED WHY THE SUN SETS IN THE WEST?
WHY THAT IS WHERE THE DAY ENDS, WHEN THE GREAT DARKNESS COMES?
YET ALL ACROSS THE WORLD, TIRED EYES TURN WEST AND TIRED MINDS DREAM OF BRAVE NEW WORLDS ACROSS THE SEA--
AND NEW BEGINNINGS FOR HEARTS THAT ONLY KNOW DESPAIR.
SO THEY COME FROM EVERYWHERE, WALKING, SAILING, FLYING FOR UTOPIA, AND LO! THE GOLDEN DOOR IS MARKED WITH LAMP HELD HIGH!

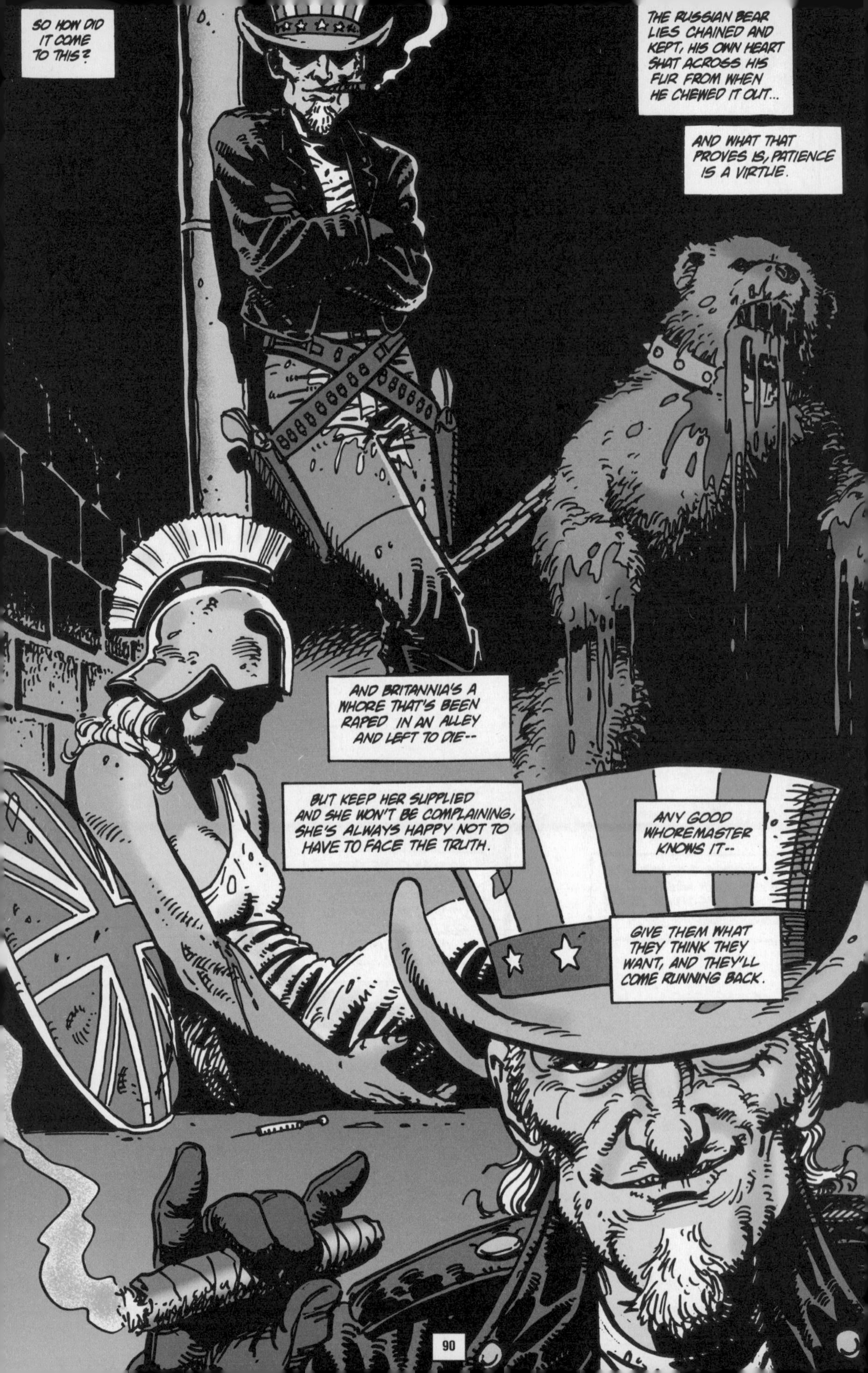

SO HOW DID IT COME TO THIS?
THE RUSSIAN BEAR LIES CHAINED AND KEPT, HIS OWN HEART SHAT ACROSS HIS FUR FROM WHEN HE CHEWED IT OUT...
AND WHAT THAT PROVES IS, PATIENCE IS A VIRTUE.
AND BRITANNIA'S A WHORE THAT'S BEEN RAPED IN AN ALLEY AND LEFT TO DIE--
BUT KEEP HER SUPPLIED AND SHE WON'T BE COMPLAINING, SHE'S ALWAYS HAPPY NOT TO HAVE TO FACE THE TRUTH.
ANY GOOD WHOREMASTER KNOWS IT--
GIVE THEM WHAT THEY THINK THEY WANT, AND THEY'LL COME RUNNING BACK.

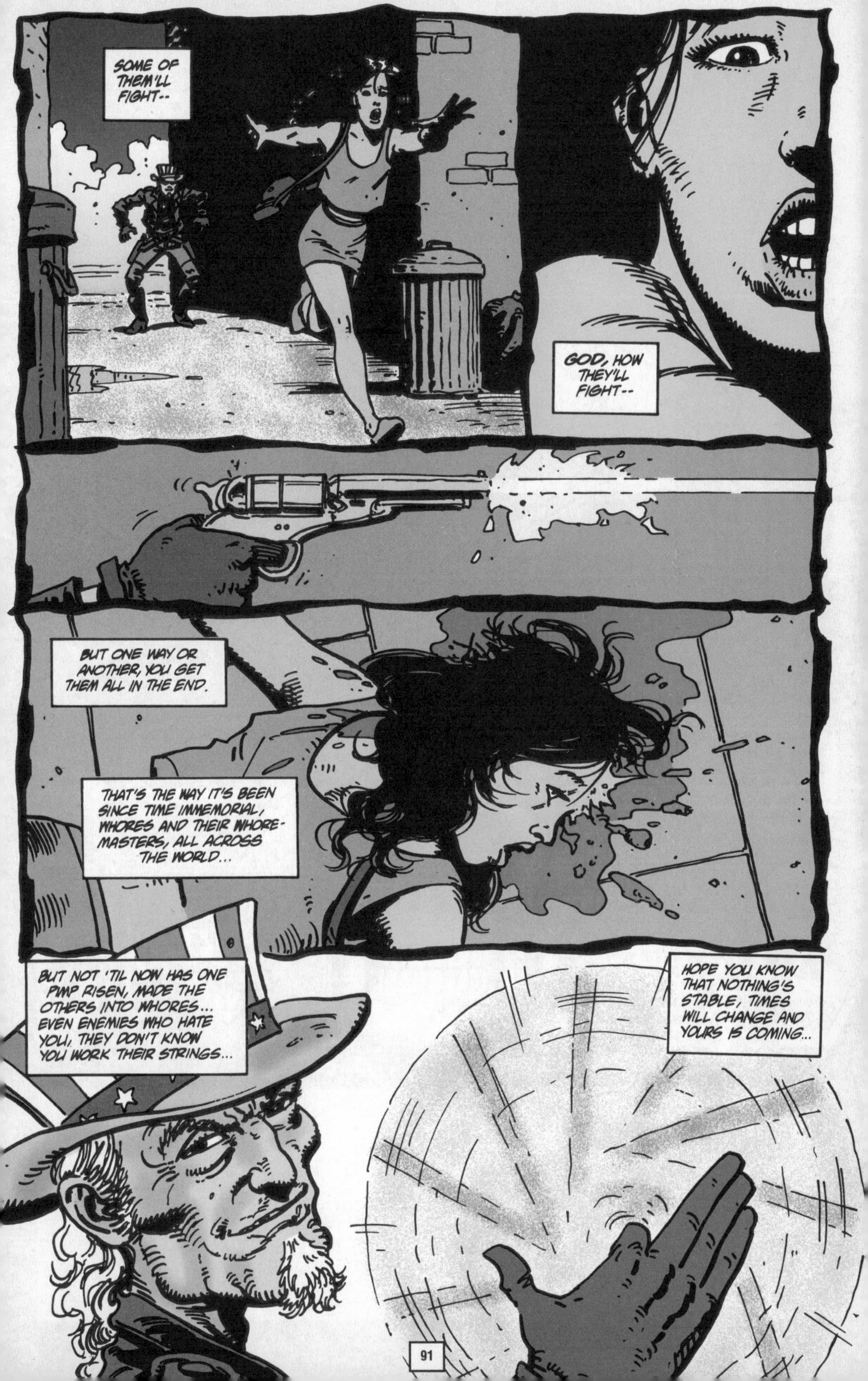
SOME OF THEM'LL FIGHT--
GOD, HOW THEY'LL FIGHT--
BUT ONE WAY OR ANOTHER, YOU GET THEM ALL IN THE END.
THAT'S THE WAY IT'S BEEN SINCE TIME IMMEMORIAL, WHORES AND THEIR WHORE-MASTERS, ALL ACROSS THE WORLD...
BUT NOT 'TIL NOW HAS ONE PIMP RISEN, MADE THE OTHERS INTO WHORES... EVEN ENEMIES WHO HATE YOU, THEY DON'T KNOW YOU WORK THEIR STRINGS...
HOPE YOU KNOW THAT NOTHING'S STABLE, TIMES WILL CHANGE AND YOURS IS COMING...

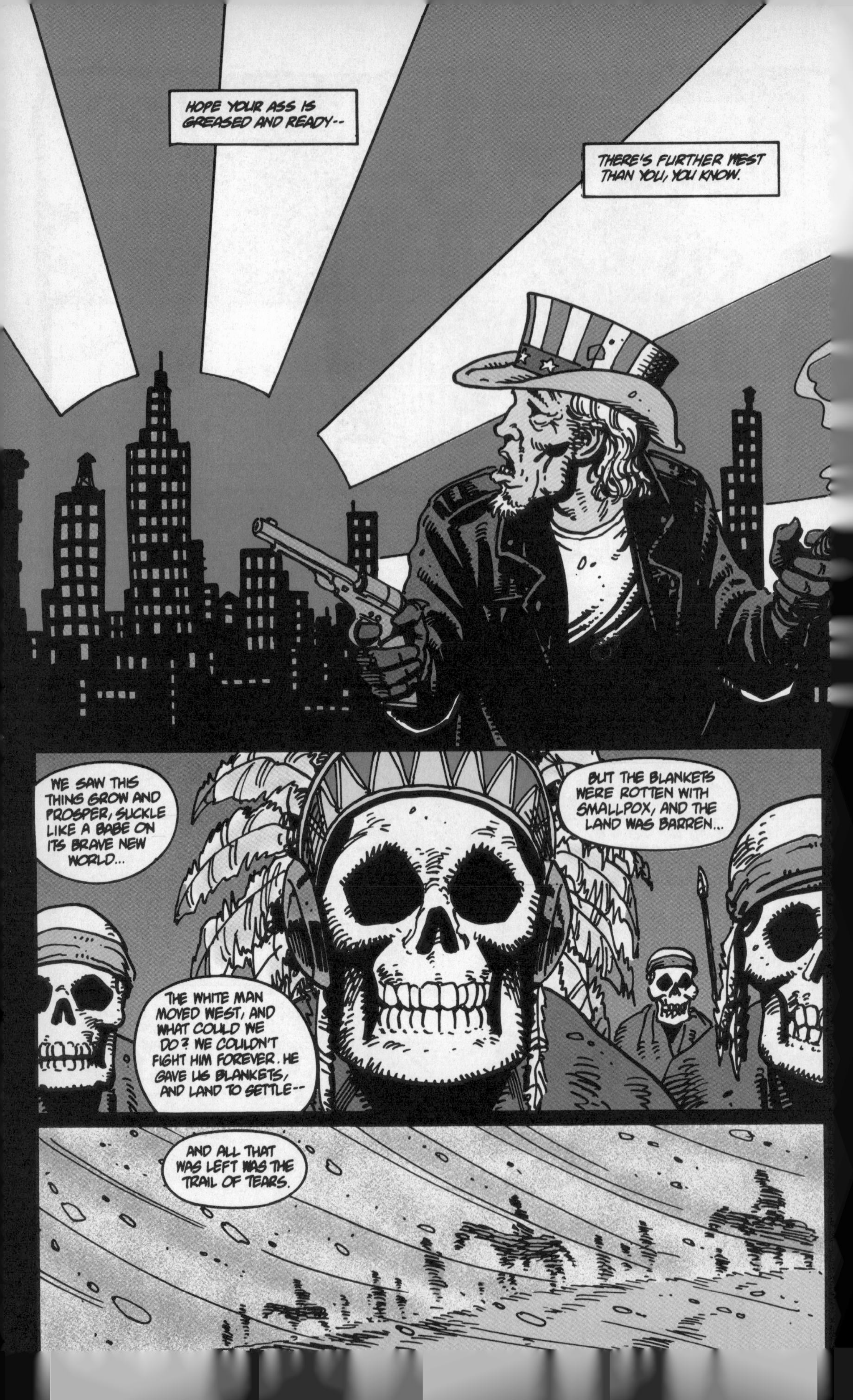

HOPE YOUR ASS IS GREASED AND READY--
THERE'S FURTHER WEST THAN YOU, YOU KNOW.
WE SAW THIS THING GROW AND PROSPER, SUCKLE LIKE A BABE ON ITS BRAVE NEW WORLD...
BUT THE BLANKETS WERE ROTTEN WITH SMALLPOX, AND THE LAND WAS BARREN...
THE WHITE MAN MOVED WEST, AND WHAT COULD WE DO? WE COULDN'T FIGHT HIM FOREVER. HE GAVE US BLANKETS, AND LAND TO SETTLE--
AND ALL THAT WAS LEFT WAS THE TRAIL OF TEARS.

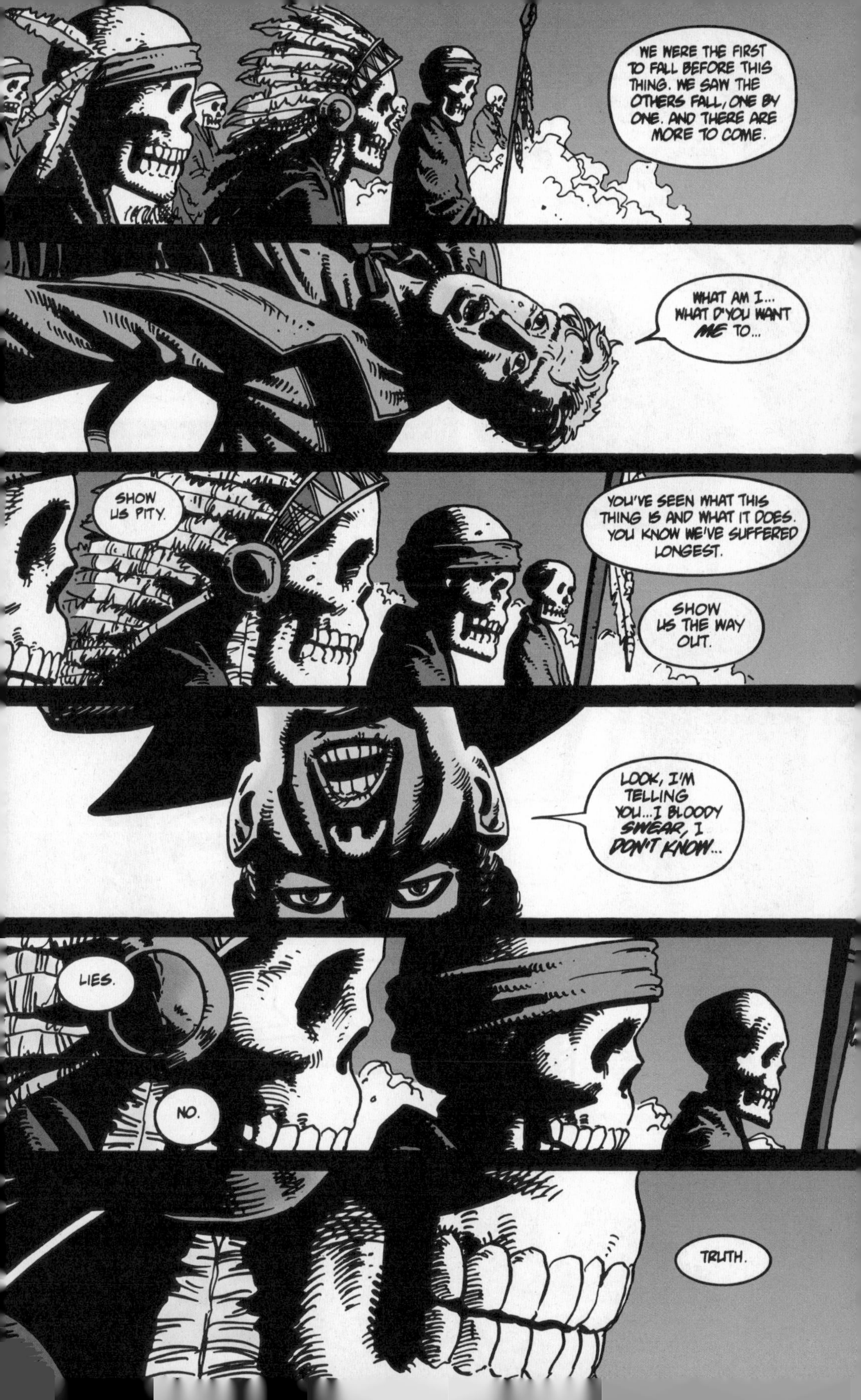

WE WERE THE FIRST TO FALL BEFORE THIS THING. WE SAW THE OTHERS FALL, ONE BY ONE. AND THERE ARE MORE TO COME.
WHAT AM I... WHAT D'YOU WANT *ME* TO...
SHOW US PITY.
YOU'VE SEEN WHAT THIS THING IS AND WHAT IT DOES. YOU KNOW WE'VE SUFFERED LONGEST.
SHOW US THE WAY OUT.
LOOK, I'M TELLING YOU...I BLOODY *SWEAR*, I *DON'T KNOW*...
LIES.
NO.
TRUTH.

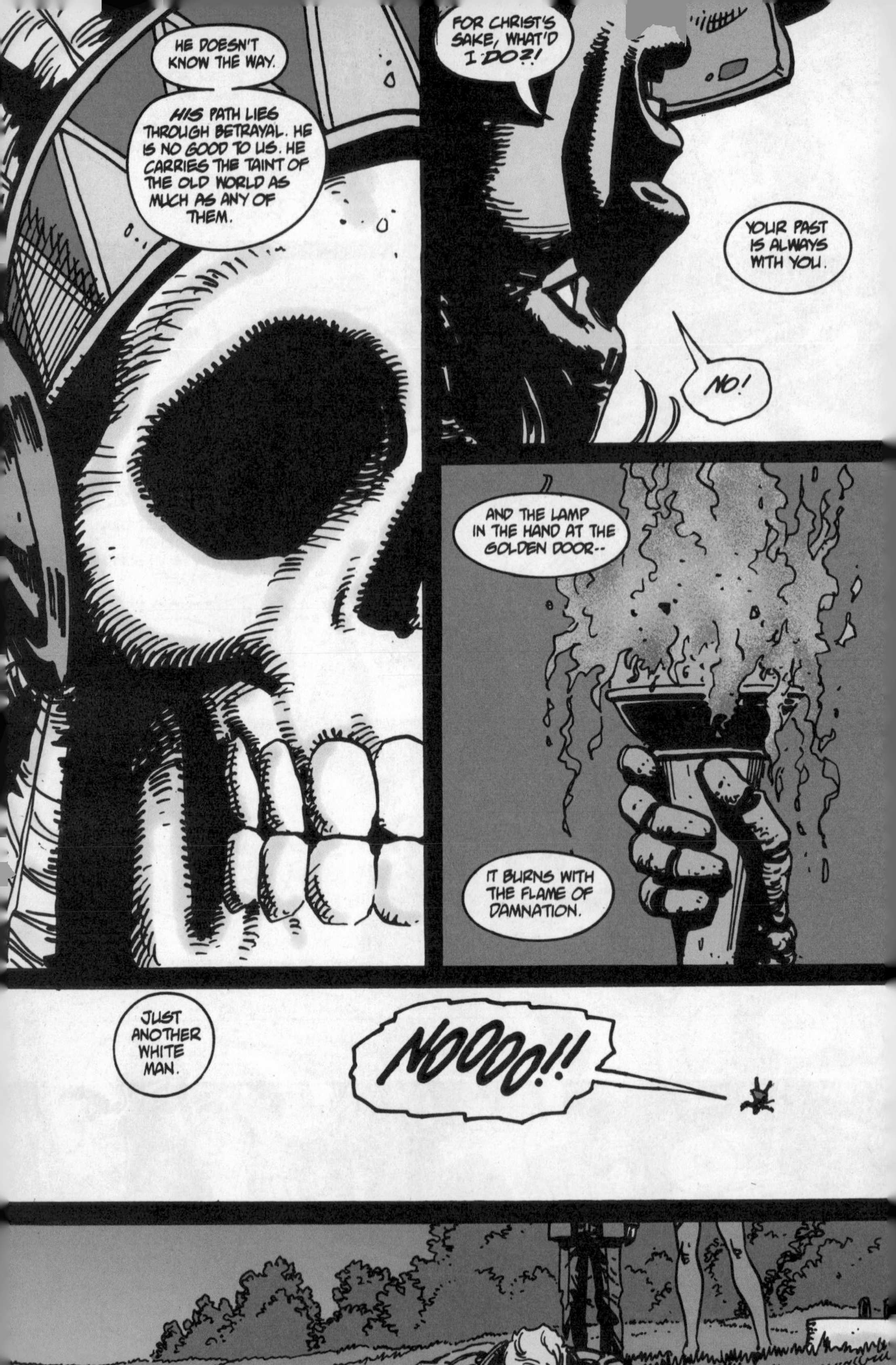
HE DOESN'T KNOW THE WAY.
HIS PATH LIES THROUGH BETRAYAL. HE IS NO GOOD TO US. HE CARRIES THE TAINT OF THE OLD WORLD AS MUCH AS ANY OF THEM.
FOR CHRIST'S SAKE, WHAT'D I DO?!
YOUR PAST IS ALWAYS WITH YOU.
NO!
AND THE LAMP IN THE HAND AT THE GOLDEN DOOR--
IT BURNS WITH THE FLAME OF DAMNATION.
JUST ANOTHER WHITE MAN.
NOOOO!!

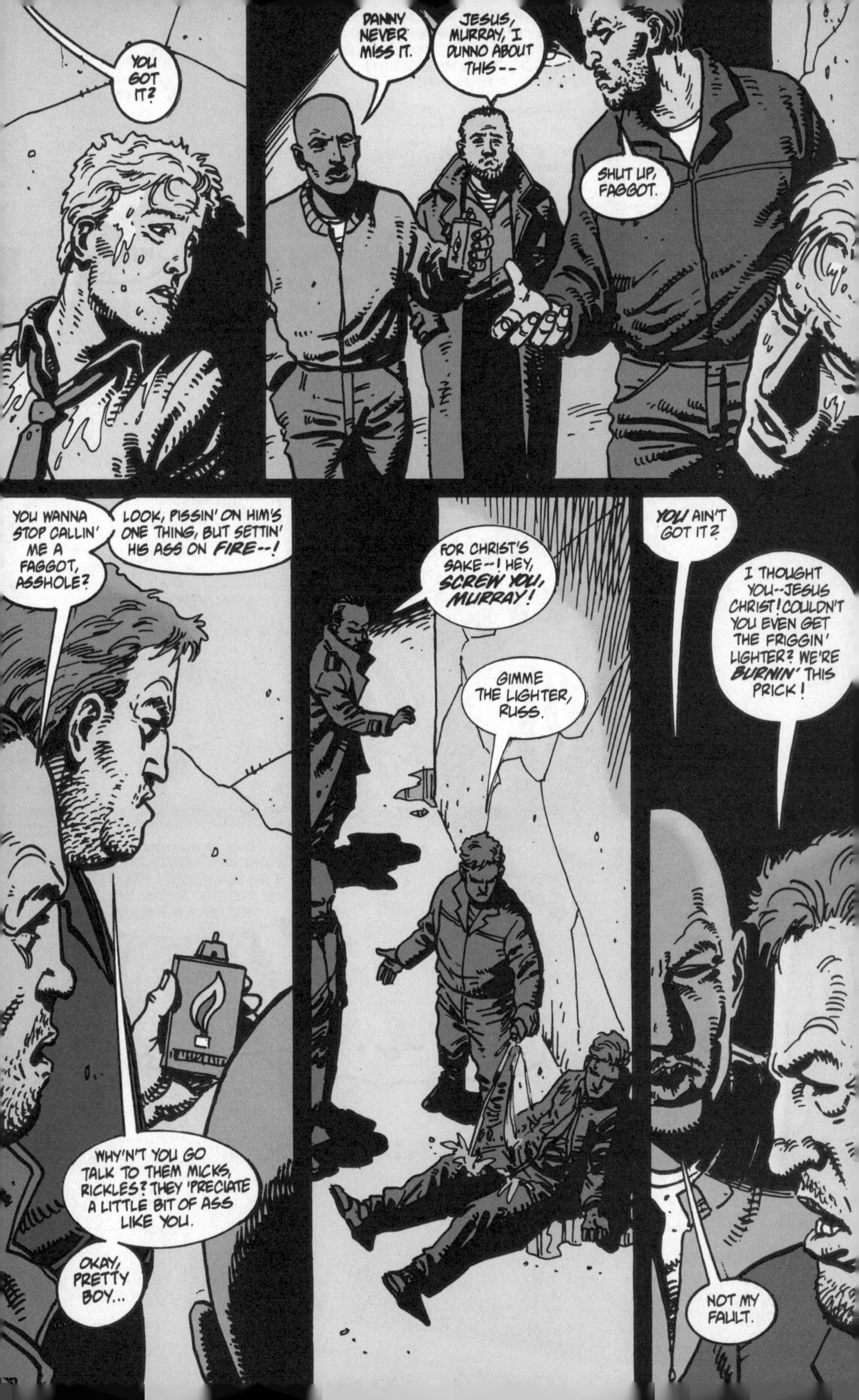
YOU GOT IT?
DANNY NEVER MISS IT.
JESUS, MURRAY, I DUNNO ABOUT THIS--
SHUT UP, FAGGOT.
YOU WANNA STOP CALLIN' ME A FAGGOT, ASSHOLE?
LOOK, PISSIN' ON HIM'S ONE THING, BUT SETTIN' HIS ASS ON FIRE--!
WHY'N'T YOU GO TALK TO THEM MICKS, RICKLES? THEY 'PRECIATE A LITTLE BIT OF ASS LIKE YOU.
OKAY, PRETTY BOY...
FOR CHRIST'S SAKE--! HEY, SCREW YOU, MURRAY!
GIMME THE LIGHTER, RUSS.
YOU AIN'T GOT IT?
I THOUGHT YOU--JESUS CHRIST! COULDN'T YOU EVEN GET THE FRIGGIN' LIGHTER? WE'RE BURNIN' THIS PRICK!
NOT MY FAULT.

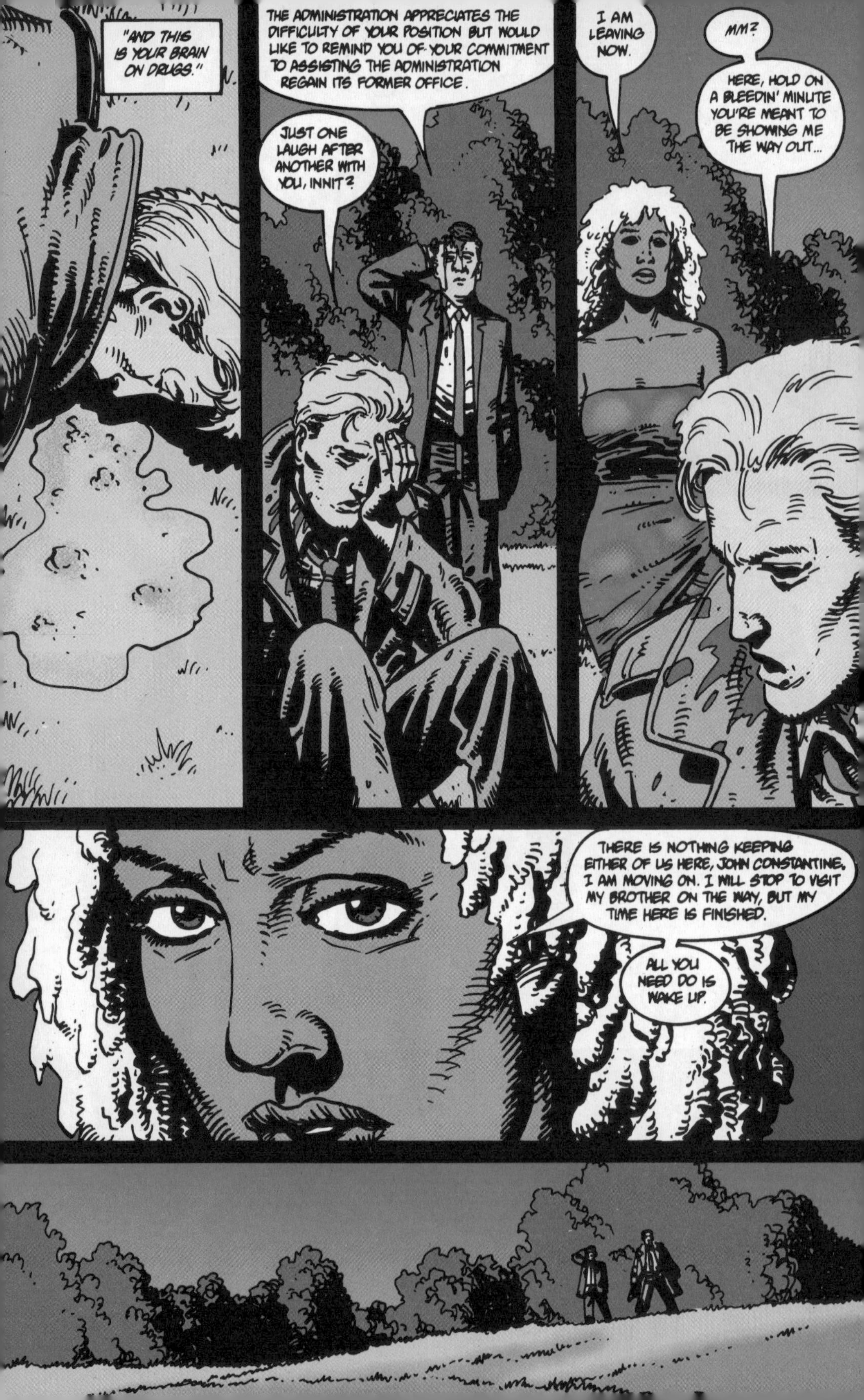
"AND THIS IS YOUR BRAIN ON DRUGS."
THE ADMINISTRATION APPRECIATES THE DIFFICULTY OF YOUR POSITION BUT WOULD LIKE TO REMIND YOU OF YOUR COMMITMENT TO ASSISTING THE ADMINISTRATION REGAIN ITS FORMER OFFICE.
JUST ONE LAUGH AFTER ANOTHER WITH YOU, INNIT?
I AM LEAVING NOW.
MM?
HERE, HOLD ON A BLEEDIN' MINUTE YOU'RE MEANT TO BE SHOWING ME THE WAY OUT...
THERE IS NOTHING KEEPING EITHER OF US HERE, JOHN CONSTANTINE. I AM MOVING ON. I WILL STOP TO VISIT MY BROTHER ON THE WAY, BUT MY TIME HERE IS FINISHED.
ALL YOU NEED DO IS WAKE UP.

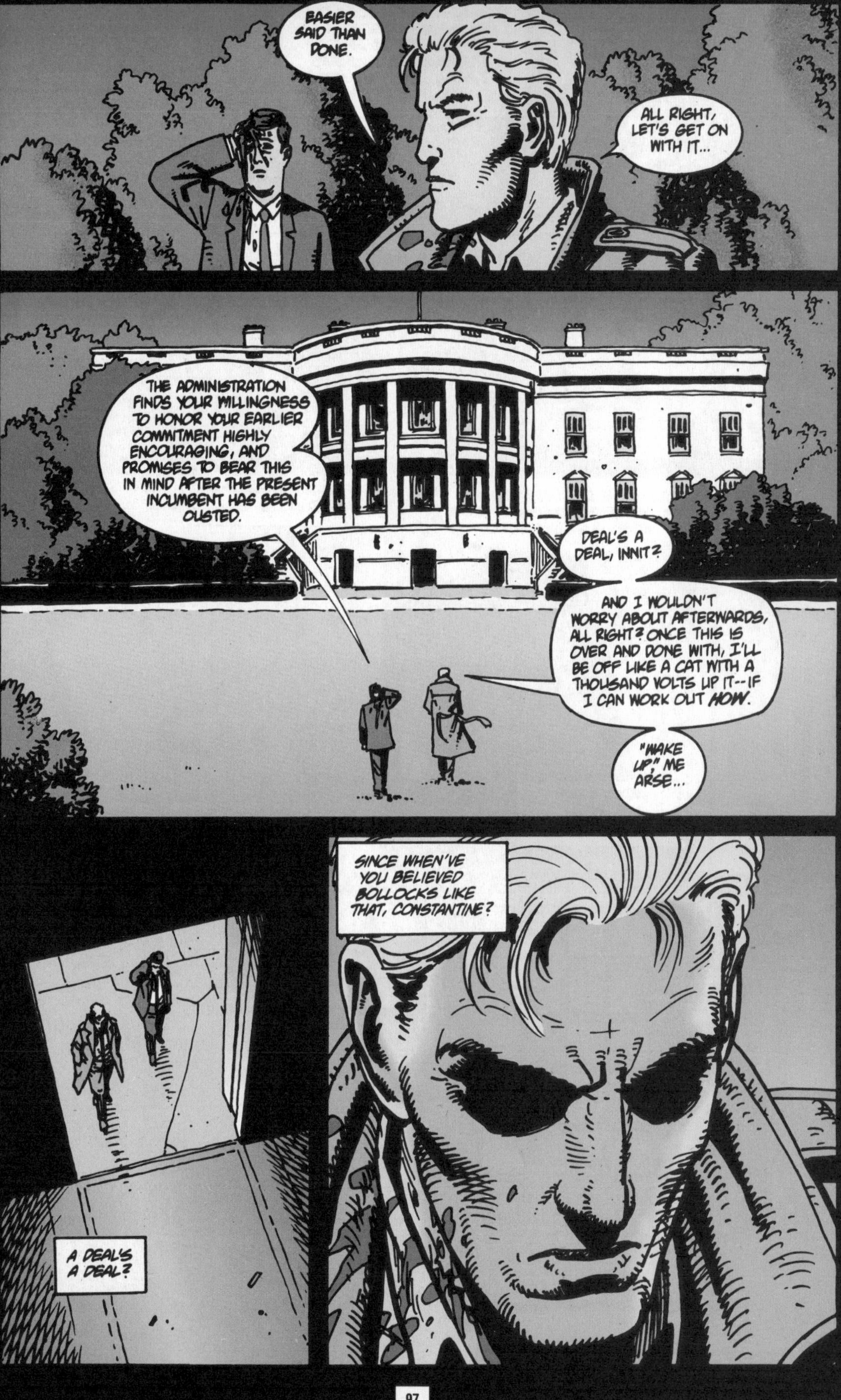

EASIER SAID THAN DONE.
ALL RIGHT, LET'S GET ON WITH IT...
THE ADMINISTRATION FINDS YOUR WILLINGNESS TO HONOR YOUR EARLIER COMMITMENT HIGHLY ENCOURAGING, AND PROMISES TO BEAR THIS IN MIND AFTER THE PRESENT INCUMBENT HAS BEEN OUSTED.
DEAL'S A DEAL, INNIT?
AND I WOULDN'T WORRY ABOUT AFTERWARDS, ALL RIGHT? ONCE THIS IS OVER AND DONE WITH, I'LL BE OFF LIKE A CAT WITH A THOUSAND VOLTS UP IT--IF I CAN WORK OUT HOW.
"WAKE UP," ME ARSE...
A DEAL'S A DEAL?
SINCE WHEN'VE YOU BELIEVED BOLLOCKS LIKE THAT, CONSTANTINE?

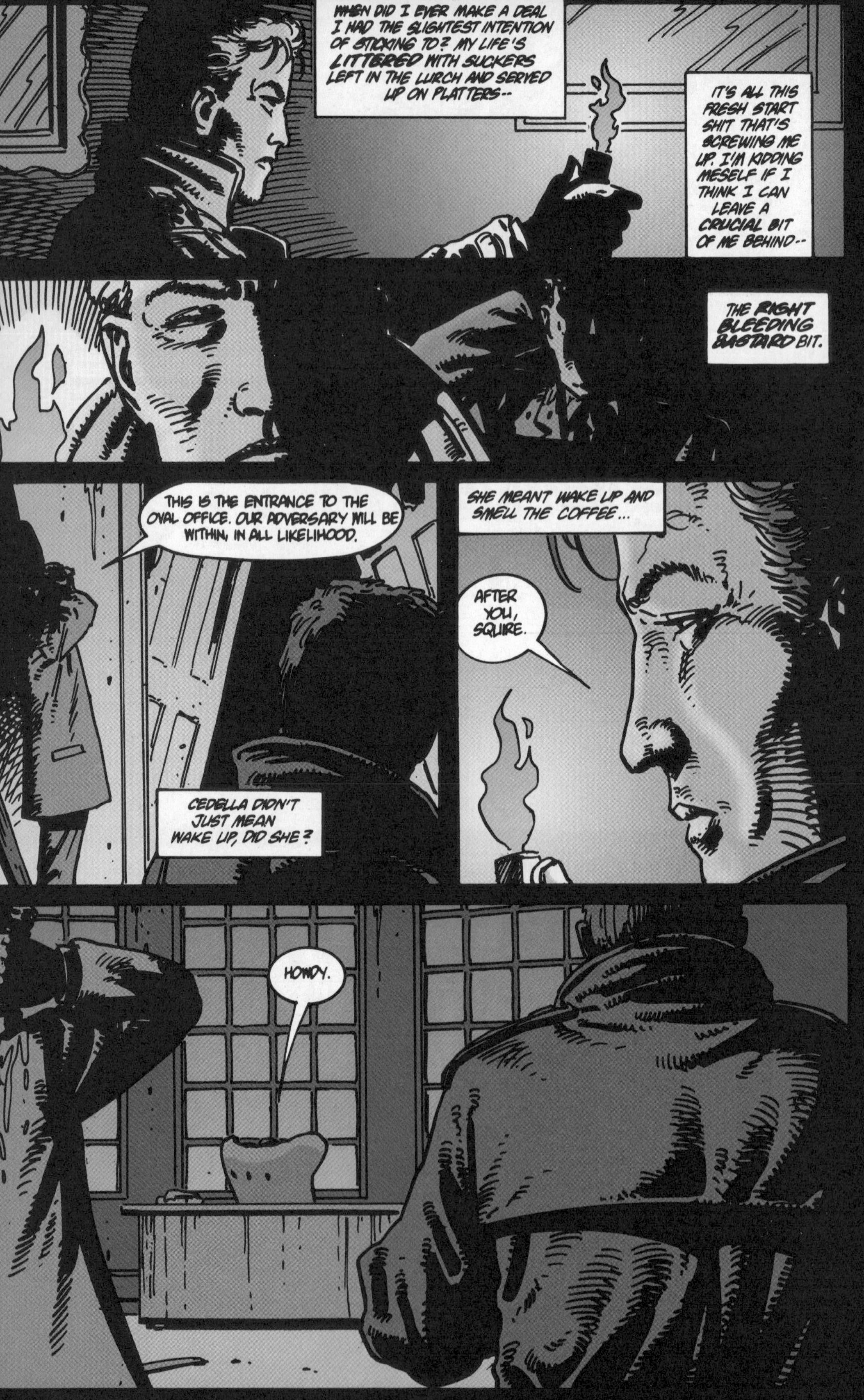
WHEN DID I EVER MAKE A DEAL I HAD THE SLIGHTEST INTENTION OF STICKING TO? MY LIFE'S LITTERED WITH SUCKERS LEFT IN THE LURCH AND SERVED UP ON PLATTERS--
IT'S ALL THIS FRESH START SHIT THAT'S SCREWING ME UP. I'M KIDDING MESELF IF I THINK I CAN LEAVE A CRUCIAL BIT OF ME BEHIND--
THE RIGHT BLEEDING BASTARD BIT.
THIS IS THE ENTRANCE TO THE OVAL OFFICE. OUR ADVERSARY WILL BE WITHIN, IN ALL LIKELIHOOD.
CEDELLA DIDN'T JUST MEAN WAKE UP, DID SHE?
SHE MEANT WAKE UP AND SMELL THE COFFEE...
AFTER YOU, SQUIRE.
HOWDY.

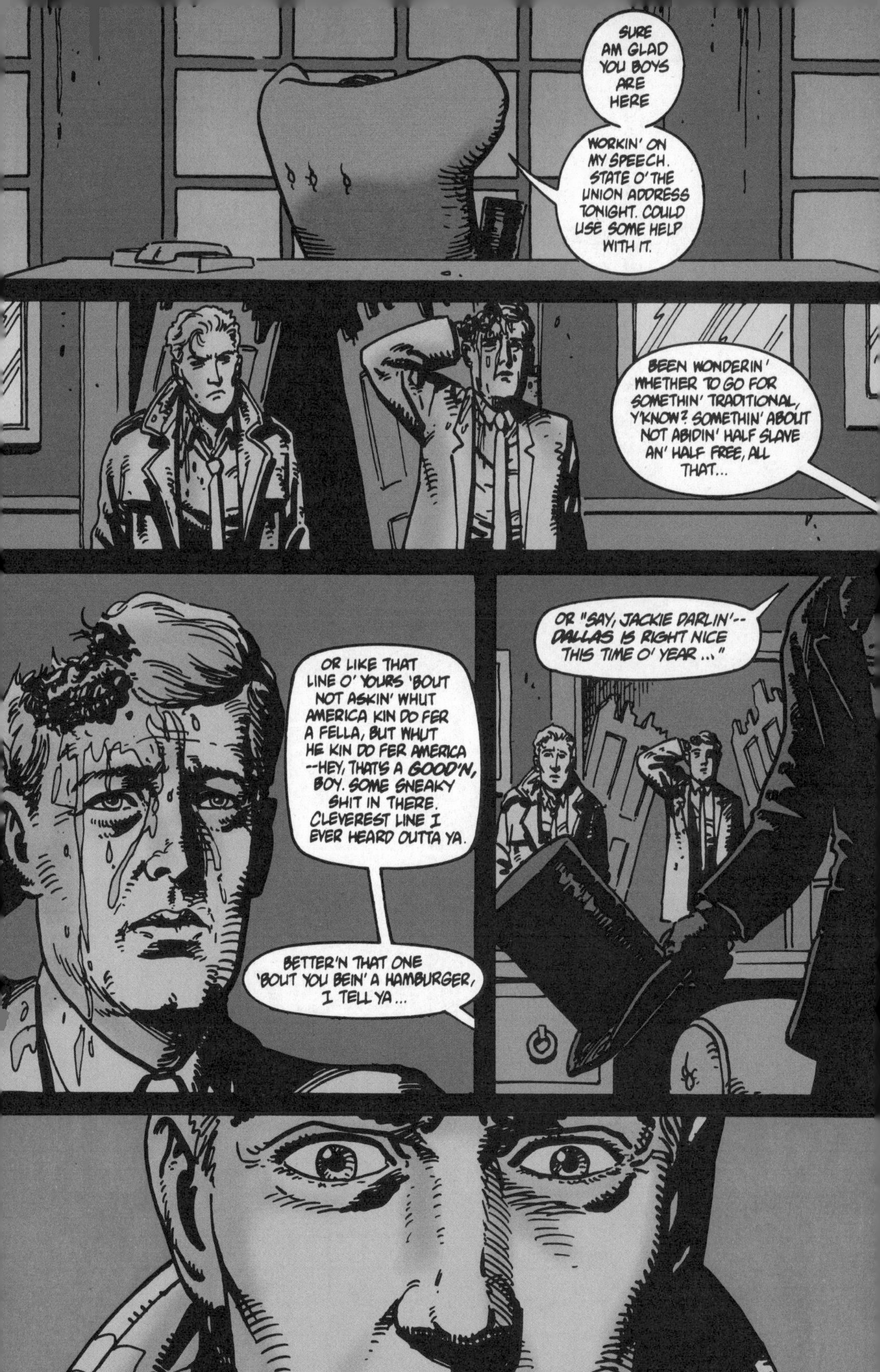
SURE AM GLAD YOU BOYS ARE HERE
WORKIN' ON MY SPEECH. STATE O' THE UNION ADDRESS TONIGHT. COULD USE SOME HELP WITH IT.
BEEN WONDERIN' WHETHER TO GO FOR SOMETHIN' TRADITIONAL, Y'KNOW? SOMETHIN' ABOUT NOT ABIDIN' HALF SLAVE AN' HALF FREE, ALL THAT...
OR LIKE THAT LINE O' YOURS 'BOUT NOT ASKIN' WHUT AMERICA KIN DO FER A FELLA, BUT WHUT HE KIN DO FER AMERICA --HEY, THAT'S A GOOD'N, BOY. SOME SNEAKY SHIT IN THERE. CLEVEREST LINE I EVER HEARD OUTTA YA.
BETTER'N THAT ONE 'BOUT YOU BEIN' A HAMBURGER, I TELL YA...
OR "SAY, JACKIE DARLIN'-- DALLAS IS RIGHT NICE THIS TIME O' YEAR..."

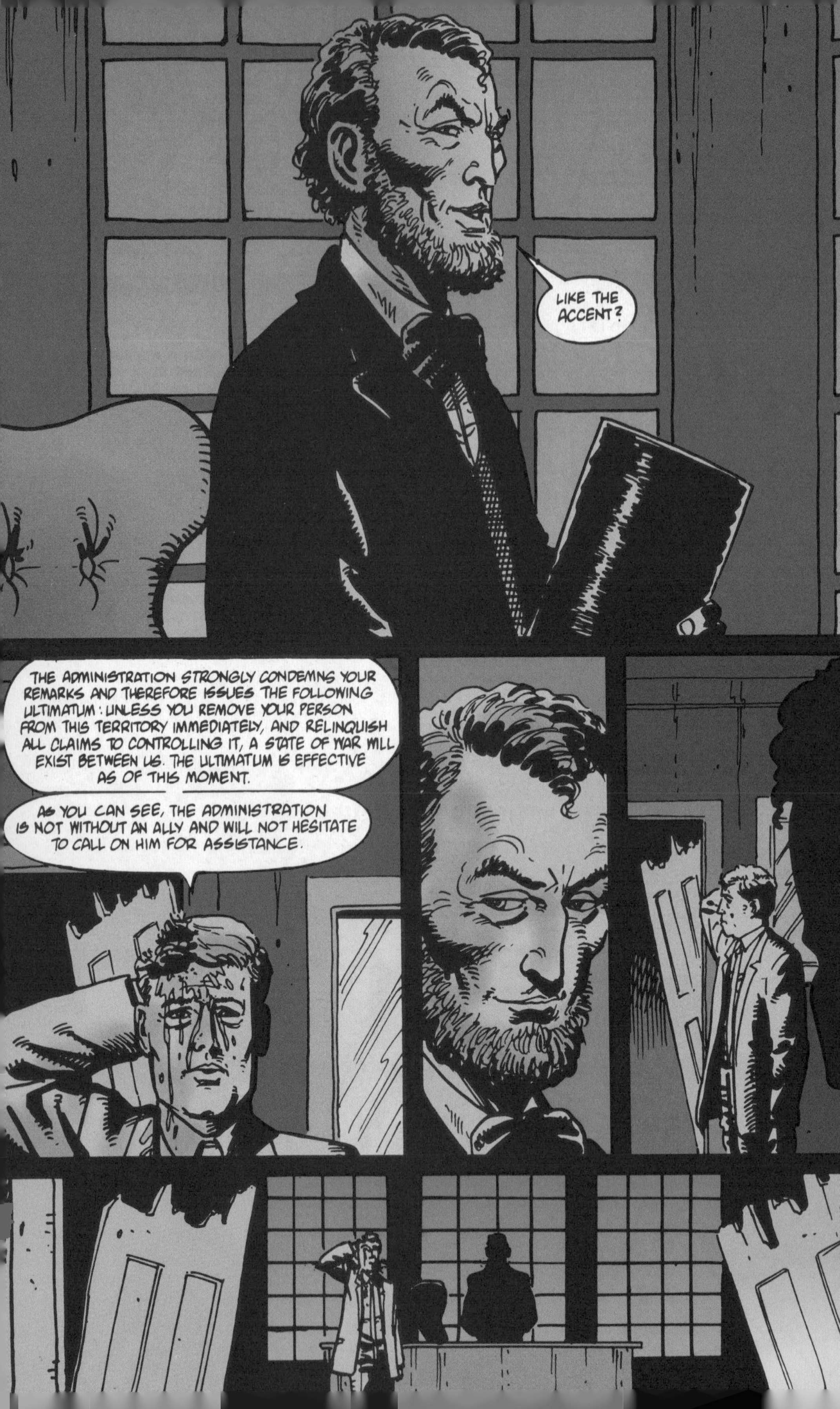

LIKE THE ACCENT?
THE ADMINISTRATION STRONGLY CONDEMNS YOUR REMARKS AND THEREFORE ISSUES THE FOLLOWING ULTIMATUM: UNLESS YOU REMOVE YOUR PERSON FROM THIS TERRITORY IMMEDIATELY, AND RELINQUISH ALL CLAIMS TO CONTROLLING IT, A STATE OF WAR WILL EXIST BETWEEN US. THE ULTIMATUM IS EFFECTIVE AS OF THIS MOMENT.
AS YOU CAN SEE, THE ADMINISTRATION IS NOT WITHOUT AN ALLY AND WILL NOT HESITATE TO CALL ON HIM FOR ASSISTANCE.

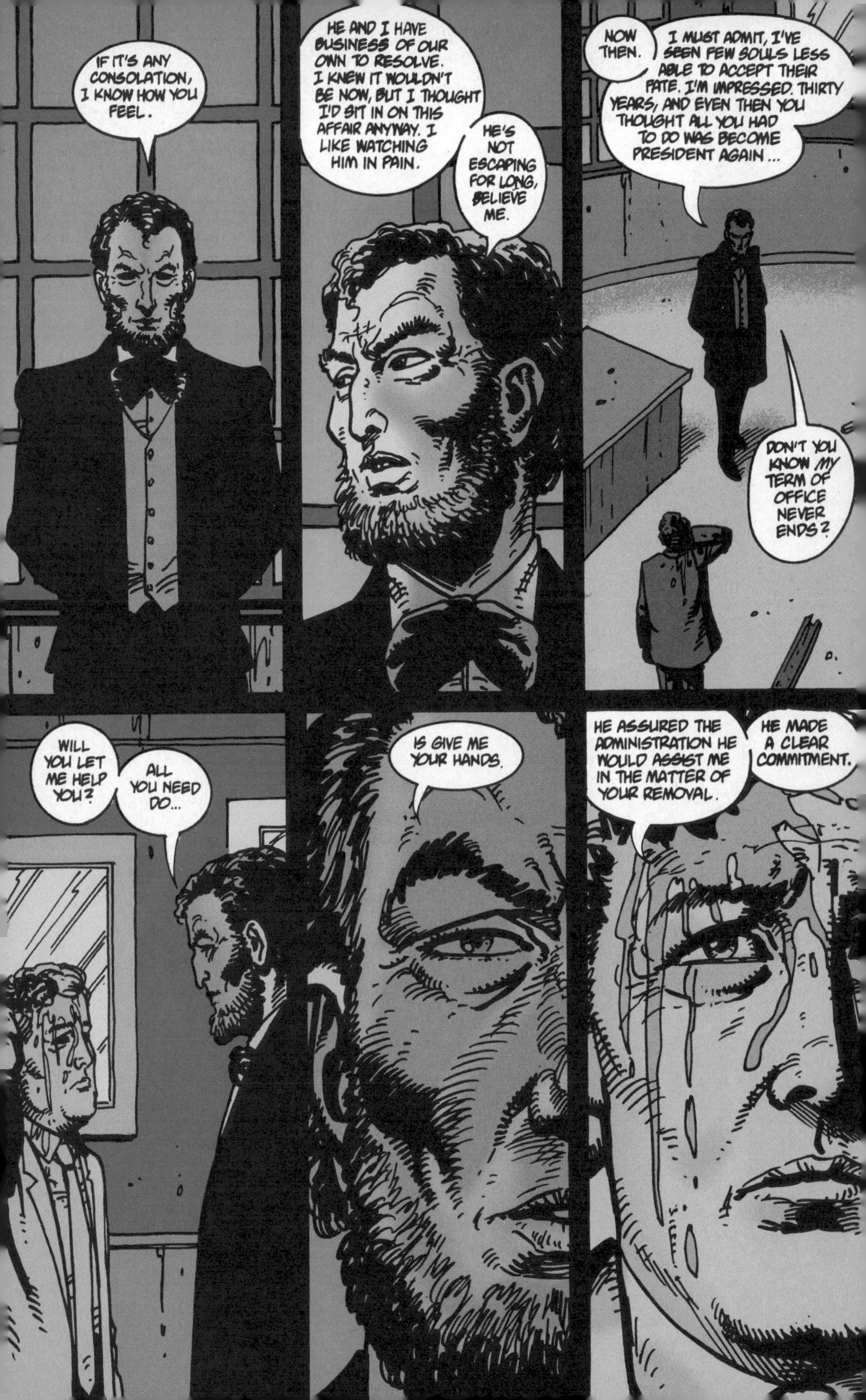
IF IT'S ANY CONSOLATION, I KNOW HOW YOU FEEL.
HE AND I HAVE BUSINESS OF OUR OWN TO RESOLVE. I KNEW IT WOULDN'T BE NOW, BUT I THOUGHT I'D SIT IN ON THIS AFFAIR ANYWAY. I LIKE WATCHING HIM IN PAIN.
HE'S NOT ESCAPING FOR LONG, BELIEVE ME.
NOW THEN.
I MUST ADMIT, I'VE SEEN FEW SOULS LESS ABLE TO ACCEPT THEIR FATE. I'M IMPRESSED. THIRTY YEARS, AND EVEN THEN YOU THOUGHT ALL YOU HAD TO DO WAS BECOME PRESIDENT AGAIN...
DON'T YOU KNOW MY TERM OF OFFICE NEVER ENDS?
WILL YOU LET ME HELP YOU?
ALL YOU NEED DO...
IS GIVE ME YOUR HANDS.
HE ASSURED THE ADMINISTRATION HE WOULD ASSIST ME IN THE MATTER OF YOUR REMOVAL.
HE MADE A CLEAR COMMITMENT.

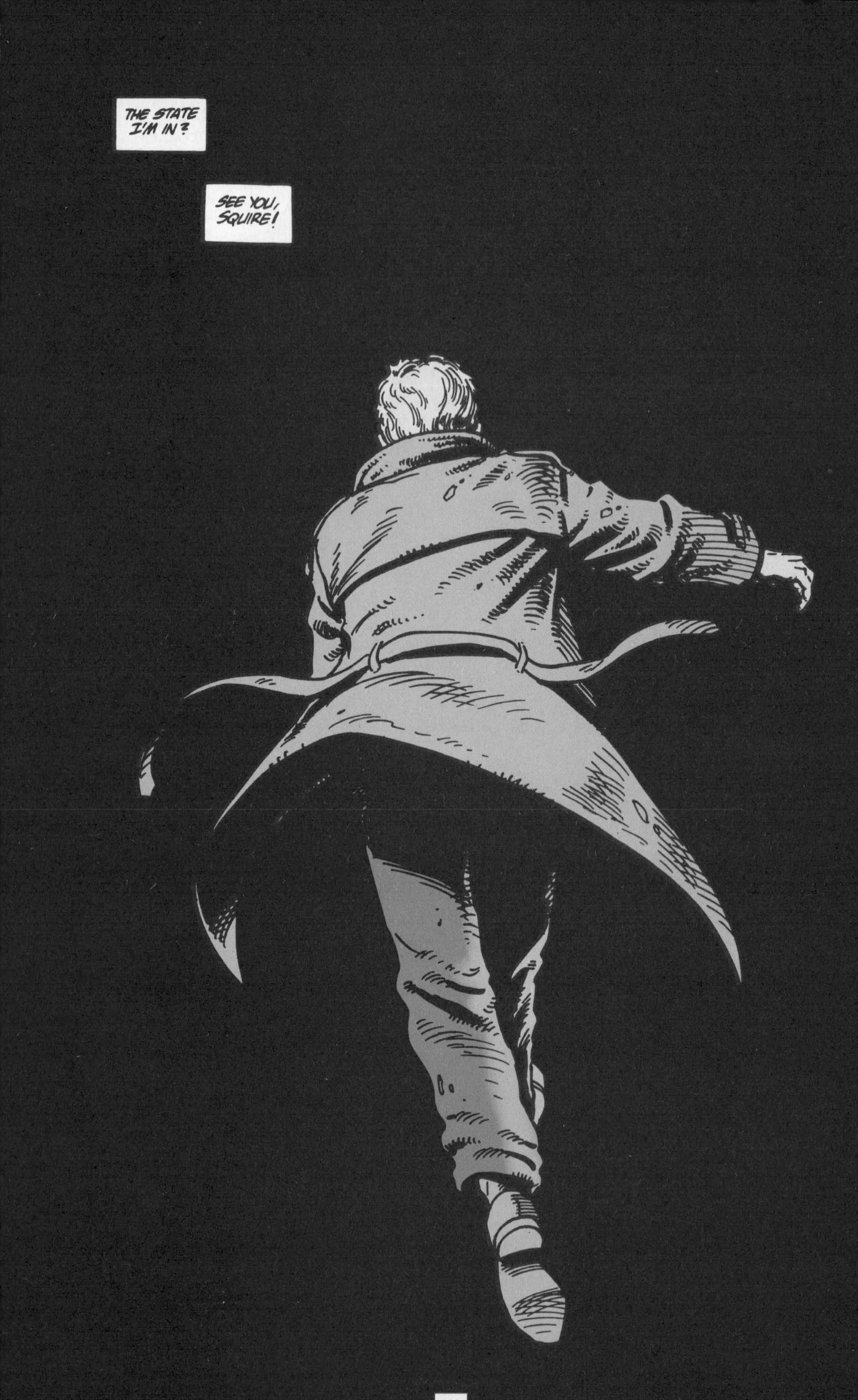
THE STATE I'M IN?
SEE YOU, SQUIRE!

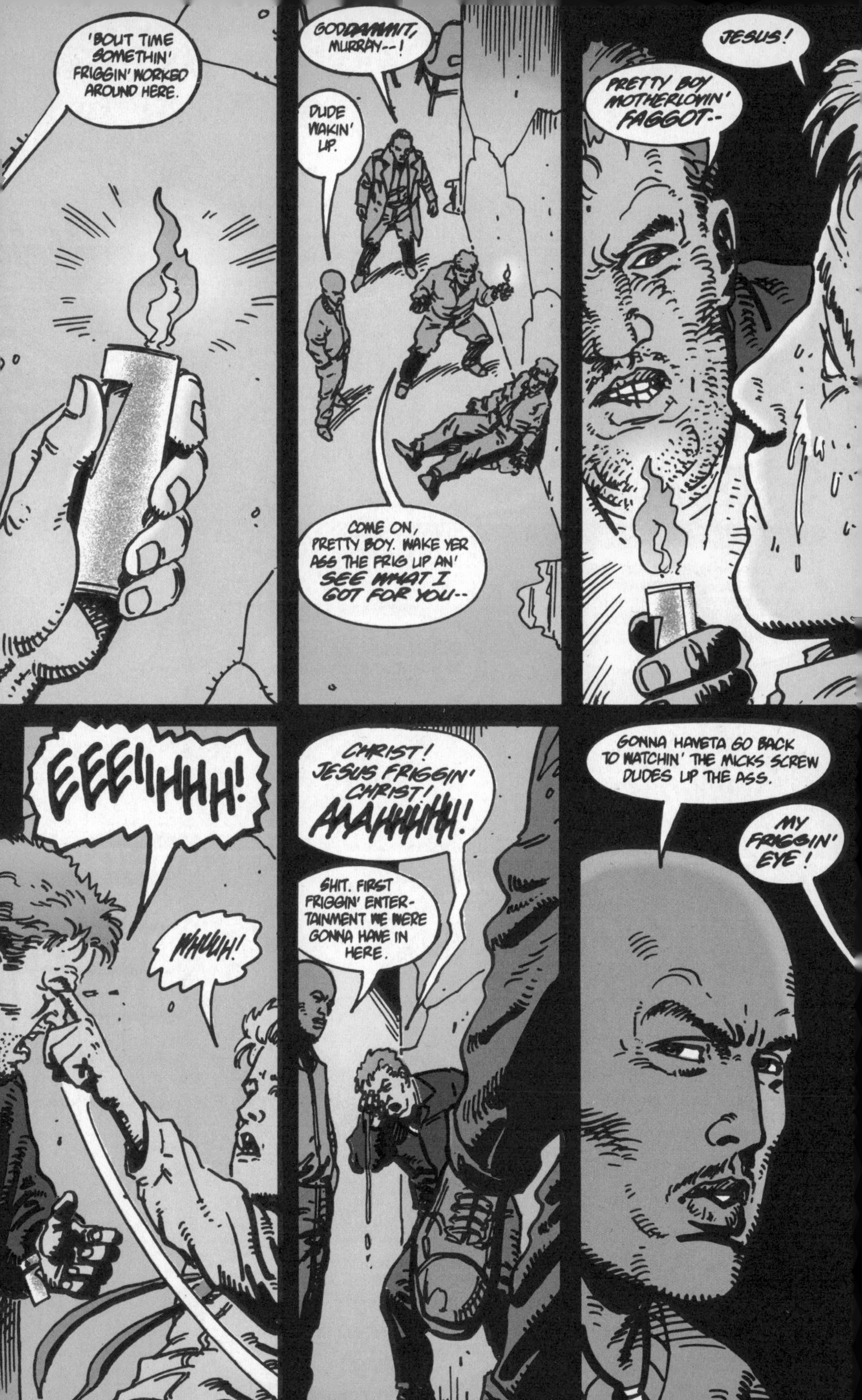
'BOUT TIME SOMETHIN' FRIGGIN' WORKED AROUND HERE.
GODDAMMIT, MURRAY--!
DUDE WAKIN' UP.
COME ON, PRETTY BOY. WAKE YER ASS THE FRIG UP AN' SEE WHAT I GOT FOR YOU--
JESUS!
PRETTY BOY MOTHERLOVIN' FAGGOT--
EEEIIHHH!
WHUUH!
CHRIST! JESUS FRIGGIN' CHRIST! AAAHHHH!
SHIT. FIRST FRIGGIN' ENTER-TAINMENT WE WERE GONNA HAVE IN HERE.
GONNA HAVETA GO BACK TO WATCHIN' THE MICKS SCREW DUDES UP THE ASS.
MY FRIGGIN' EYE!

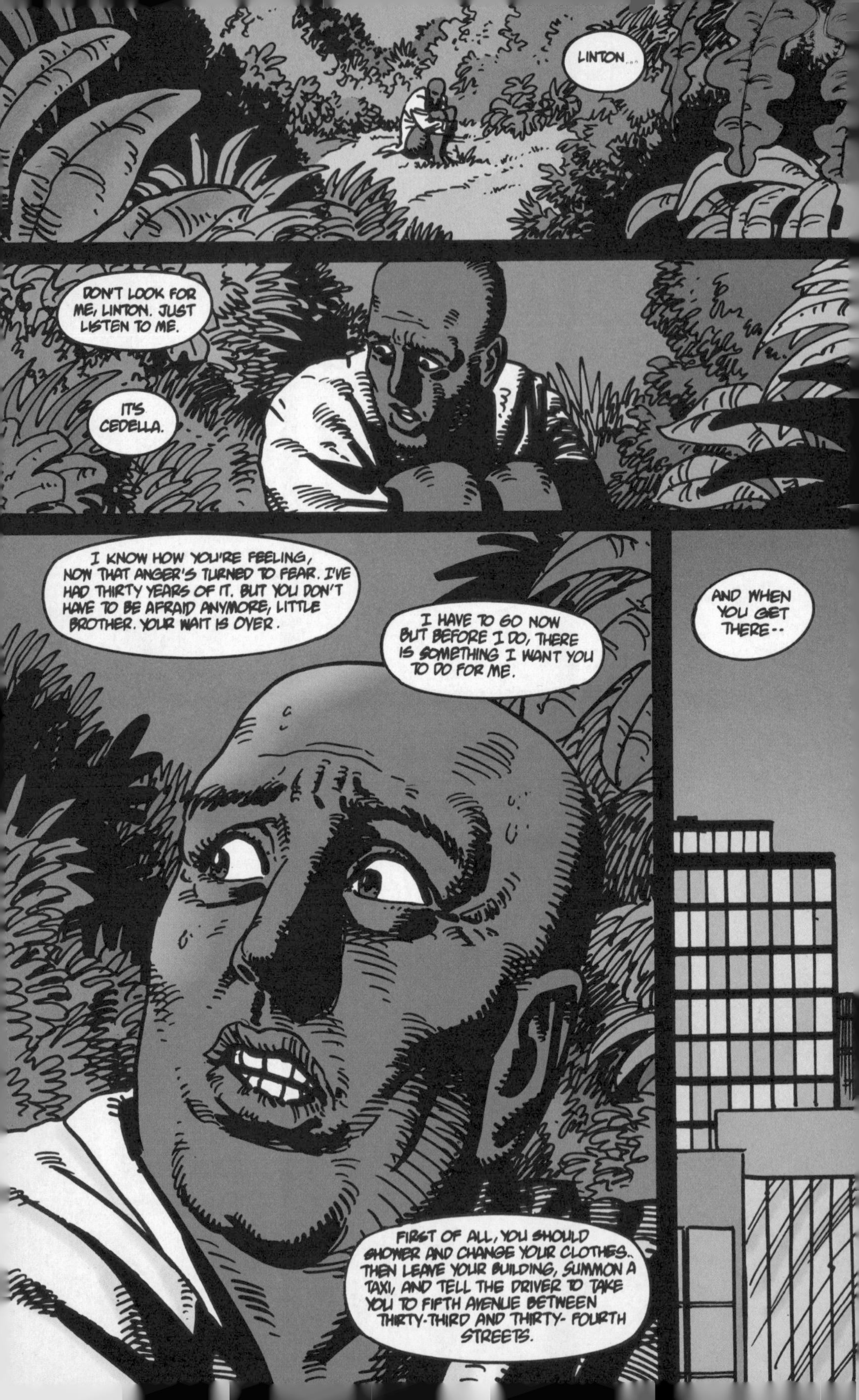
LINTON...
DON'T LOOK FOR ME, LINTON. JUST LISTEN TO ME.
IT'S CEDELLA.
I KNOW HOW YOU'RE FEELING, NOW THAT ANGER'S TURNED TO FEAR. I'VE HAD THIRTY YEARS OF IT. BUT YOU DON'T HAVE TO BE AFRAID ANYMORE, LITTLE BROTHER. YOUR WAIT IS OVER.
I HAVE TO GO NOW BUT BEFORE I DO, THERE IS SOMETHING I WANT YOU TO DO FOR ME.
FIRST OF ALL, YOU SHOULD SHOWER AND CHANGE YOUR CLOTHES. THEN LEAVE YOUR BUILDING, SUMMON A TAXI, AND TELL THE DRIVER TO TAKE YOU TO FIFTH AVENUE BETWEEN THIRTY-THIRD AND THIRTY-FOURTH STREETS.
AND WHEN YOU GET THERE--

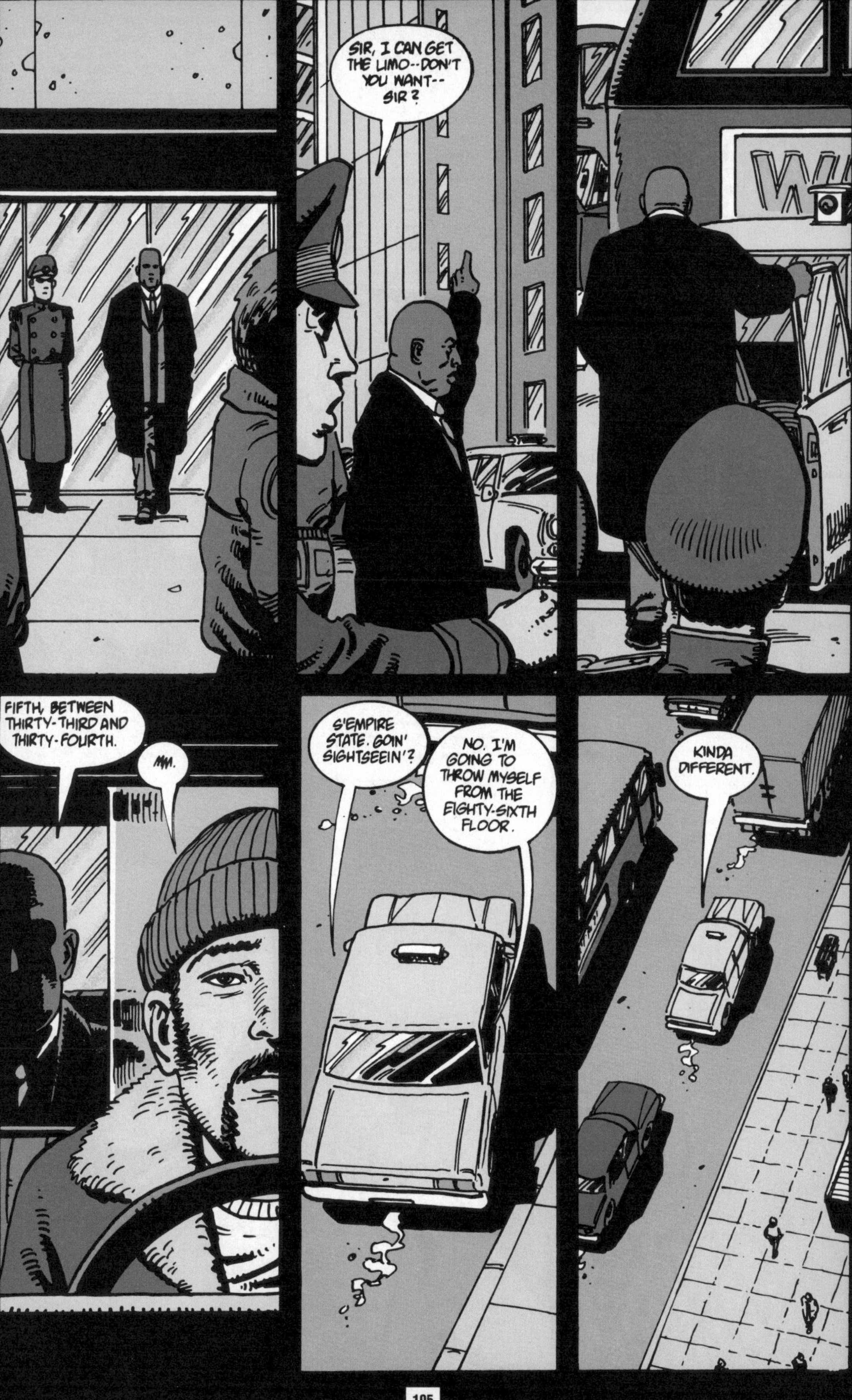

SIR, I CAN GET THE LIMO--DON'T YOU WANT-- SIR?
FIFTH, BETWEEN THIRTY-THIRD AND THIRTY-FOURTH.
MM.
S'EMPIRE STATE. GOIN' SIGHTSEEIN'?
NO. I'M GOING TO THROW MYSELF FROM THE EIGHTY-SIXTH FLOOR.
KINDA DIFFERENT.

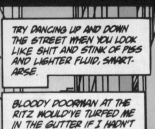

TRY DANCING UP AND DOWN THE STREET WHEN YOU LOOK LIKE SHIT AND STINK OF PISS AND LIGHTER FLUID, SMART-ARSE.

BLOODY DOORMAN AT THE RITZ WOULD'VE TURFED ME IN THE GUTTER IF I HADN'T PUT THE ZAP ON HIM...

THE GIT.

BUT YEAH, FRIG IT. ONCE I WAS IN, ALL I HAD TO DO WAS NICK THE FAT BLOKE'S WALLET, CLEAN UP AND THEN GO SHOPPING FOR CLOTHES.

THIS THING'LL DO 'TIL I GET HOME, I S'POSE...

ENJOY.

YOU BET.

IT'S NOTHING NEW, THIS PLACE. IT'S JUST THE SAME OLD SHIT OUT WEST. AND IF IT WHISPERS LIES YOU WANT SO BADLY TO BELIEVE--

DON'T.

JUST STICK TO THE ESSENTIAL TRUTHS:

AAH...

FIRST OF THE DAY ALWAYS TASTES THE BEST.

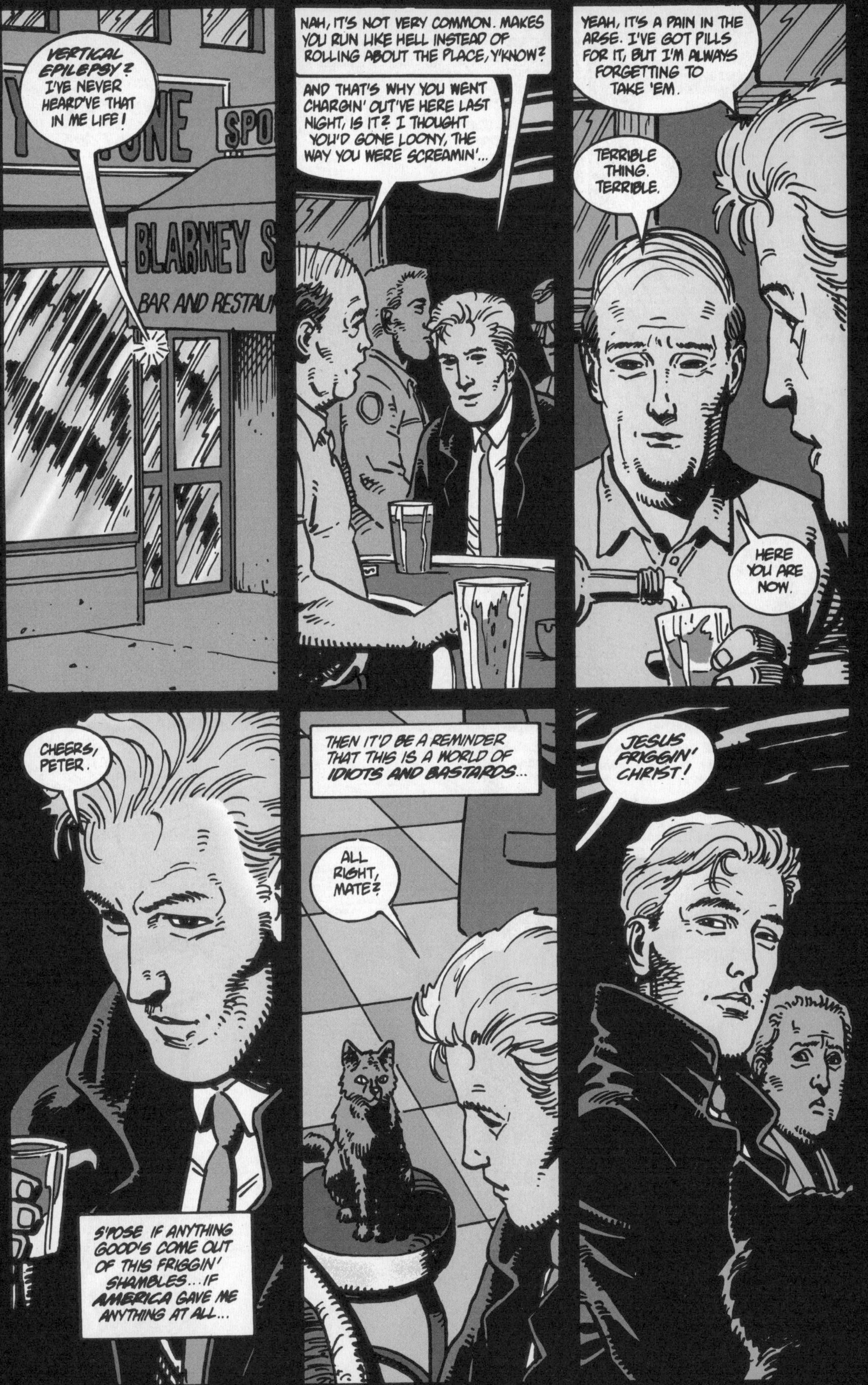
VERTICAL EPILEPSY? I'VE NEVER HEARD'VE THAT IN ME LIFE!
BLARNEY S
BAR AND RESTAU
NAH, IT'S NOT VERY COMMON. MAKES YOU RUN LIKE HELL INSTEAD OF ROLLING ABOUT THE PLACE, Y'KNOW?
AND THAT'S WHY YOU WENT CHARGIN' OUT'VE HERE LAST NIGHT, IS IT? I THOUGHT YOU'D GONE LOONY, THE WAY YOU WERE SCREAMIN'...
YEAH, IT'S A PAIN IN THE ARSE. I'VE GOT PILLS FOR IT, BUT I'M ALWAYS FORGETTING TO TAKE 'EM.
TERRIBLE THING. TERRIBLE.
HERE YOU ARE NOW.
CHEERS, PETER.
S'POSE IF ANYTHING GOOD'S COME OUT OF THIS FRIGGIN' SHAMBLES... IF AMERICA GAVE ME ANYTHING AT ALL...
THEN IT'D BE A REMINDER THAT THIS IS A WORLD OF IDIOTS AND BASTARDS...
ALL RIGHT, MATE?
JESUS FRIGGIN' CHRIST!

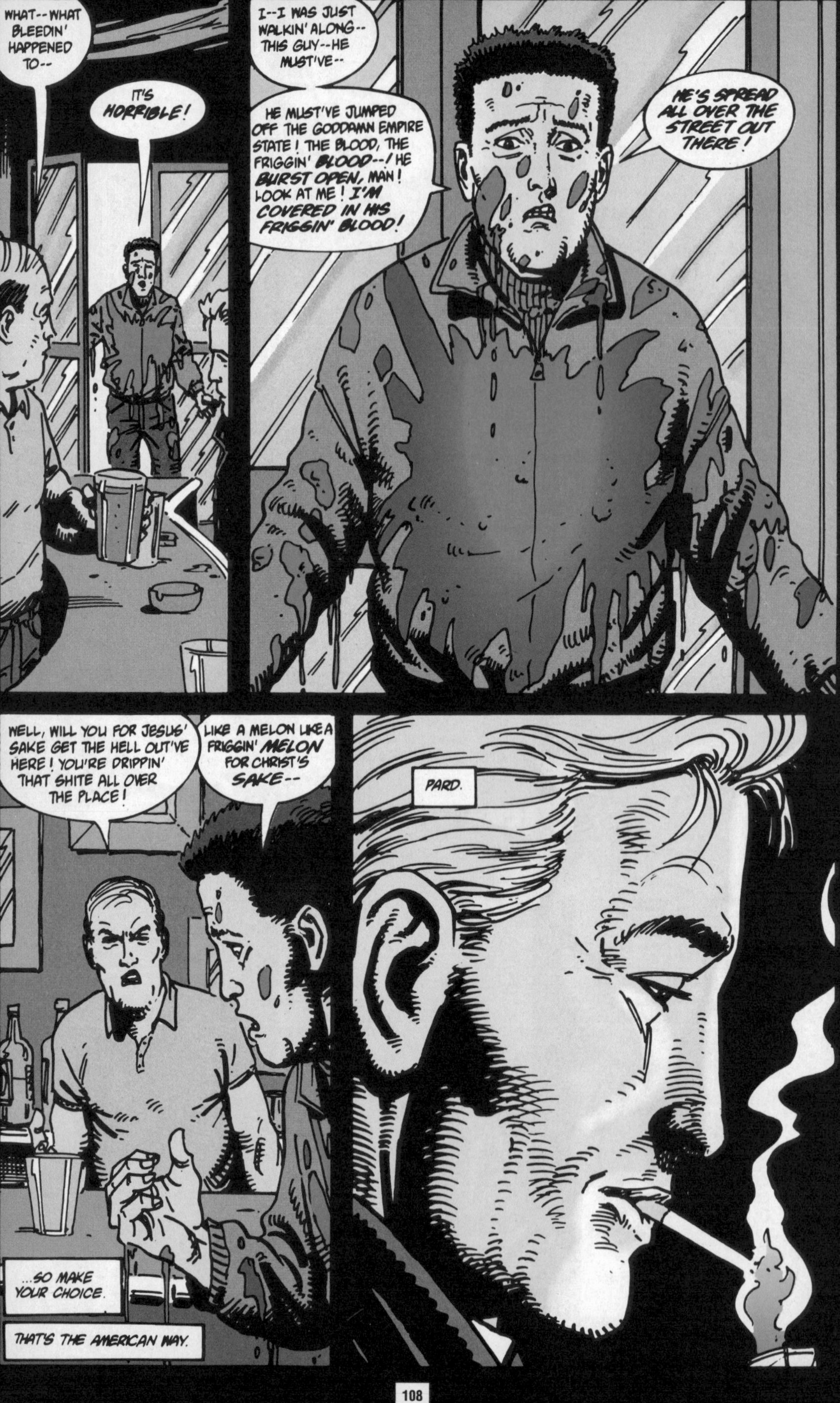

WHAT--WHAT BLEEDIN' HAPPENED TO--
IT'S HORRIBLE!
I--I WAS JUST WALKIN' ALONG-- THIS GUY--HE MUST'VE--
HE MUST'VE JUMPED OFF THE GODDAMN EMPIRE STATE! THE BLOOD, THE FRIGGIN' BLOOD--! HE BURST OPEN, MAN! LOOK AT ME! I'M COVERED IN HIS FRIGGIN' BLOOD!
HE'S SPREAD ALL OVER THE STREET OUT THERE!
WELL, WILL YOU FOR JESUS' SAKE GET THE HELL OUT'VE HERE! YOU'RE DRIPPIN' THAT SHITE ALL OVER THE PLACE!
LIKE A MELON LIKE A FRIGGIN' MELON FOR CHRIST'S SAKE--
PARD.
...SO MAKE YOUR CHOICE.
THAT'S THE AMERICAN WAY.

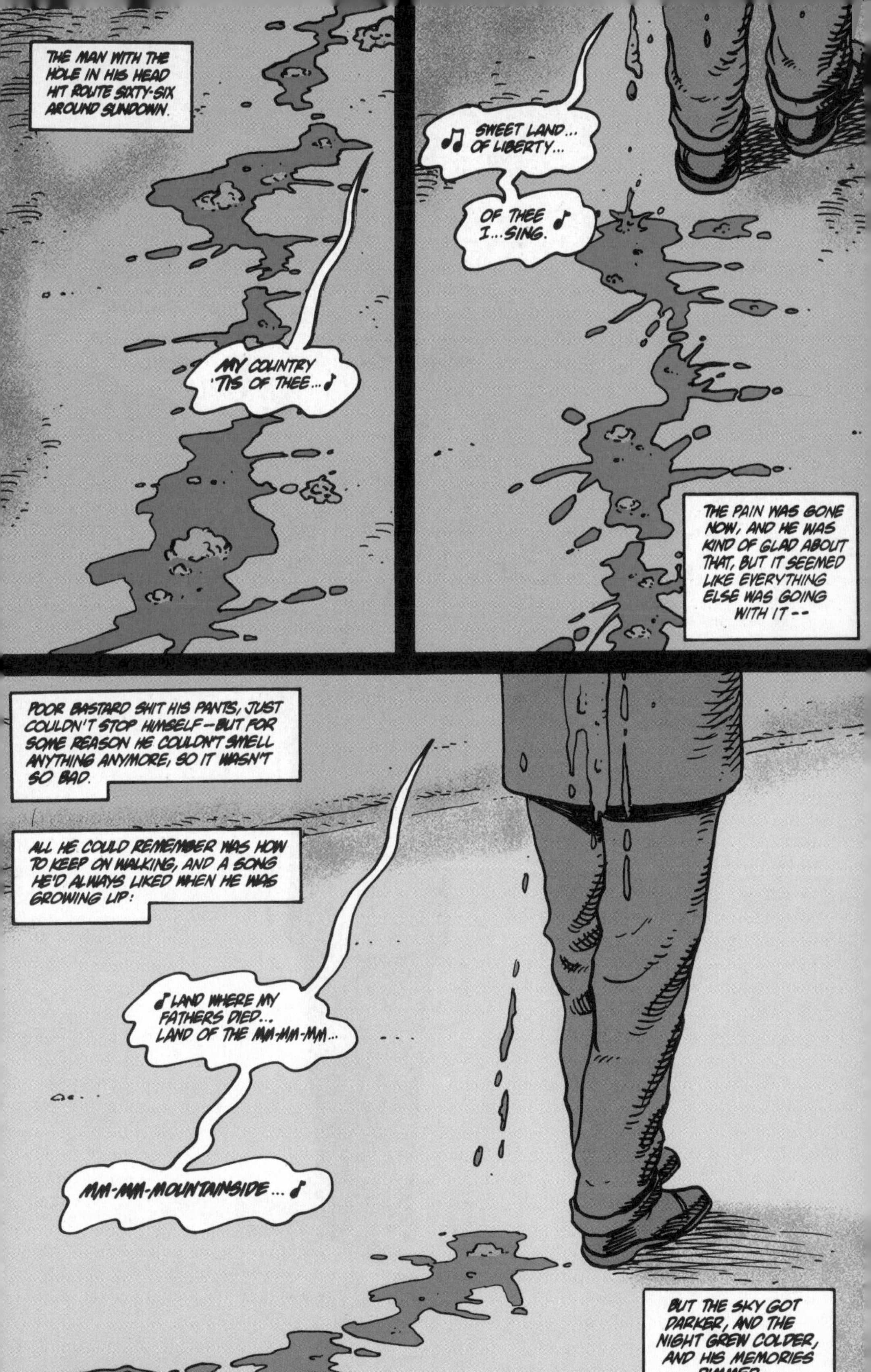
THE MAN WITH THE HOLE IN HIS HEAD HIT ROUTE SIXTY-SIX AROUND SUNDOWN.
MY COUNTRY 'TIS OF THEE... ♪
♫ SWEET LAND... OF LIBERTY...
OF THEE I... SING. ♪
THE PAIN WAS GONE NOW, AND HE WAS KIND OF GLAD ABOUT THAT, BUT IT SEEMED LIKE EVERYTHING ELSE WAS GOING WITH IT --
POOR BASTARD SHIT HIS PANTS, JUST COULDN'T STOP HIMSELF--BUT FOR SOME REASON HE COULDN'T SMELL ANYTHING ANYMORE, SO IT WASN'T SO BAD.
ALL HE COULD REMEMBER WAS HOW TO KEEP ON WALKING, AND A SONG HE'D ALWAYS LIKED WHEN HE WAS GROWING UP:
♪ LAND WHERE MY FATHERS DIED... LAND OF THE MM-MM-MM...
MM-MM-MOUNTAINSIDE... ♪
BUT THE SKY GOT DARKER, AND THE NIGHT GREW COLDER, AND HIS MEMORIES DIMMED...

...AND AFTER A WHILE HE FORGOT THE WORDS.
♪MMM...HMM...HMM...HMM... HMMM.
THE END

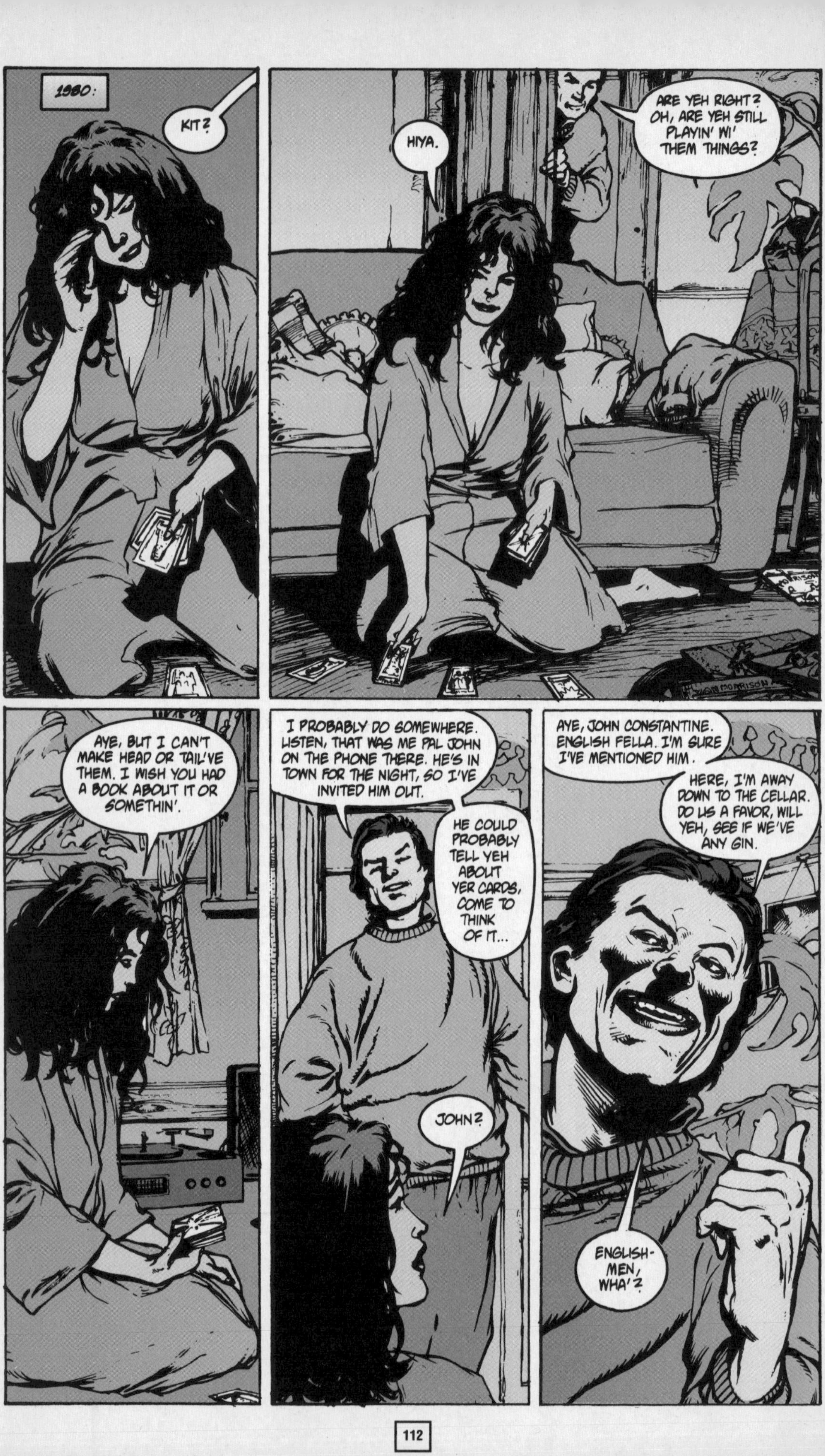
1980:
KIT?
HIYA.
ARE YEH RIGHT? OH, ARE YEH STILL PLAYIN' WI' THEM THINGS?
AYE, BUT I CAN'T MAKE HEAD OR TAIL'VE THEM. I WISH YOU HAD A BOOK ABOUT IT OR SOMETHIN'.
I PROBABLY DO SOMEWHERE. LISTEN, THAT WAS ME PAL JOHN ON THE PHONE THERE. HE'S IN TOWN FOR THE NIGHT, SO I'VE INVITED HIM OUT.
HE COULD PROBABLY TELL YEH ABOUT YER CARDS, COME TO THINK OF IT...
JOHN?
AYE, JOHN CONSTANTINE. ENGLISH FELLA. I'M SURE I'VE MENTIONED HIM.
HERE, I'M AWAY DOWN TO THE CELLAR. DO US A FAVOR, WILL YEH, SEE IF WE'VE ANY GIN.
ENGLISH-MEN, WHA'?

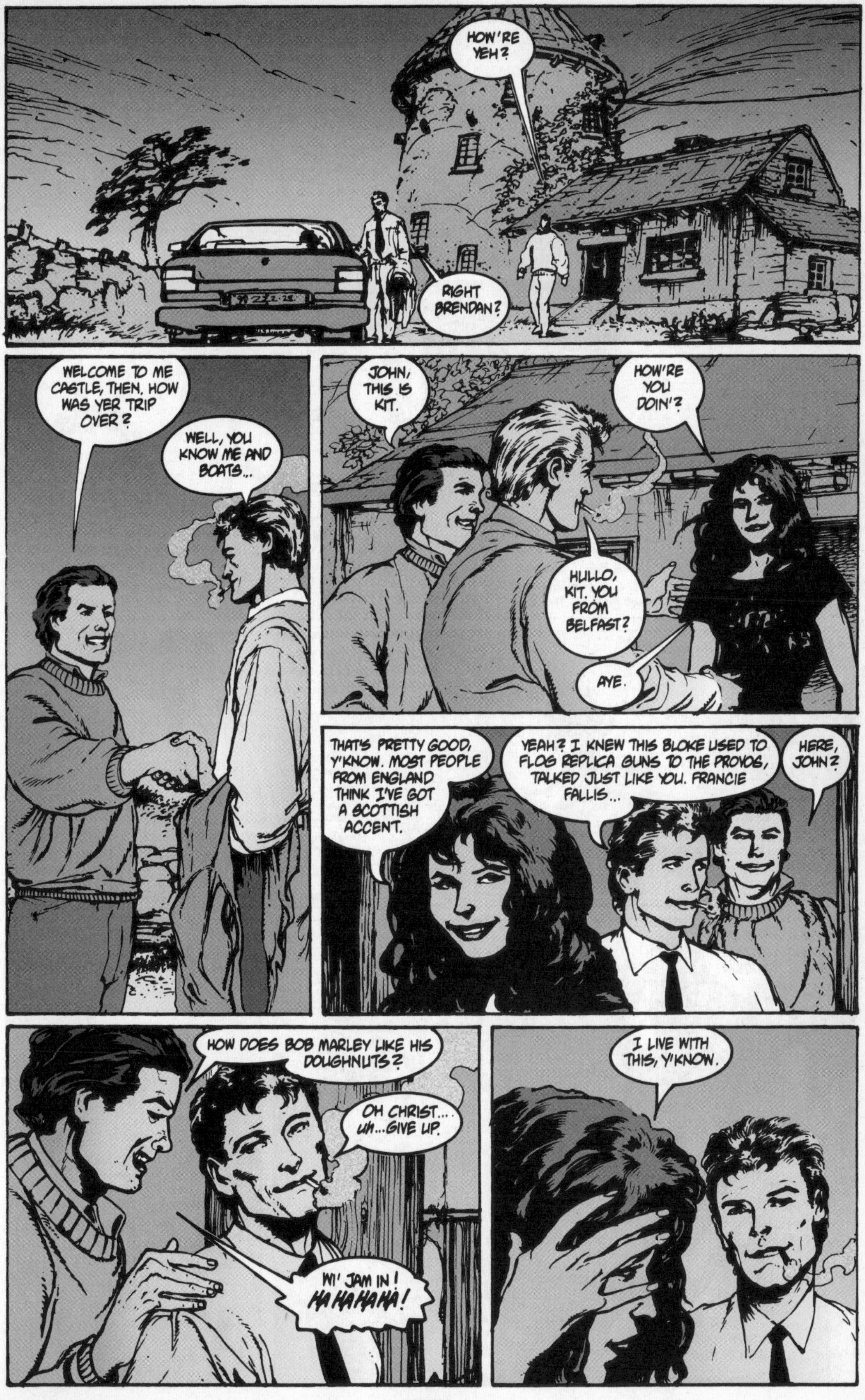
HOW'RE YEH?
RIGHT BRENDAN?
WELCOME TO ME CASTLE, THEN. HOW WAS YER TRIP OVER?
WELL, YOU KNOW ME AND BOATS...
JOHN, THIS IS KIT.
HOW'RE YOU DOIN'?
HULLO, KIT. YOU FROM BELFAST?
AYE.
THAT'S PRETTY GOOD, Y'KNOW. MOST PEOPLE FROM ENGLAND THINK I'VE GOT A SCOTTISH ACCENT.
YEAH? I KNEW THIS BLOKE USED TO FLOG REPLICA GUNS TO THE PROVOS, TALKED JUST LIKE YOU. FRANCIE FALLIS...
HERE, JOHN?
HOW DOES BOB MARLEY LIKE HIS DOUGHNUTS?
OH CHRIST.... uh...GIVE UP.
WI' JAM IN! HA HA HA HA!
I LIVE WITH THIS, Y'KNOW.

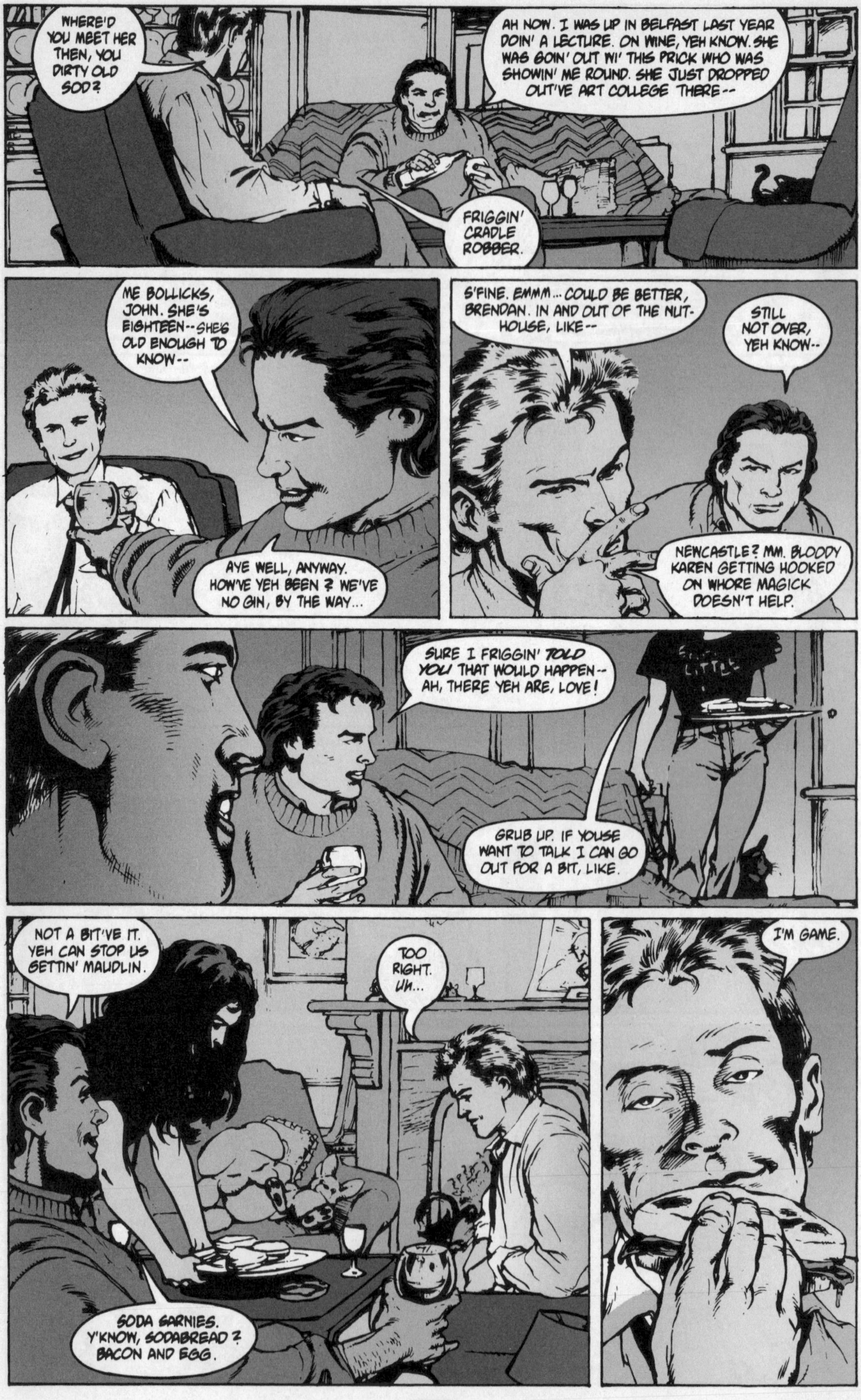
WHERE'D YOU MEET HER THEN, YOU DIRTY OLD SOD?
AH NOW. I WAS UP IN BELFAST LAST YEAR DOIN' A LECTURE. ON WINE, YEH KNOW. SHE WAS GOIN' OUT WI' THIS PRICK WHO WAS SHOWIN' ME ROUND. SHE JUST DROPPED OUT'VE ART COLLEGE THERE--
FRIGGIN' CRADLE ROBBER.
ME BOLLICKS, JOHN. SHE'S EIGHTEEN--SHE'S OLD ENOUGH TO KNOW--
AYE WELL, ANYWAY. HOW'VE YEH BEEN? WE'VE NO GIN, BY THE WAY...
S'FINE. EMMM... COULD BE BETTER, BRENDAN. IN AND OUT OF THE NUT-HOUSE, LIKE--
STILL NOT OVER, YEH KNOW--
NEWCASTLE? MM. BLOODY KAREN GETTING HOOKED ON WHORE MAGICK DOESN'T HELP.
SURE I FRIGGIN' *TOLD YOU* THAT WOULD HAPPEN-- AH, THERE YEH ARE, LOVE!
GRUB UP. IF YOUSE WANT TO TALK I CAN GO OUT FOR A BIT, LIKE.
NOT A BIT'VE IT. YEH CAN STOP US GETTIN' MAUDLIN.
TOO RIGHT. UH...
SODA GARNIES. Y'KNOW, SODABREAD? BACON AND EGG.
I'M GAME.

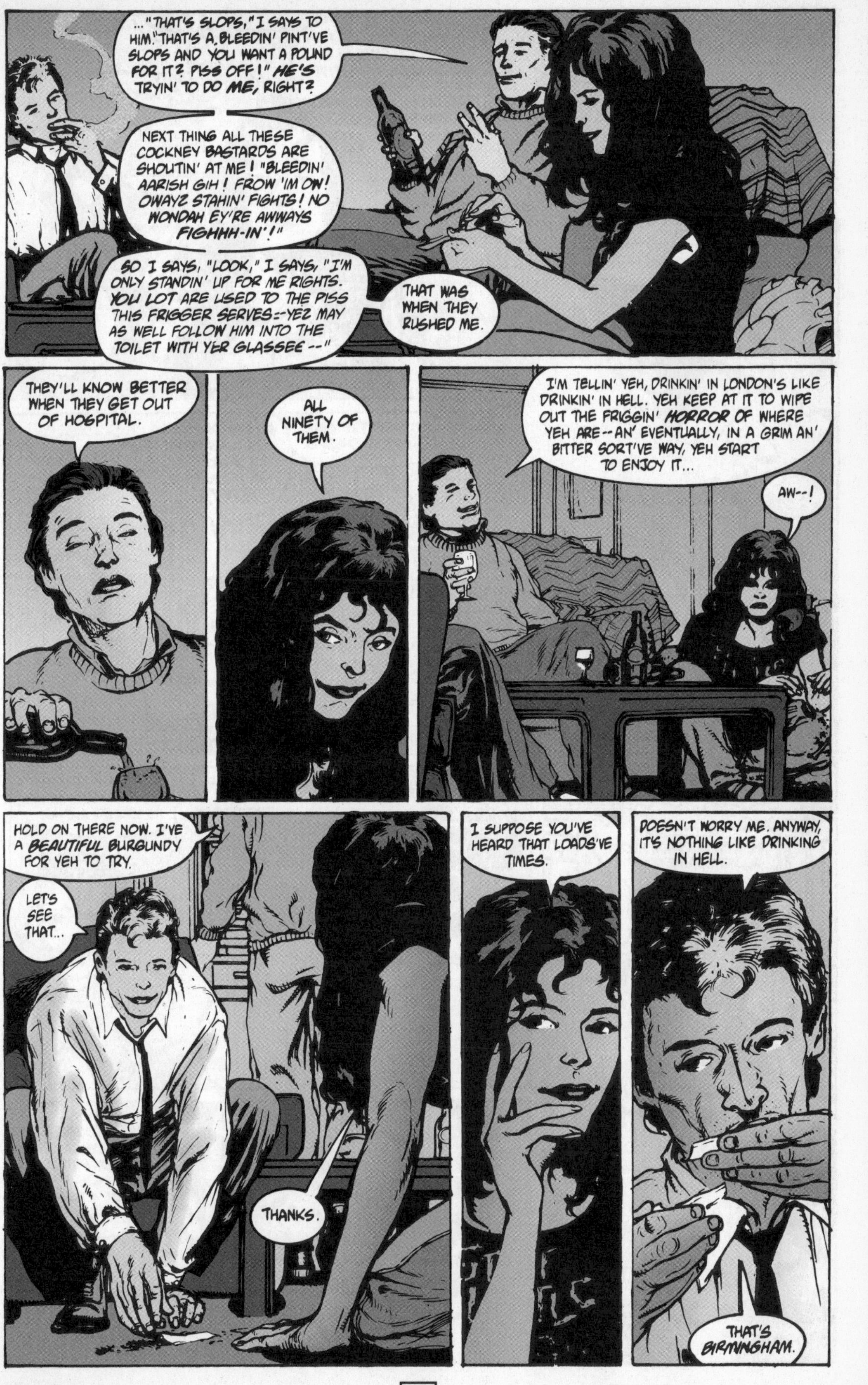

..."THAT'S SLOPS," I SAYS TO HIM."THAT'S A BLEEDIN' PINT'VE SLOPS AND YOU WANT A POUND FOR IT? PISS OFF!" HE'S TRYIN' TO DO ME, RIGHT?
NEXT THING ALL THESE COCKNEY BASTARDS ARE SHOUTIN' AT ME! "BLEEDIN' AARISH GIH! FROW 'IM OW! OWAYZ STAHIN' FIGHTS! NO WONDAH EY'RE AWWAYS FIGHHH-IN'!"
SO I SAYS, "LOOK," I SAYS, "I'M ONLY STANDIN' UP FOR ME RIGHTS. YOU LOT ARE USED TO THE PISS THIS FRIGGER SERVES:-YEZ MAY AS WELL FOLLOW HIM INTO THE TOILET WITH YER GLASSES--"
THAT WAS WHEN THEY RUSHED ME.
THEY'LL KNOW BETTER WHEN THEY GET OUT OF HOSPITAL.
ALL NINETY OF THEM.
I'M TELLIN' YEH, DRINKIN' IN LONDON'S LIKE DRINKIN' IN HELL. YEH KEEP AT IT TO WIPE OUT THE FRIGGIN' HORROR OF WHERE YEH ARE--AN' EVENTUALLY, IN A GRIM AN' BITTER SORT'VE WAY, YEH START TO ENJOY IT...
AW--!
HOLD ON THERE NOW. I'VE A BEAUTIFUL BURGUNDY FOR YEH TO TRY.
LET'S SEE THAT...
THANKS.
I SUPPOSE YOU'VE HEARD THAT LOADS'VE TIMES.
DOESN'T WORRY ME. ANYWAY, IT'S NOTHING LIKE DRINKING IN HELL.
THAT'S BIRMINGHAM.

AH! SMOKIN' THE EVIL WEED!

I BROUGHT A CASE'VE STOUT UP TOO. VARIETY'S THE SPICE'VE LIFE, WHA'Z

"HERE YEH ARE, MR. FINN. YER BLOOD TYPE IS O GUINNESS POSITIVE. YE'RE A UNIVERSAL RECIPIENT." UNIVERSAL AN' THEN SOME...

PHFFFFFOW WOULD YOU KNOW? YOU DRINK NOTHIN' ELSE, SURE.

HAVE MERCY ON A POOR OLD MAN, WILL YEH?

AH, I SORT'VE GAVE UP--SOD IT. CHEERS.

SO BRENDAN SAID YOU KNEW ABOUT THE TAROT-- AN' BRENDAN, DON'T!

HMFOOHH--

HE WENT TO GIVE BLOOD LAST WEEK, JOHN. THEY TOOK HALF A PINT OUT'VE HIM AND IT HAD A HEAD ON IT.

WHCCCHTT--TOOOFT!

BETTER OUT THAN IN. AYE, YEH KNOW ABOUT ALL THAT STUFF, DON'T YEH?

A BIT. IT'S ALL DOWN TO INTERPRETATION--

IN OTHER WORDS IT'S DOWN TO MAKIN' IT UP AS YOU GO ALONG.

I HAD THIS MATE'VE MINE USED TO DO PEOPLE'S CARDS ON GRAFTON STREET-- YEH KNOW, FOR TWENTY PEE? SO ONE DAY...

116

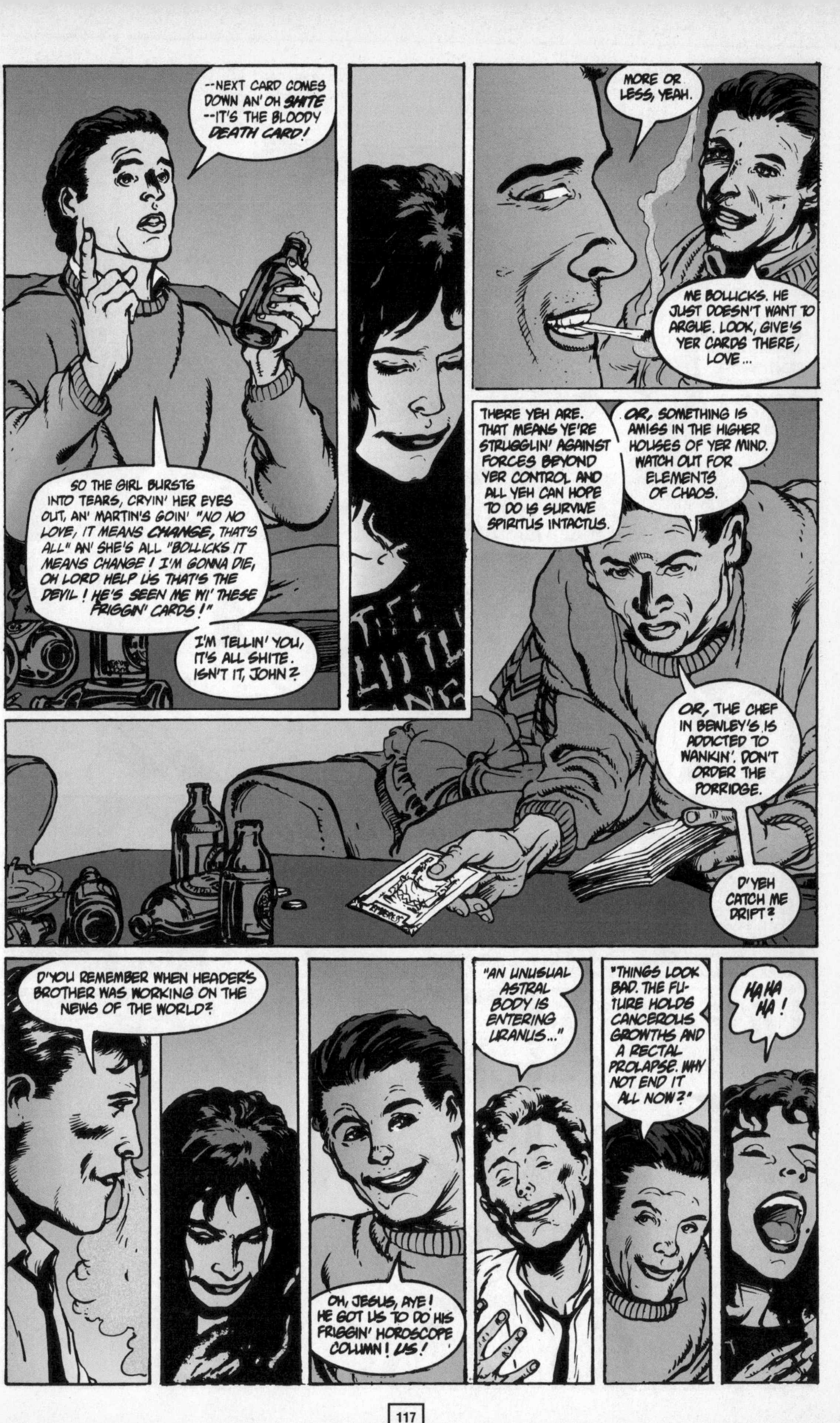
--NEXT CARD COMES DOWN AN' OH SHITE --IT'S THE BLOODY DEATH CARD!
SO THE GIRL BURSTS INTO TEARS, CRYIN' HER EYES OUT, AN' MARTIN'S GOIN' "NO NO LOVE, IT MEANS CHANGE, THAT'S ALL" AN' SHE'S ALL "BOLLICKS IT MEANS CHANGE! I'M GONNA DIE, OH LORD HELP US THAT'S THE DEVIL! HE'S SEEN ME WI' THESE FRIGGIN' CARDS!"
I'M TELLIN' YOU, IT'S ALL SHITE. ISN'T IT, JOHN?
MORE OR LESS, YEAH.
ME BOLLICKS. HE JUST DOESN'T WANT TO ARGUE. LOOK, GIVE'S YER CARDS THERE, LOVE...
THERE YEH ARE. THAT MEANS YE'RE STRUGGLIN' AGAINST FORCES BEYOND YER CONTROL AND ALL YEH CAN HOPE TO DO IS SURVIVE SPIRITUS INTACTUS.
OR, SOMETHING IS AMISS IN THE HIGHER HOUSES OF YER MIND. WATCH OUT FOR ELEMENTS OF CHAOS.
OR, THE CHEF IN BEWLEY'S IS ADDICTED TO WANKIN'. DON'T ORDER THE PORRIDGE.
D'YEH CATCH ME DRIFT?
D'YOU REMEMBER WHEN HEADER'S BROTHER WAS WORKING ON THE NEWS OF THE WORLD?
OH, JESUS, AYE! HE GOT US TO DO HIS FRIGGIN' HOROSCOPE COLUMN! US!
"AN UNUSUAL ASTRAL BODY IS ENTERING URANUS..."
"THINGS LOOK BAD. THE FUTURE HOLDS CANCEROUS GROWTHS AND A RECTAL PROLAPSE. WHY NOT END IT ALL NOW?"
HA HA HA!

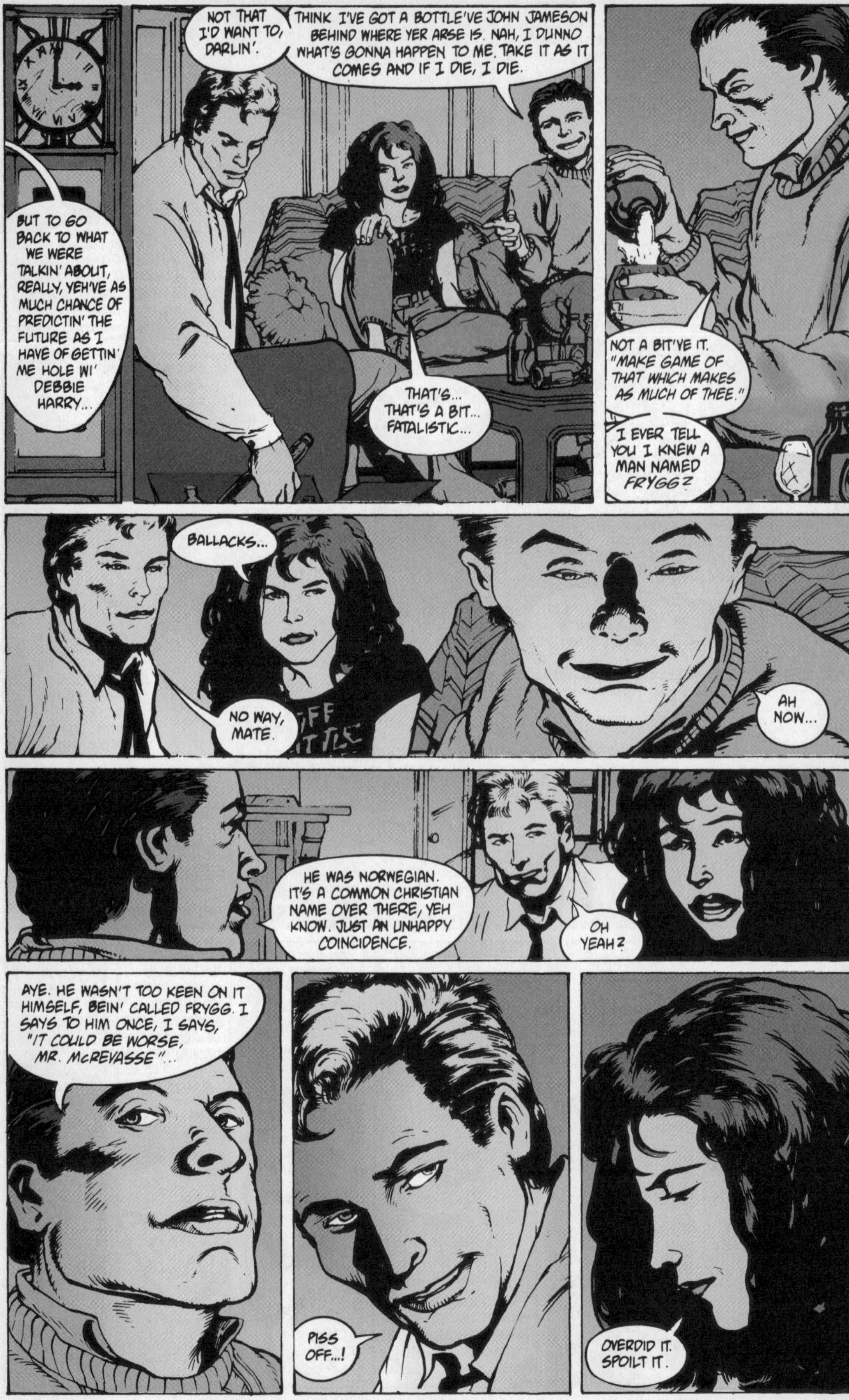

NOT THAT I'D WANT TO, DARLIN'.
BUT TO GO BACK TO WHAT WE WERE TALKIN' ABOUT, REALLY, YEH'VE AS MUCH CHANCE OF PREDICTIN' THE FUTURE AS I HAVE OF GETTIN' ME HOLE WI' DEBBIE HARRY...
THINK I'VE GOT A BOTTLE'VE JOHN JAMESON BEHIND WHERE YER ARSE IS. NAH, I DUNNO WHAT'S GONNA HAPPEN TO ME. TAKE IT AS IT COMES AND IF I DIE, I DIE.
THAT'S... THAT'S A BIT... FATALISTIC...
NOT A BIT'VE IT. "MAKE GAME OF THAT WHICH MAKES AS MUCH OF THEE."
I EVER TELL YOU I KNEW A MAN NAMED FRYGG?
BALLACKS...
NO WAY, MATE.
AH NOW...
HE WAS NORWEGIAN. IT'S A COMMON CHRISTIAN NAME OVER THERE, YEH KNOW. JUST AN UNHAPPY COINCIDENCE.
OH YEAH?
AYE. HE WASN'T TOO KEEN ON IT HIMSELF, BEIN' CALLED FRYGG. I SAYS TO HIM ONCE, I SAYS, "IT COULD BE WORSE, MR. McREVASSE"...
PISS OFF...!
OVERDID IT. SPOILT IT.

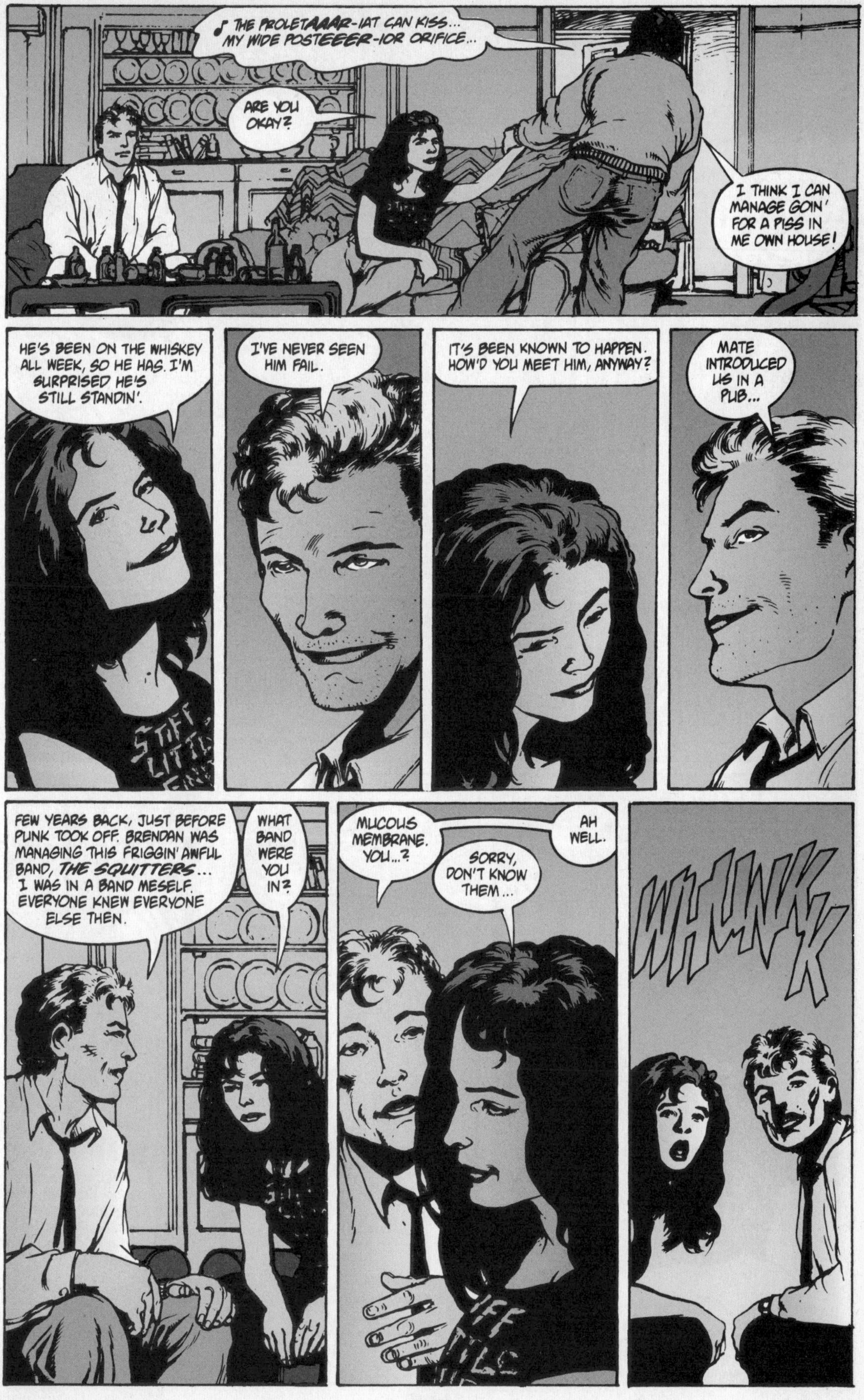

♪ THE PROLETAAAR-IAT CAN KISS... MY WIDE POSTEEEER-IOR ORIFICE...
ARE YOU OKAY?
I THINK I CAN MANAGE GOIN' FOR A PISS IN ME OWN HOUSE!
HE'S BEEN ON THE WHISKEY ALL WEEK, SO HE HAS. I'M SURPRISED HE'S STILL STANDIN'.
I'VE NEVER SEEN HIM FAIL.
IT'S BEEN KNOWN TO HAPPEN. HOW'D YOU MEET HIM, ANYWAY?
MATE INTRODUCED US IN A PUB...
FEW YEARS BACK, JUST BEFORE PUNK TOOK OFF. BRENDAN WAS MANAGING THIS FRIGGIN' AWFUL BAND, THE SQUITTERS... I WAS IN A BAND MESELF. EVERYONE KNEW EVERYONE ELSE THEN.
WHAT BAND WERE YOU IN?
MUCOUS MEMBRANE. YOU...?
AH WELL.
SORRY, DON'T KNOW THEM...
WHUNK

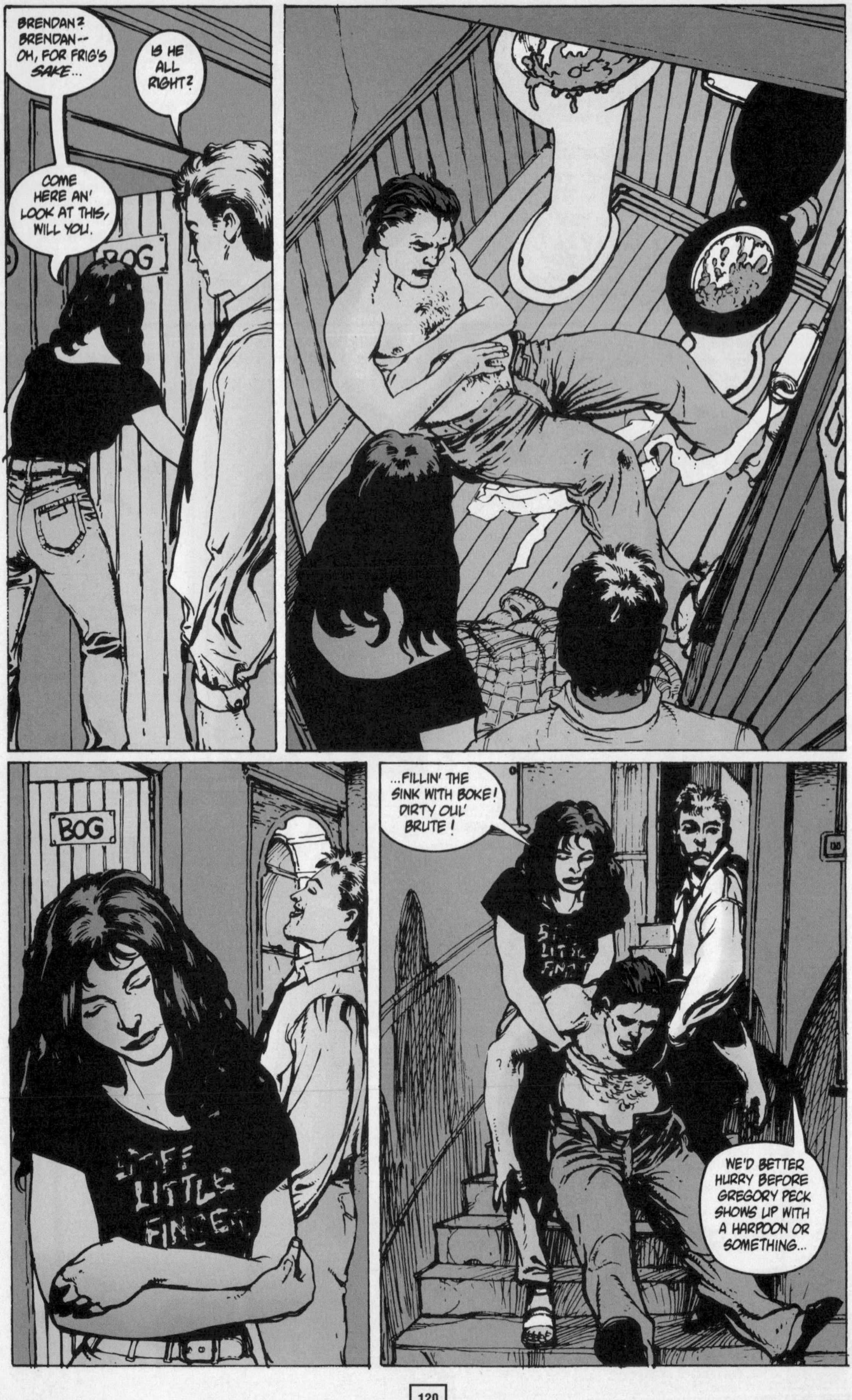
BRENDAN? BRENDAN-- OH, FOR FRIG'S SAKE...
IS HE ALL RIGHT?
COME HERE AN' LOOK AT THIS, WILL YOU.
BOG
BOG
...FILLIN' THE SINK WITH BOKE! DIRTY OUL' BRUTE!
WE'D BETTER HURRY BEFORE GREGORY PECK SHOWS UP WITH A HARPOON OR SOMETHING...

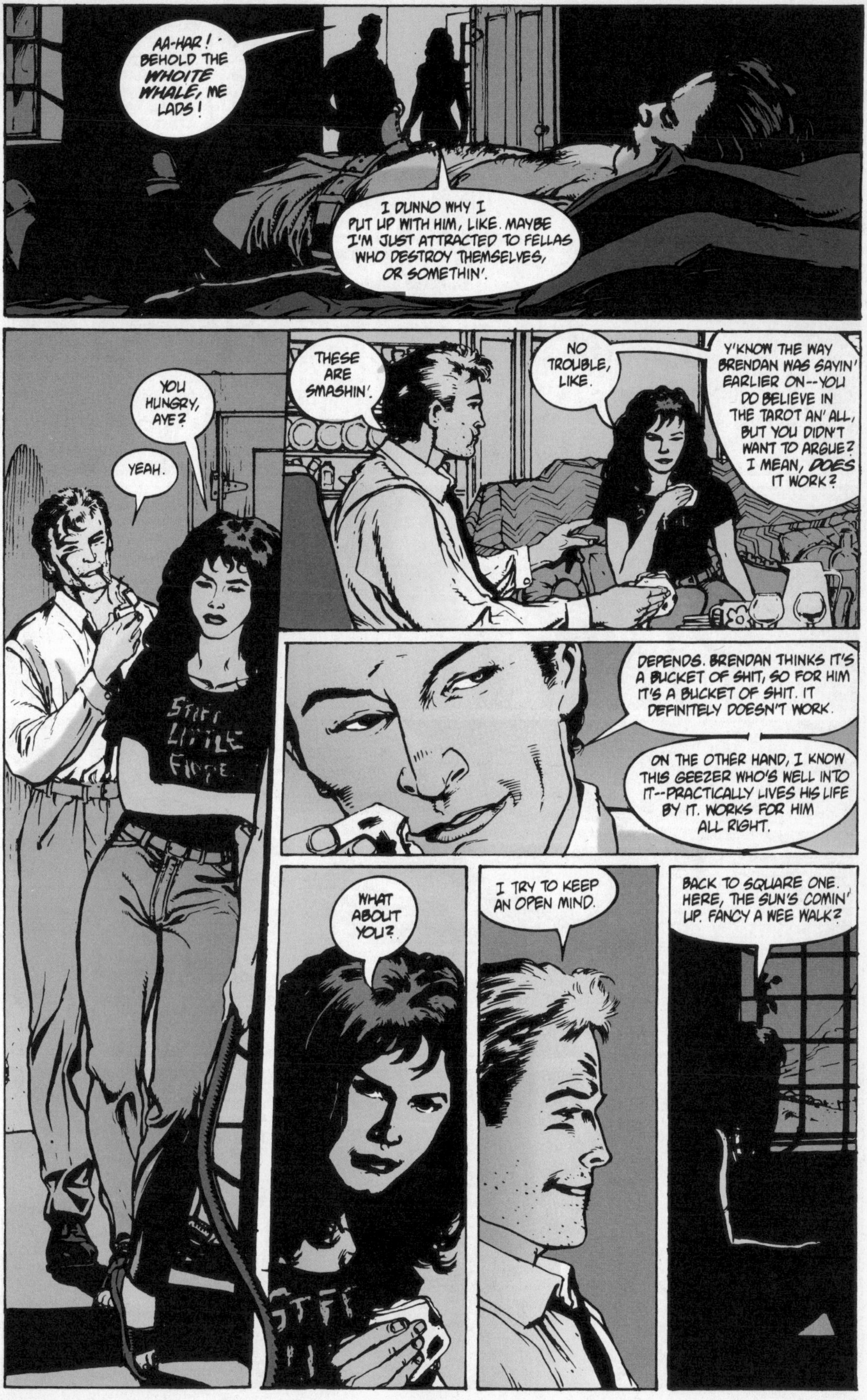
AA-HAR! BEHOLD THE WHOITE WHALE, ME LADS!
I DUNNO WHY I PUT UP WITH HIM, LIKE. MAYBE I'M JUST ATTRACTED TO FELLAS WHO DESTROY THEMSELVES, OR SOMETHIN'.
YOU HUNGRY, AYE?
YEAH.
STIFF LITTLE FINGERS
THESE ARE SMASHIN'.
NO TROUBLE, LIKE.
Y'KNOW THE WAY BRENDAN WAS SAYIN' EARLIER ON--YOU DO BELIEVE IN THE TAROT AN' ALL, BUT YOU DIDN'T WANT TO ARGUE? I MEAN, DOES IT WORK?
DEPENDS. BRENDAN THINKS IT'S A BUCKET OF SHIT, SO FOR HIM IT'S A BUCKET OF SHIT. IT DEFINITELY DOESN'T WORK.
ON THE OTHER HAND, I KNOW THIS GEEZER WHO'S WELL INTO IT--PRACTICALLY LIVES HIS LIFE BY IT. WORKS FOR HIM ALL RIGHT.
WHAT ABOUT YOU?
I TRY TO KEEP AN OPEN MIND.
BACK TO SQUARE ONE. HERE, THE SUN'S COMIN' UP. FANCY A WEE WALK?

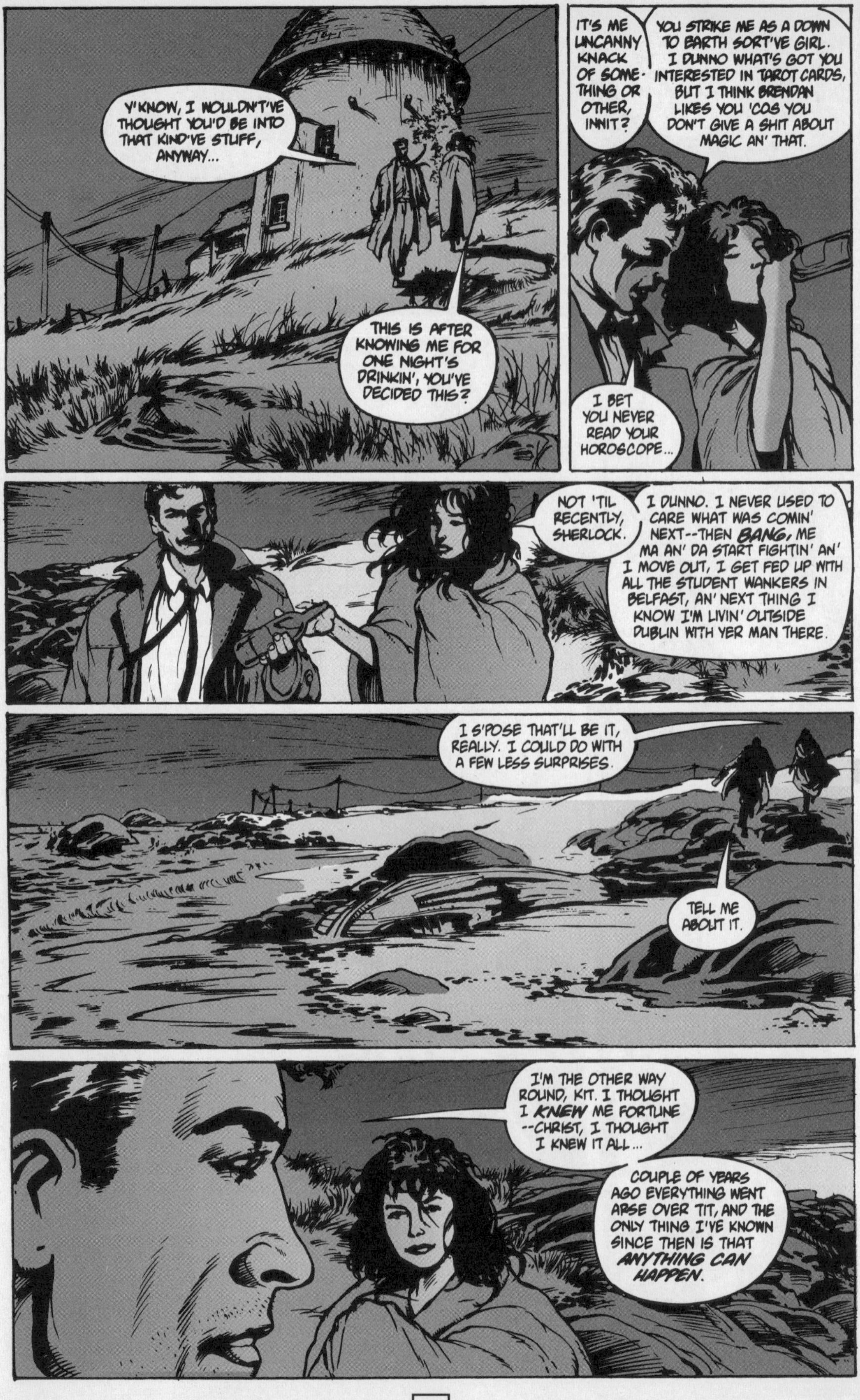

Y'KNOW, I WOULDN'T'VE THOUGHT YOU'D BE INTO THAT KIND'VE STUFF, ANYWAY...
THIS IS AFTER KNOWING ME FOR ONE NIGHT'S DRINKIN', YOU'VE DECIDED THIS?
IT'S ME UNCANNY KNACK OF SOME-THING OR OTHER, INNIT?
YOU STRIKE ME AS A DOWN TO EARTH SORT'VE GIRL. I DUNNO WHAT'S GOT YOU INTERESTED IN TAROT CARDS, BUT I THINK BRENDAN LIKES YOU 'COS YOU DON'T GIVE A SHIT ABOUT MAGIC AN' THAT.
I BET YOU NEVER READ YOUR HOROSCOPE...
NOT 'TIL RECENTLY, SHERLOCK.
I DUNNO. I NEVER USED TO CARE WHAT WAS COMIN' NEXT--THEN BANG, ME MA AN' DA START FIGHTIN' AN' I MOVE OUT, I GET FED UP WITH ALL THE STUDENT WANKERS IN BELFAST, AN' NEXT THING I KNOW I'M LIVIN' OUTSIDE DUBLIN WITH YER MAN THERE.
I S'POSE THAT'LL BE IT, REALLY. I COULD DO WITH A FEW LESS SURPRISES.
TELL ME ABOUT IT.
I'M THE OTHER WAY ROUND, KIT. I THOUGHT I KNEW ME FORTUNE --CHRIST, I THOUGHT I KNEW IT ALL...
COUPLE OF YEARS AGO EVERYTHING WENT ARSE OVER TIT, AND THE ONLY THING I'VE KNOWN SINCE THEN IS THAT ANYTHING CAN HAPPEN.

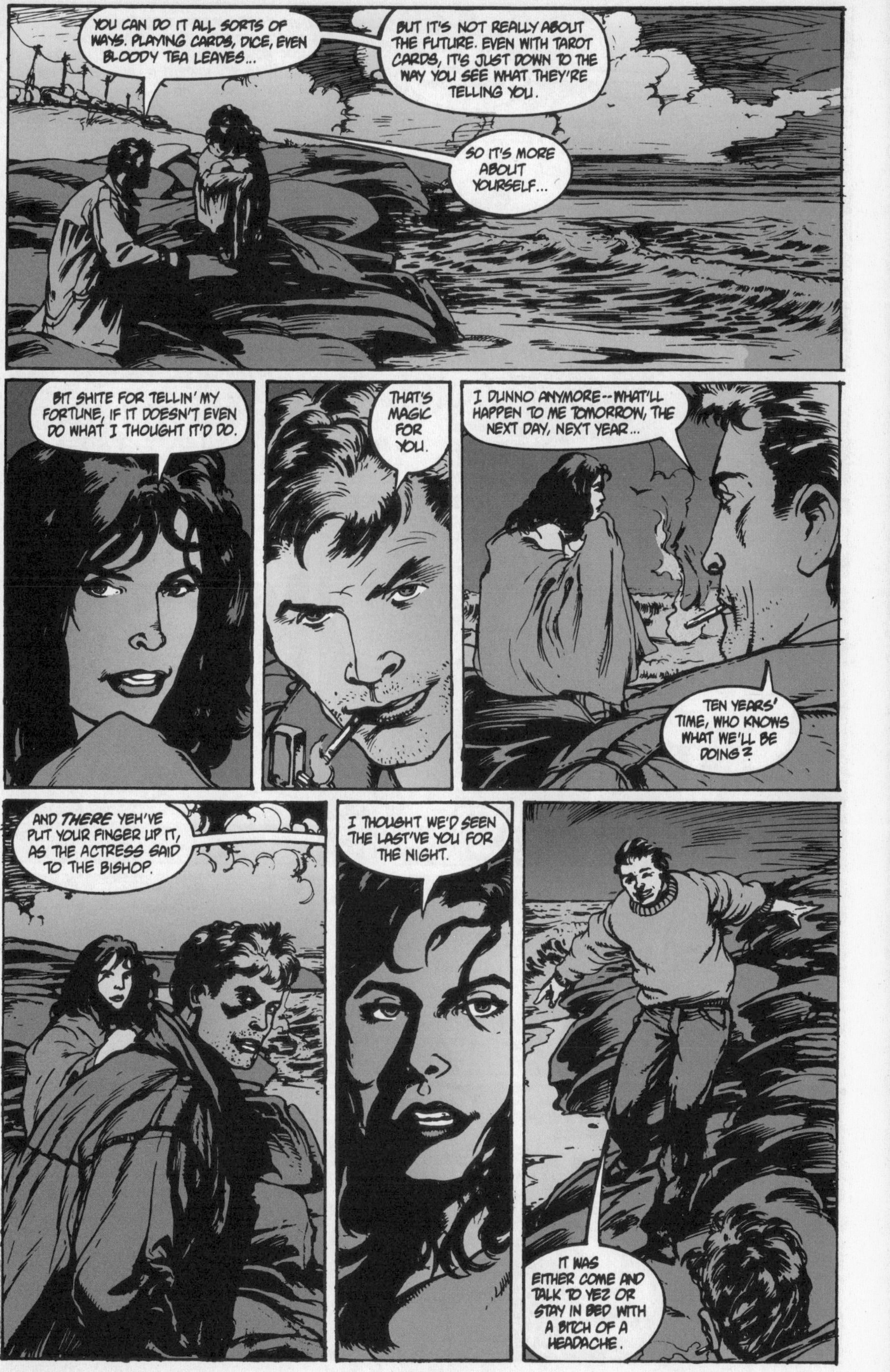
YOU CAN DO IT ALL SORTS OF WAYS. PLAYING CARDS, DICE, EVEN BLOODY TEA LEAVES...
BUT IT'S NOT REALLY ABOUT THE FUTURE. EVEN WITH TAROT CARDS, IT'S JUST DOWN TO THE WAY YOU SEE WHAT THEY'RE TELLING YOU.
SO IT'S MORE ABOUT YOURSELF...
BIT SHITE FOR TELLIN' MY FORTUNE, IF IT DOESN'T EVEN DO WHAT I THOUGHT IT'D DO.
THAT'S MAGIC FOR YOU.
I DUNNO ANYMORE--WHAT'LL HAPPEN TO ME TOMORROW, THE NEXT DAY, NEXT YEAR...
TEN YEARS' TIME, WHO KNOWS WHAT WE'LL BE DOING?
AND THERE YEH'VE PUT YOUR FINGER UP IT, AS THE ACTRESS SAID TO THE BISHOP.
I THOUGHT WE'D SEEN THE LAST'VE YOU FOR THE NIGHT.
IT WAS EITHER COME AND TALK TO YEZ OR STAY IN BED WITH A BITCH OF A HEADACHE.

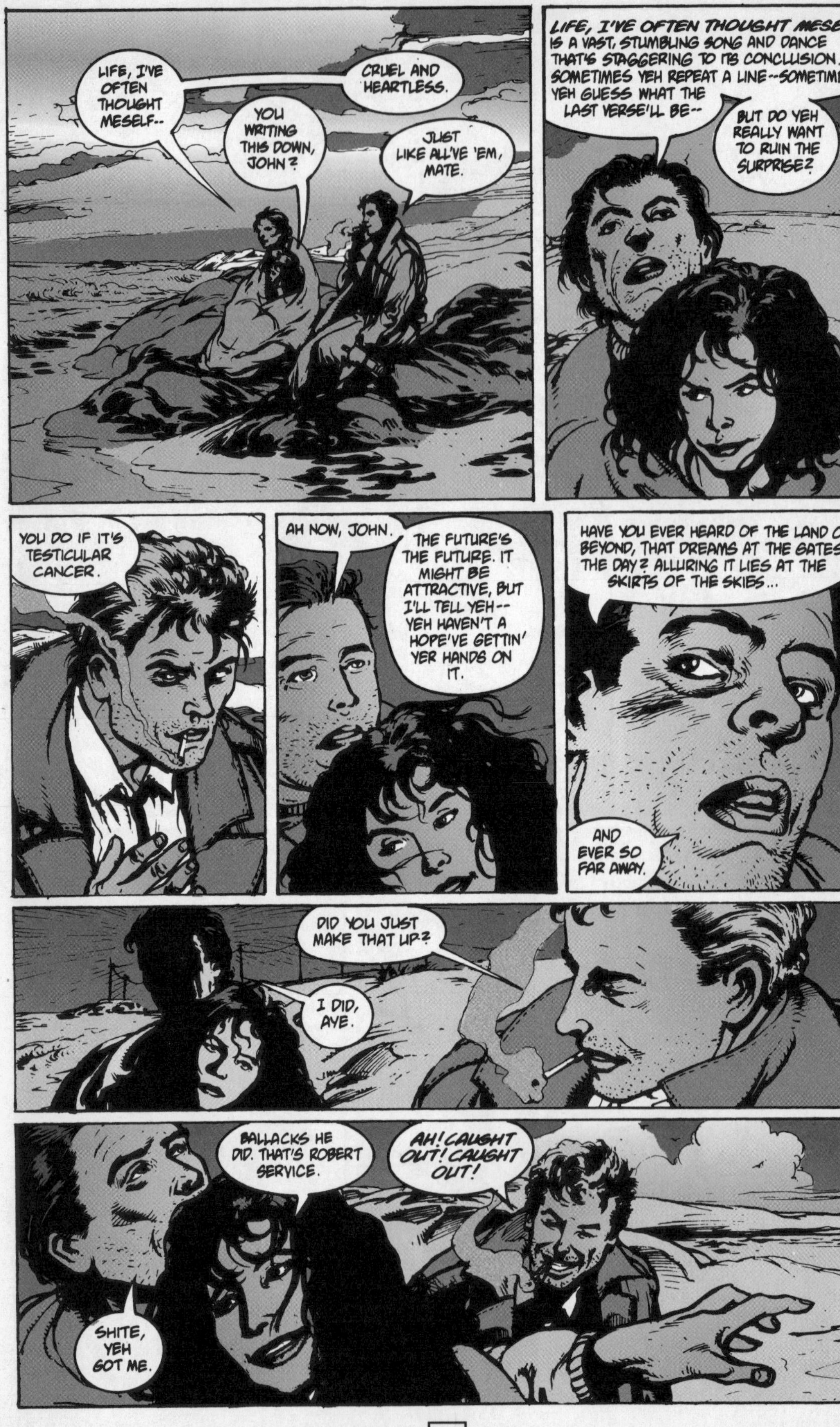
LIFE, I'VE OFTEN THOUGHT MESELF--
YOU WRITING THIS DOWN, JOHN?
CRUEL AND HEARTLESS.
JUST LIKE ALL'VE 'EM, MATE.
LIFE, I'VE OFTEN THOUGHT MESELF, IS A VAST, STUMBLING SONG AND DANCE THAT'S STAGGERING TO ITS CONCLUSION. SOMETIMES YEH REPEAT A LINE--SOMETIMES YEH GUESS WHAT THE LAST VERSE'LL BE--
BUT DO YEH REALLY WANT TO RUIN THE SURPRISE?
YOU DO IF IT'S TESTICULAR CANCER.
AH NOW, JOHN.
THE FUTURE'S THE FUTURE. IT MIGHT BE ATTRACTIVE, BUT I'LL TELL YEH-- YEH HAVEN'T A HOPE'VE GETTIN' YER HANDS ON IT.
HAVE YOU EVER HEARD OF THE LAND OF BEYOND, THAT DREAMS AT THE GATES OF THE DAY? ALLURING IT LIES AT THE SKIRTS OF THE SKIES...
AND EVER SO FAR AWAY.
DID YOU JUST MAKE THAT UP?
I DID, AYE.
BALLACKS HE DID. THAT'S ROBERT SERVICE.
AH! CAUGHT OUT! CAUGHT OUT!
SHITE, YEH GOT ME.

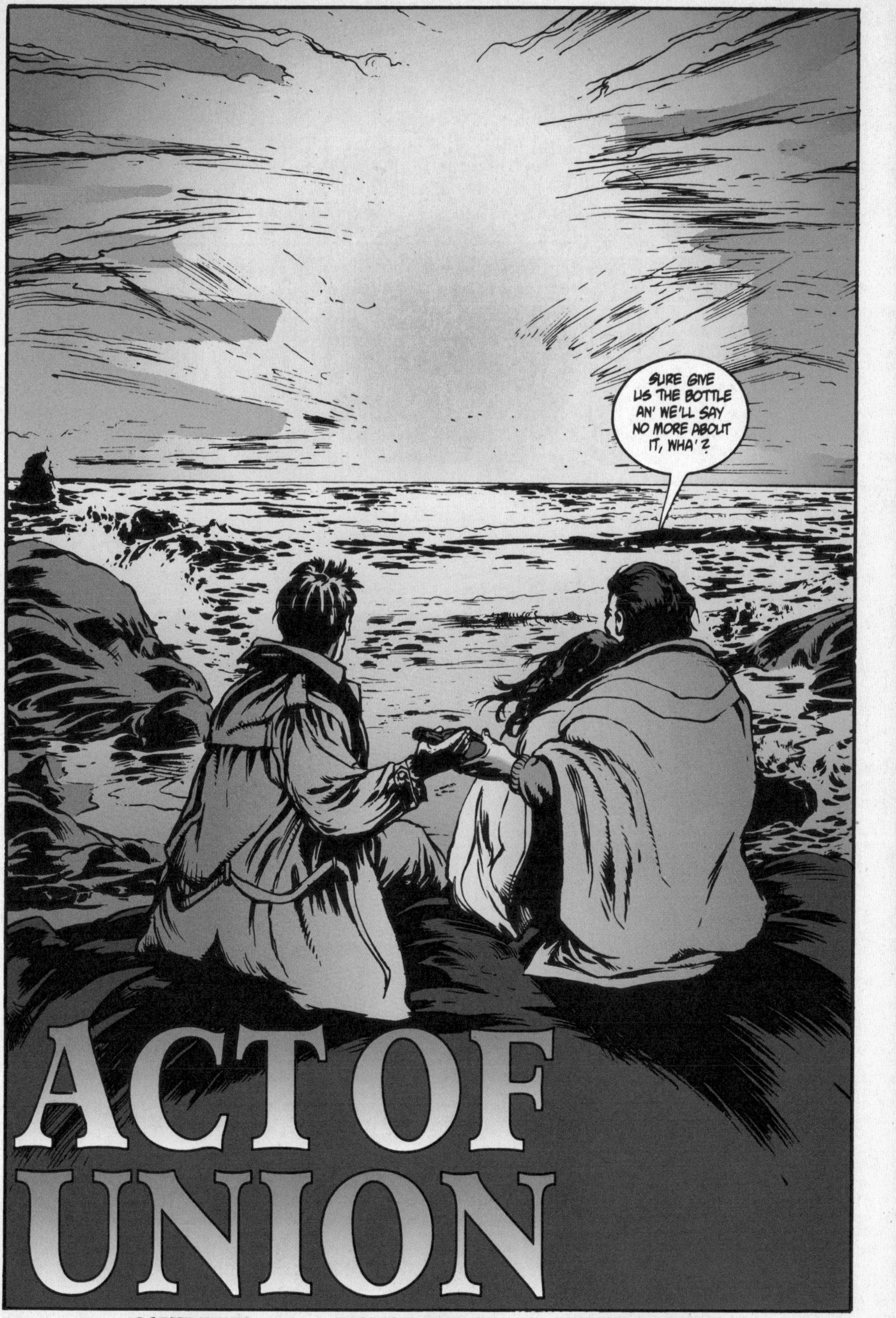
SURE GIVE US THE BOTTLE AN' WE'LL SAY NO MORE ABOUT IT, WHA'?
ACT OF UNION

GARTH ENNIS
writer
CLEM ROBINS
letterer

WILLIAM SIMPSON
artist
JULIE ROTTENBERG
asst. editor

STUART CHAIFETZ
colorist
STUART MOORE
editor

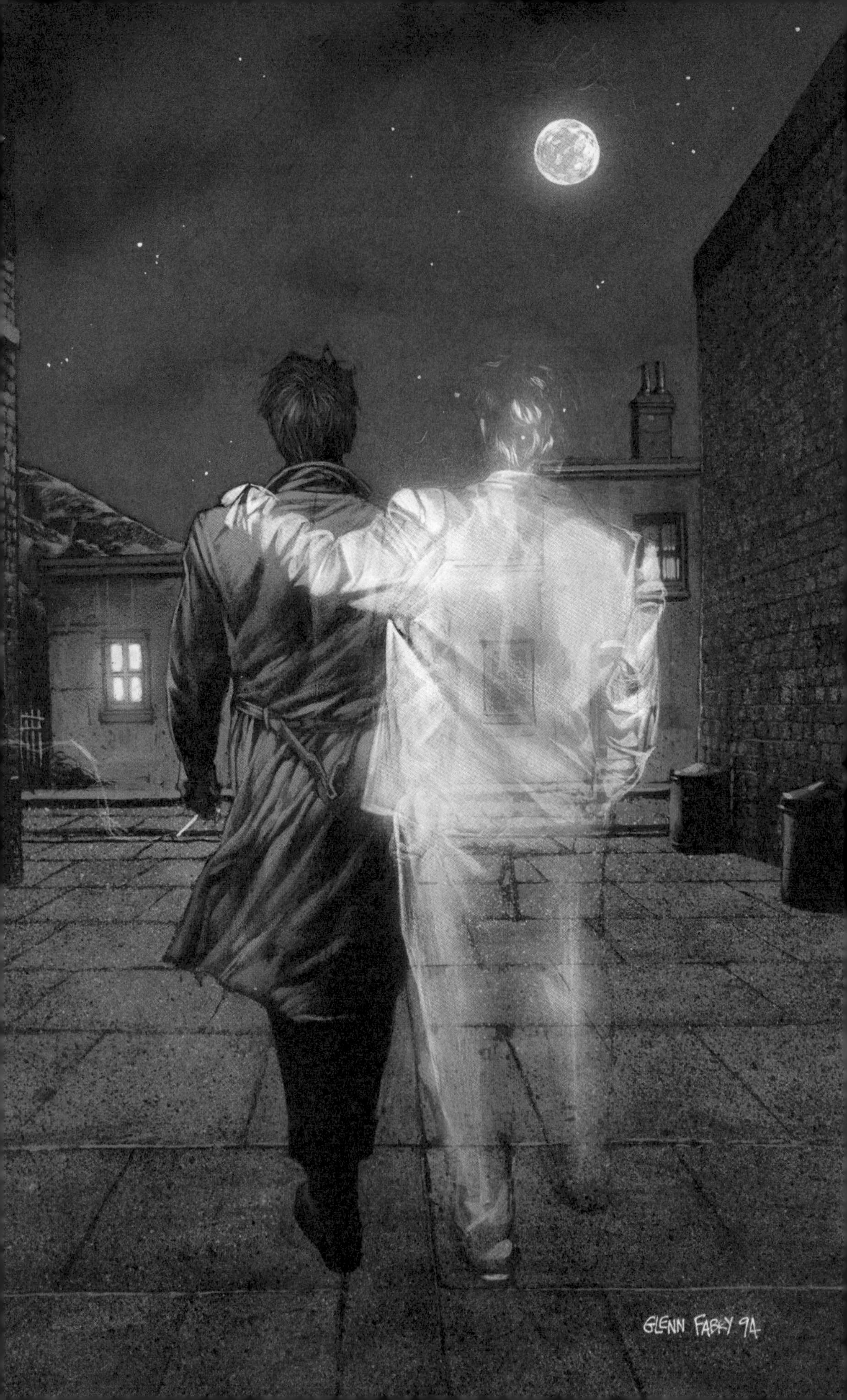
GLENN FABRY 94

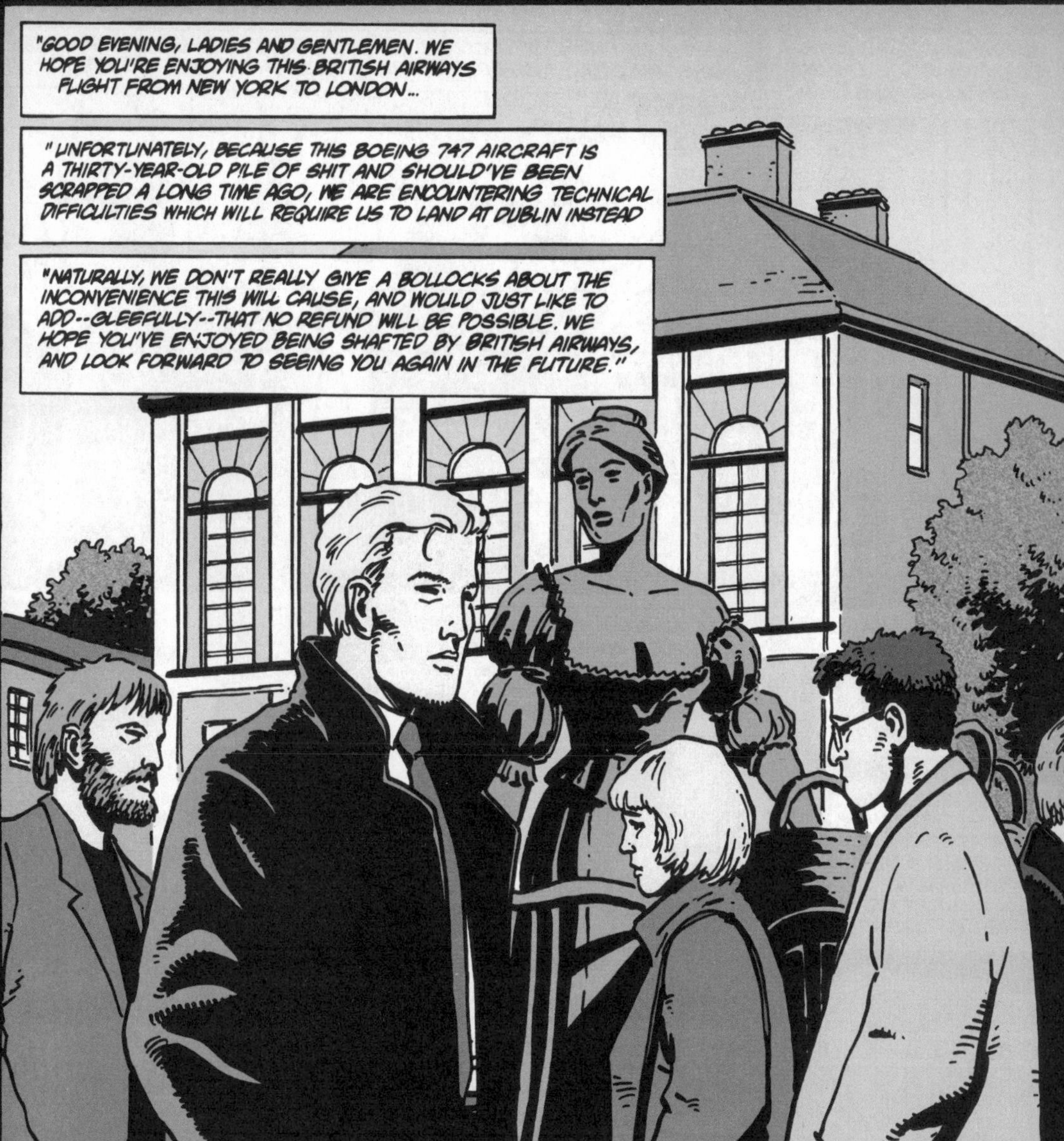
"GOOD EVENING, LADIES AND GENTLEMEN. WE HOPE YOU'RE ENJOYING THIS BRITISH AIRWAYS FLIGHT FROM NEW YORK TO LONDON...
"UNFORTUNATELY, BECAUSE THIS BOEING 747 AIRCRAFT IS A THIRTY-YEAR-OLD PILE OF SHIT AND SHOULD'VE BEEN SCRAPPED A LONG TIME AGO, WE ARE ENCOUNTERING TECHNICAL DIFFICULTIES WHICH WILL REQUIRE US TO LAND AT DUBLIN INSTEAD
"NATURALLY, WE DON'T REALLY GIVE A BOLLOCKS ABOUT THE INCONVENIENCE THIS WILL CAUSE, AND WOULD JUST LIKE TO ADD--GLEEFULLY--THAT NO REFUND WILL BE POSSIBLE. WE HOPE YOU'VE ENJOYED BEING SHAFTED BY BRITISH AIRWAYS, AND LOOK FORWARD TO SEEING YOU AGAIN IN THE FUTURE."
THAT WASN'T EXACTLY WHAT THEY SAID, BUT YOU GET THE IDEA.

CONFESSIONS OF AN IRISH REBEL

GARTH ENNIS • *writer* **STEVE DILLON** • *artist* **TOM ZIUKO** • *colors*
CLEM ROBINS • *letters* **JULIE ROTTENBERG** • *asst. editor* **STUART MOORE** • *editor*

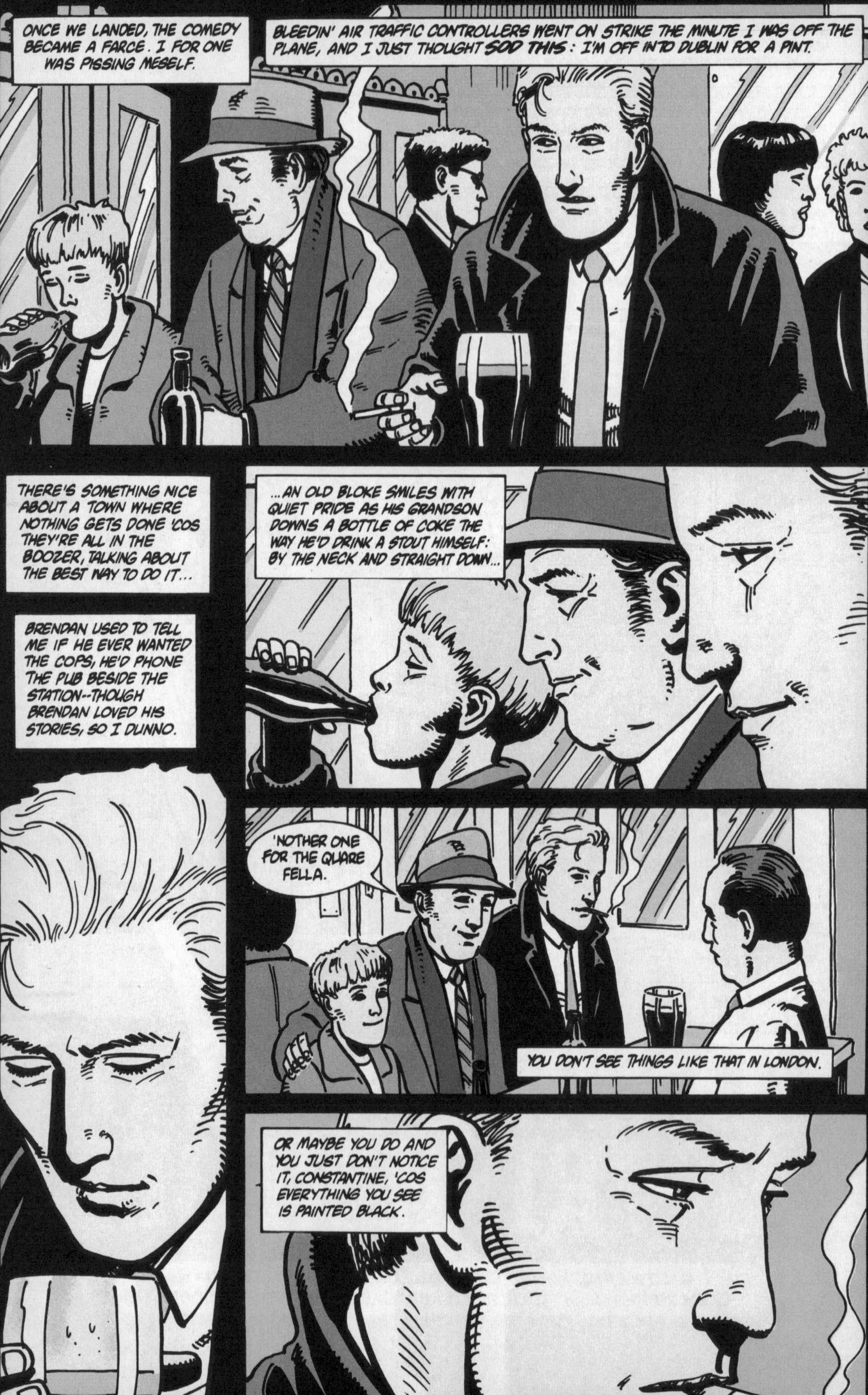

ONCE WE LANDED, THE COMEDY BECAME A FARCE. I FOR ONE WAS PISSING MESELF.
BLEEDIN' AIR TRAFFIC CONTROLLERS WENT ON STRIKE THE MINUTE I WAS OFF THE PLANE, AND I JUST THOUGHT SOD THIS: I'M OFF INTO DUBLIN FOR A PINT.
THERE'S SOMETHING NICE ABOUT A TOWN WHERE NOTHING GETS DONE 'COS THEY'RE ALL IN THE BOOZER, TALKING ABOUT THE BEST WAY TO DO IT...
BRENDAN USED TO TELL ME IF HE EVER WANTED THE COPS, HE'D PHONE THE PUB BESIDE THE STATION--THOUGH BRENDAN LOVED HIS STORIES, SO I DUNNO.
...AN OLD BLOKE SMILES WITH QUIET PRIDE AS HIS GRANDSON DOWNS A BOTTLE OF COKE THE WAY HE'D DRINK A STOUT HIMSELF: BY THE NECK AND STRAIGHT DOWN...
'NOTHER ONE FOR THE QUARE FELLA.
YOU DON'T SEE THINGS LIKE THAT IN LONDON.
OR MAYBE YOU DO AND YOU JUST DON'T NOTICE IT, CONSTANTINE, 'COS EVERYTHING YOU SEE IS PAINTED BLACK.

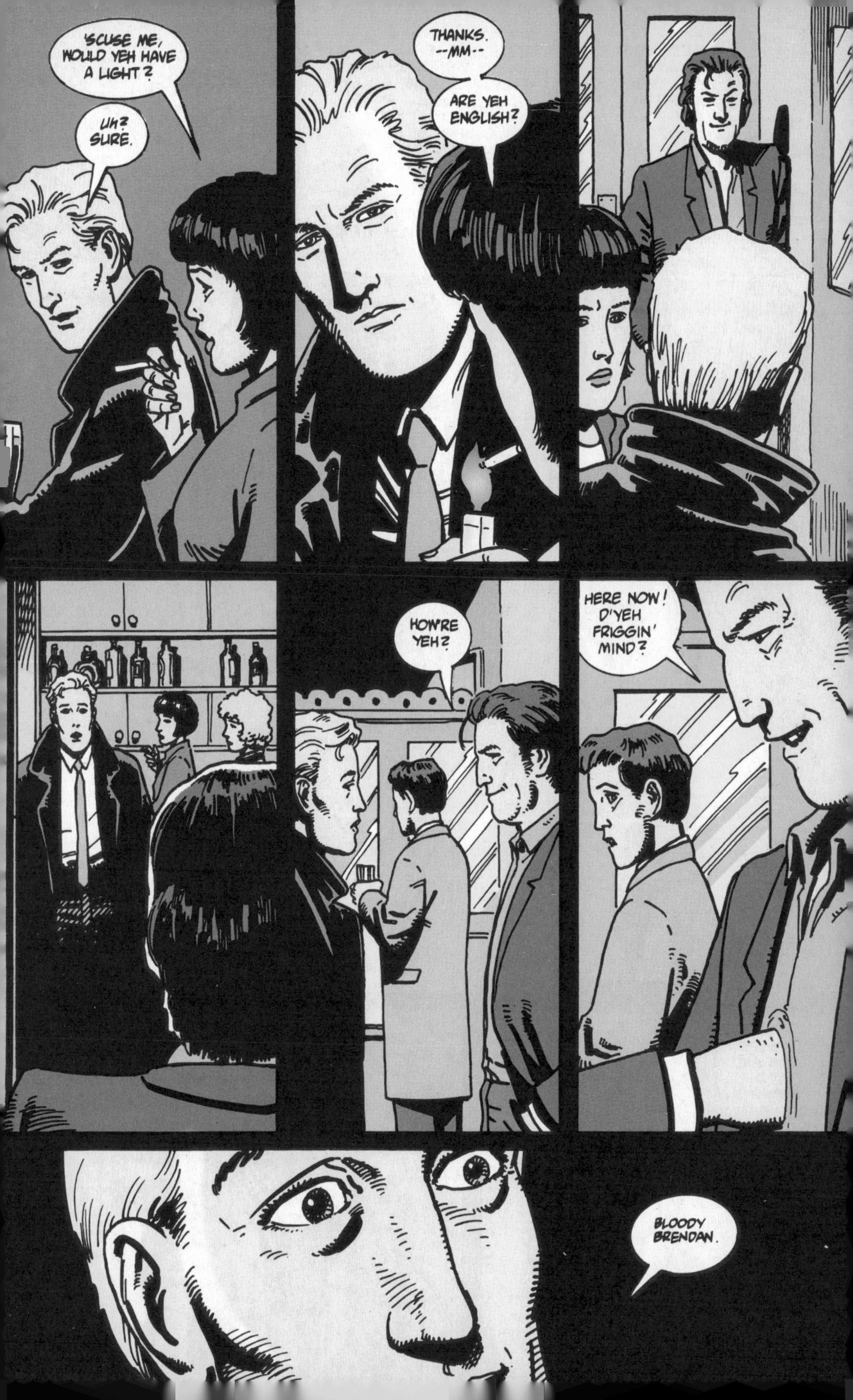
'SCUSE ME, WOULD YEH HAVE A LIGHT?
UH? SURE.
THANKS. --MM--
ARE YEH ENGLISH?
HOW'RE YEH?
HERE NOW! D'YEH FRIGGIN' MIND?
BLOODY BRENDAN.

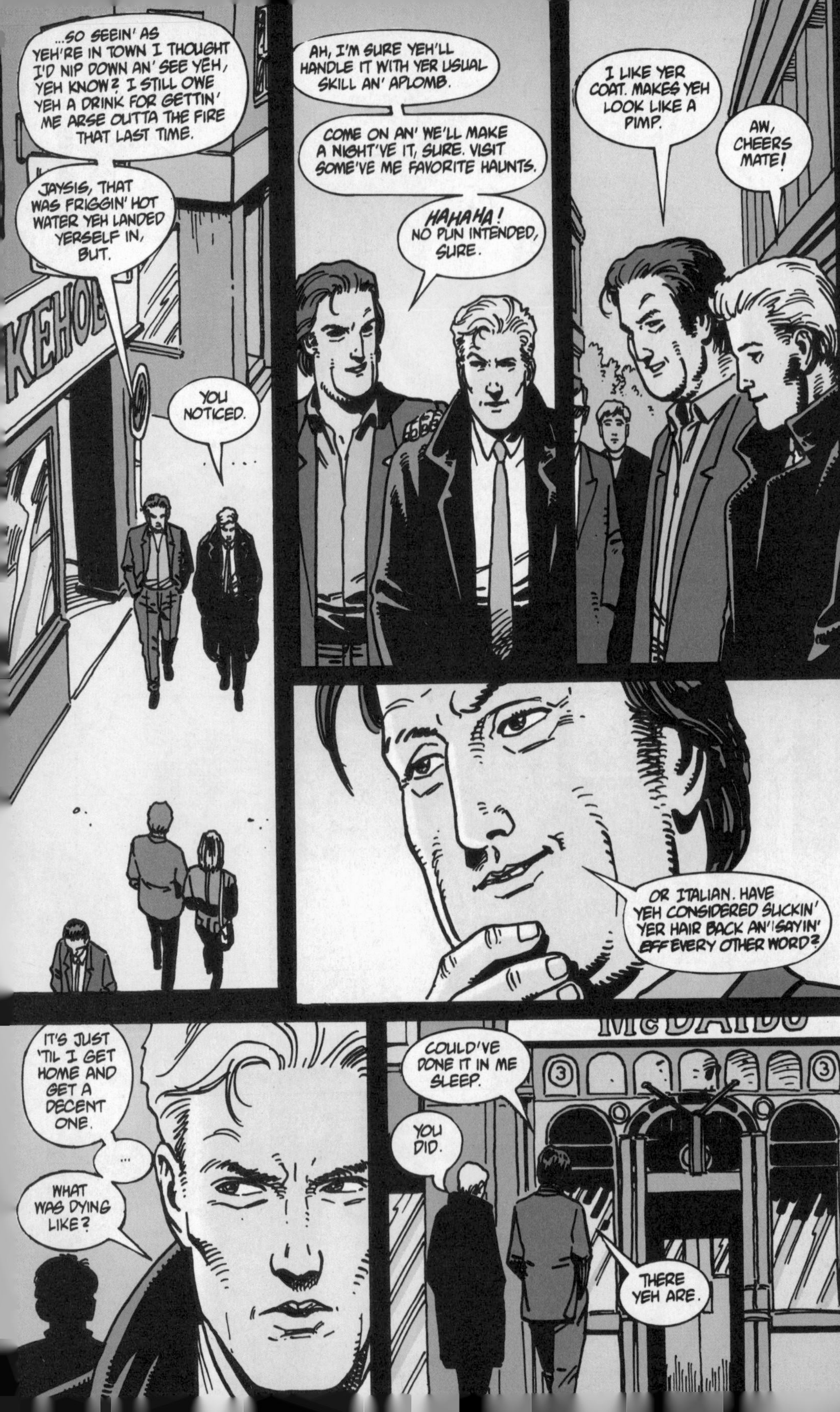
...SO SEEIN' AS YEH'RE IN TOWN I THOUGHT I'D NIP DOWN AN' SEE YEH, YEH KNOW? I STILL OWE YEH A DRINK FOR GETTIN' ME ARSE OUTTA THE FIRE THAT LAST TIME.
JAYSIS, THAT WAS FRIGGIN' HOT WATER YEH LANDED YERSELF IN, BUT.
KEHOE
YOU NOTICED.
...
AH, I'M SURE YEH'LL HANDLE IT WITH YER USUAL SKILL AN' APLOMB.
COME ON AN' WE'LL MAKE A NIGHT'VE IT, SURE. VISIT SOME'VE ME FAVORITE HAUNTS.
HAHAHA! NO PUN INTENDED, SURE.
I LIKE YER COAT. MAKES YEH LOOK LIKE A PIMP.
AW, CHEERS MATE!
OR ITALIAN. HAVE YEH CONSIDERED SLICKIN' YER HAIR BACK AN' SAYIN' EFF EVERY OTHER WORD?
IT'S JUST 'TIL I GET HOME AND GET A DECENT ONE.
...
WHAT WAS DYING LIKE?
COULD'VE DONE IT IN ME SLEEP.
YOU DID.
THERE YEH ARE.

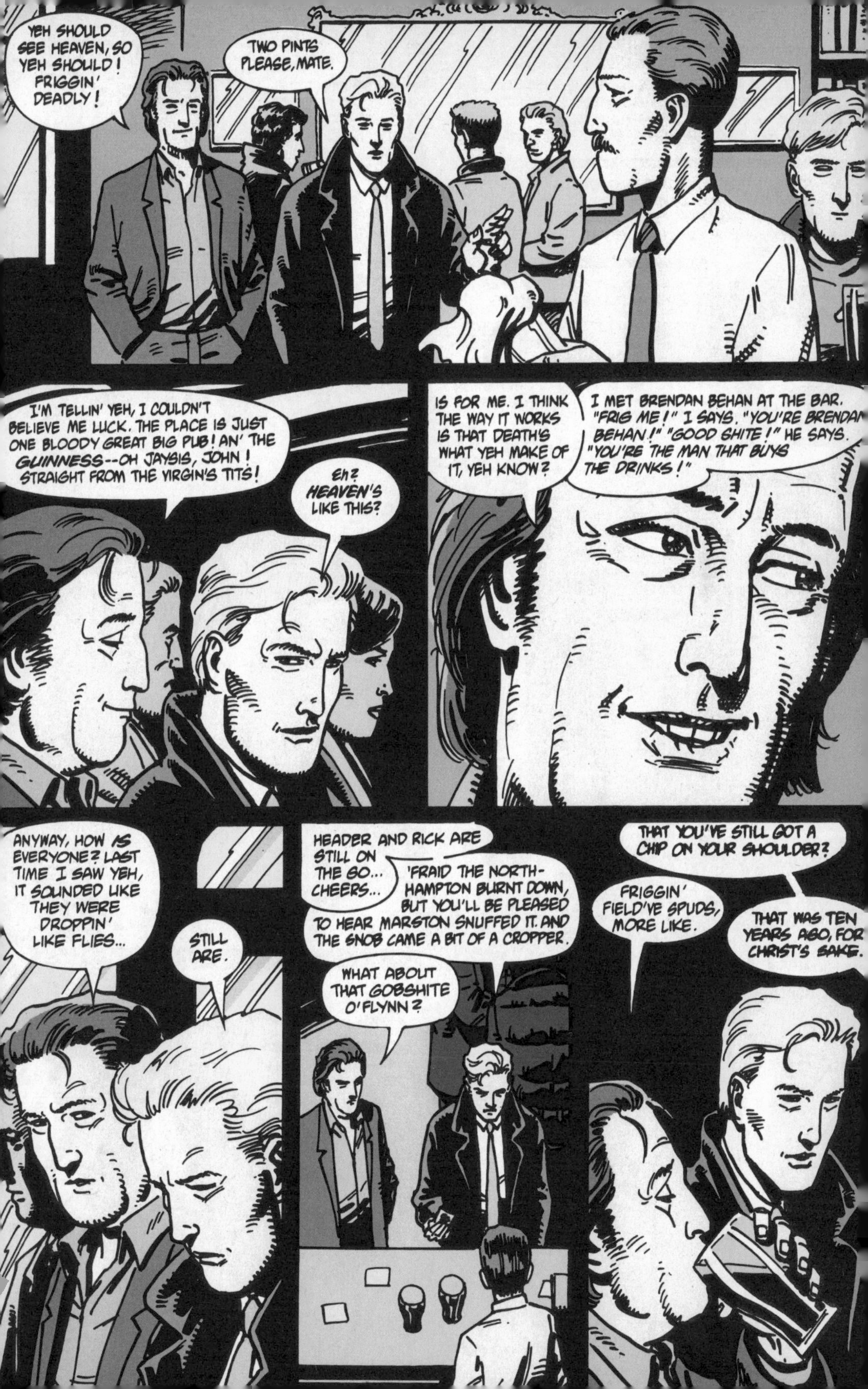

YEH SHOULD SEE HEAVEN, SO YEH SHOULD! FRIGGIN' DEADLY!
TWO PINTS PLEASE, MATE.
I'M TELLIN' YEH, I COULDN'T BELIEVE ME LUCK. THE PLACE IS JUST ONE BLOODY GREAT BIG PUB! AN' THE GUINNESS--OH JAYSIS, JOHN! STRAIGHT FROM THE VIRGIN'S TITS!
EH? HEAVEN'S LIKE THIS?
IS FOR ME. I THINK THE WAY IT WORKS IS THAT DEATH'S WHAT YEH MAKE OF IT, YEH KNOW?
I MET BRENDAN BEHAN AT THE BAR. "FRIG ME!" I SAYS. "YOU'RE BRENDAN BEHAN!" "GOOD SHITE!" HE SAYS. "YOU'RE THE MAN THAT BUYS THE DRINKS!"
ANYWAY, HOW IS EVERYONE? LAST TIME I SAW YEH, IT SOUNDED LIKE THEY WERE DROPPIN' LIKE FLIES...
STILL ARE.
HEADER AND RICK ARE STILL ON THE GO... CHEERS...
'FRAID THE NORTH-HAMPTON BURNT DOWN, BUT YOU'LL BE PLEASED TO HEAR MARSTON SNUFFED IT. AND THE SNOB CAME A BIT OF A CROPPER.
WHAT ABOUT THAT GOBSHITE O'FLYNN?
THAT YOU'VE STILL GOT A CHIP ON YOUR SHOULDER?
FRIGGIN' FIELD'VE SPUDS, MORE LIKE.
THAT WAS TEN YEARS AGO, FOR CHRIST'S SAKE.

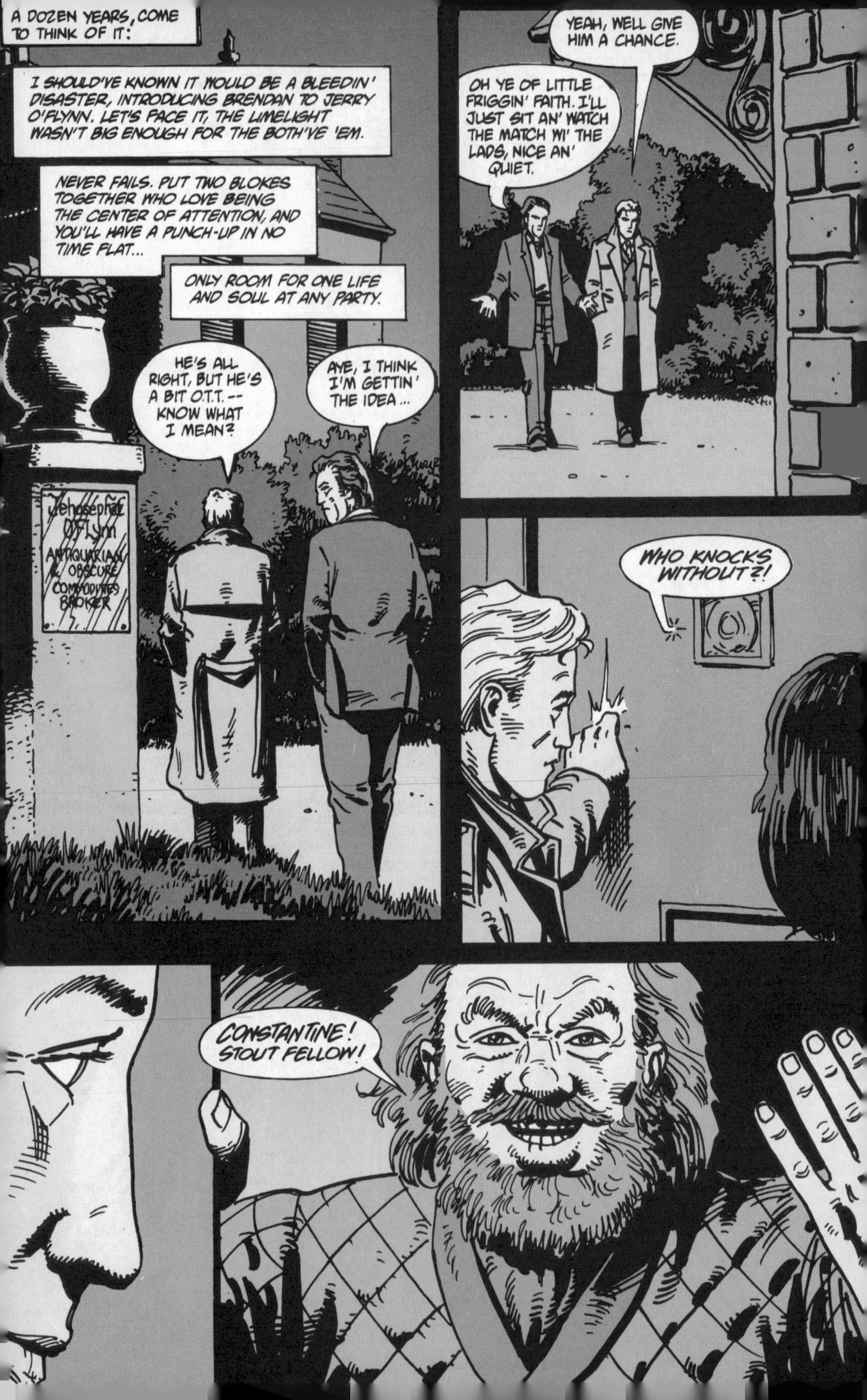
A DOZEN YEARS, COME TO THINK OF IT:
I SHOULD'VE KNOWN IT WOULD BE A BLEEDIN' DISASTER, INTRODUCING BRENDAN TO JERRY O'FLYNN. LET'S FACE IT, THE LIMELIGHT WASN'T BIG ENOUGH FOR THE BOTH'VE 'EM.
NEVER FAILS. PUT TWO BLOKES TOGETHER WHO LOVE BEING THE CENTER OF ATTENTION, AND YOU'LL HAVE A PUNCH-UP IN NO TIME FLAT...
ONLY ROOM FOR ONE LIFE AND SOUL AT ANY PARTY.
HE'S ALL RIGHT, BUT HE'S A BIT O.T.T. -- KNOW WHAT I MEAN?
AYE, I THINK I'M GETTIN' THE IDEA...
Jehosephat O'Flynn
ANTIQUARIAN & OBSCURE COMMODITIES BROKER
YEAH, WELL GIVE HIM A CHANCE.
OH YE OF LITTLE FRIGGIN' FAITH. I'LL JUST SIT AN' WATCH THE MATCH WI' THE LADS, NICE AN' QUIET.
WHO KNOCKS WITHOUT?!
CONSTANTINE! STOUT FELLOW!

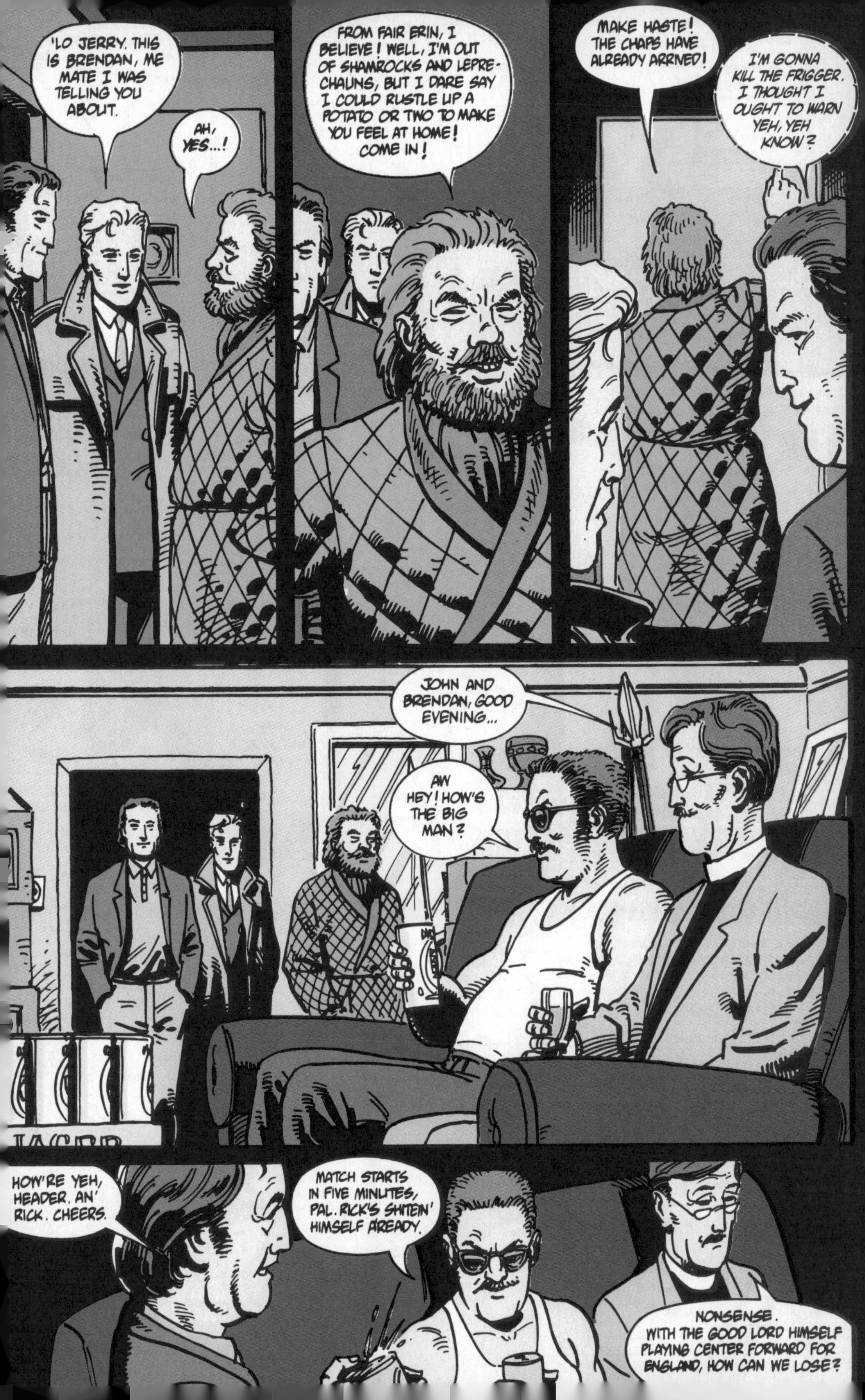

'LO JERRY. THIS IS BRENDAN, ME MATE I WAS TELLING YOU ABOUT.
AH, YES...!
FROM FAIR ERIN, I BELIEVE! WELL, I'M OUT OF SHAMROCKS AND LEPRE-CHAUNS, BUT I DARE SAY I COULD RUSTLE UP A POTATO OR TWO TO MAKE YOU FEEL AT HOME! COME IN!
MAKE HASTE! THE CHAPS HAVE ALREADY ARRIVED!
I'M GONNA KILL THE FRIGGER. I THOUGHT I OUGHT TO WARN YEH, YEH KNOW?
JOHN AND BRENDAN, GOOD EVENING...
AW HEY! HOW'S THE BIG MAN?
HOW'RE YEH, HEADER. AN' RICK. CHEERS.
MATCH STARTS IN FIVE MINUTES, PAL. RICK'S SHITEIN' HIMSELF AREADY.
NONSENSE. WITH THE GOOD LORD HIMSELF PLAYING CENTER FORWARD FOR ENGLAND, HOW CAN WE LOSE?

COME OAN, YA BASTARD! TACKLE HIM! BREAK HIS FRIGGIN' LEGS! YES! *SCOT-LAND!!*

YOU'RE REALLY GOING AFTER IT?

YEAH, NEXT WEEK. TOMMY COX HAS SET US UP WITH SOME BLOKE, UH, *ZEERKE* I THINK HIS NAME IS. THAT'S WHY I CAME ROUND...

I DIDN'T THINK IT WAS FOR THE SOCCER, DEAR BOY. HOW MUCH IS HE ASKING?

HALF A MILLION.

HALF A MILLION FOR THE ACE OF WINCHESTERS!... A *PLAYER,* THIS *ZEERKE!*

LITTLE SHIT, ACCORDING TO COX.

YOU PUT UP HALF, MATE, AND IN TWO WEEKS THE BOAT COMES IN FOR ALL OF US.

THAT'S IT! *THAT'S IT!* ALL THE FRIGGIN' WAY! GO OAN! SHOOT!

SCOT-LAND! SCOT-LAND! **SCOT-LAND.**

YA WEE BEWTY!

OH! A REMARKABLE TACKLE AND *ENGLAND* REGAIN POSSESSION! OH! HE'S GOING ALL THE WAY! HE BEATS ONE MAN--TWO-- JUST THE GOALKEEPER TO-- HE SHOOTS!

YES! IT'S ONE NIL! AND WHAT *MUST* THEY BE THINKING IN SCOTLAND NOW...?

ENG-LAND.

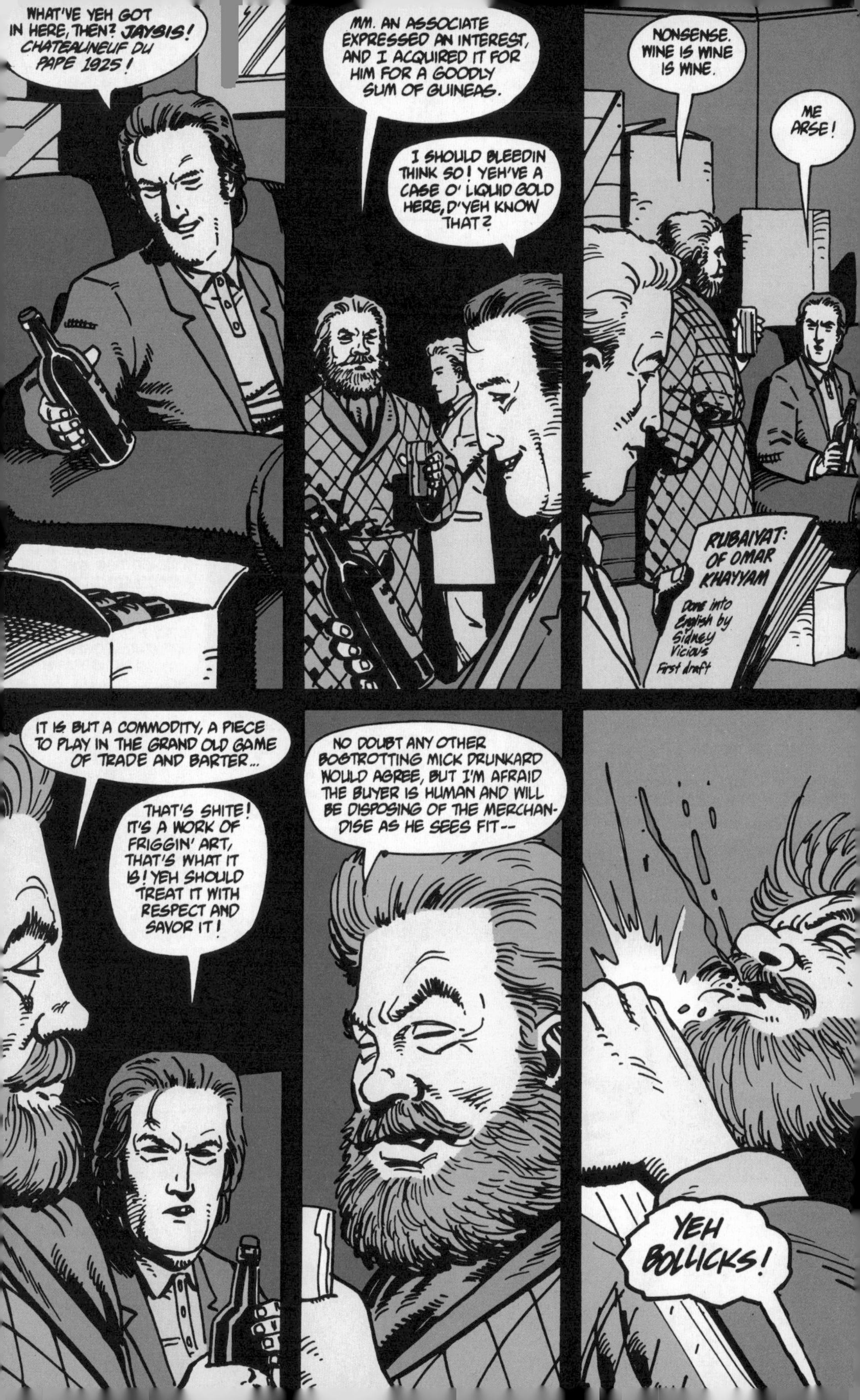
WHAT'VE YEH GOT IN HERE, THEN? JAYSIS! CHATEAUNEUF DU PAPE 1925!
MM. AN ASSOCIATE EXPRESSED AN INTEREST, AND I ACQUIRED IT FOR HIM FOR A GOODLY SUM OF GUINEAS.
I SHOULD BLEEDIN THINK SO! YEH'VE A CASE O' LIQUID GOLD HERE, D'YEH KNOW THAT?
NONSENSE. WINE IS WINE IS WINE.
ME ARSE!
RUBAIYAT: OF OMAR KHAYYAM
Done into English by Sidney Vicious
First draft
IT IS BUT A COMMODITY, A PIECE TO PLAY IN THE GRAND OLD GAME OF TRADE AND BARTER...
THAT'S SHITE! IT'S A WORK OF FRIGGIN' ART, THAT'S WHAT IT IS! YEH SHOULD TREAT IT WITH RESPECT AND SAVOR IT!
NO DOUBT ANY OTHER BOGTROTTING MICK DRUNKARD WOULD AGREE, BUT I'M AFRAID THE BUYER IS HUMAN AND WILL BE DISPOSING OF THE MERCHANDISE AS HE SEES FIT--
YEH BOLLICKS!

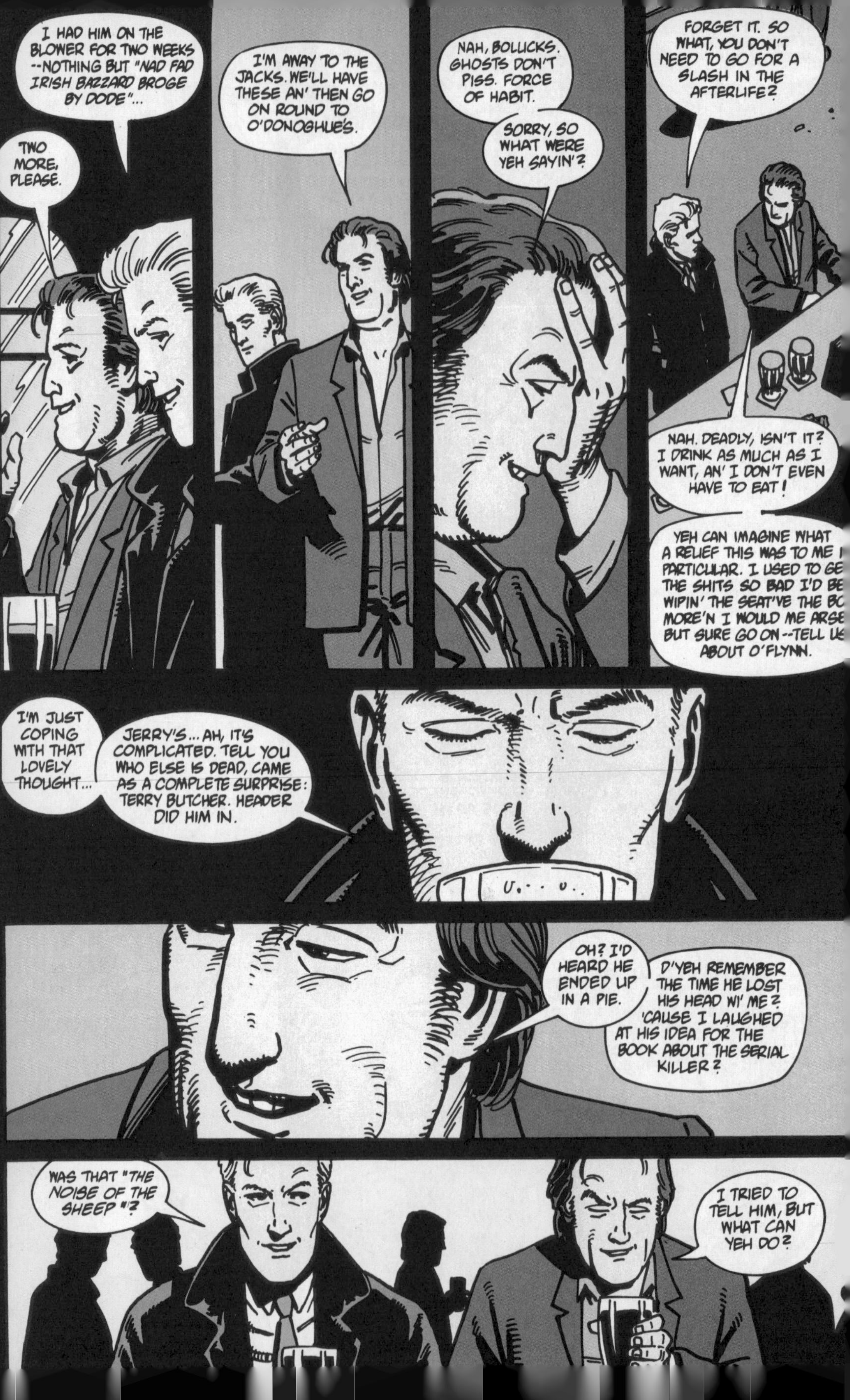

I HAD HIM ON THE BLOWER FOR TWO WEEKS --NOTHING BUT "NAD FAD IRISH BAZZARD BROGE BY DODE"...
TWO MORE, PLEASE.
I'M AWAY TO THE JACKS. WE'LL HAVE THESE AN' THEN GO ON ROUND TO O'DONOGHUE'S.
NAH, BOLLUCKS. GHOSTS DON'T PISS. FORCE OF HABIT.
SORRY, SO WHAT WERE YEH SAYIN'?
FORGET IT. SO WHAT, YOU DON'T NEED TO GO FOR A SLASH IN THE AFTERLIFE?
NAH. DEADLY, ISN'T IT? I DRINK AS MUCH AS I WANT, AN' I DON'T EVEN HAVE TO EAT!
YEH CAN IMAGINE WHAT A RELIEF THIS WAS TO ME PARTICULAR. I USED TO GE THE SHITS SO BAD I'D BE WIPIN' THE SEAT'VE THE BO MORE'N I WOULD ME ARSE BUT SURE GO ON --TELL U ABOUT O'FLYNN.
I'M JUST COPING WITH THAT LOVELY THOUGHT...
JERRY'S... AH, IT'S COMPLICATED. TELL YOU WHO ELSE IS DEAD, CAME AS A COMPLETE SURPRISE: TERRY BUTCHER. HEADER DID HIM IN.
OH? I'D HEARD HE ENDED UP IN A PIE.
D'YEH REMEMBER THE TIME HE LOST HIS HEAD WI' ME? 'CAUSE I LAUGHED AT HIS IDEA FOR THE BOOK ABOUT THE SERIAL KILLER?
WAS THAT "THE NOISE OF THE SHEEP"?
I TRIED TO TELL HIM, BUT WHAT CAN YEH DO?

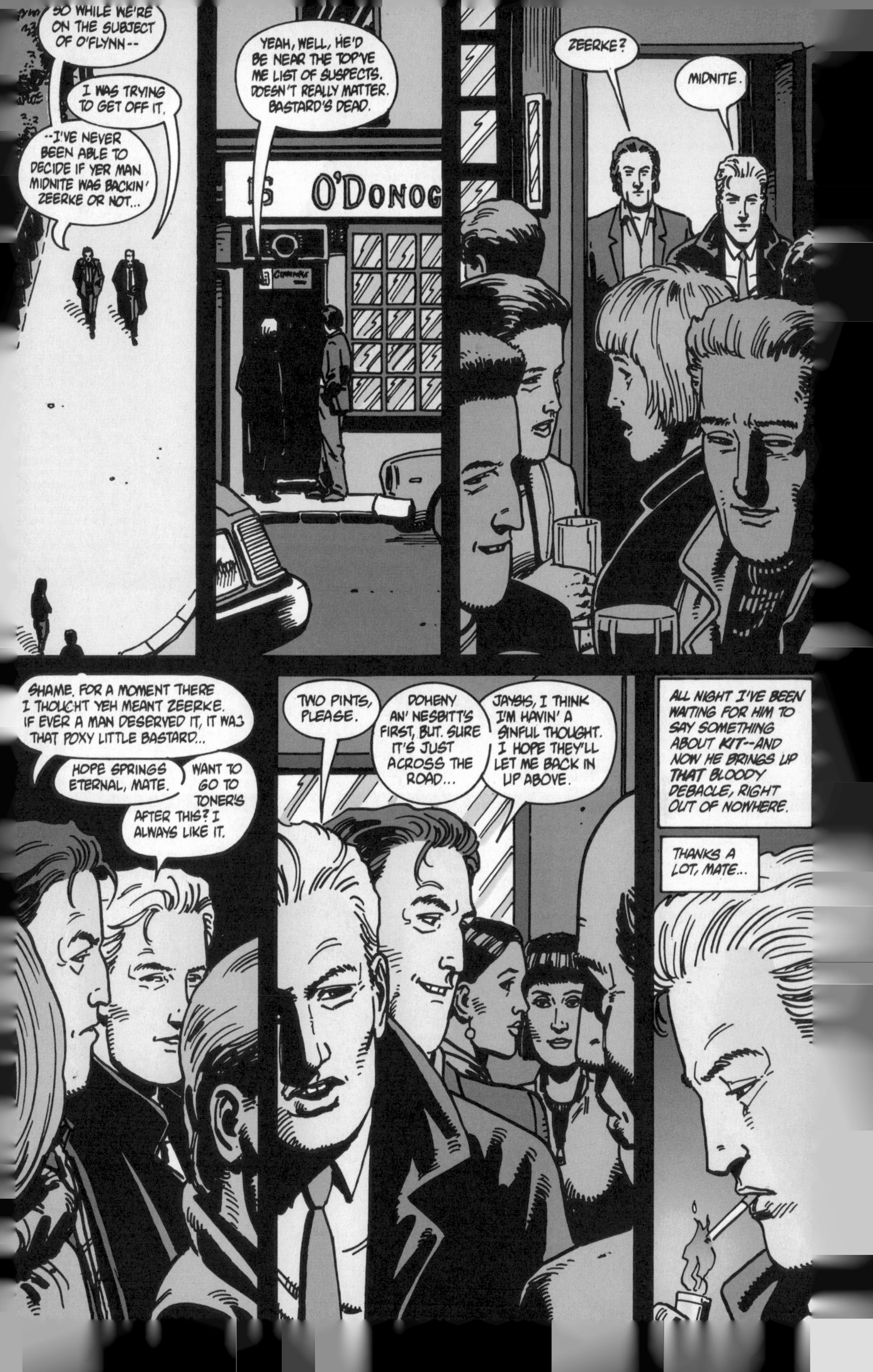
SO WHILE WE'RE ON THE SUBJECT OF O'FLYNN--
I WAS TRYING TO GET OFF IT.
--I'VE NEVER BEEN ABLE TO DECIDE IF YER MAN MIDNITE WAS BACKIN' ZEERKE OR NOT...
YEAH, WELL, HE'D BE NEAR THE TOP'VE ME LIST OF SUSPECTS. DOESN'T REALLY MATTER. BASTARD'S DEAD.
O'DONOG
ZEERKE?
MIDNITE.
SHAME. FOR A MOMENT THERE I THOUGHT YEH MEANT ZEERKE. IF EVER A MAN DESERVED IT, IT WAS THAT POXY LITTLE BASTARD...
HOPE SPRINGS ETERNAL, MATE.
WANT TO GO TO TONER'S AFTER THIS? I ALWAYS LIKE IT.
TWO PINTS, PLEASE.
DOHENY AN' NESBITT'S FIRST, BUT. SURE IT'S JUST ACROSS THE ROAD...
JAYSIS, I THINK I'M HAVIN' A SINFUL THOUGHT. I HOPE THEY'LL LET ME BACK IN UP ABOVE.
ALL NIGHT I'VE BEEN WAITING FOR HIM TO SAY SOMETHING ABOUT KIT--AND NOW HE BRINGS UP THAT BLOODY DEBACLE, RIGHT OUT OF NOWHERE.
THANKS A LOT, MATE...

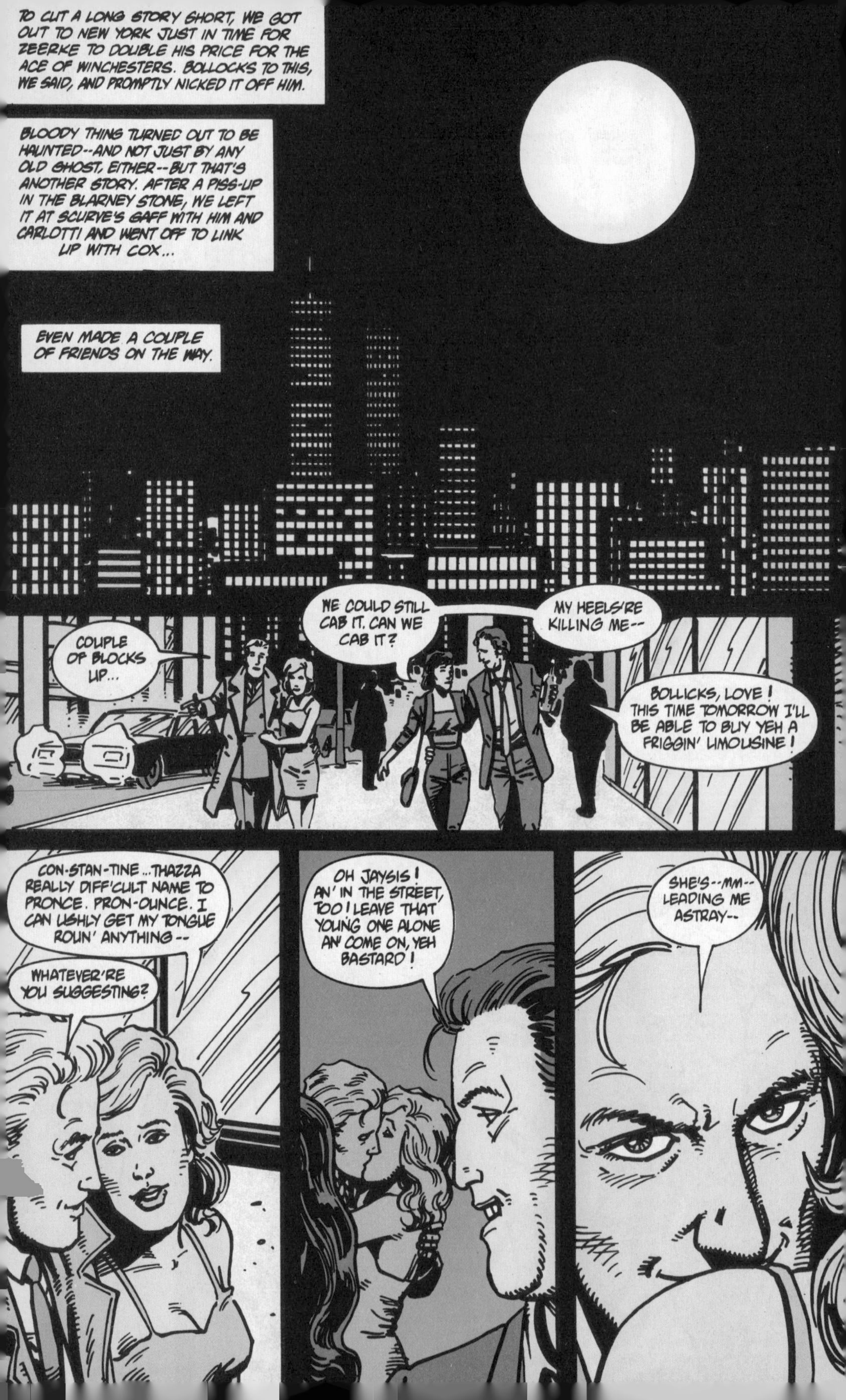
TO CUT A LONG STORY SHORT, WE GOT OUT TO NEW YORK JUST IN TIME FOR ZEERKE TO DOUBLE HIS PRICE FOR THE ACE OF WINCHESTERS. BOLLOCKS TO THIS, WE SAID, AND PROMPTLY NICKED IT OFF HIM.
BLOODY THING TURNED OUT TO BE HAUNTED--AND NOT JUST BY ANY OLD GHOST, EITHER--BUT THAT'S ANOTHER STORY. AFTER A PISS-UP IN THE BLARNEY STONE, WE LEFT IT AT SCURVE'S GAFF WITH HIM AND CARLOTTI AND WENT OFF TO LINK UP WITH COX...
EVEN MADE A COUPLE OF FRIENDS ON THE WAY.
COUPLE OF BLOCKS UP...
WE COULD STILL CAB IT. CAN WE CAB IT?
MY HEELS'RE KILLING ME--
BOLLICKS, LOVE! THIS TIME TOMORROW I'LL BE ABLE TO BUY YEH A FRIGGIN' LIMOUSINE!
CON-STAN-TINE...THAZZA REALLY DIFF'CULT NAME TO PRONCE. PRON-OUNCE. I CAN USHLY GET MY TONGUE ROUN' ANYTHING--
WHATEVER'RE YOU SUGGESTING?
OH JAYSIS! AN' IN THE STREET, TOO! LEAVE THAT YOUNG ONE ALONE AN' COME ON, YEH BASTARD!
SHE'S--MM--LEADING ME ASTRAY--

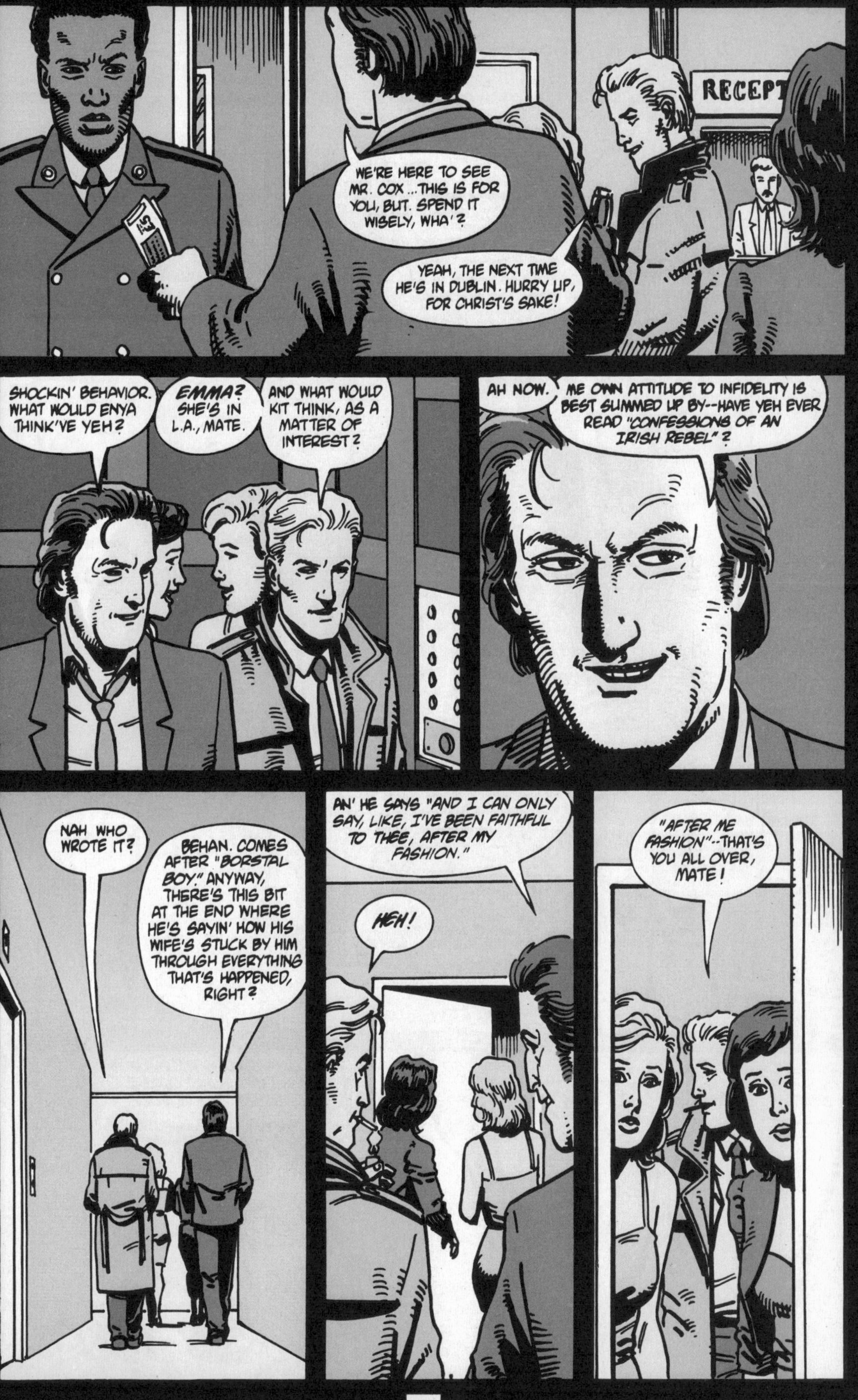
RECEPT
WE'RE HERE TO SEE MR. COX ... THIS IS FOR YOU, BUT. SPEND IT WISELY, WHA'?
YEAH, THE NEXT TIME HE'S IN DUBLIN. HURRY UP, FOR CHRIST'S SAKE!
SHOCKIN' BEHAVIOR. WHAT WOULD ENYA THINK'VE YEH?
EMMA? SHE'S IN L.A., MATE.
AND WHAT WOULD KIT THINK, AS A MATTER OF INTEREST?
AH NOW.
ME OWN ATTITUDE TO INFIDELITY IS BEST SUMMED UP BY--HAVE YEH EVER READ "CONFESSIONS OF AN IRISH REBEL"?
NAH WHO WROTE IT?
BEHAN. COMES AFTER "BORSTAL BOY." ANYWAY, THERE'S THIS BIT AT THE END WHERE HE'S SAYIN' HOW HIS WIFE'S STUCK BY HIM THROUGH EVERYTHING THAT'S HAPPENED, RIGHT?
AN' HE SAYS "AND I CAN ONLY SAY, LIKE, I'VE BEEN FAITHFUL TO THEE, AFTER MY FASHION."
HEH!
"AFTER ME FASHION"--THAT'S YOU ALL OVER, MATE!

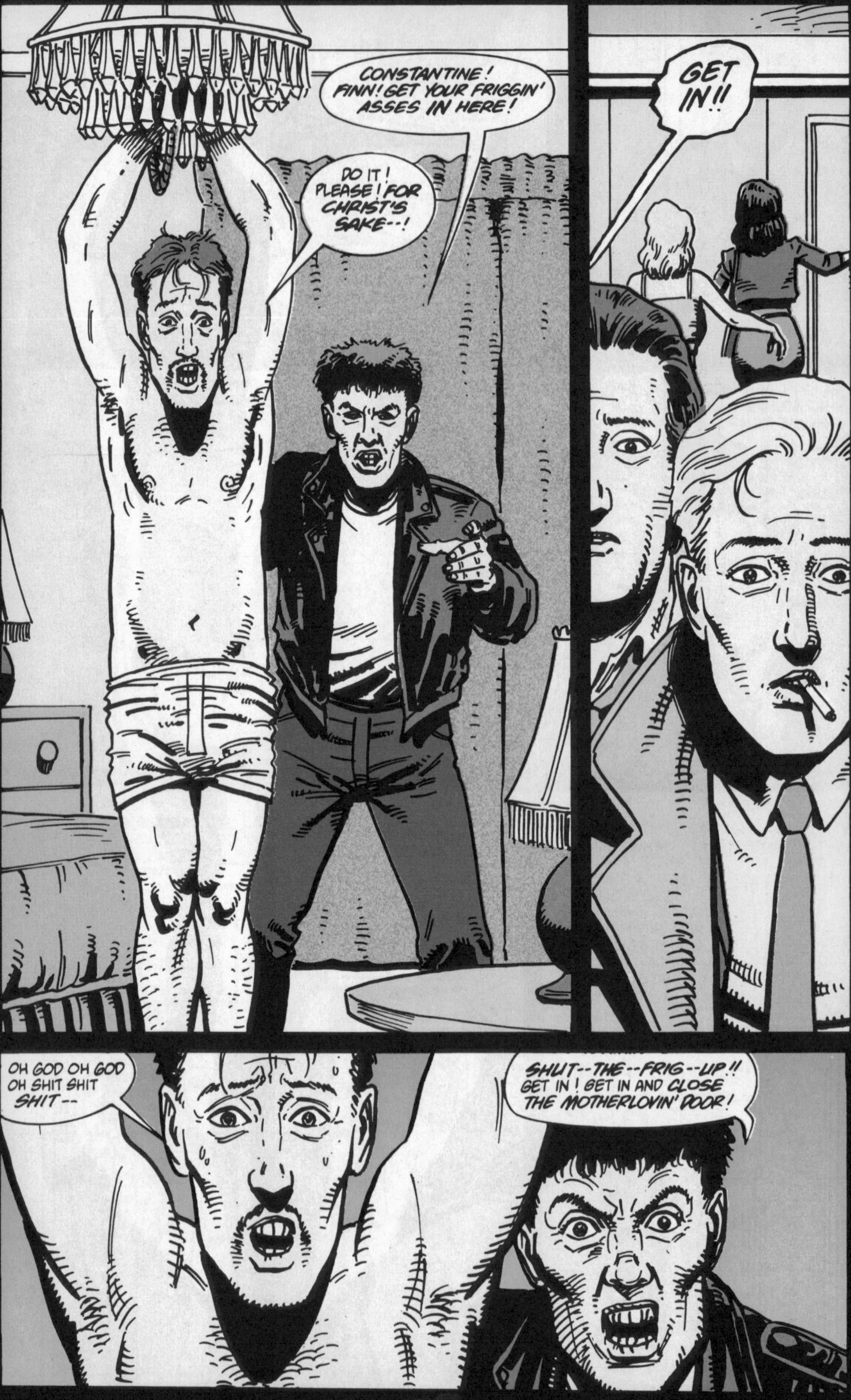
CONSTANTINE! FINN! GET YOUR FRIGGIN' ASSES IN HERE!
DO IT! PLEASE! FOR CHRIST'S SAKE--!
GET IN!!
OH GOD OH GOD OH SHIT SHIT SHIT--
SHUT--THE--FRIG--UP!! GET IN! GET IN AND CLOSE THE MOTHERLOVIN' DOOR!

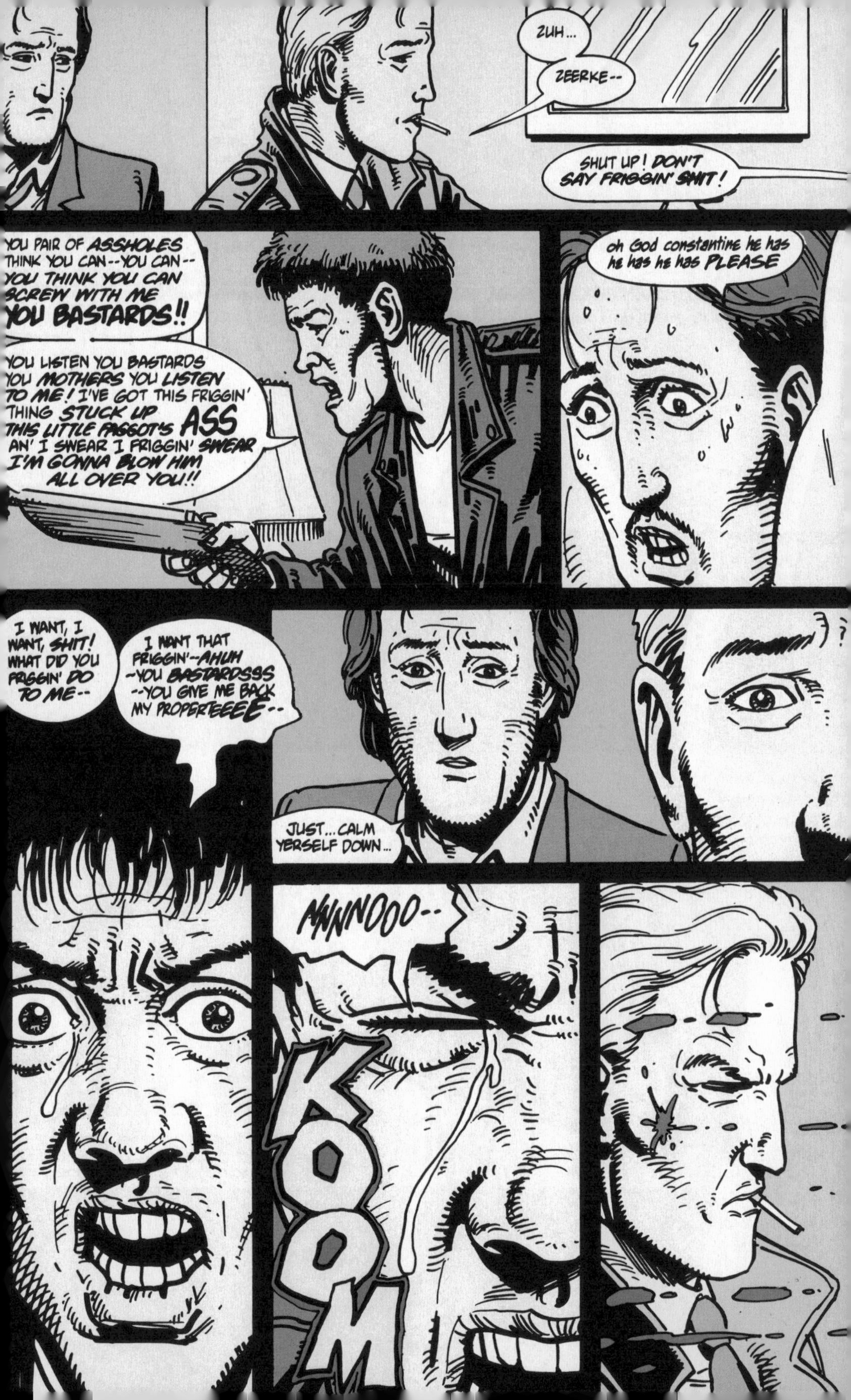
ZUH...
ZEERKE--
SHUT UP! DON'T SAY FRIGGIN' SHIT!
YOU PAIR OF ASSHOLES THINK YOU CAN--YOU CAN--YOU THINK YOU CAN SCREW WITH ME YOU BASTARDS!!
YOU LISTEN YOU BASTARDS YOU MOTHERS YOU LISTEN TO ME! I'VE GOT THIS FRIGGIN' THING STUCK UP THIS LITTLE FAGGOT'S ASS AN' I SWEAR I FRIGGIN' SWEAR I'M GONNA BLOW HIM ALL OVER YOU!!
oh God constantine he has he has he has PLEASE
I WANT, I WANT, SHIT! WHAT DID YOU FRIGGIN' DO TO ME--
I WANT THAT FRIGGIN'--AHUH --YOU BASTARDSSS --YOU GIVE ME BACK MY PROPERTEEEE--
JUST... CALM YERSELF DOWN...
MNNNOOO--
KOOM

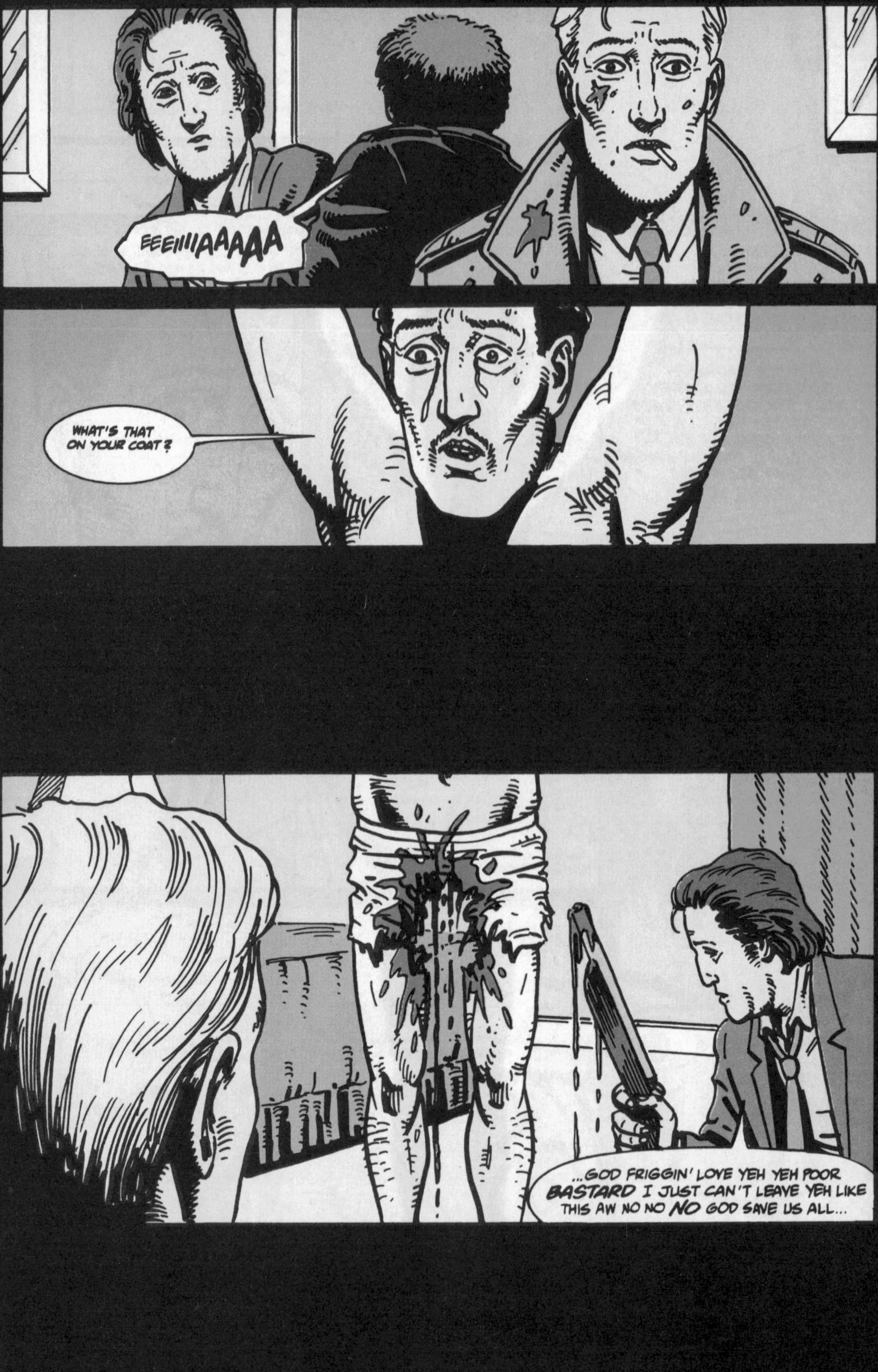
EEEIIIIAAAAA
WHAT'S THAT ON YOUR COAT?
...GOD FRIGGIN' LOVE YEH YEH POOR BASTARD I JUST CAN'T LEAVE YEH LIKE THIS AW NO NO NO GOD SAVE US ALL...

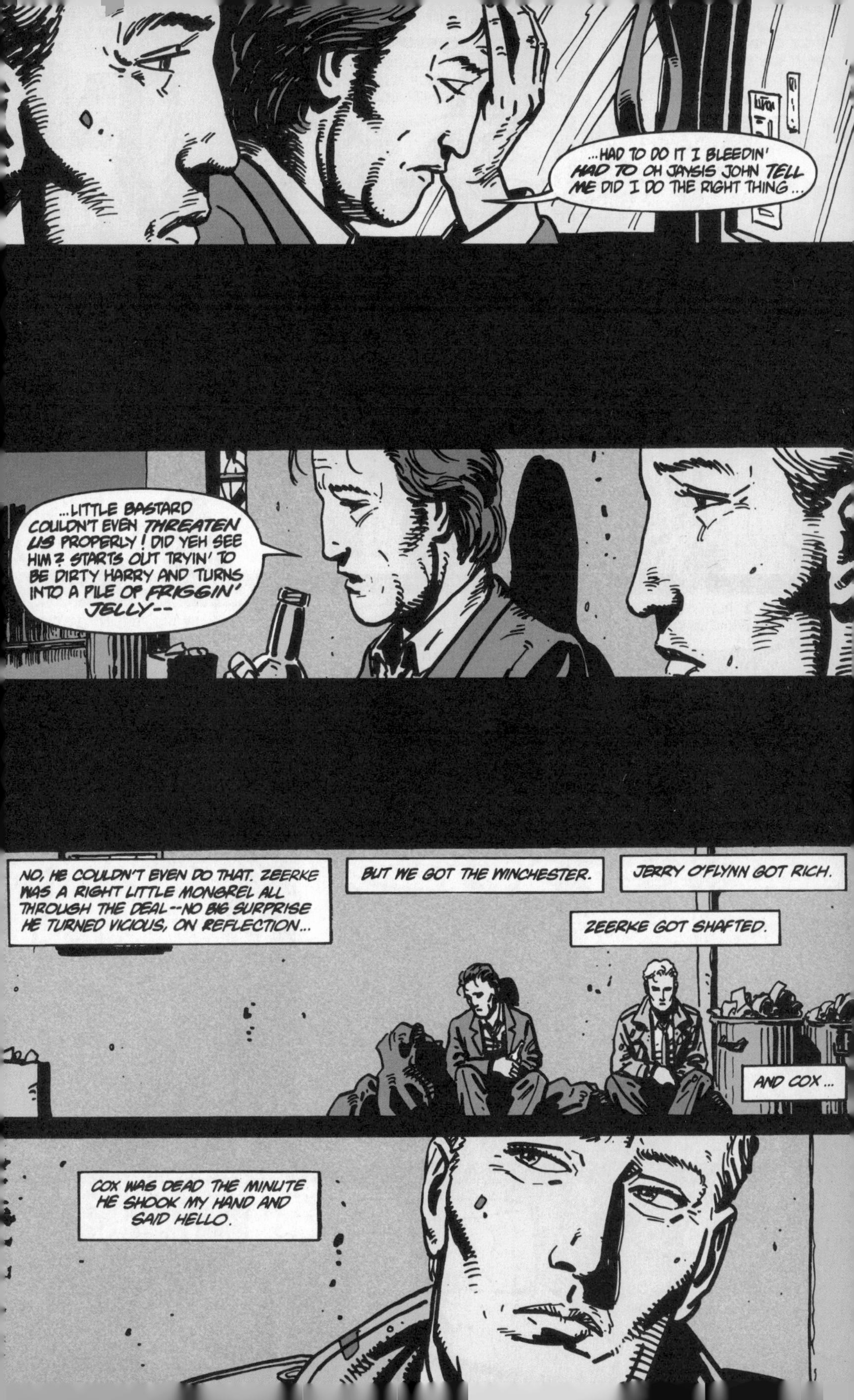
...HAD TO DO IT I BLEEDIN' HAD TO OH JAYSIS JOHN TELL ME DID I DO THE RIGHT THING...
...LITTLE BASTARD COULDN'T EVEN THREATEN US PROPERLY! DID YEH SEE HIM? STARTS OUT TRYIN' TO BE DIRTY HARRY AND TURNS INTO A PILE OF FRIGGIN' JELLY--
NO, HE COULDN'T EVEN DO THAT. ZEERKE WAS A RIGHT LITTLE MONGREL ALL THROUGH THE DEAL--NO BIG SURPRISE HE TURNED VICIOUS, ON REFLECTION...
BUT WE GOT THE WINCHESTER.
JERRY O'FLYNN GOT RICH.
ZEERKE GOT SHAFTED.
AND COX...
COX WAS DEAD THE MINUTE HE SHOOK MY HAND AND SAID HELLO.

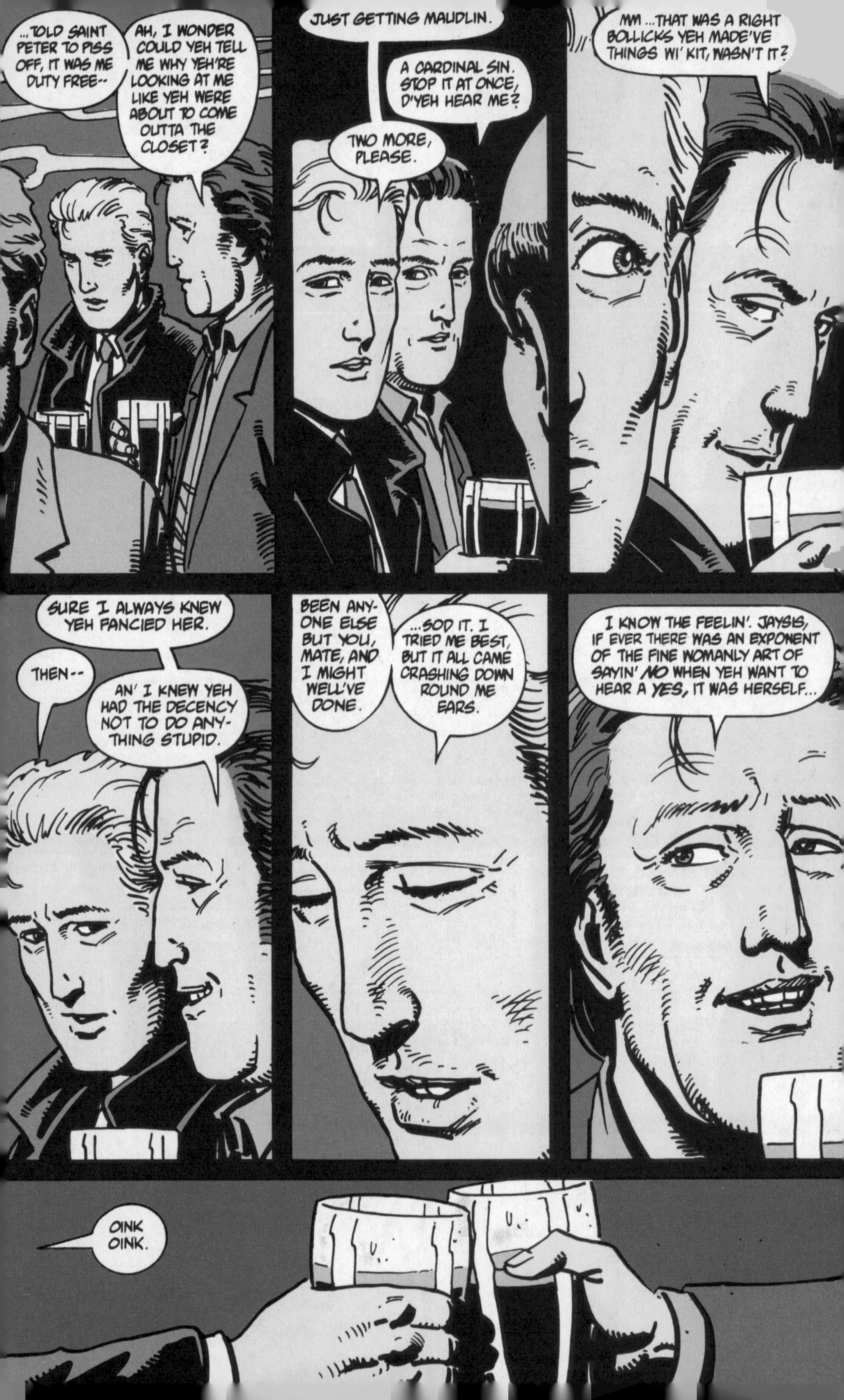
...TOLD SAINT PETER TO PISS OFF, IT WAS ME DUTY FREE--
AH, I WONDER COULD YEH TELL ME WHY YEH'RE LOOKING AT ME LIKE YEH WERE ABOUT TO COME OUTTA THE CLOSET?
JUST GETTING MAUDLIN.
A CARDINAL SIN. STOP IT AT ONCE, D'YEH HEAR ME?
TWO MORE, PLEASE.
MM ...THAT WAS A RIGHT BOLLICKS YEH MADE'VE THINGS WI' KIT, WASN'T IT?
SURE I ALWAYS KNEW YEH FANCIED HER.
THEN--
AN' I KNEW YEH HAD THE DECENCY NOT TO DO ANYTHING STUPID.
BEEN ANYONE ELSE BUT YOU, MATE, AN' I MIGHT WELL'VE DONE.
...SOD IT. I TRIED ME BEST, BUT IT ALL CAME CRASHING DOWN ROUND ME EARS.
I KNOW THE FEELIN'. JAYSIS, IF EVER THERE WAS AN EXPONENT OF THE FINE WOMANLY ART OF SAYIN' *NO* WHEN YEH WANT TO HEAR A *YES*, IT WAS HERSELF...
OINK OINK.

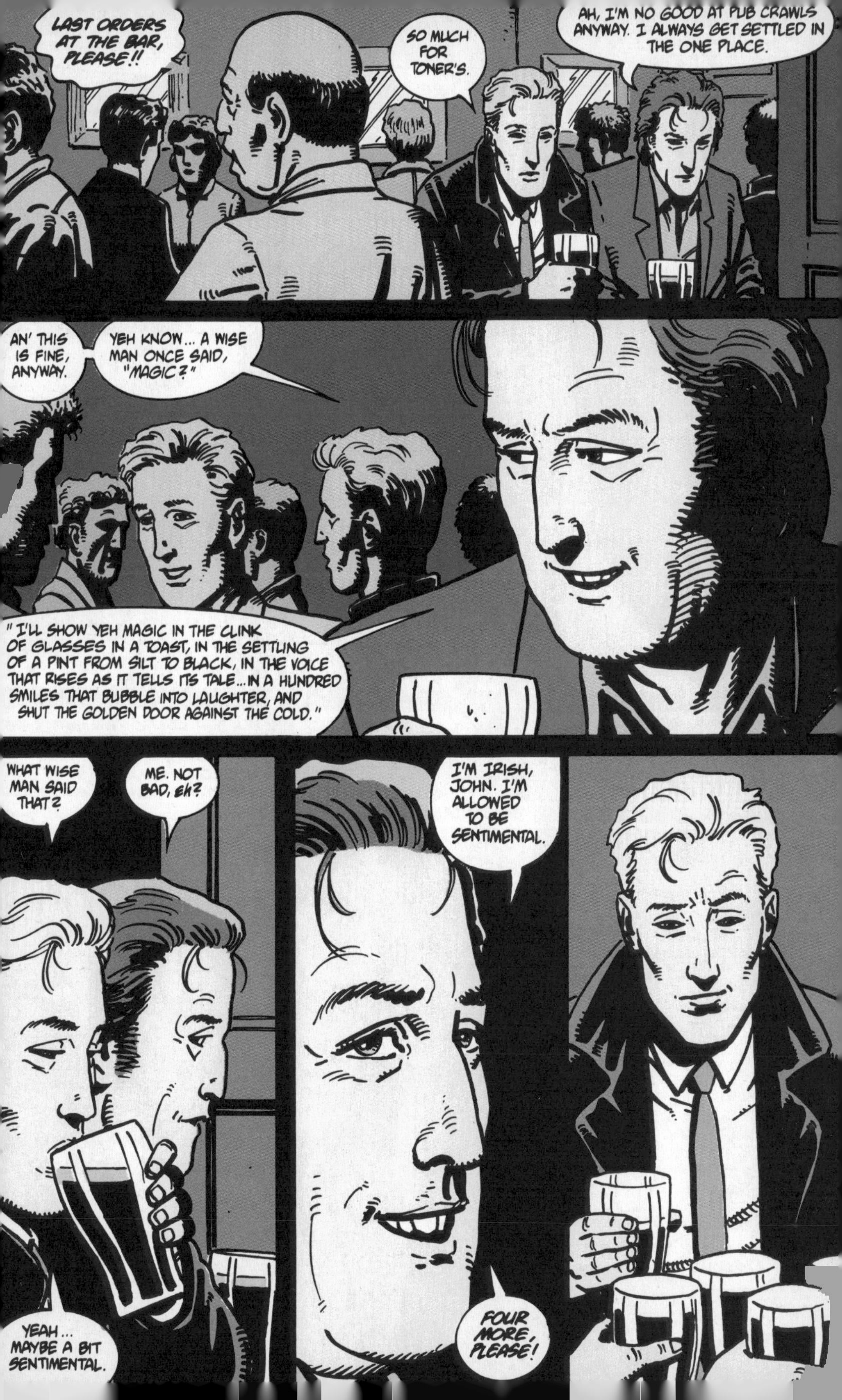
LAST ORDERS AT THE BAR, PLEASE!!
SO MUCH FOR TONER'S.
AH, I'M NO GOOD AT PUB CRAWLS ANYWAY. I ALWAYS GET SETTLED IN THE ONE PLACE.
AN' THIS IS FINE, ANYWAY.
YEH KNOW... A WISE MAN ONCE SAID, "MAGIC?"
"I'LL SHOW YEH MAGIC IN THE CLINK OF GLASSES IN A TOAST, IN THE SETTLING OF A PINT FROM SILT TO BLACK, IN THE VOICE THAT RISES AS IT TELLS ITS TALE... IN A HUNDRED SMILES THAT BUBBLE INTO LAUGHTER, AND SHUT THE GOLDEN DOOR AGAINST THE COLD."
WHAT WISE MAN SAID THAT?
ME. NOT BAD, EH?
YEAH... MAYBE A BIT SENTIMENTAL.
I'M IRISH, JOHN. I'M ALLOWED TO BE SENTIMENTAL.
FOUR MORE, PLEASE!

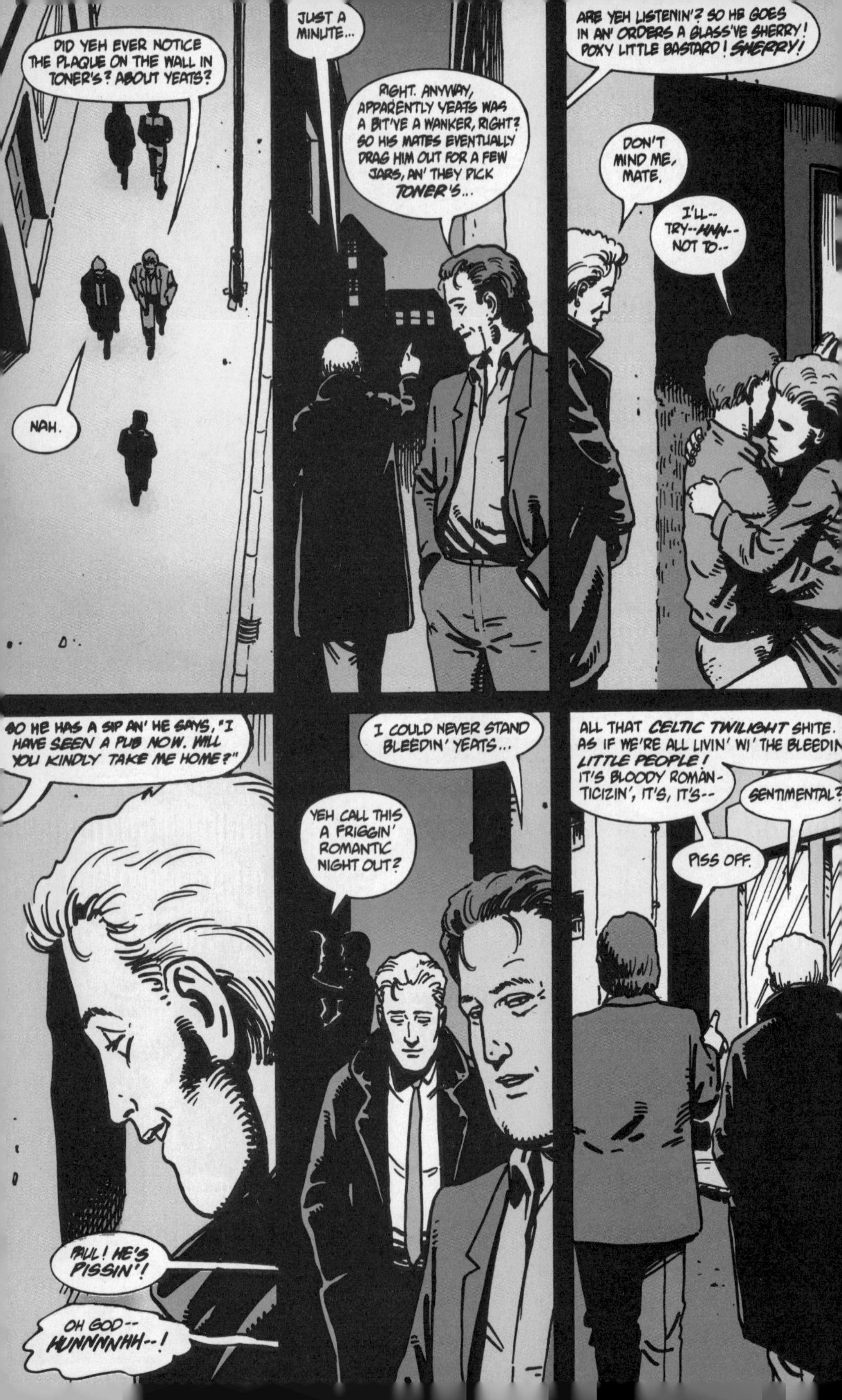
DID YEH EVER NOTICE THE PLAQUE ON THE WALL IN TONER'S? ABOUT YEATS?
NAH.
JUST A MINUTE...
RIGHT. ANYWAY, APPARENTLY YEATS WAS A BIT'VE A WANKER, RIGHT? SO HIS MATES EVENTUALLY DRAG HIM OUT FOR A FEW JARS, AN' THEY PICK TONER'S...
ARE YEH LISTENIN'? SO HE GOES IN AN' ORDERS A GLASS'VE SHERRY! POXY LITTLE BASTARD! SHERRY!
DON'T MIND ME, MATE.
I'LL-- TRY--HNN-- NOT TO--
SO HE HAS A SIP AN' HE SAYS, "I HAVE SEEN A PUB NOW. WILL YOU KINDLY TAKE ME HOME?"
PAUL! HE'S PISSIN'!
OH GOD-- HUNNNNHH--!
I COULD NEVER STAND BLEEDIN' YEATS...
YEH CALL THIS A FRIGGIN' ROMANTIC NIGHT OUT?
ALL THAT CELTIC TWILIGHT SHITE. AS IF WE'RE ALL LIVIN' WI' THE BLEEDIN LITTLE PEOPLE! IT'S BLOODY ROMAN-TICIZIN', IT'S, IT'S--
SENTIMENTAL?
PISS OFF.

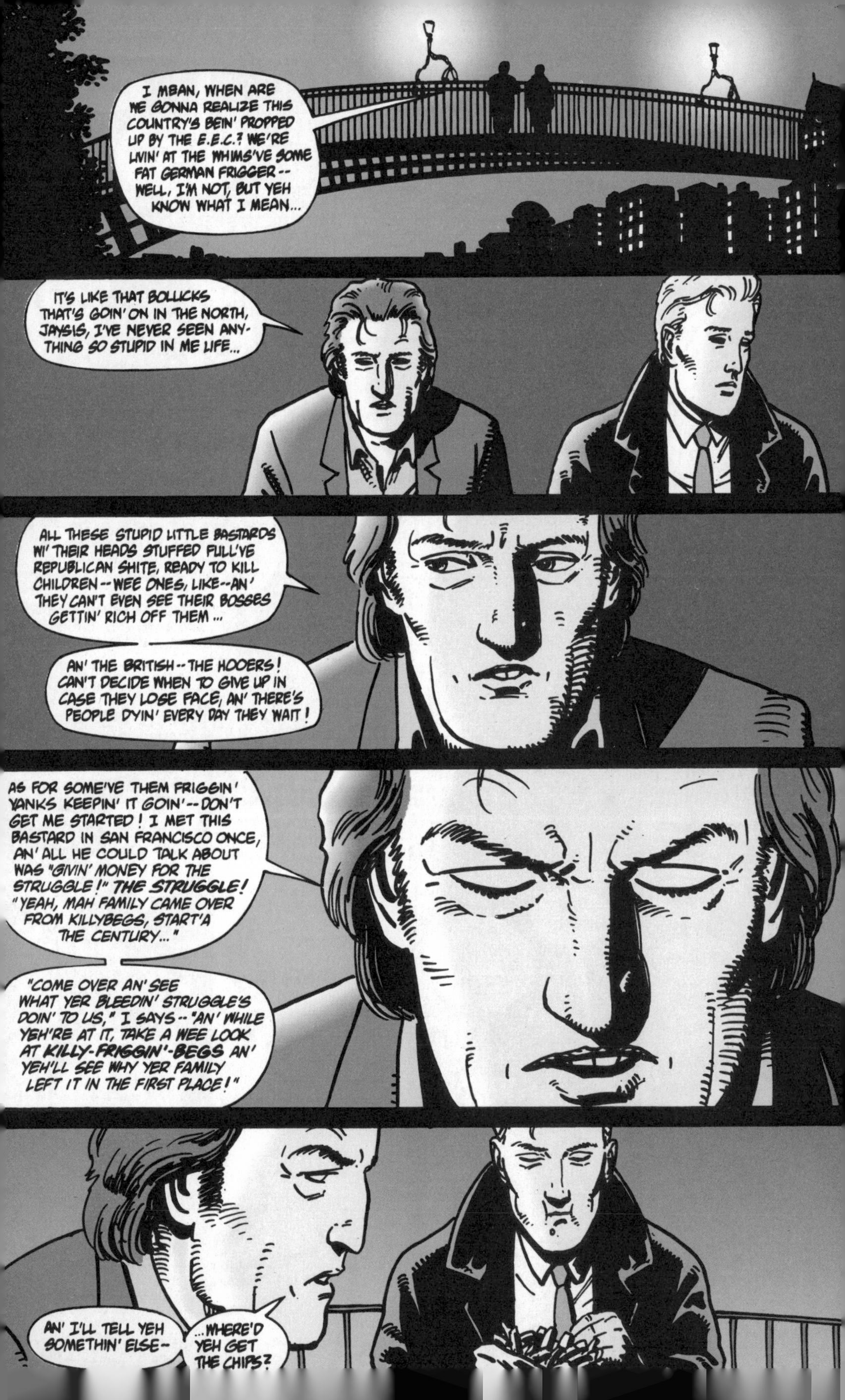
I MEAN, WHEN ARE WE GONNA REALIZE THIS COUNTRY'S BEIN' PROPPED UP BY THE E.E.C.? WE'RE LIVIN' AT THE WHIMS'VE SOME FAT GERMAN FRIGGER-- WELL, I'M NOT, BUT YEH KNOW WHAT I MEAN...
IT'S LIKE THAT BOLLICKS THAT'S GOIN' ON IN THE NORTH, JAYSIS, I'VE NEVER SEEN ANYTHING SO STUPID IN ME LIFE...
ALL THESE STUPID LITTLE BASTARDS WI' THEIR HEADS STUFFED FULL'VE REPUBLICAN SHITE, READY TO KILL CHILDREN--WEE ONES, LIKE--AN' THEY CAN'T EVEN SEE THEIR BOSSES GETTIN' RICH OFF THEM...
AN' THE BRITISH--THE HOOERS! CAN'T DECIDE WHEN TO GIVE UP IN CASE THEY LOSE FACE, AN' THERE'S PEOPLE DYIN' EVERY DAY THEY WAIT!
AS FOR SOME'VE THEM FRIGGIN' YANKS KEEPIN' IT GOIN'--DON'T GET ME STARTED! I MET THIS BASTARD IN SAN FRANCISCO ONCE, AN' ALL HE COULD TALK ABOUT WAS "GIVIN' MONEY FOR THE STRUGGLE!" *THE STRUGGLE!* "YEAH, MAH FAMILY CAME OVER FROM KILLYBEGS, START'A THE CENTURY..."
"COME OVER AN' SEE WHAT YER BLEEDIN' STRUGGLE'S DOIN' TO US," I SAYS--"AN' WHILE YEH'RE AT IT, TAKE A WEE LOOK AT *KILLY-FRIGGIN'-BEGS* AN' YEH'LL SEE WHY YER FAMILY LEFT IT IN THE FIRST PLACE!"
AN' I'LL TELL YEH SOMETHIN' ELSE-
...WHERE'D YEH GET THE CHIPS?

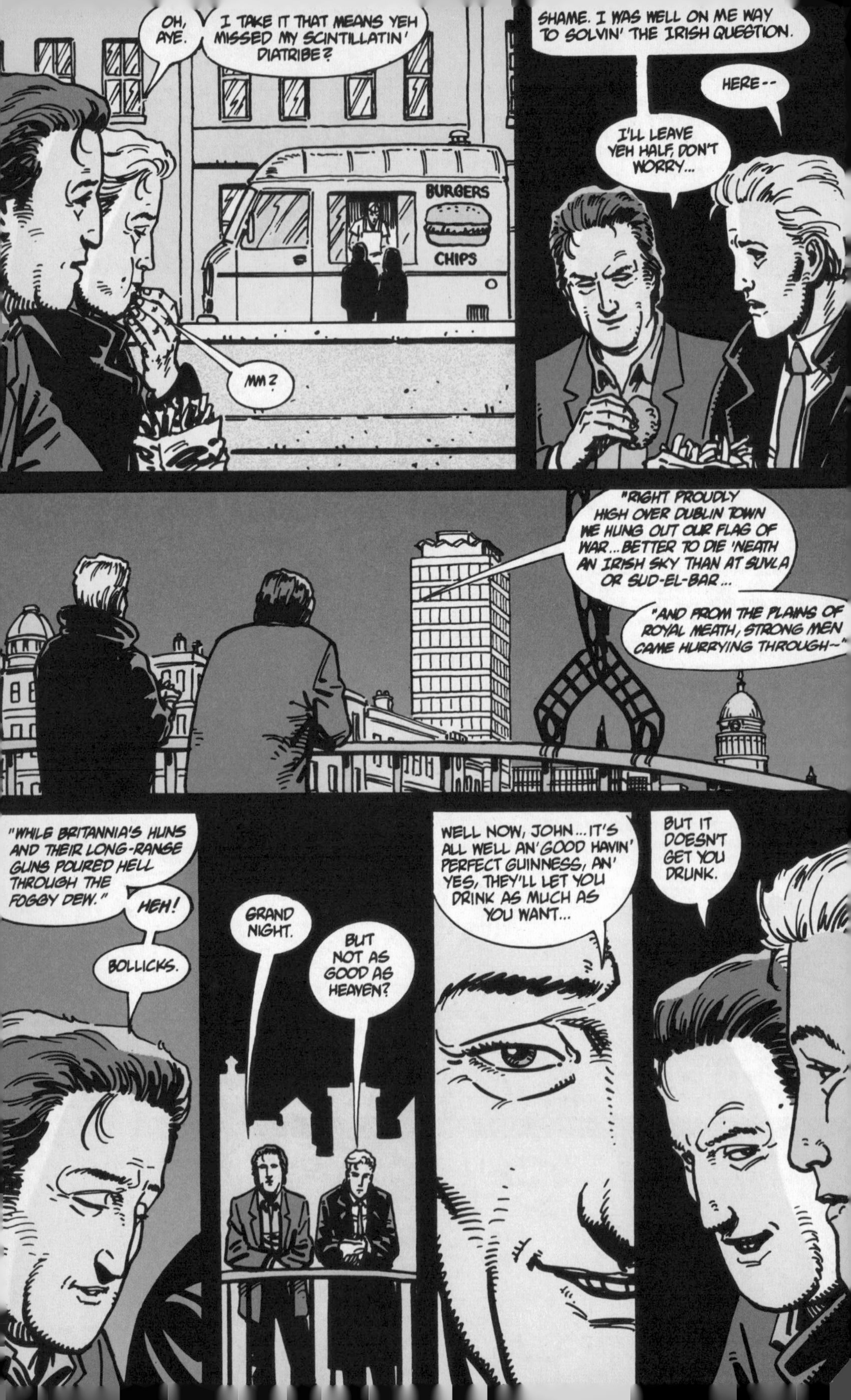
OH, AYE.
I TAKE IT THAT MEANS YEH MISSED MY SCINTILLATIN' DIATRIBE?
BURGERS
CHIPS
MM?
SHAME. I WAS WELL ON ME WAY TO SOLVIN' THE IRISH QUESTION.
HERE--
I'LL LEAVE YEH HALF, DON'T WORRY...
"RIGHT PROUDLY HIGH OVER DUBLIN TOWN WE HUNG OUT OUR FLAG OF WAR...BETTER TO DIE 'NEATH AN IRISH SKY THAN AT SUVLA OR SUD-EL-BAR...
"AND FROM THE PLAINS OF ROYAL MEATH, STRONG MEN CAME HURRYING THROUGH--"
"WHILE BRITANNIA'S HUNS AND THEIR LONG-RANGE GUNS POURED HELL THROUGH THE FOGGY DEW."
HEH!
BOLLICKS.
GRAND NIGHT.
BUT NOT AS GOOD AS HEAVEN?
WELL NOW, JOHN...IT'S ALL WELL AN' GOOD HAVIN' PERFECT GUINNESS, AN' YES, THEY'LL LET YOU DRINK AS MUCH AS YOU WANT...
BUT IT DOESN'T GET YOU DRUNK.

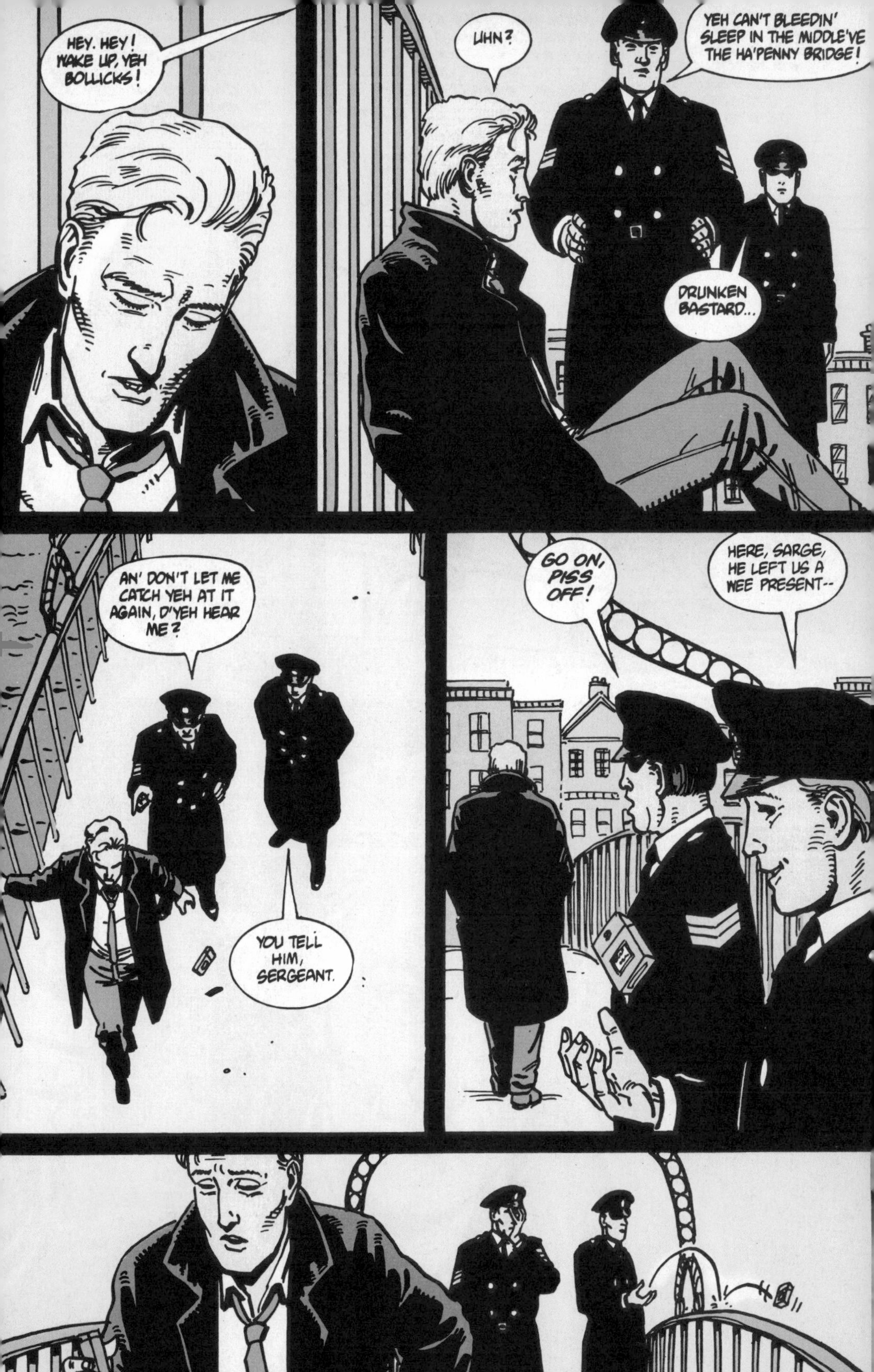
HEY. HEY! WAKE UP, YEH BOLLICKS!
UHN?
YEH CAN'T BLEEDIN' SLEEP IN THE MIDDLE'VE THE HA'PENNY BRIDGE!
DRUNKEN BASTARD...
AN' DON'T LET ME CATCH YEH AT IT AGAIN, D'YEH HEAR ME?
YOU TELL HIM, SERGEANT.
GO ON, PISS OFF!
HERE, SARGE, HE LEFT US A WEE PRESENT--

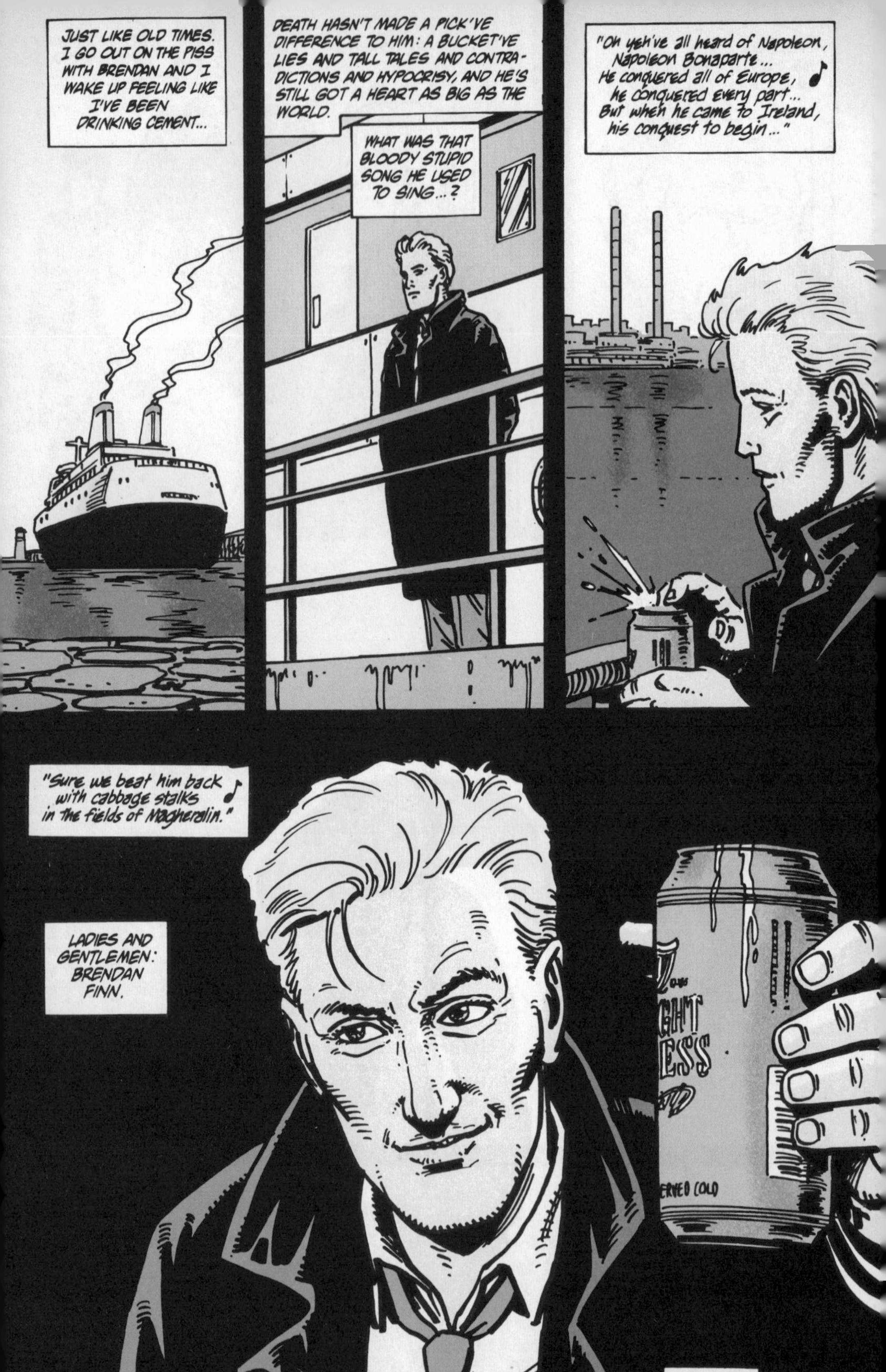
JUST LIKE OLD TIMES. I GO OUT ON THE PISS WITH BRENDAN AND I WAKE UP FEELING LIKE I'VE BEEN DRINKING CEMENT...
DEATH HASN'T MADE A PICK'VE DIFFERENCE TO HIM: A BUCKET'VE LIES AND TALL TALES AND CONTRADICTIONS AND HYPOCRISY, AND HE'S STILL GOT A HEART AS BIG AS THE WORLD.
WHAT WAS THAT BLOODY STUPID SONG HE USED TO SING...?
"Oh yeh've all heard of Napoleon, Napoleon Bonaparte... He conquered all of Europe, he conquered every part... But when he came to Ireland, his conquest to begin..."
"Sure we beat him back with cabbage stalks in the fields of Magheralin."
LADIES AND GENTLEMEN: BRENDAN FINN.
The End

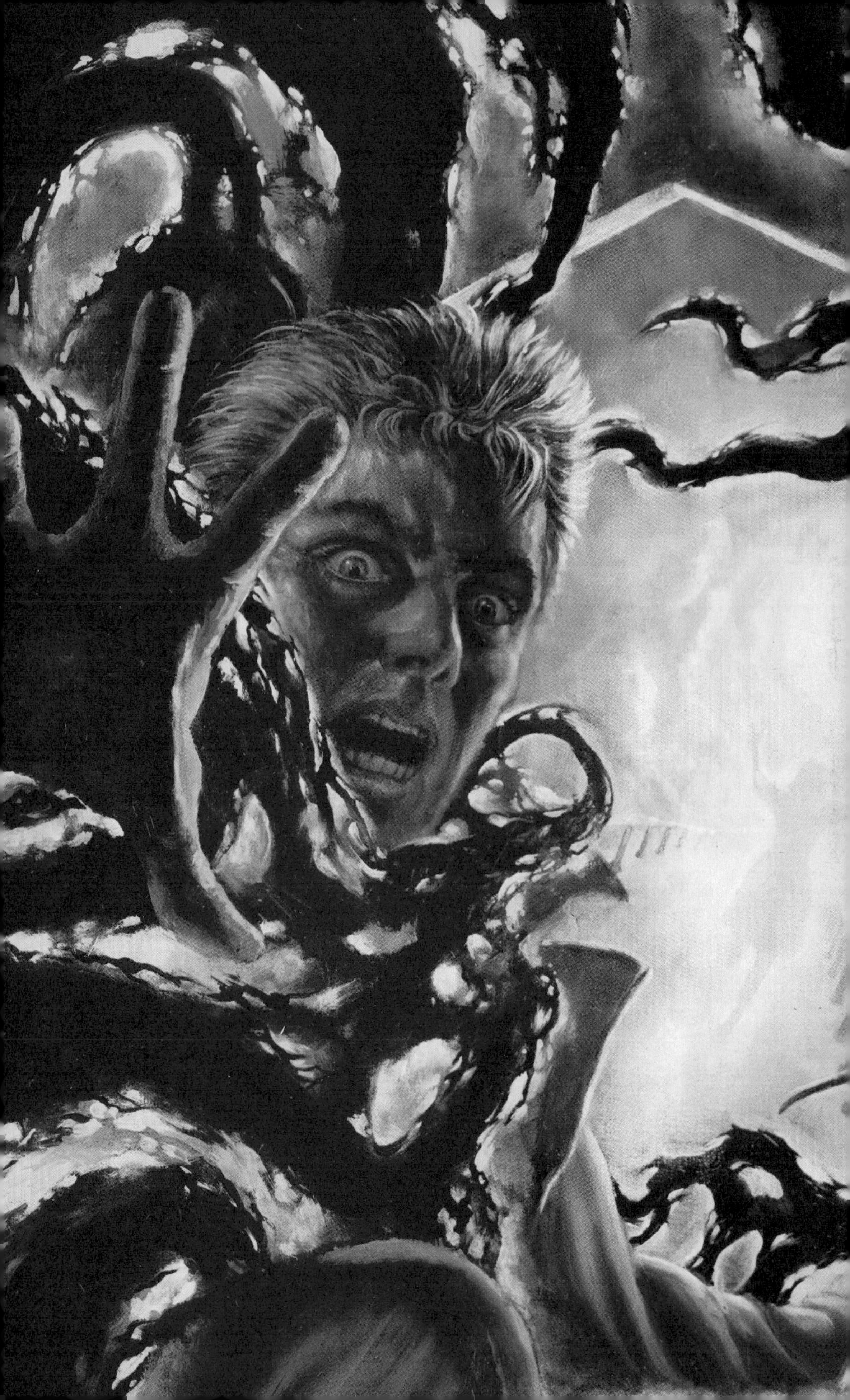

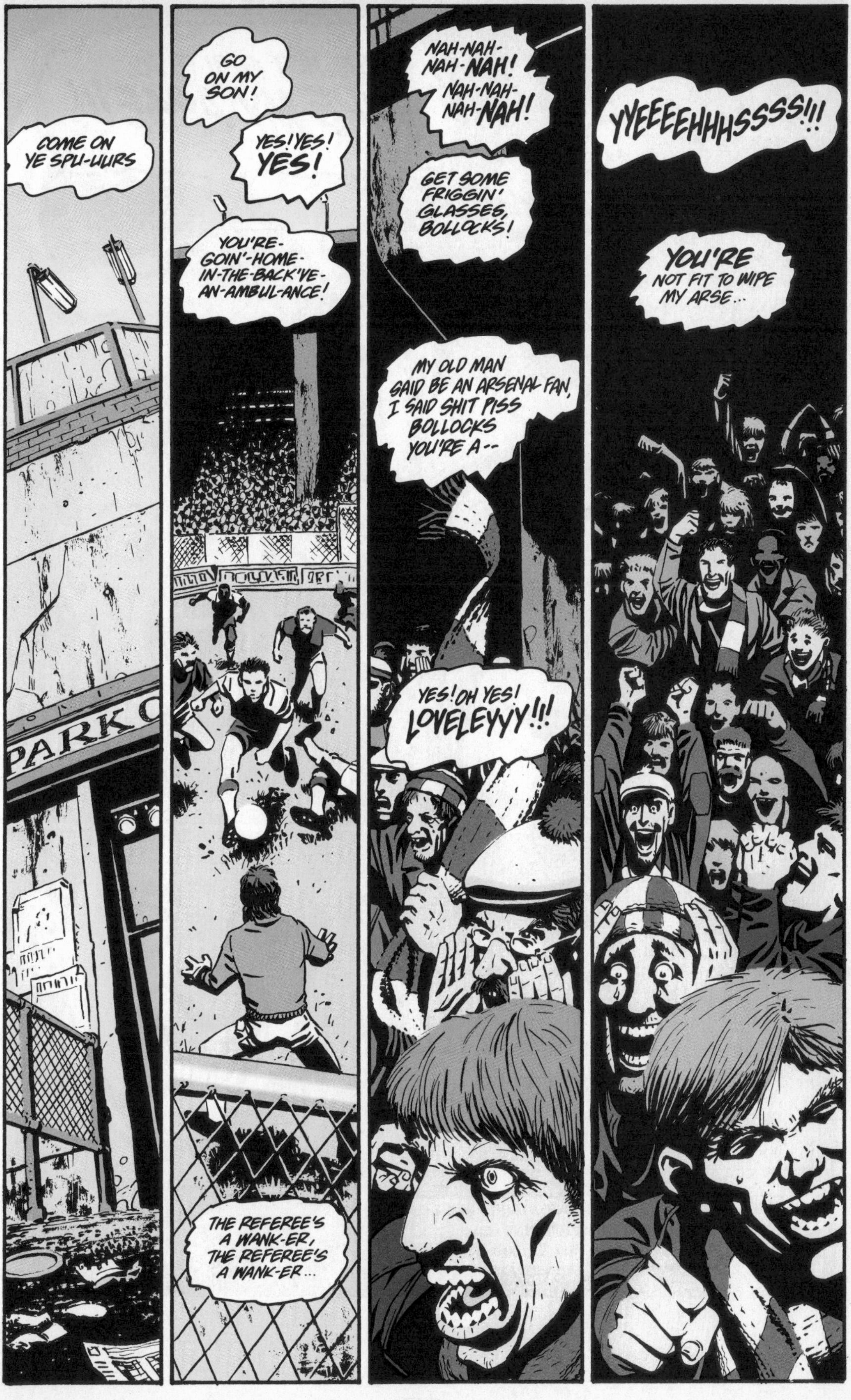
COME ON YE SPU-UURS
GO ON MY SON!
YES! YES! YES!
YOU'RE-GOIN'-HOME-IN-THE-BACK'YE-AN-AMBUL-ANCE!
THE REFEREE'S A WANK-ER, THE REFEREE'S A WANK-ER...
NAH-NAH-NAH-NAH! NAH-NAH-NAH-NAH!
GET SOME FRIGGIN' GLASSES, BOLLOCKS!
MY OLD MAN SAID BE AN ARSENAL FAN, I SAID SHIT PISS BOLLOCKS YOU'RE A--
YES! OH YES! LOVELEYYY!!!
YYEEEEHHHSSSS!!!
YOU'RE NOT FIT TO WIPE MY ARSE...
PARK

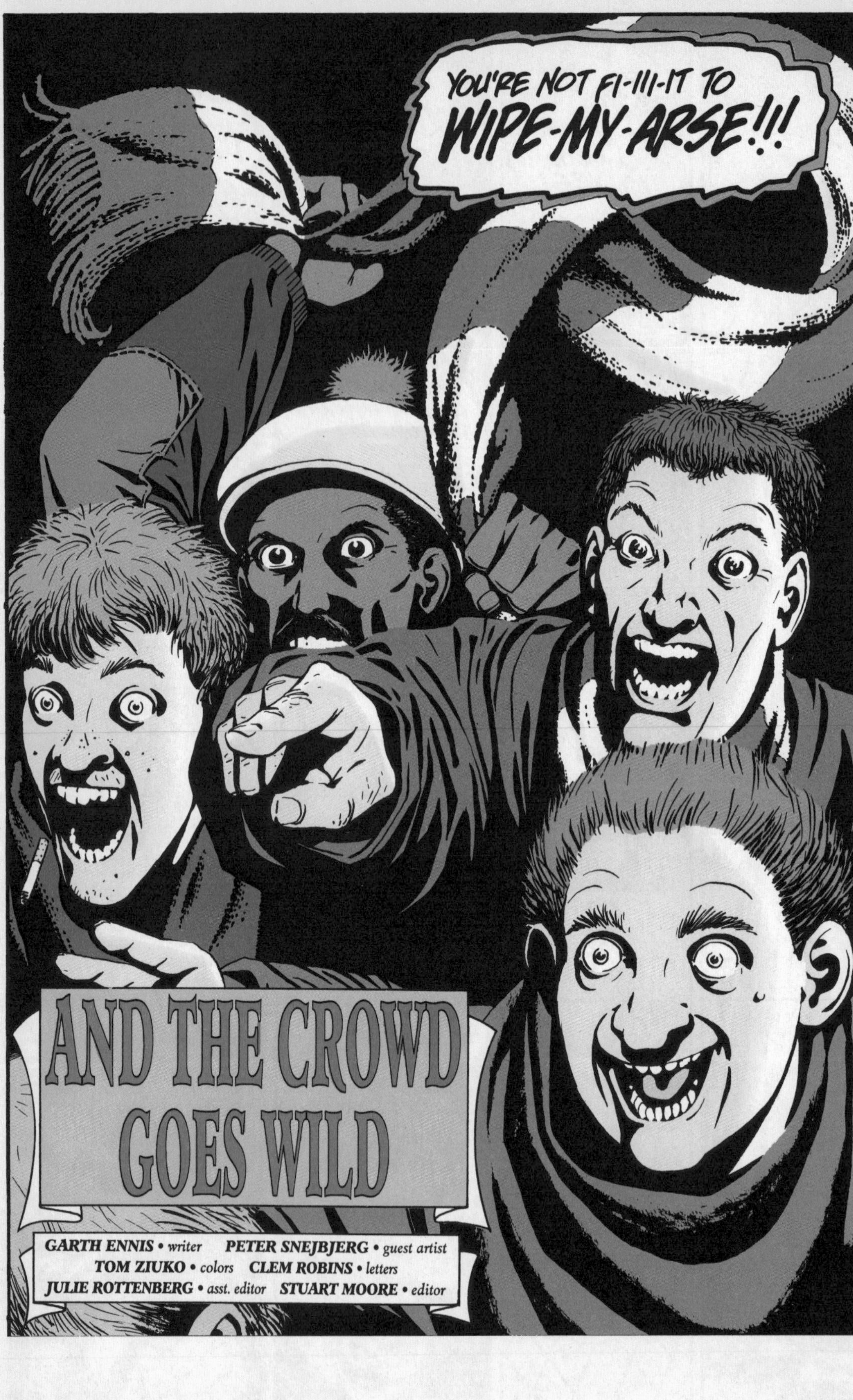
YOU'RE NOT FI-III-IT TO WIPE-MY-ARSE!!!
AND THE CROWD GOES WILD
GARTH ENNIS • writer PETER SNEJBJERG • guest artist
TOM ZIUKO • colors CLEM ROBINS • letters
JULIE ROTTENBERG • asst. editor STUART MOORE • editor

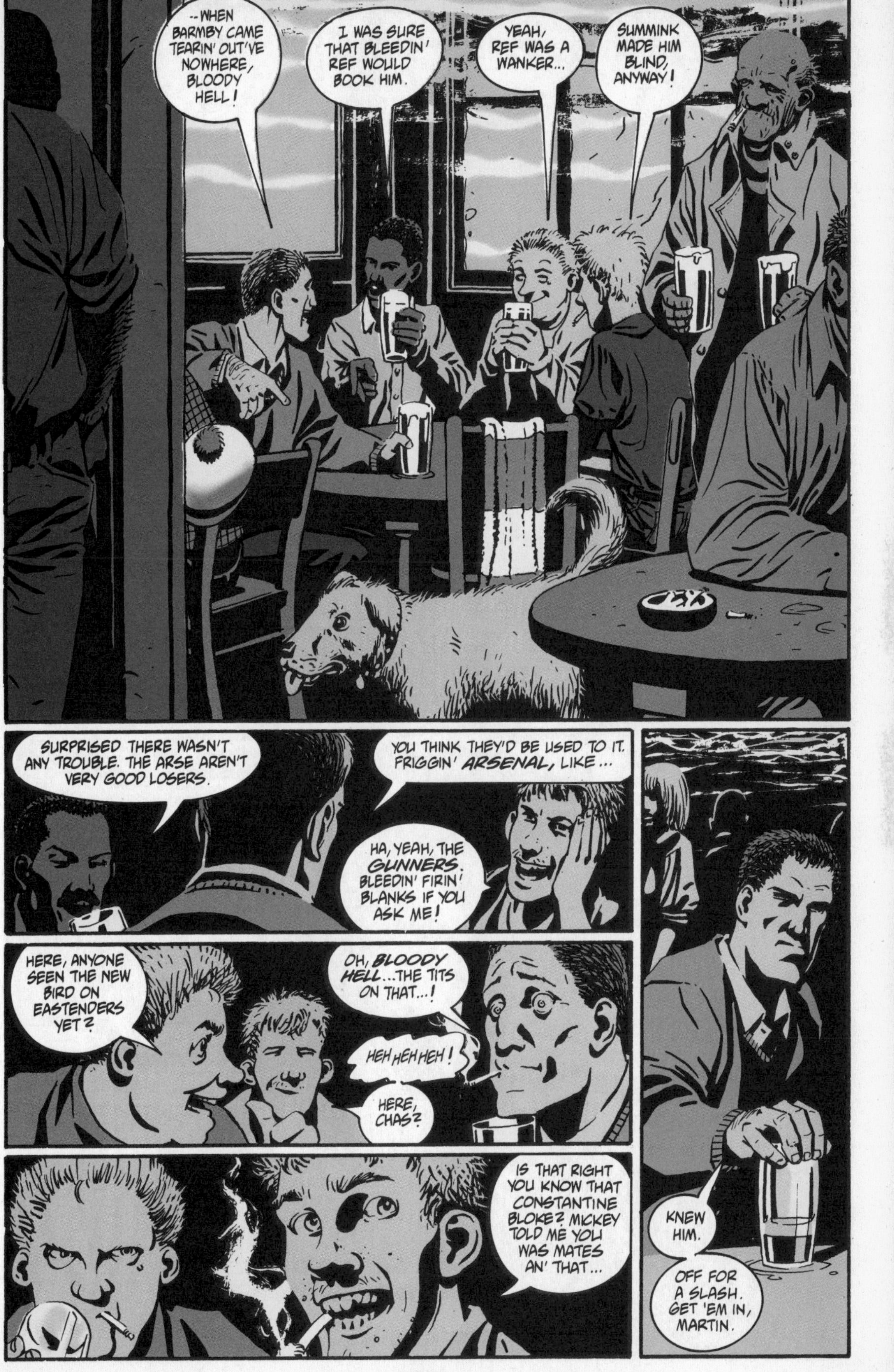
--WHEN BARMBY CAME TEARIN' OUT'VE NOWHERE, BLOODY HELL!
I WAS SURE THAT BLEEDIN' REF WOULD BOOK HIM.
YEAH, REF WAS A WANKER...
SUMMINK MADE HIM BLIND, ANYWAY!
SURPRISED THERE WASN'T ANY TROUBLE. THE ARSE AREN'T VERY GOOD LOSERS.
YOU THINK THEY'D BE USED TO IT. FRIGGIN' ARSENAL, LIKE...
HA, YEAH, THE GUNNERS. BLEEDIN' FIRIN' BLANKS IF YOU ASK ME!
HERE, ANYONE SEEN THE NEW BIRD ON EASTENDERS YET?
OH, BLOODY HELL...THE TITS ON THAT...!
HEH HEH HEH!
HERE, CHAS?
IS THAT RIGHT YOU KNOW THAT CONSTANTINE BLOKE? MICKEY TOLD ME YOU WAS MATES AN' THAT...
KNEW HIM.
OFF FOR A SLASH. GET 'EM IN, MARTIN.

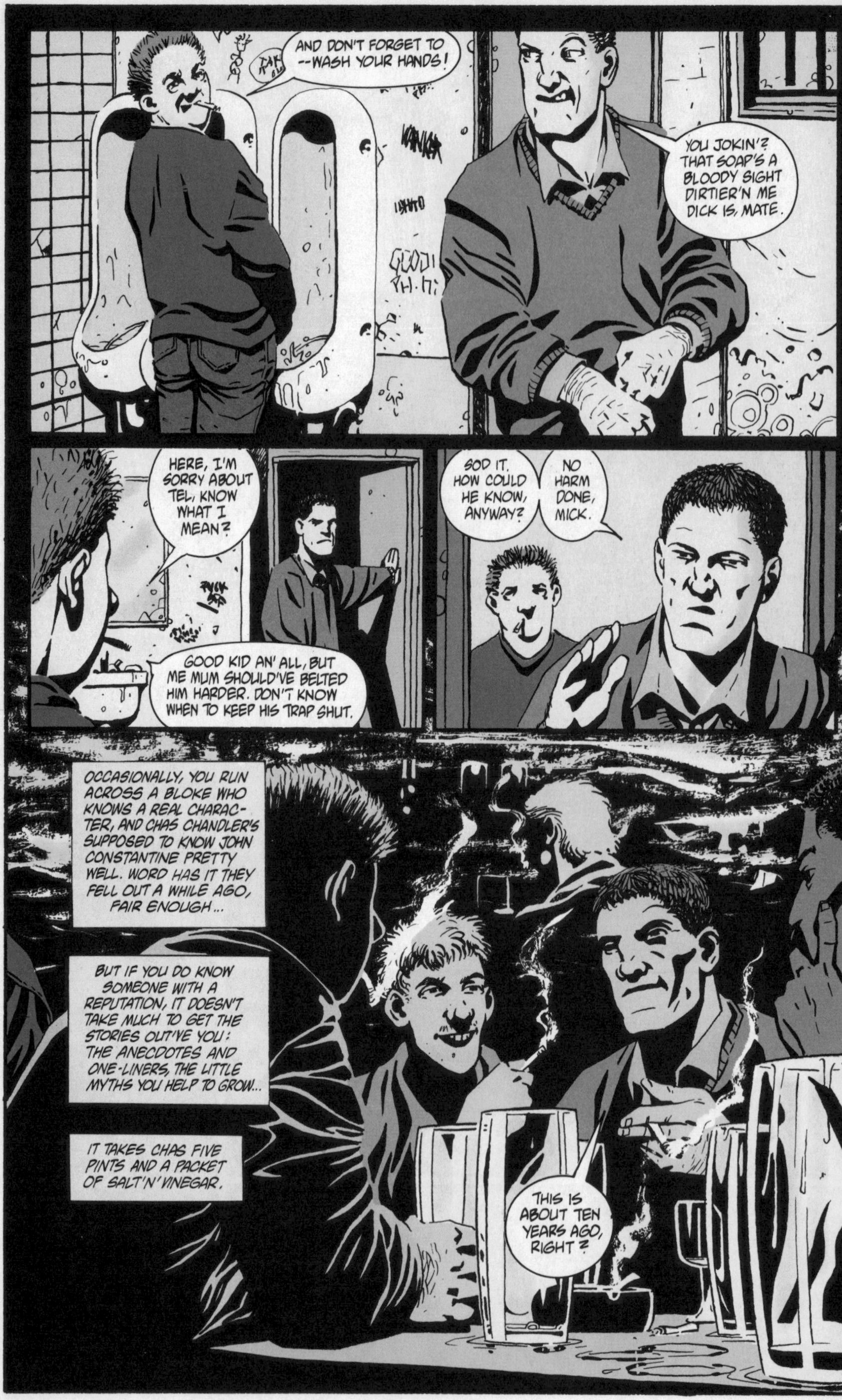
AND DON'T FORGET TO --WASH YOUR HANDS!
YOU JOKIN'? THAT SOAP'S A BLOODY SIGHT DIRTIER'N ME DICK IS, MATE.
HERE, I'M SORRY ABOUT TEL, KNOW WHAT I MEAN?
GOOD KID AN' ALL, BUT ME MUM SHOULD'VE BELTED HIM HARDER. DON'T KNOW WHEN TO KEEP HIS TRAP SHUT.
SOD IT. HOW COULD HE KNOW, ANYWAY?
NO HARM DONE, MICK.
OCCASIONALLY, YOU RUN ACROSS A BLOKE WHO KNOWS A REAL CHARACTER, AND CHAS CHANDLER'S SUPPOSED TO KNOW JOHN CONSTANTINE PRETTY WELL. WORD HAS IT THEY FELL OUT A WHILE AGO, FAIR ENOUGH...
BUT IF YOU DO KNOW SOMEONE WITH A REPUTATION, IT DOESN'T TAKE MUCH TO GET THE STORIES OUT'VE YOU: THE ANECDOTES AND ONE-LINERS, THE LITTLE MYTHS YOU HELP TO GROW...
IT TAKES CHAS FIVE PINTS AND A PACKET OF SALT'N'VINEGAR.
THIS IS ABOUT TEN YEARS AGO, RIGHT?

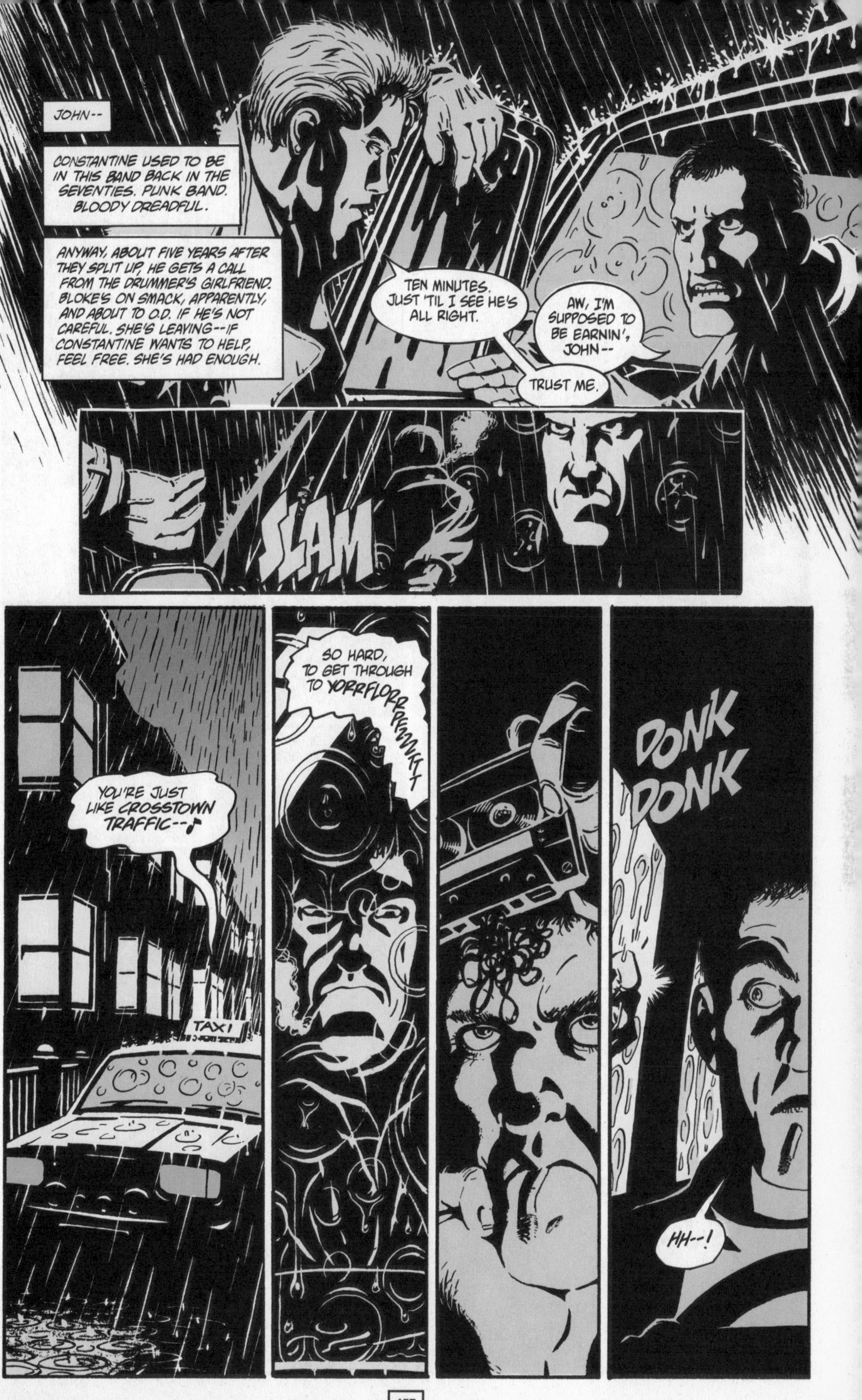
JOHN--
CONSTANTINE USED TO BE IN THIS BAND BACK IN THE SEVENTIES. PUNK BAND. BLOODY DREADFUL.
ANYWAY, ABOUT FIVE YEARS AFTER THEY SPLIT UP, HE GETS A CALL FROM THE DRUMMER'S GIRLFRIEND. BLOKE'S ON SMACK, APPARENTLY, AND ABOUT TO O.D. IF HE'S NOT CAREFUL. SHE'S LEAVING--IF CONSTANTINE WANTS TO HELP, FEEL FREE. SHE'S HAD ENOUGH.
TEN MINUTES. JUST 'TIL I SEE HE'S ALL RIGHT.
AW, I'M SUPPOSED TO BE EARNIN', JOHN--
TRUST ME.
SLAM
TAXI
YOU'RE JUST LIKE CROSSTOWN TRAFFIC--♪
SO HARD, TO GET THROUGH TO YORRFLORRRZZKKT
DONK
DONK
HH--!

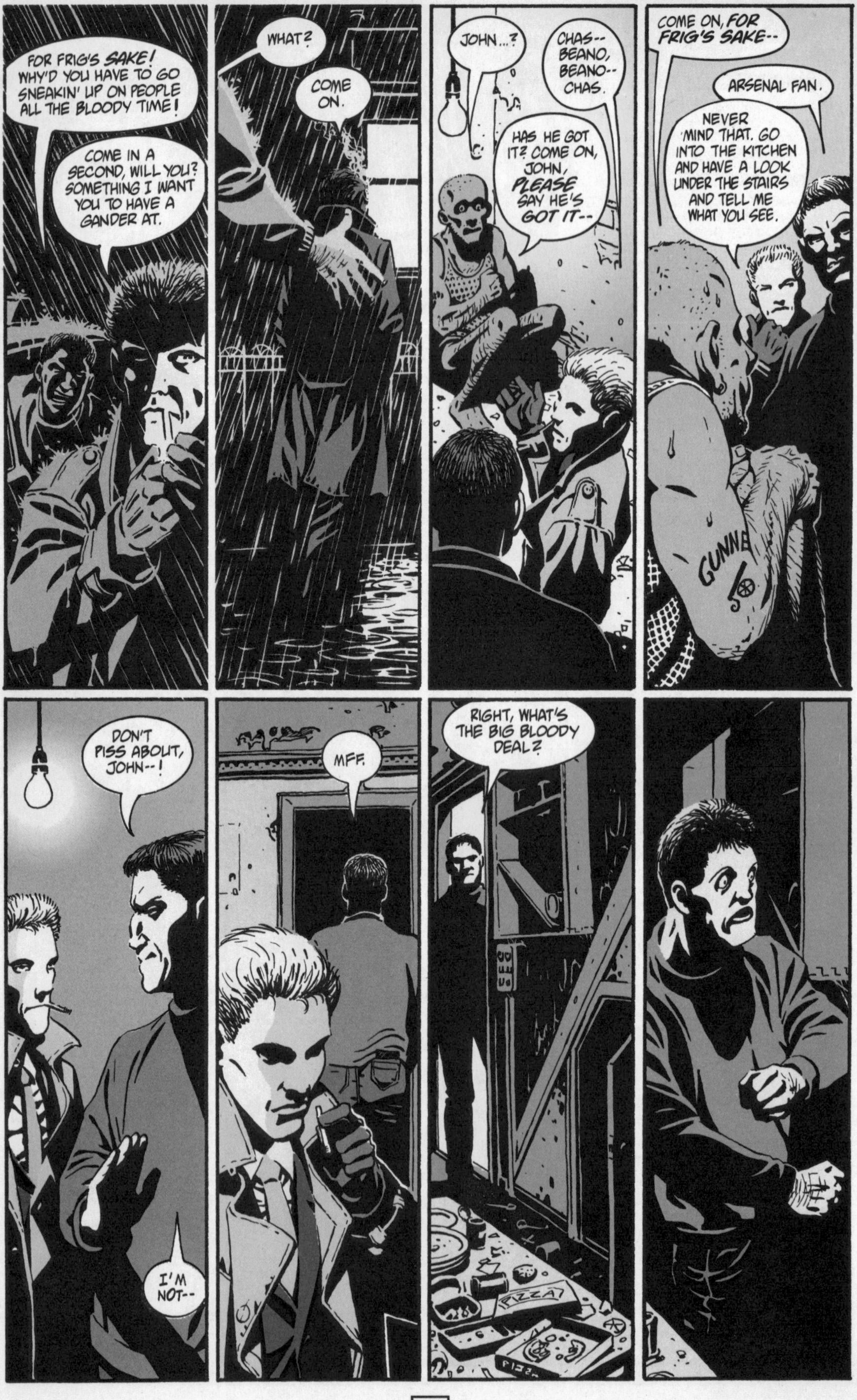
FOR FRIG'S SAKE! WHY'D YOU HAVE TO GO SNEAKIN' UP ON PEOPLE ALL THE BLOODY TIME!
COME IN A SECOND, WILL YOU? SOMETHING I WANT YOU TO HAVE A GANDER AT.
WHAT?
COME ON.
JOHN...?
CHAS-- BEANO, BEANO-- CHAS.
HAS HE GOT IT? COME ON, JOHN, PLEASE SAY HE'S GOT IT--
COME ON, FOR FRIG'S SAKE--
ARSENAL FAN.
NEVER MIND THAT. GO INTO THE KITCHEN AND HAVE A LOOK UNDER THE STAIRS AND TELL ME WHAT YOU SEE.
GUNNE
DON'T PISS ABOUT, JOHN--!
I'M NOT--
MFF.
RIGHT, WHAT'S THE BIG BLOODY DEAL?
PIZZA

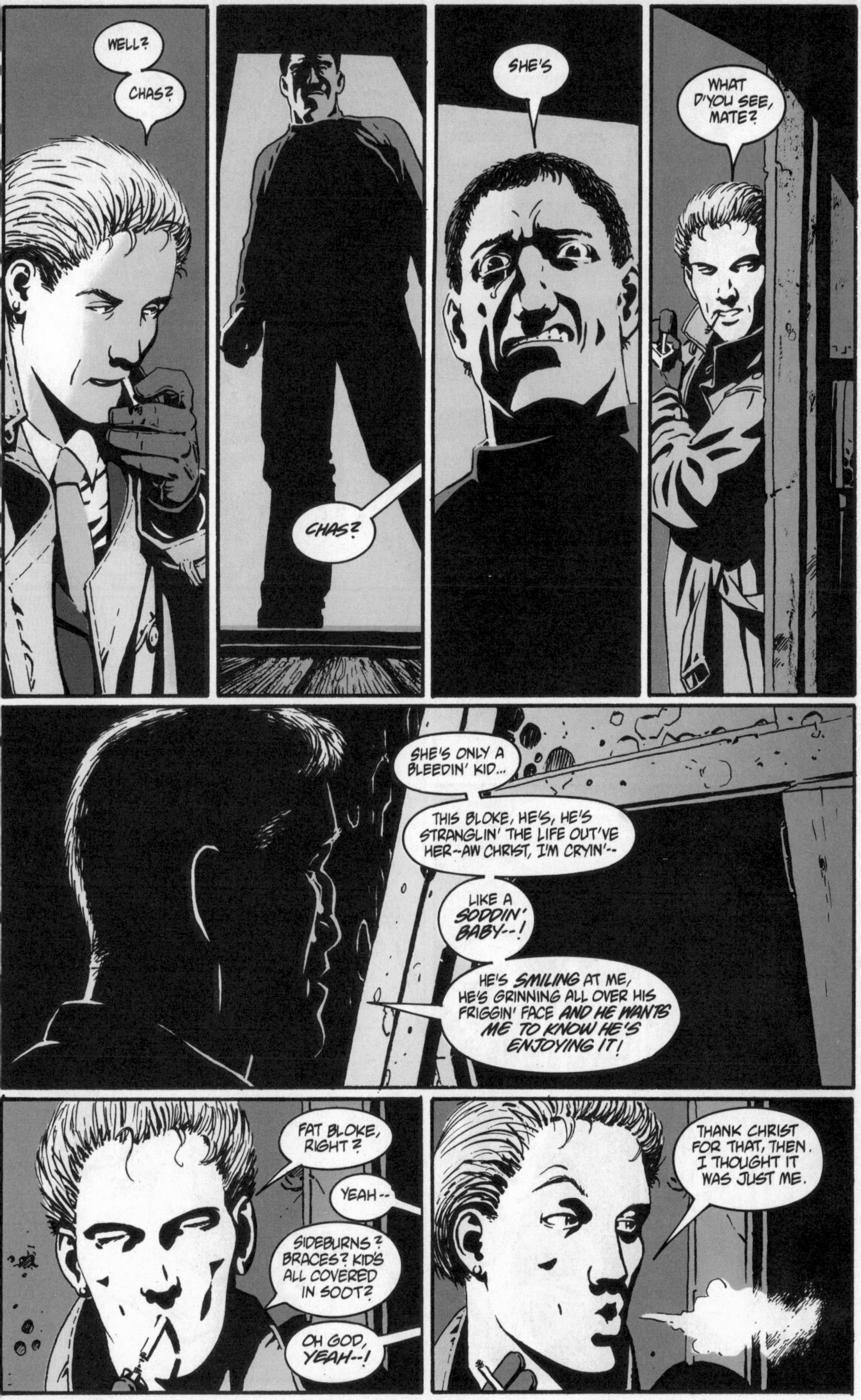
WELL?
CHAS?
CHAS?
SHE'S
WHAT D'YOU SEE, MATE?
SHE'S ONLY A BLEEDIN' KID...
THIS BLOKE, HE'S, HE'S STRANGLIN' THE LIFE OUT'VE HER--AW CHRIST, I'M CRYIN'--
LIKE A SODDIN' BABY--!
HE'S SMILING AT ME, HE'S GRINNING ALL OVER HIS FRIGGIN' FACE AND HE WANTS ME TO KNOW HE'S ENJOYING IT!
FAT BLOKE, RIGHT?
YEAH--
SIDEBURNS? BRACES? KID'S ALL COVERED IN SOOT?
OH GOD, YEAH--!
THANK CHRIST FOR THAT, THEN. I THOUGHT IT WAS JUST ME.

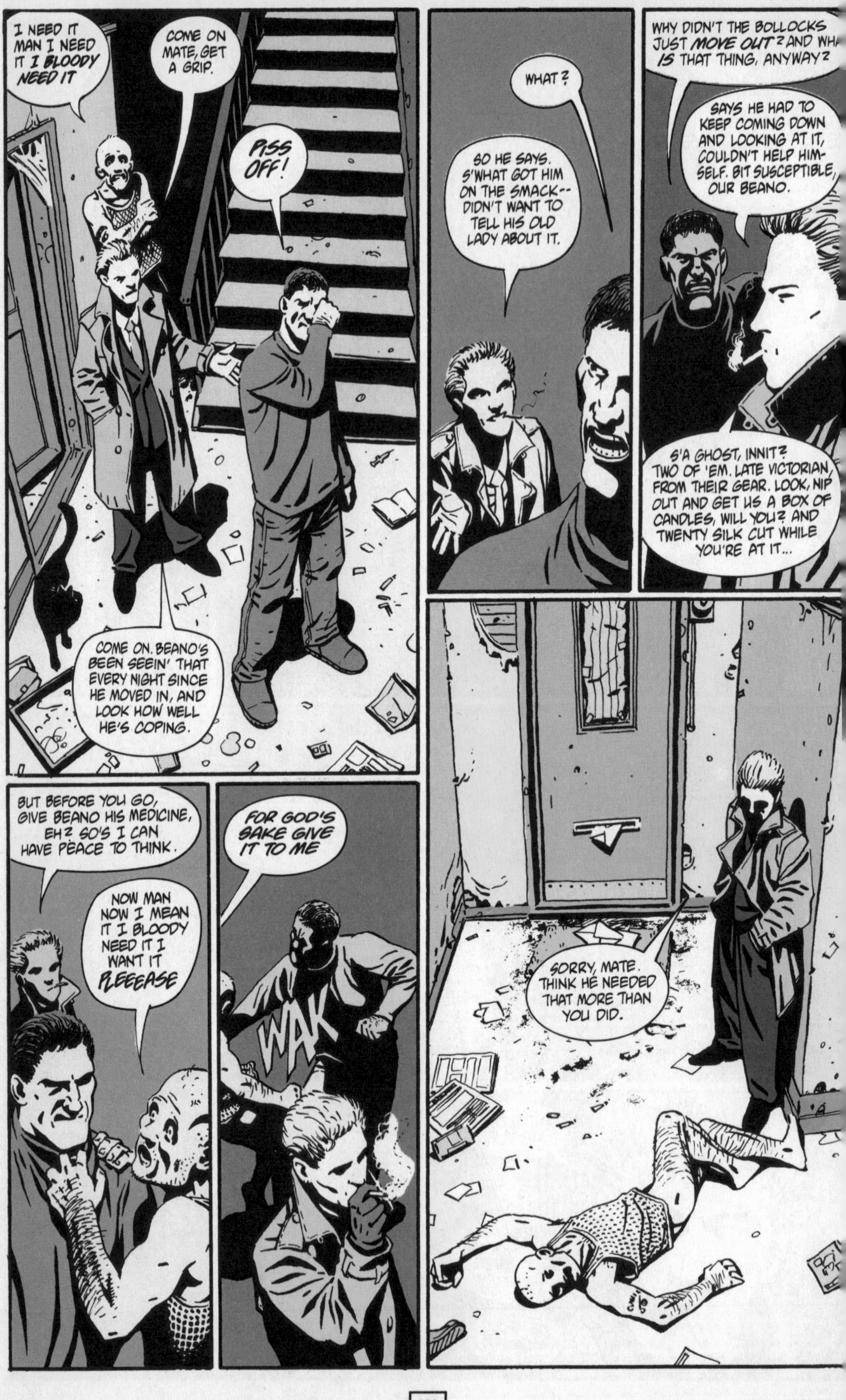
I NEED IT MAN I NEED IT I BLOODY NEED IT
COME ON MATE, GET A GRIP.
PISS OFF!
COME ON. BEANO'S BEEN SEEIN' THAT EVERY NIGHT SINCE HE MOVED IN, AND LOOK HOW WELL HE'S COPING.
WHAT?
SO HE SAYS. S'WHAT GOT HIM ON THE SMACK-- DIDN'T WANT TO TELL HIS OLD LADY ABOUT IT.
WHY DIDN'T THE BOLLOCKS JUST MOVE OUT? AND WHA IS THAT THING, ANYWAY?
SAYS HE HAD TO KEEP COMING DOWN AND LOOKING AT IT, COULDN'T HELP HIMSELF. BIT SUSCEPTIBLE, OUR BEANO.
S'A GHOST, INNIT? TWO OF 'EM. LATE VICTORIAN, FROM THEIR GEAR. LOOK, NIP OUT AND GET US A BOX OF CANDLES, WILL YOU? AND TWENTY SILK CUT WHILE YOU'RE AT IT...
BUT BEFORE YOU GO, GIVE BEANO HIS MEDICINE, EH? SO'S I CAN HAVE PEACE TO THINK.
NOW MAN NOW I MEAN IT I BLOODY NEED IT I WANT IT PLEEEASE
FOR GOD'S SAKE GIVE IT TO ME
WAK
SORRY, MATE. THINK HE NEEDED THAT MORE THAN YOU DID.

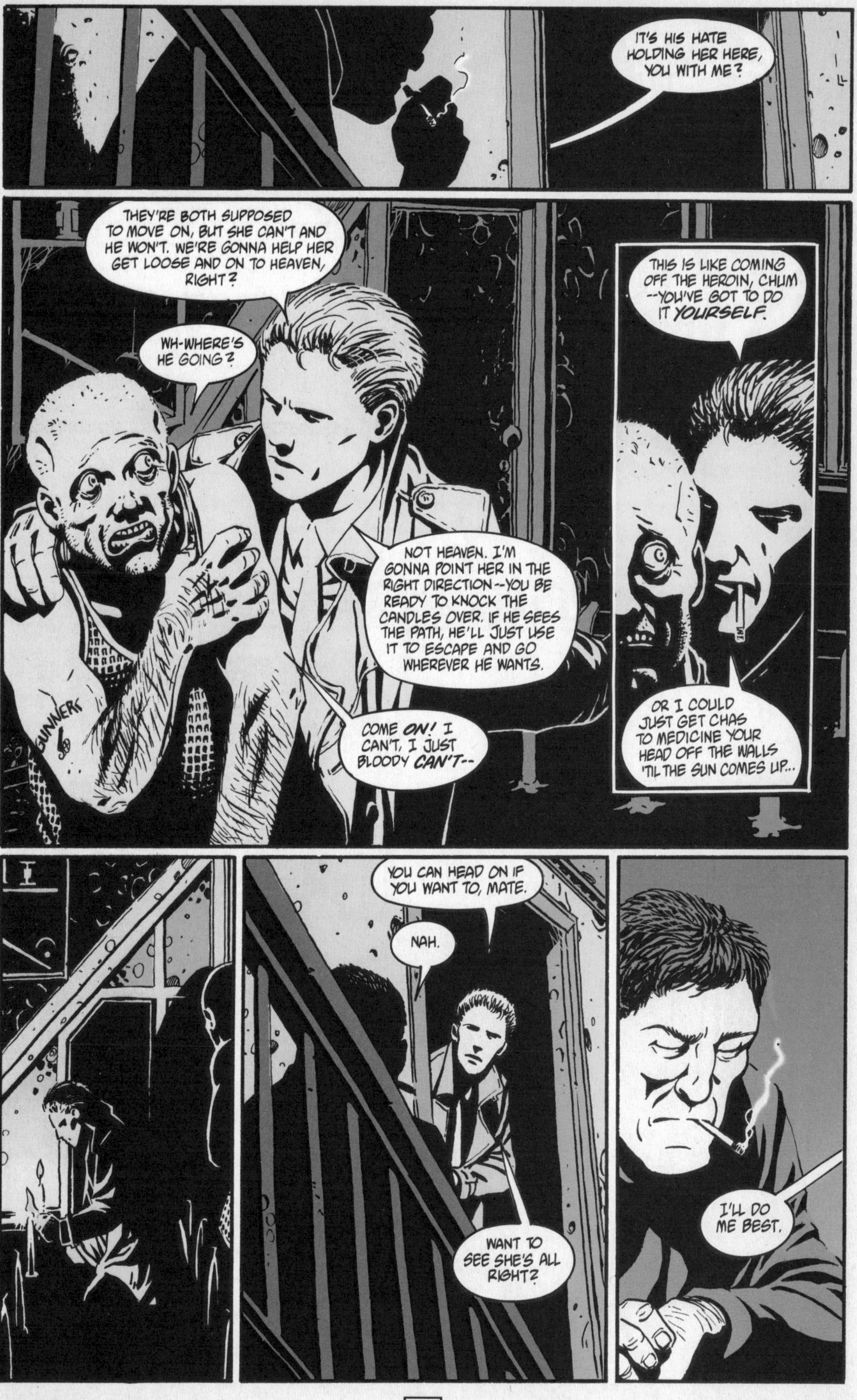
IT'S HIS HATE HOLDING HER HERE, YOU WITH ME?
THEY'RE BOTH SUPPOSED TO MOVE ON, BUT SHE CAN'T AND HE WON'T. WE'RE GONNA HELP HER GET LOOSE AND ON TO HEAVEN, RIGHT?
WH-WHERE'S HE GOING?
NOT HEAVEN. I'M GONNA POINT HER IN THE RIGHT DIRECTION--YOU BE READY TO KNOCK THE CANDLES OVER. IF HE SEES THE PATH, HE'LL JUST USE IT TO ESCAPE AND GO WHEREVER HE WANTS.
COME ON! I CAN'T, I JUST BLOODY CAN'T--
GUNNERS
THIS IS LIKE COMING OFF THE HEROIN, CHUM --YOU'VE GOT TO DO IT YOURSELF.
OR I COULD JUST GET CHAS TO MEDICINE YOUR HEAD OFF THE WALLS 'TIL THE SUN COMES UP...
YOU CAN HEAD ON IF YOU WANT TO, MATE.
NAH.
WANT TO SEE SHE'S ALL RIGHT?
I'LL DO ME BEST.

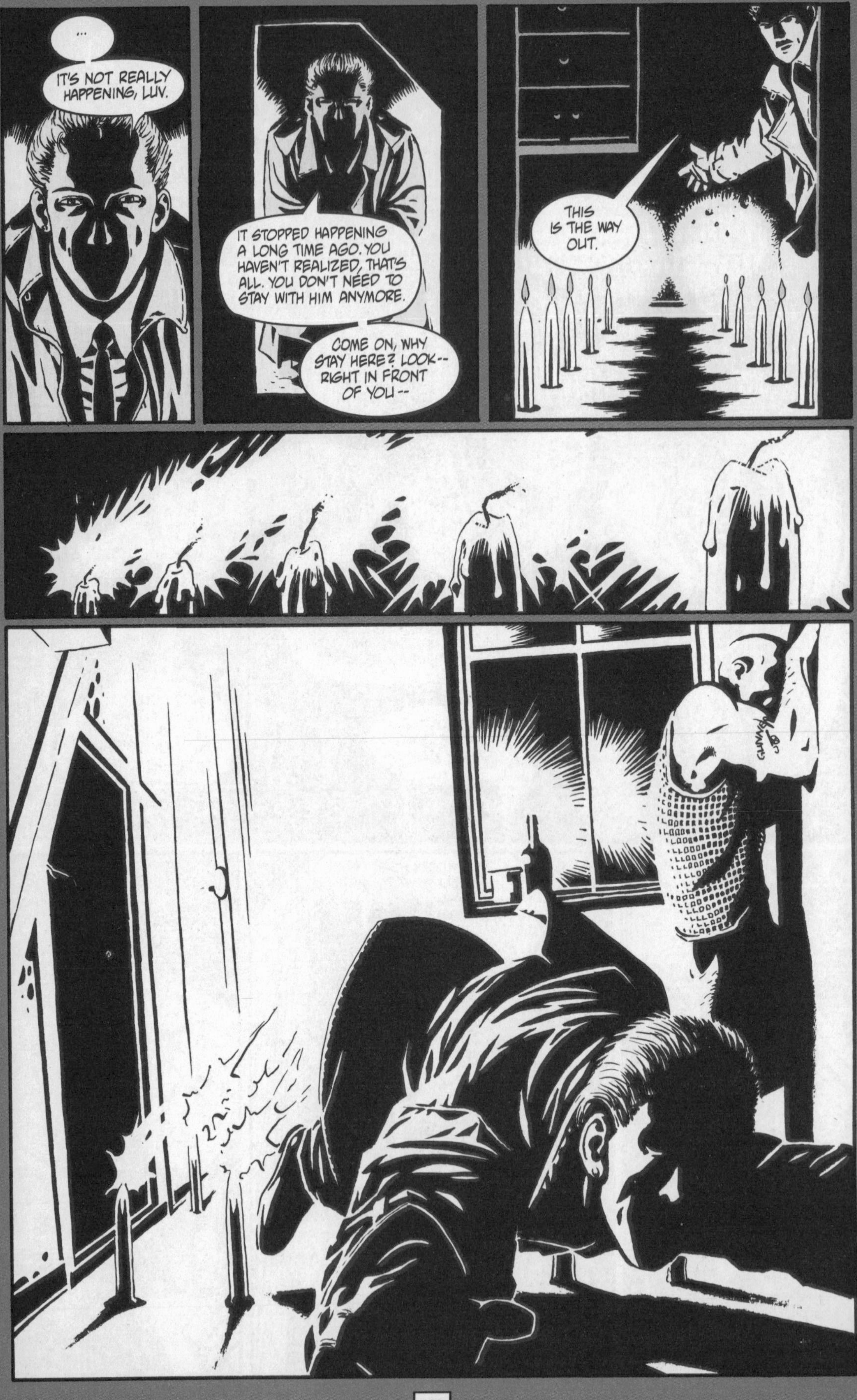
...
IT'S NOT REALLY HAPPENING, LUV.
IT STOPPED HAPPENING A LONG TIME AGO. YOU HAVEN'T REALIZED, THAT'S ALL. YOU DON'T NEED TO STAY WITH HIM ANYMORE.
COME ON, WHY STAY HERE? LOOK-- RIGHT IN FRONT OF YOU --
THIS IS THE WAY OUT.

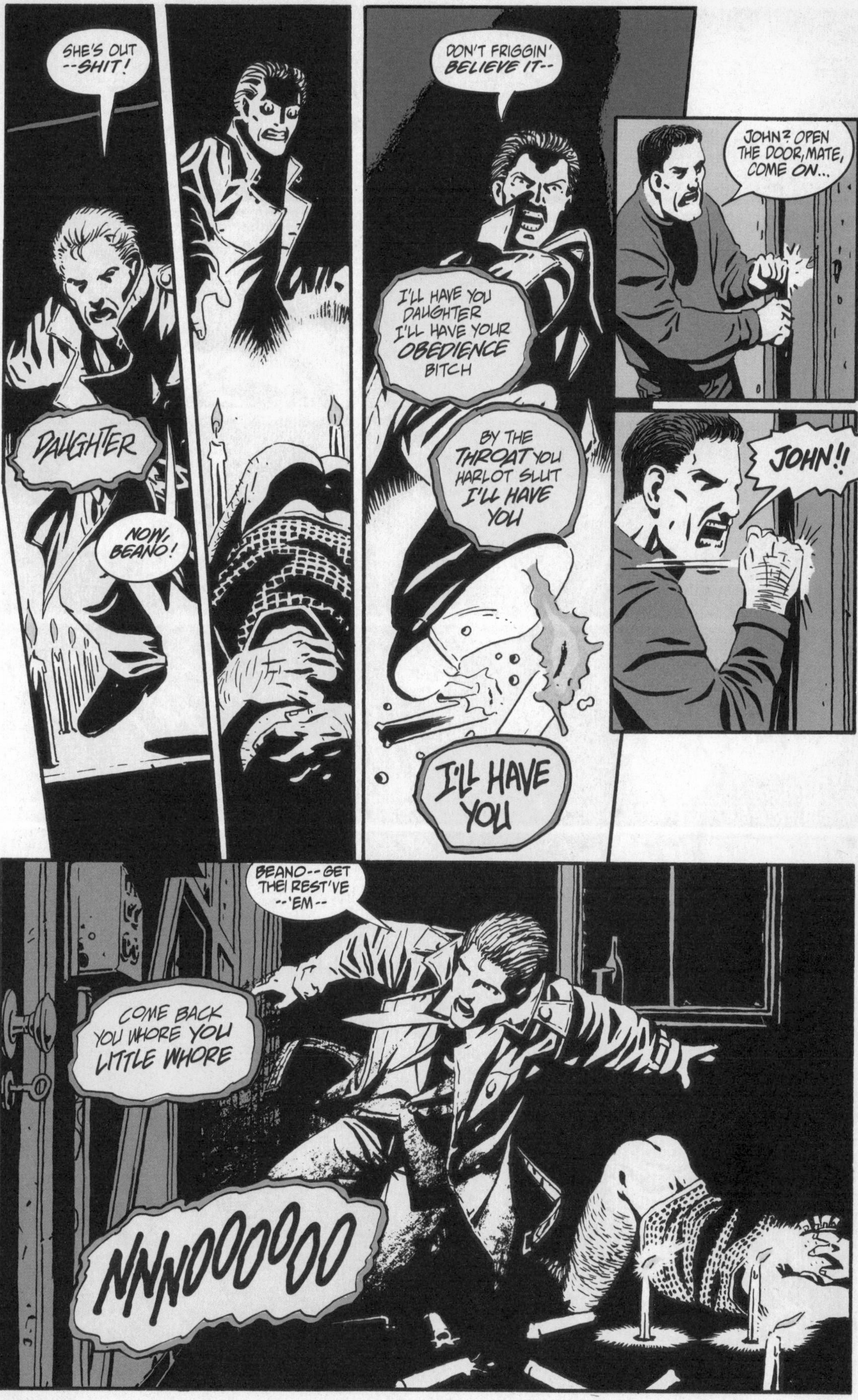
SHE'S OUT --SHIT!
DAUGHTER
NOW, BEANO!
DON'T FRIGGIN' BELIEVE IT--
I'LL HAVE YOU DAUGHTER I'LL HAVE YOUR OBEDIENCE BITCH
BY THE THROAT YOU HARLOT SLUT I'LL HAVE YOU
I'LL HAVE YOU
JOHN? OPEN THE DOOR, MATE, COME ON...
JOHN!!
BEANO--GET THE! REST'VE --'EM--
COME BACK YOU WHORE YOU LITTLE WHORE
NNNOOOOOO

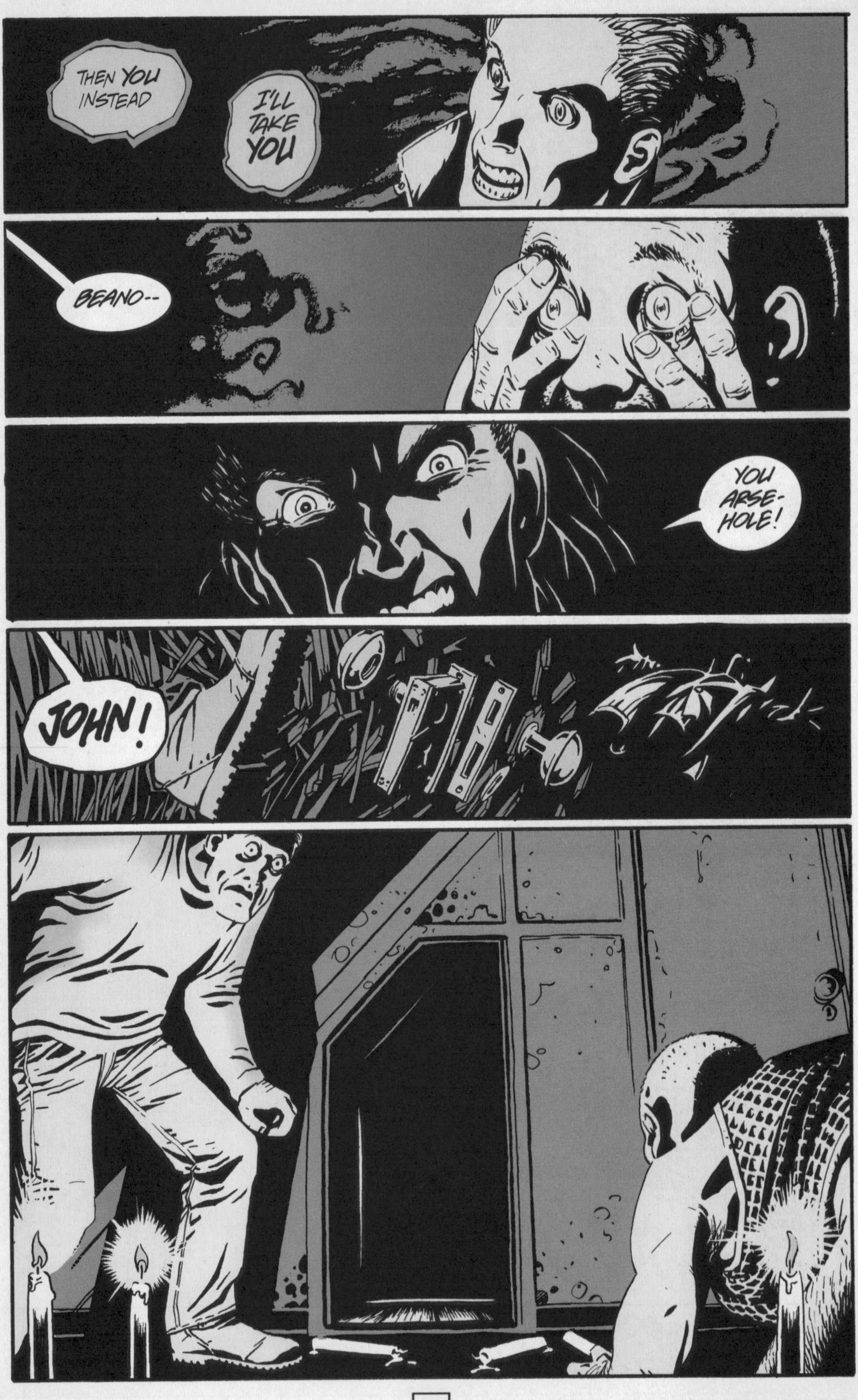
THEN YOU INSTEAD
I'LL TAKE YOU
BEANO--
YOU ARSE-HOLE!
JOHN!

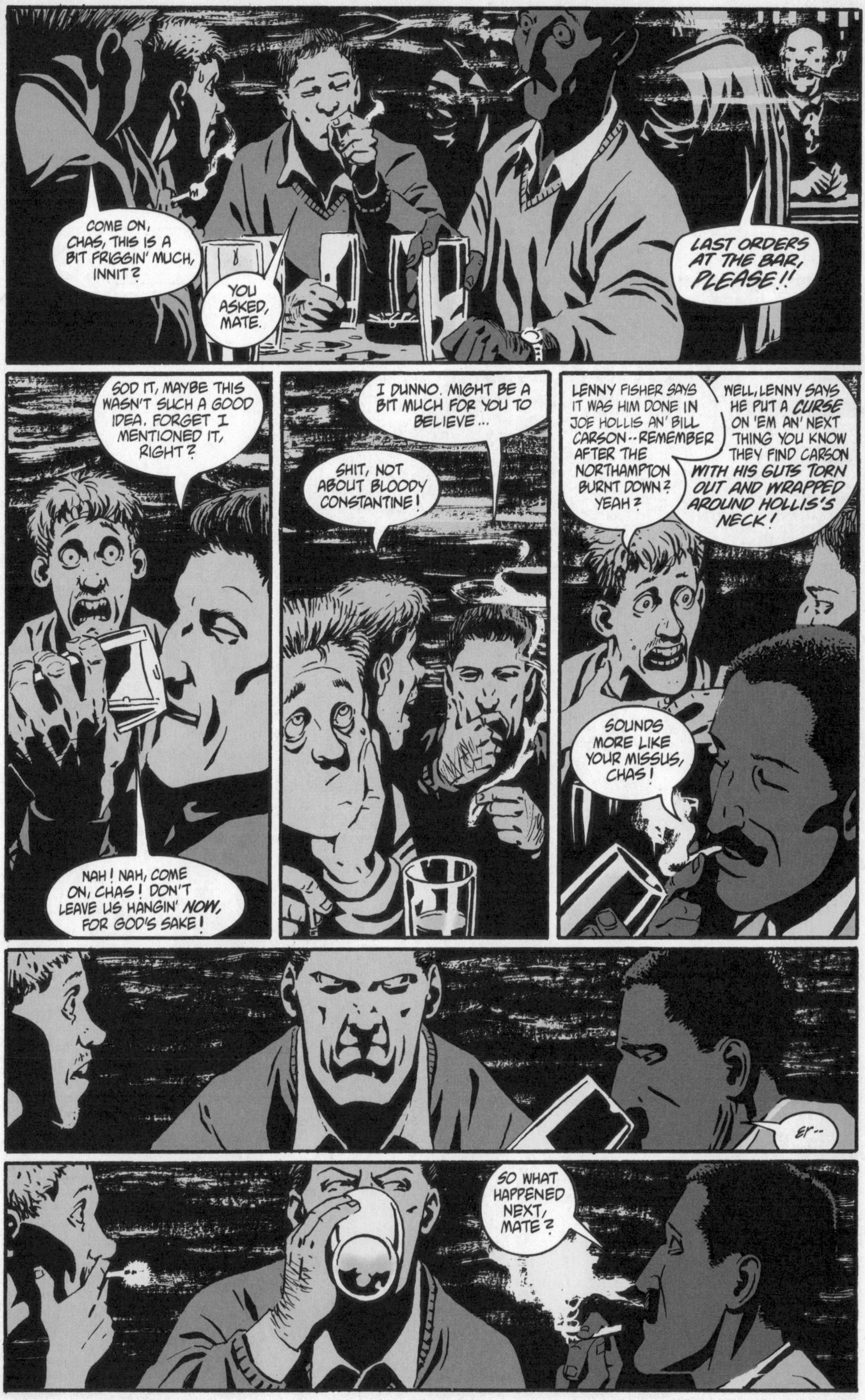
COME ON, CHAS, THIS IS A BIT FRIGGIN' MUCH, INNIT?
YOU ASKED, MATE.
LAST ORDERS AT THE BAR, PLEASE!!
SOD IT, MAYBE THIS WASN'T SUCH A GOOD IDEA. FORGET I MENTIONED IT, RIGHT?
NAH! NAH, COME ON, CHAS! DON'T LEAVE US HANGIN' NOW, FOR GOD'S SAKE!
I DUNNO. MIGHT BE A BIT MUCH FOR YOU TO BELIEVE...
SHIT, NOT ABOUT BLOODY CONSTANTINE!
LENNY FISHER SAYS IT WAS HIM DONE IN JOE HOLLIS AN' BILL CARSON--REMEMBER AFTER THE NORTHAMPTON BURNT DOWN? YEAH?
WELL, LENNY SAYS HE PUT A CURSE ON 'EM AN' NEXT THING YOU KNOW THEY FIND CARSON WITH HIS GUTS TORN OUT AND WRAPPED AROUND HOLLIS'S NECK!
SOUNDS MORE LIKE YOUR MISSUS, CHAS!
Er--
SO WHAT HAPPENED NEXT, MATE?

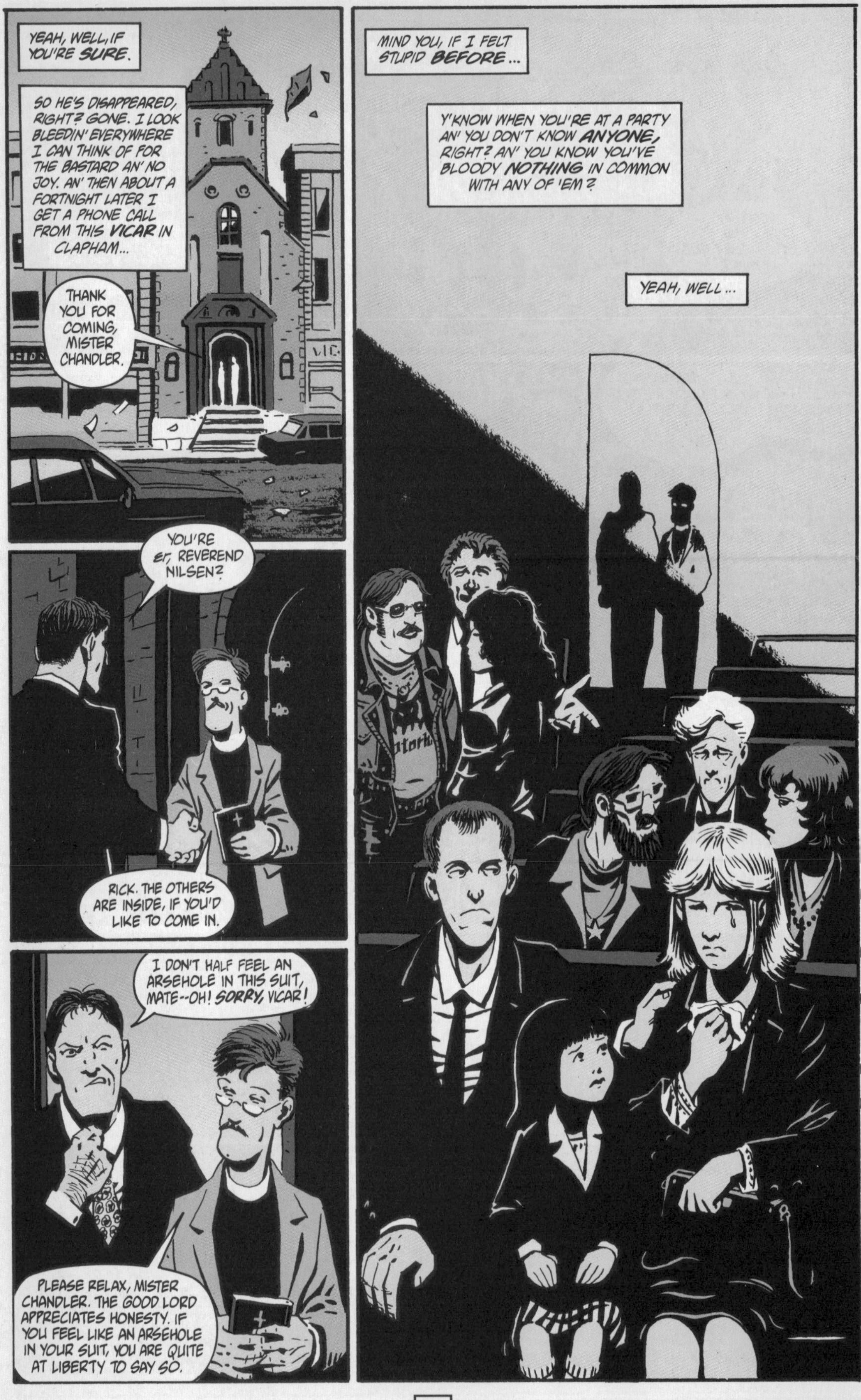
YEAH, WELL, IF YOU'RE SURE.
SO HE'S DISAPPEARED, RIGHT? GONE. I LOOK BLEEDIN' EVERYWHERE I CAN THINK OF FOR THE BASTARD AN' NO JOY. AN' THEN ABOUT A FORTNIGHT LATER I GET A PHONE CALL FROM THIS VICAR IN CLAPHAM...
THANK YOU FOR COMING, MISTER CHANDLER.
YOU'RE er, REVEREND NILSEN?
RICK. THE OTHERS ARE INSIDE, IF YOU'D LIKE TO COME IN.
I DON'T HALF FEEL AN ARSEHOLE IN THIS SUIT, MATE--OH! SORRY, VICAR!
PLEASE RELAX, MISTER CHANDLER. THE GOOD LORD APPRECIATES HONESTY. IF YOU FEEL LIKE AN ARSEHOLE IN YOUR SUIT, YOU ARE QUITE AT LIBERTY TO SAY SO.
MIND YOU, IF I FELT STUPID BEFORE...
Y'KNOW WHEN YOU'RE AT A PARTY AN' YOU DON'T KNOW ANYONE, RIGHT? AN' YOU KNOW YOU'VE BLOODY NOTHING IN COMMON WITH ANY OF 'EM?
YEAH, WELL...

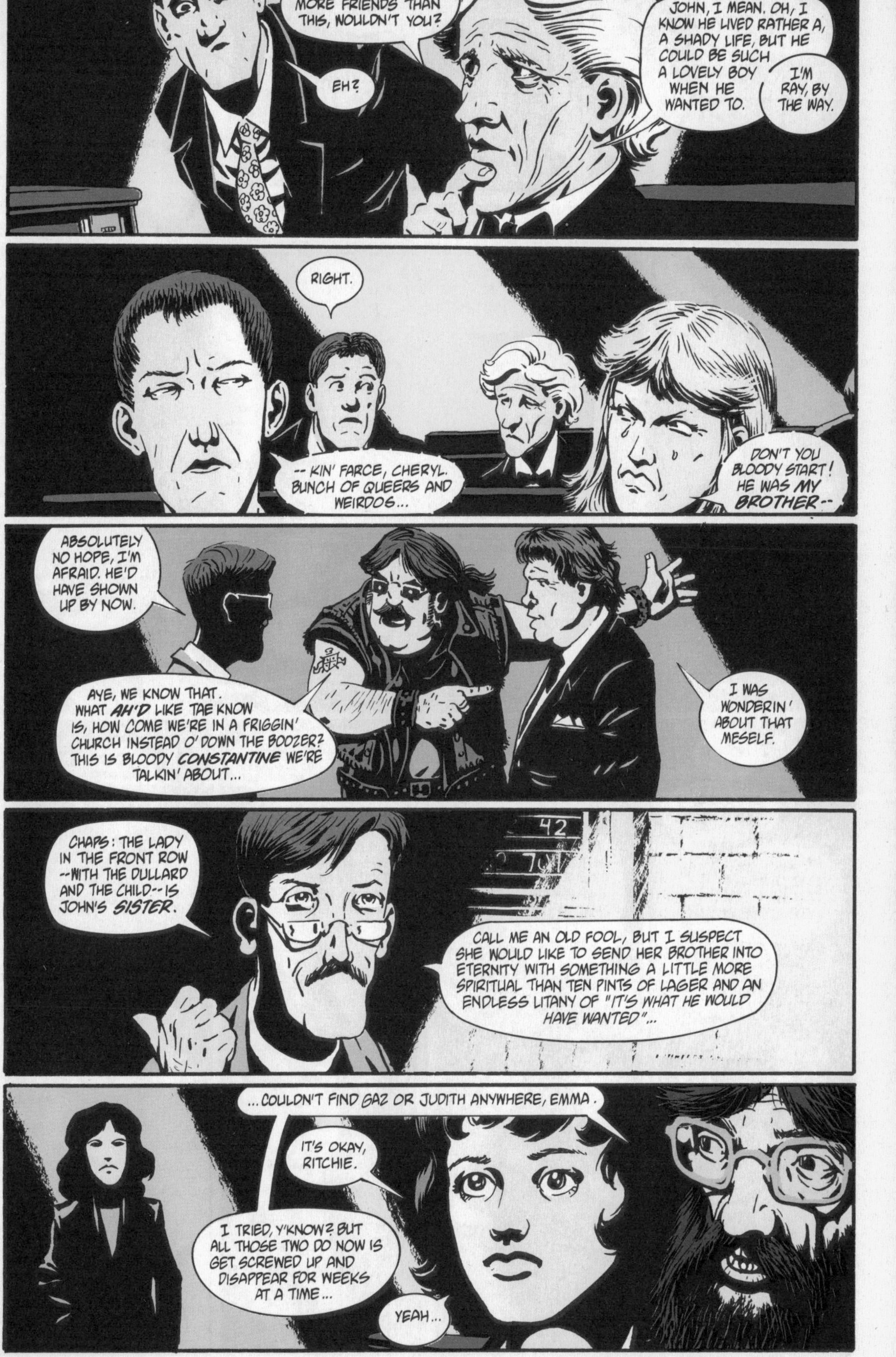

YOU'D THINK HE'D HAVE MORE FRIENDS THAN THIS, WOULDN'T YOU?
EH?
JOHN, I MEAN. OH, I KNOW HE LIVED RATHER A, A SHADY LIFE, BUT HE COULD BE SUCH A LOVELY BOY WHEN HE WANTED TO.
I'M RAY, BY THE WAY.
RIGHT.
--KIN' FARCE, CHERYL. BUNCH OF QUEERS AND WEIRDOS...
DON'T YOU BLOODY START! HE WAS MY BROTHER--
ABSOLUTELY NO HOPE, I'M AFRAID. HE'D HAVE SHOWN UP BY NOW.
AYE, WE KNOW THAT. WHAT AH'D LIKE TAE KNOW IS, HOW COME WE'RE IN A FRIGGIN' CHURCH INSTEAD O' DOWN THE BOOZER? THIS IS BLOODY CONSTANTINE WE'RE TALKIN' ABOUT...
I WAS WONDERIN' ABOUT THAT MESELF.
CHAPS: THE LADY IN THE FRONT ROW --WITH THE DULLARD AND THE CHILD--IS JOHN'S SISTER.
CALL ME AN OLD FOOL, BUT I SUSPECT SHE WOULD LIKE TO SEND HER BROTHER INTO ETERNITY WITH SOMETHING A LITTLE MORE SPIRITUAL THAN TEN PINTS OF LAGER AND AN ENDLESS LITANY OF "IT'S WHAT HE WOULD HAVE WANTED"...
...COULDN'T FIND GAZ OR JUDITH ANYWHERE, EMMA.
IT'S OKAY, RITCHIE.
I TRIED, Y'KNOW? BUT ALL THOSE TWO DO NOW IS GET SCREWED UP AND DISAPPEAR FOR WEEKS AT A TIME...
YEAH...

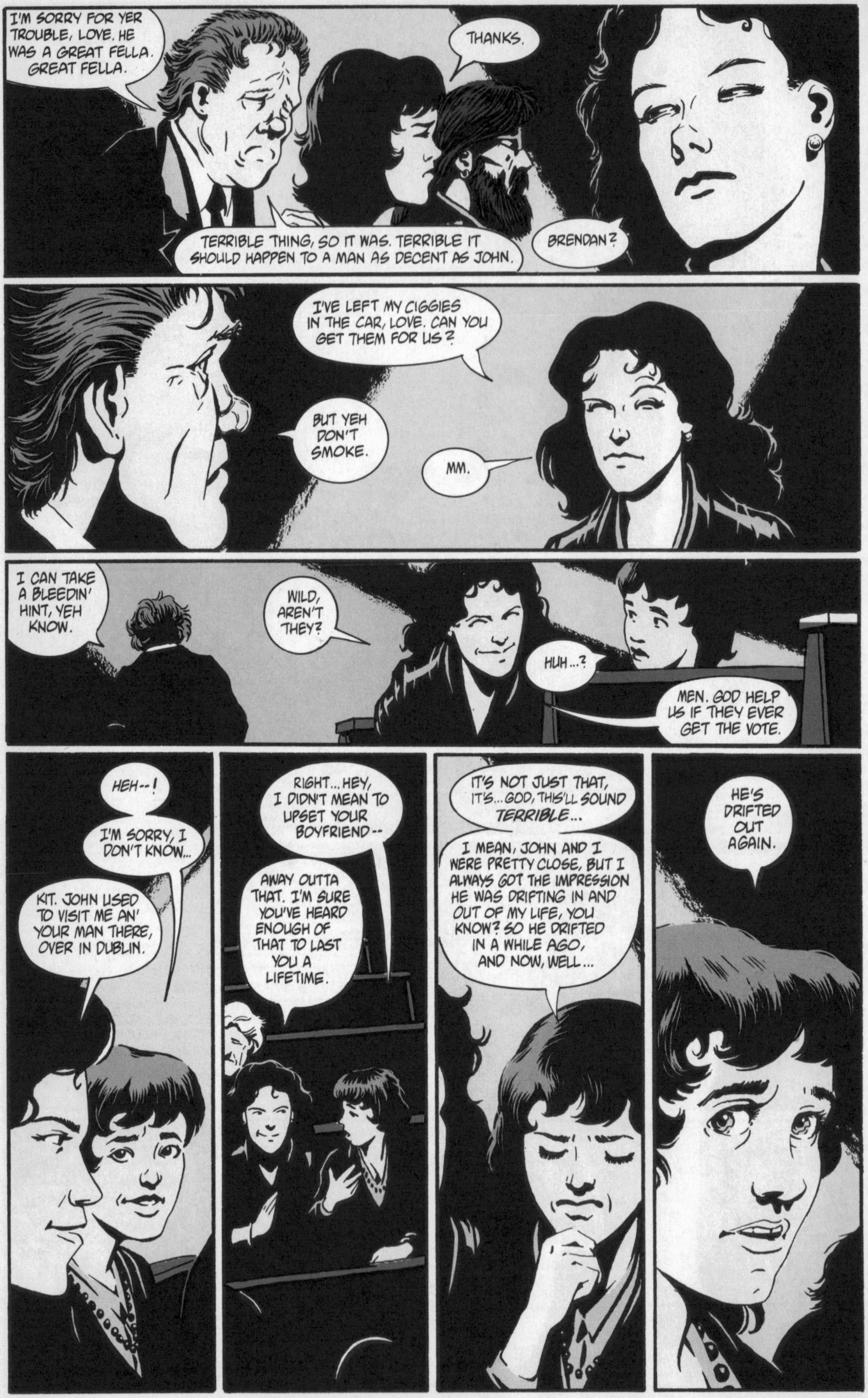
I'M SORRY FOR YER TROUBLE, LOVE. HE WAS A GREAT FELLA. GREAT FELLA.
THANKS.
TERRIBLE THING, SO IT WAS. TERRIBLE IT SHOULD HAPPEN TO A MAN AS DECENT AS JOHN.
BRENDAN?
I'VE LEFT MY CIGGIES IN THE CAR, LOVE. CAN YOU GET THEM FOR US?
BUT YEH DON'T SMOKE.
MM.
I CAN TAKE A BLEEDIN' HINT, YEH KNOW.
WILD, AREN'T THEY?
HUH...?
MEN. GOD HELP US IF THEY EVER GET THE VOTE.
HEH--!
I'M SORRY, I DON'T KNOW...
KIT. JOHN USED TO VISIT ME AN' YOUR MAN THERE, OVER IN DUBLIN.
RIGHT... HEY, I DIDN'T MEAN TO UPSET YOUR BOYFRIEND--
AWAY OUTTA THAT. I'M SURE YOU'VE HEARD ENOUGH OF THAT TO LAST YOU A LIFETIME.
IT'S NOT JUST THAT, IT'S... GOD, THIS'LL SOUND TERRIBLE...
I MEAN, JOHN AND I WERE PRETTY CLOSE, BUT I ALWAYS GOT THE IMPRESSION HE WAS DRIFTING IN AND OUT OF MY LIFE, YOU KNOW? SO HE DRIFTED IN A WHILE AGO, AND NOW, WELL...
HE'S DRIFTED OUT AGAIN.

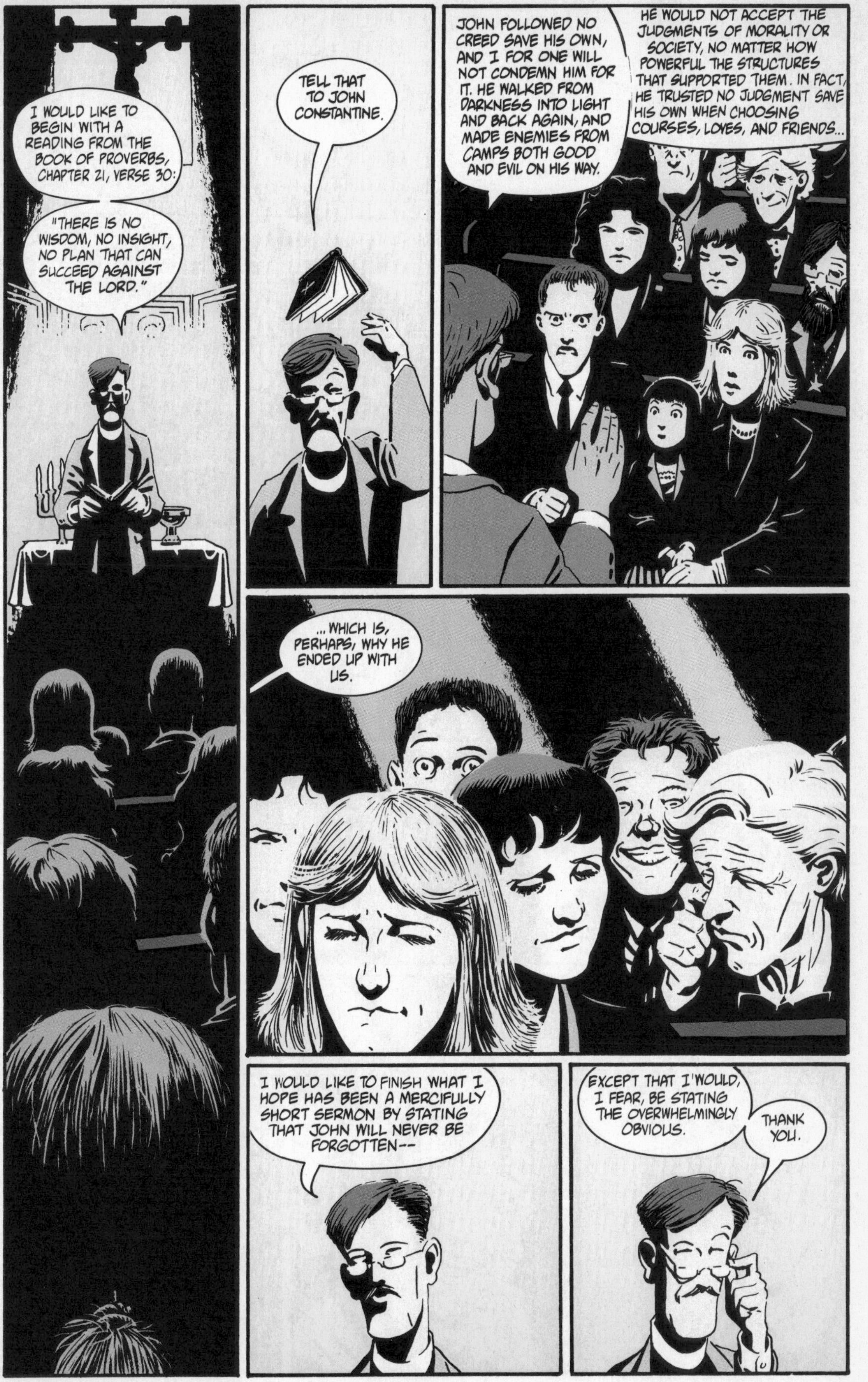
I WOULD LIKE TO BEGIN WITH A READING FROM THE BOOK OF PROVERBS, CHAPTER 21, VERSE 30:
"THERE IS NO WISDOM, NO INSIGHT, NO PLAN THAT CAN SUCCEED AGAINST THE LORD."
TELL THAT TO JOHN CONSTANTINE.
JOHN FOLLOWED NO CREED SAVE HIS OWN, AND I FOR ONE WILL NOT CONDEMN HIM FOR IT. HE WALKED FROM DARKNESS INTO LIGHT AND BACK AGAIN, AND MADE ENEMIES FROM CAMPS BOTH GOOD AND EVIL ON HIS WAY.
HE WOULD NOT ACCEPT THE JUDGMENTS OF MORALITY OR SOCIETY, NO MATTER HOW POWERFUL THE STRUCTURES THAT SUPPORTED THEM. IN FACT, HE TRUSTED NO JUDGMENT SAVE HIS OWN WHEN CHOOSING COURSES, LOVES, AND FRIENDS...
...WHICH IS, PERHAPS, WHY HE ENDED UP WITH US.
I WOULD LIKE TO FINISH WHAT I HOPE HAS BEEN A MERCIFULLY SHORT SERMON BY STATING THAT JOHN WILL NEVER BE FORGOTTEN--
EXCEPT THAT I WOULD, I FEAR, BE STATING THE OVERWHELMINGLY OBVIOUS.
THANK YOU.

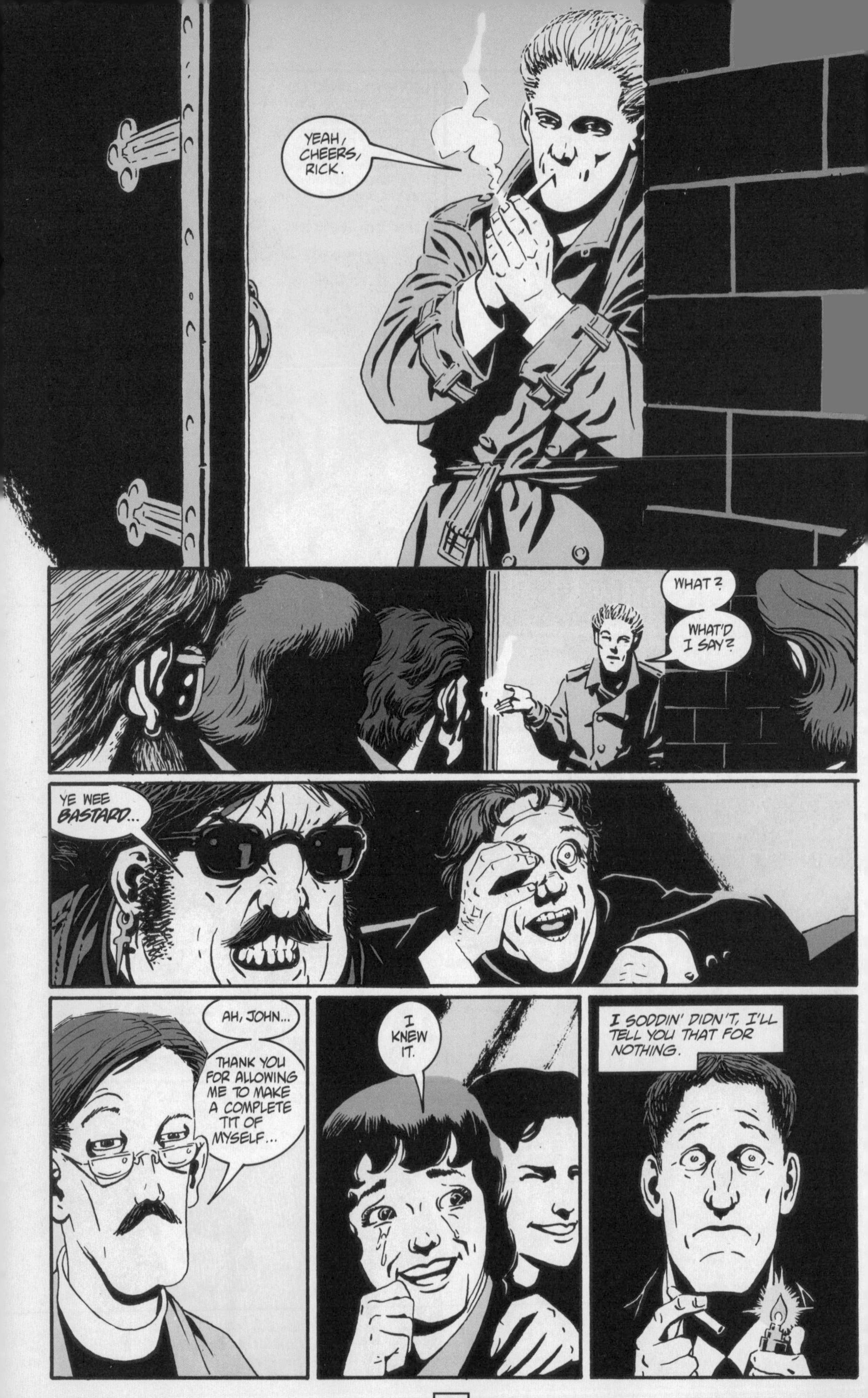

YEAH, CHEERS, RICK.
WHAT?
WHAT'D I SAY?
YE WEE BASTARD...
AH, JOHN...
THANK YOU FOR ALLOWING ME TO MAKE A COMPLETE TIT OF MYSELF...
I KNEW IT.
I SODDIN' DIDN'T, I'LL TELL YOU THAT FOR NOTHING.

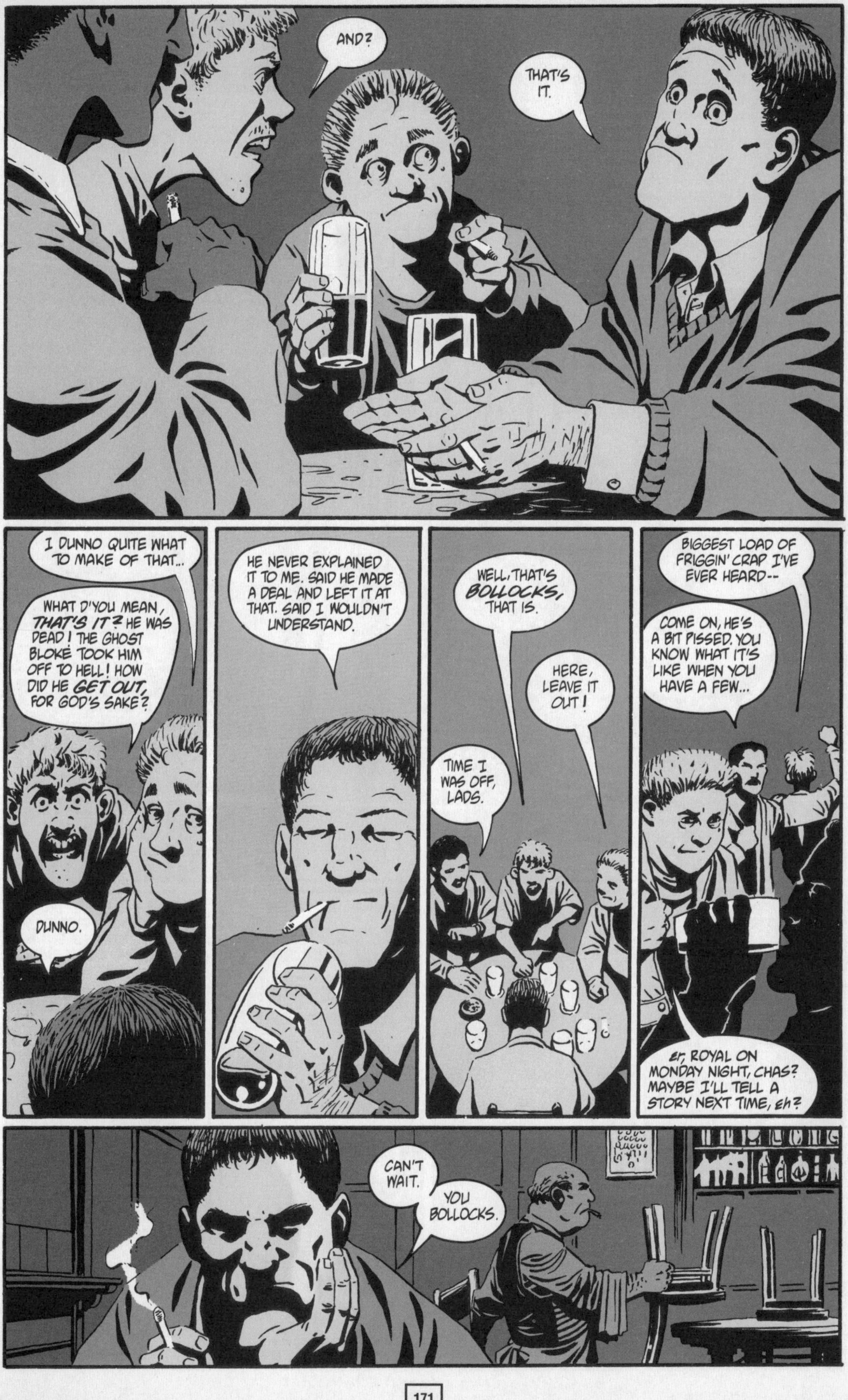
AND?
THAT'S IT.
I DUNNO QUITE WHAT TO MAKE OF THAT...
WHAT D'YOU MEAN, THAT'S IT? HE WAS DEAD! THE GHOST BLOKE TOOK HIM OFF TO HELL! HOW DID HE GET OUT, FOR GOD'S SAKE?
DUNNO.
HE NEVER EXPLAINED IT TO ME. SAID HE MADE A DEAL AND LEFT IT AT THAT. SAID I WOULDN'T UNDERSTAND.
WELL, THAT'S BOLLOCKS, THAT IS.
HERE, LEAVE IT OUT!
TIME I WAS OFF, LADS.
BIGGEST LOAD OF FRIGGIN' CRAP I'VE EVER HEARD--
COME ON, HE'S A BIT PISSED. YOU KNOW WHAT IT'S LIKE WHEN YOU HAVE A FEW...
eh, ROYAL ON MONDAY NIGHT, CHAS? MAYBE I'LL TELL A STORY NEXT TIME, eh?
CAN'T WAIT.
YOU BOLLOCKS.

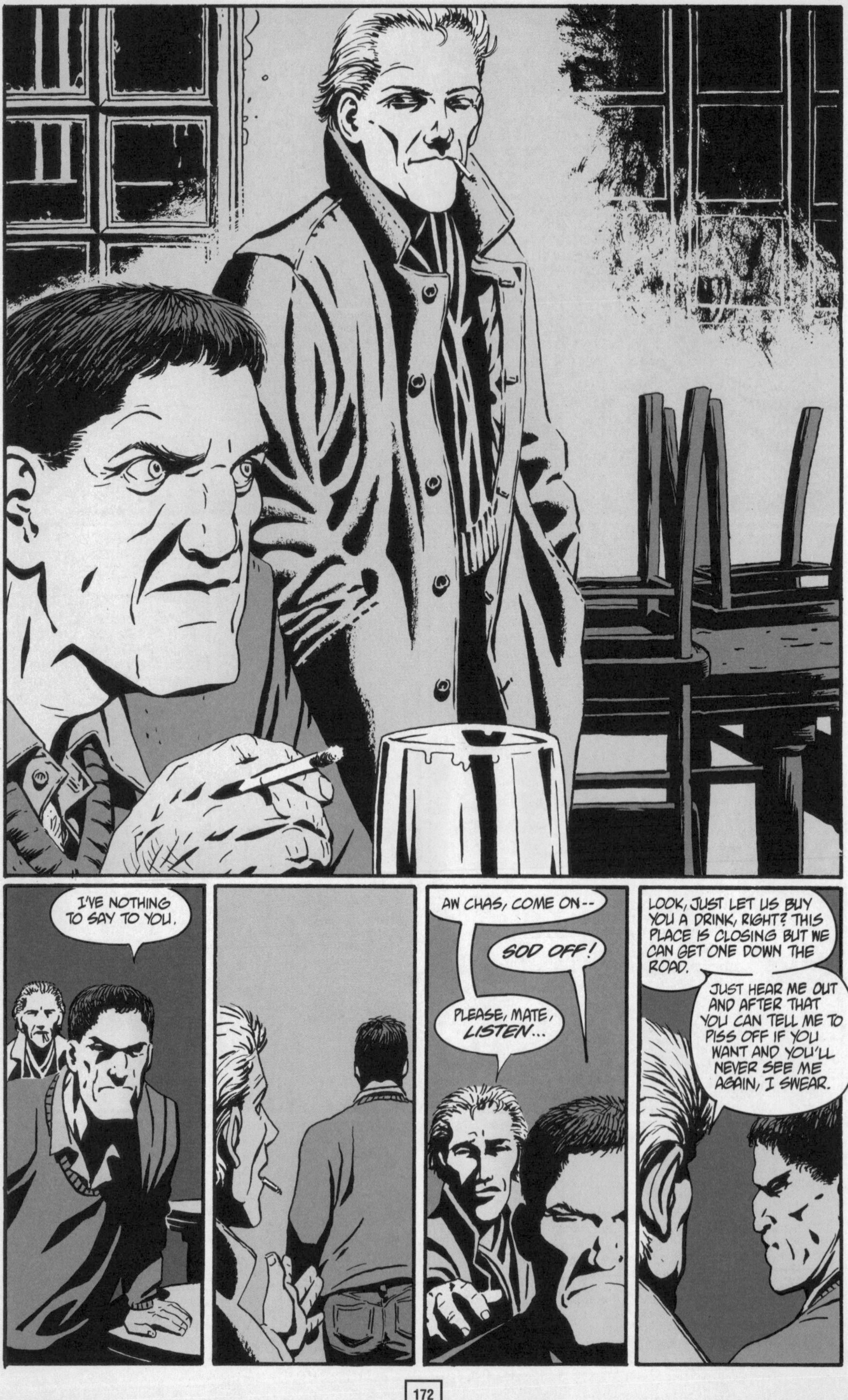
I'VE NOTHING TO SAY TO YOU.
AW CHAS, COME ON--
SOD OFF!
PLEASE, MATE, LISTEN...
LOOK, JUST LET US BUY YOU A DRINK, RIGHT? THIS PLACE IS CLOSING BUT WE CAN GET ONE DOWN THE ROAD.
JUST HEAR ME OUT AND AFTER THAT YOU CAN TELL ME TO PISS OFF IF YOU WANT AND YOU'LL NEVER SEE ME AGAIN, I SWEAR.

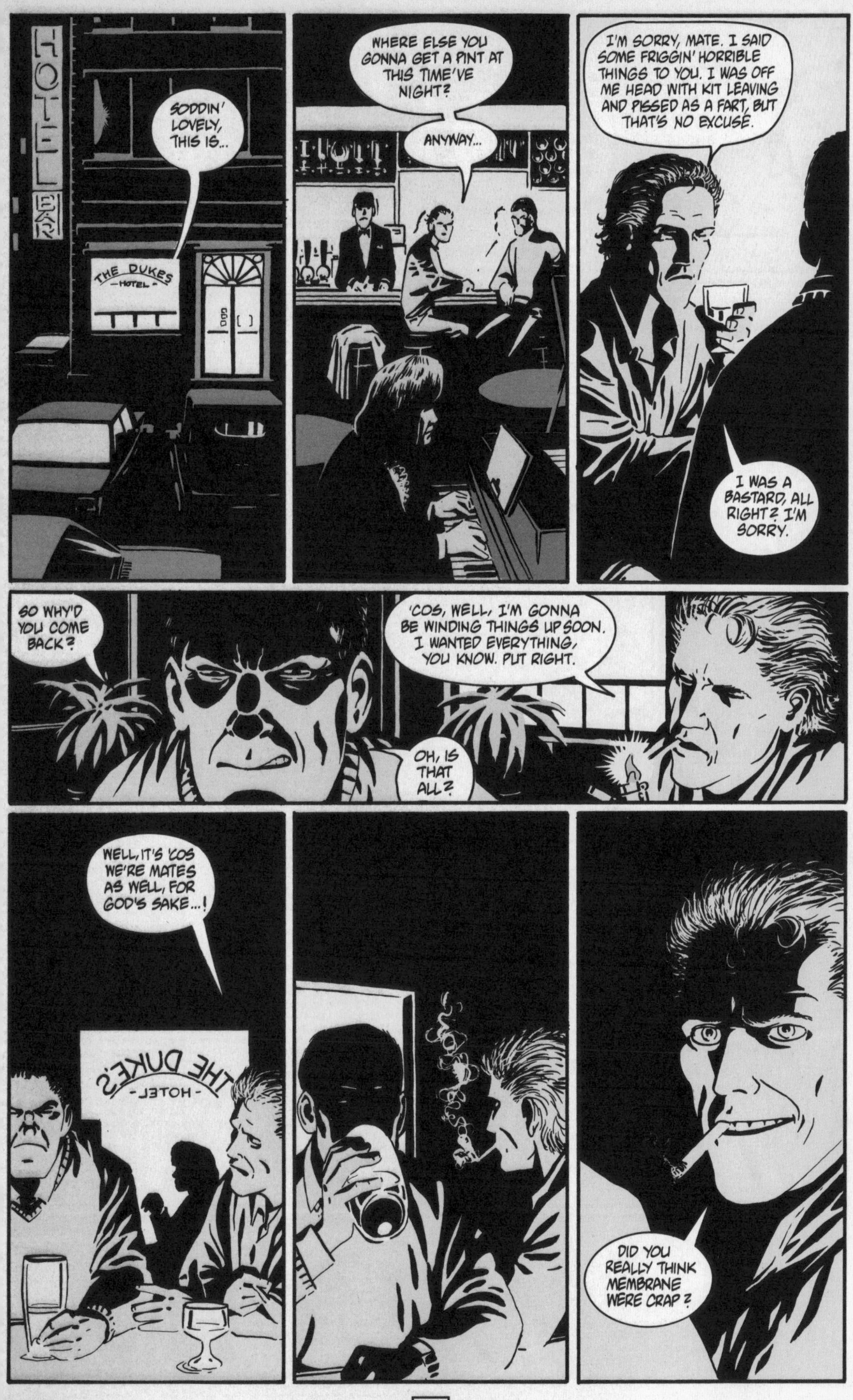
HOTEL
BAR
THE DUKES HOTEL
SODDIN' LOVELY, THIS IS...
WHERE ELSE YOU GONNA GET A PINT AT THIS TIME'VE NIGHT?
ANYWAY...
I'M SORRY, MATE. I SAID SOME FRIGGIN' HORRIBLE THINGS TO YOU. I WAS OFF ME HEAD WITH KIT LEAVING AND PISSED AS A FART, BUT THAT'S NO EXCUSE.
I WAS A BASTARD, ALL RIGHT? I'M SORRY.
SO WHY'D YOU COME BACK?
'COS, WELL, I'M GONNA BE WINDING THINGS UP SOON. I WANTED EVERYTHING, YOU KNOW. PUT RIGHT.
OH, IS THAT ALL?
WELL, IT'S 'COS WE'RE MATES AS WELL, FOR GOD'S SAKE...!
THE DUKE'S HOTEL
DID YOU REALLY THINK MEMBRANE WERE CRAP?

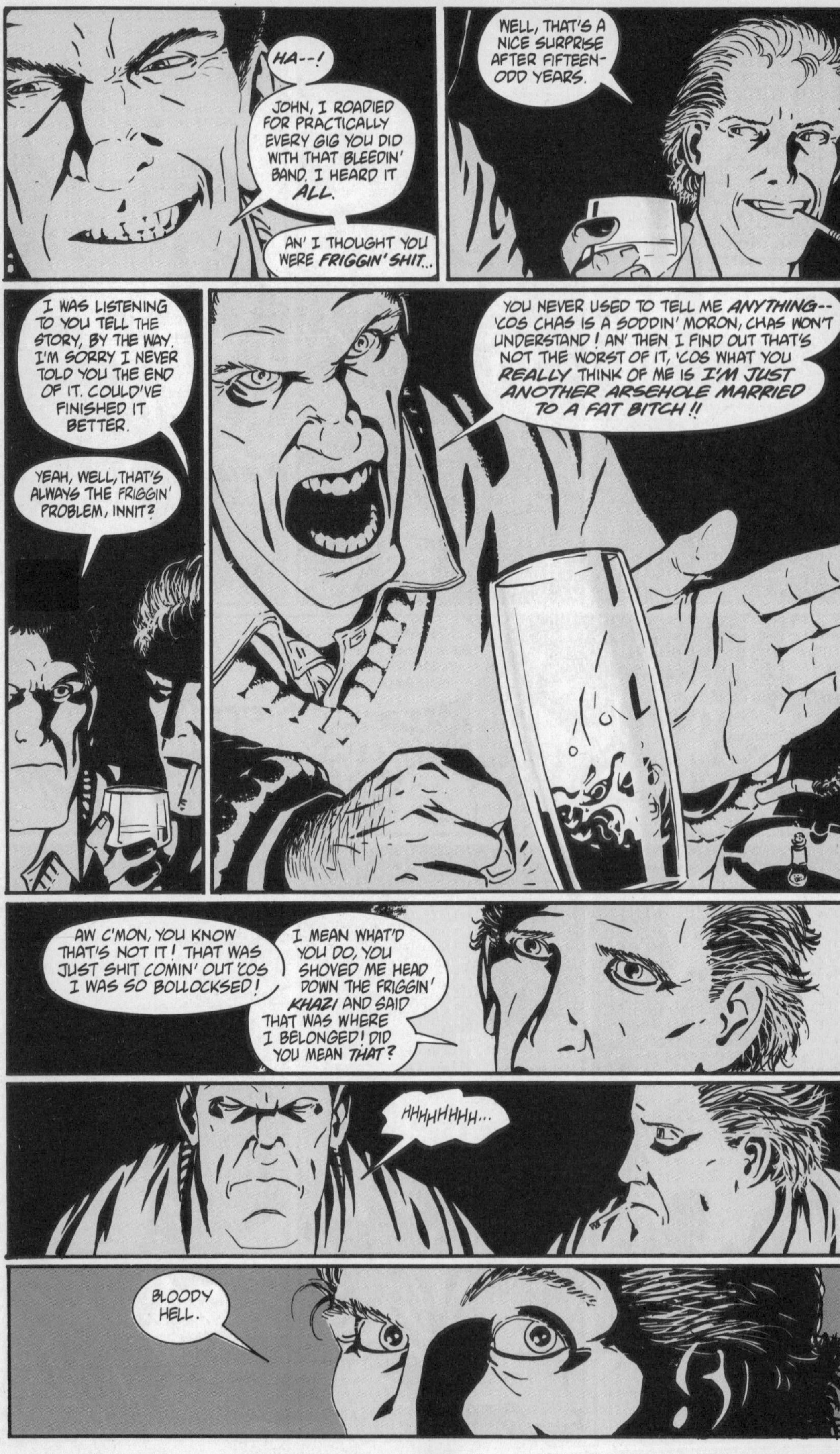
HA--!
JOHN, I ROADIED FOR PRACTICALLY EVERY GIG YOU DID WITH THAT BLEEDIN' BAND. I HEARD IT ALL.
AN' I THOUGHT YOU WERE FRIGGIN' SHIT...
WELL, THAT'S A NICE SURPRISE AFTER FIFTEEN-ODD YEARS.
I WAS LISTENING TO YOU TELL THE STORY, BY THE WAY. I'M SORRY I NEVER TOLD YOU THE END OF IT. COULD'VE FINISHED IT BETTER.
YEAH, WELL, THAT'S ALWAYS THE FRIGGIN' PROBLEM, INNIT?
YOU NEVER USED TO TELL ME ANYTHING-- 'COS CHAS IS A SODDIN' MORON, CHAS WON'T UNDERSTAND! AN' THEN I FIND OUT THAT'S NOT THE WORST OF IT, 'COS WHAT YOU REALLY THINK OF ME IS I'M JUST ANOTHER ARSEHOLE MARRIED TO A FAT BITCH!!
AW C'MON, YOU KNOW THAT'S NOT IT! THAT WAS JUST SHIT COMIN' OUT 'COS I WAS SO BOLLOCKSED!
I MEAN WHAT'D YOU DO, YOU SHOVED ME HEAD DOWN THE FRIGGIN' KHAZI AND SAID THAT WAS WHERE I BELONGED! DID YOU MEAN THAT?
HHHHHHHH...
BLOODY HELL.

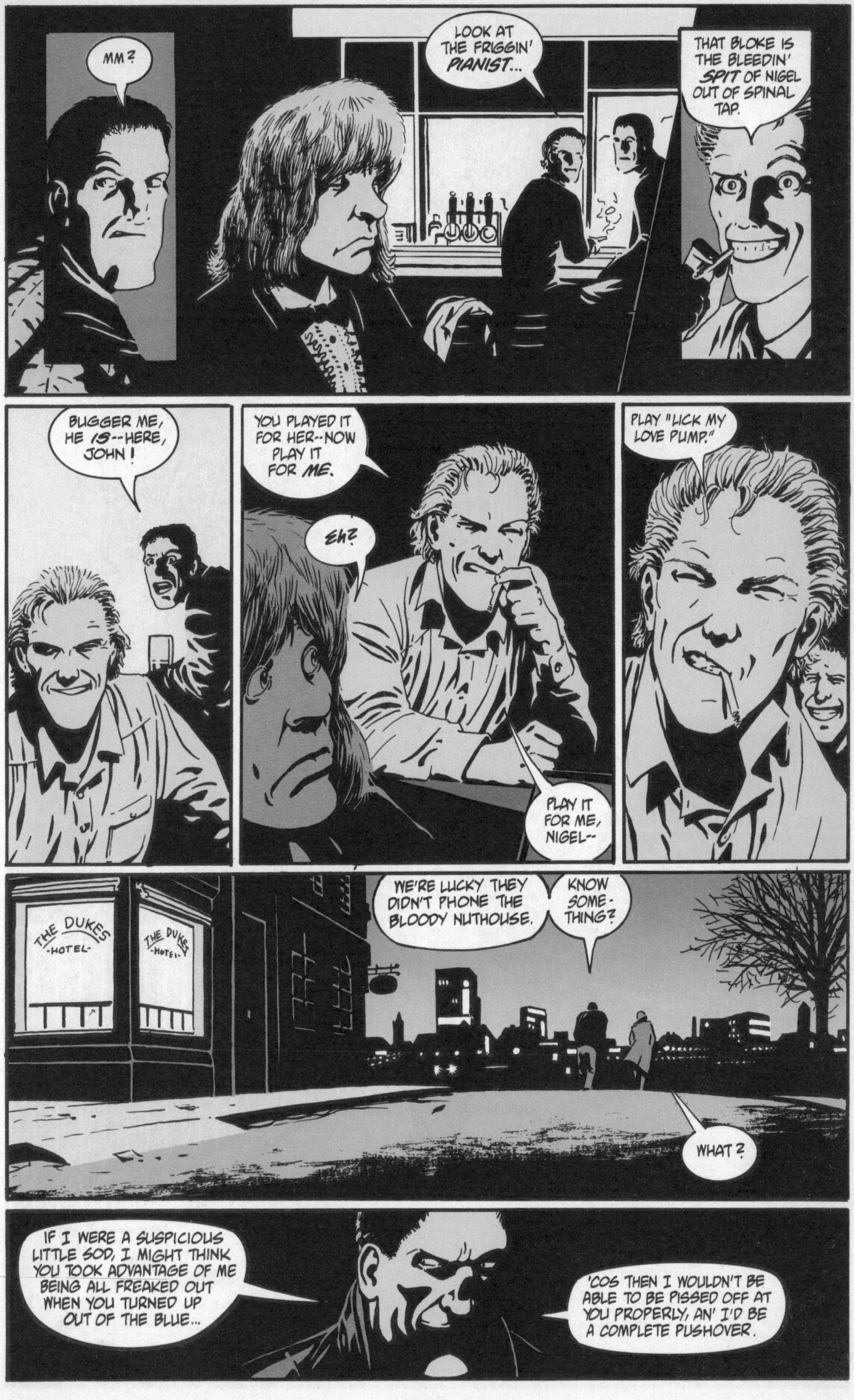
MM?
LOOK AT THE FRIGGIN' PIANIST...
THAT BLOKE IS THE BLEEDIN' SPIT OF NIGEL OUT OF SPINAL TAP.
BUGGER ME, HE IS--HERE, JOHN!
YOU PLAYED IT FOR HER--NOW PLAY IT FOR ME.
Eh?
PLAY IT FOR ME, NIGEL--
PLAY "LICK MY LOVE PUMP."
THE DUKES -HOTEL-
THE DUKES -HOTEL-
WE'RE LUCKY THEY DIDN'T PHONE THE BLOODY NUTHOUSE.
KNOW SOME-THING?
WHAT?
IF I WERE A SUSPICIOUS LITTLE SOD, I MIGHT THINK YOU TOOK ADVANTAGE OF ME BEING ALL FREAKED OUT WHEN YOU TURNED UP OUT OF THE BLUE...
'COS THEN I WOULDN'T BE ABLE TO BE PISSED OFF AT YOU PROPERLY, AN' I'D BE A COMPLETE PUSHOVER.

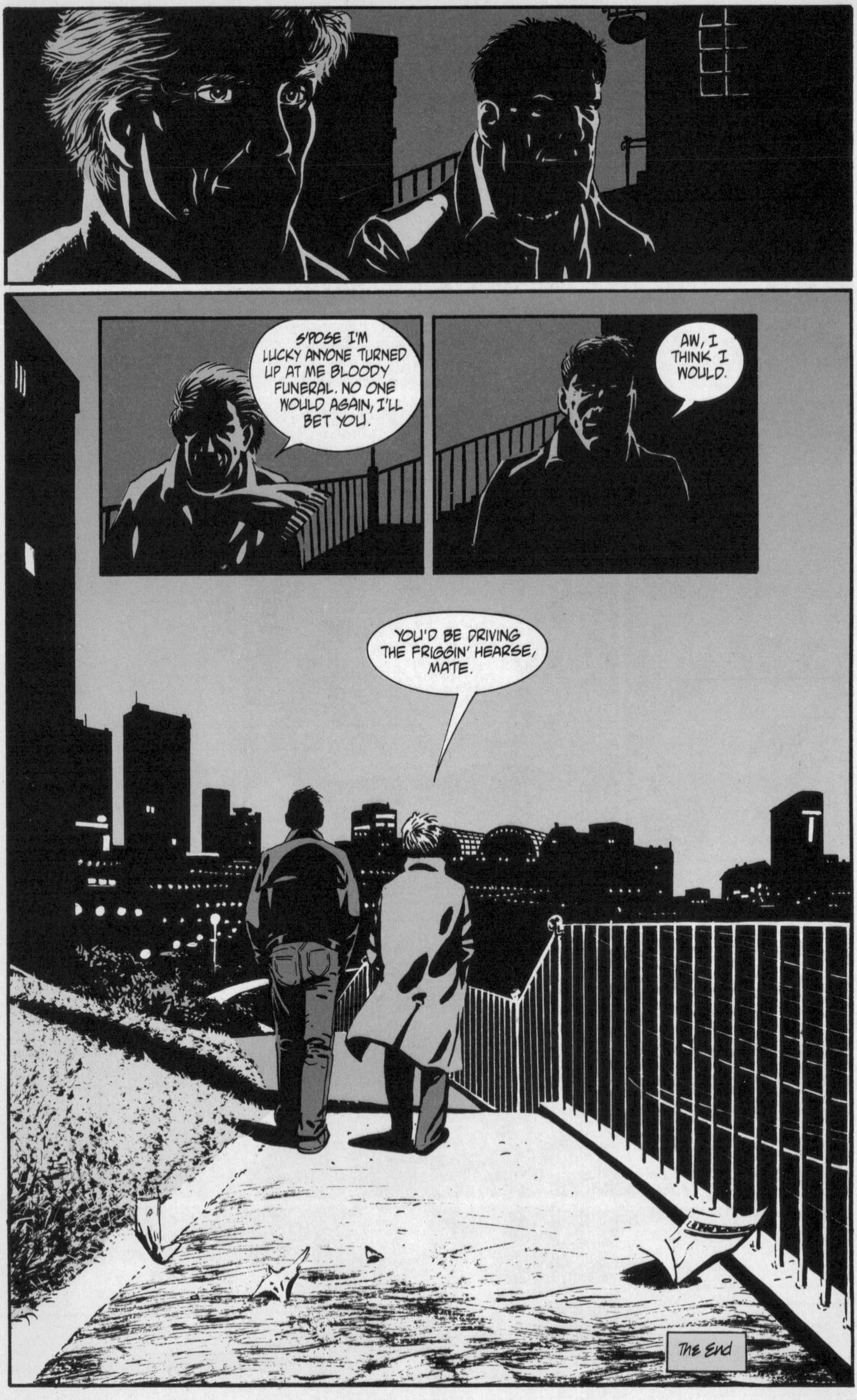
S'POSE I'M LUCKY ANYONE TURNED UP AT ME BLOODY FUNERAL. NO ONE WOULD AGAIN, I'LL BET YOU.
AW, I THINK I WOULD.
YOU'D BE DRIVING THE FRIGGIN' HEARSE, MATE.
The End